D1315854

V·I·C·K·I

VICKI

JOYCE MILTON
AND
ANN LOUISE BARDACH

ST. MARTIN'S PRESS
New York

The authors gratefully acknowledge permission to reprint from the following:

The Great Gatsby, by F. Scott Fitzgerald. Copyright 1925 Charles Scribner's Sons; copyright renewed 1953 Frances Scott Fitzgerald Lanahan. Reprinted with the permission of Charles Scribner's Sons.
The Day of the Locust, by Nathanael West. Copyright 1939 by the estate of Nathanael West, copyright renewed 1966 by Laura Perelman. Reprinted by permission of New Directions Publishing Corporation.
The Crack-Up, by F. Scott Fitzgerald. Copyright 1944. New Directions Publishing Corporation. Reprinted by permission of New Directions.

VICKI. Copyright © 1986 by Joyce Milton and Ann Louise Bardach. All rights reserved. Printed in the United States of America. No part of this book may be used or reproduced in any manner whatsoever without written permission except in the case of brief quotations embodied in critical articles or reviews. For information, address St. Martin's Press, 175 Fifth Avenue, New York, N.Y. 10010.

Design by Beth Tondreau

Library of Congress Cataloging in Publication Data

Milton, Joyce.
    Vicki.

    1. Morgan, Victoria Lynn, 1953-1983.   2. Mistresses—
California—Biography.   3. Murder—California—Case
studies.   I. Bardach, Ann Louise.   II. Title.
HQ806.M55   1986   364.1′523′0924 [B]   85-25129
ISBN 0-312-83923-5

First Edition

10 9 8 7 6 5 4 3 2 1

They were careless people, Tom and Daisy—they smashed up things and creatures and then retreated back into their money or their vast carelessness, or whatever it was that kept them together, and let other people clean up the mess they had made.

F. SCOTT FITZGERALD
THE GREAT GATSBY

The authors gratefully acknowledge the help and assistance of Barbara Lowenstein, Karen Hitsig, and Ron Bernstein. Special thanks to our editor, Joyce Engelson.

Contents

A SELECTION OF PHOTOGRAPHS FOLLOWS PAGE 152.

I wouldn't work in California for nothing. They don't have normal crime out there.

**AN NYPD DETECTIVE,
THIRD HOMICIDE DIVISION,
MANHATTAN**

A SIMPLE HOMICIDE

//

From the point of view of the LAPD, it was a very simple homicide, a normal sort of crime born out of thwarted desire and petty domestic irritation.

The killing first came to their attention at 3:20 A.M. on July 7, 1983, when desk officer Keith Wong of the North Hollywood division noticed a male Caucasian, thin and sandy-haired, with an acne-pitted complexion, standing just inside the door of the stationhouse. There had been a fatal shooting earlier in the evening, a street killing. The police had issued a call for witnesses, and Officer Wong assumed he was dealing with a bystander who'd come in, not very enthusiastically by the look of him, to volunteer information. "Are you a witness?" he asked.

The civilian seemed momentarily dumbfounded. "No. I just killed someone."

"Could you repeat that?"

"I just killed someone. She's at 4171 Colfax Avenue, Apartment D. I left the door open, but look out for the Doberman."

It took a few seconds for the words to sink in. Wong's adrenaline started to flow, but he noted with relief that the subject's hands were empty and there didn't appear to be any suspicious bulges under his blue sateen windbreaker. But the guy wasn't laughing either. This was no joke.

Wong conducted a quick patdown and had the young man handcuffed to the prisoner's bench in the rear hallway. The guy looked as if he might break down in tears at any minute, but he was still calm and seemed rational. Wong popped his head into the detectives' room and saw Detective Ramsdell seated at his desk doing some followup on the evening's earlier homicide call. "You'll never guess what we've got out here," Wong told him.

Minutes later a mobile unit dispatched by Officer Wong arrived at the Colfax Avenue address. They found the door unlocked, just as the subject had indicated. Officer Ken Henkle, was the first to enter the condo, followed by his partner Officer Geller and uniformed Sergeant Millar. The interior was very dimly lit, and Henkle switched on his flashlight to guide himself through the maze of cartons and packing crates and up the carpeted staircase.

Probing his flashlight inside what appeared to be the master bedroom, Henkle saw a woman's form stretched out on the bed wearing a yellow T-shirt, bikini panties, and fire-engine red toenail polish. The next thing he noticed, after fumbling for the lightswitch and flicking it on, was an adult Doberman pinscher curled up on the floor beside the bed. He and the other officers took a cautious step backward, but the dog regarded them without great interest and made no attempt to resist when Geller took it by the collar and led it out of the room.

In the meantime, Henkle had noticed a chewed-up-looking baseball bat laid across the woman's body, its heavy end resting on the sheet beside her. At first, though, there didn't seem to be a lot of blood. Henkle tried unsuccessfully to find a pulse.

"I get nothing," he told Sergeant Millar. "But she's still warm. Call the paramedics."

After the call went out, Henkle took a closer look and saw that the woman's injuries were worse than he'd first thought. The whole side of her skull had been bashed in, apparently by multiple blows with a blunt instrument. There was a splatter of blood on the wall above the headboard and blood on the baseball bat and on the gray designer sheet where the heavy end of the bat had come to rest. When the paramedics arrived, they confirmed what he'd already had time to conclude on his own. This victim was beyond any resuscitation efforts.

The paramedics pronounced death and departed on another call where their presence might do some good. Henkle went to help his partner take the dog down to the basement-level garage, where they locked it out of their way for the time being, while Sergeant Millar called the report into Homicide. "Looks like we got another one," he said. "The guy was telling the truth."

At ten minutes after five that same morning, Detective Jay Rush ushered the prisoner into the interrogation room and set him up with a cup of black coffee and an ashtray.

The prisoner identified himself as Marvin Pancoast, thirty-three years old, born November 13, 1949, with a previous record of arrests for traffic warrants and lewd conduct. He waived his right to remain silent with a shrug, saying, "Feel free."

"Okay," said Rush. "What happened? Let's just start from Square One. . . . People don't normally just wake up in the middle of the night and hit somebody with a baseball bat. So when did this all start? How long have you known her?"

"I met Vicki in October 1979."

"October 1979. That's almost four years? Okay. So you've known her—"

"Do you know who she is?" Pancoast interrupted. "Are you aware of the background of her?"

Rush hesitated. "Now somebody . . . she had a palimony suit against somebody or—"

"Alfred Bloomingdale."

"Uh-huh."

"A year ago this month, she filed. Her suit was five million against him before he died. Alfred Bloomingdale, of course, is Bloomingdale's department store—"

"Right."

"—in New York. And Diner's Club, he founded that. And Vicki was his mistress for twelve years."

Pancoast went on to complain that Vicki Morgan had been "coked out," "Valiumed out," "alcoholicked out." He'd been living with her for three weeks, he said, and he was "paying for everything." In the meantime, she'd wrecked the car he'd given her and treated him like a lackey. Then, the previous night, she'd reconciled with her lover, "the writer" Gordon, and he, Marvin, had been "given a kiss on the lips and told to go to bed." And this morning, Vicki had sent him out like an errand boy to buy coffee and bagels with his own money so she and Gordon could have some breakfast before they hit the sack together.

Pancoast talked so freely that it was hardly an interrogation at all. The only real problem Rush had was keeping him on the subject of the murder, since he seemed far more interested in gossiping about his victim's past.

Rush kept trying to steer the discussion toward the events of earlier that evening, but Pancoast kept wandering back to who she was:

". . . A year ago July, when all this hit the newspapers, and it was a very—it was on the front page of every newspaper," he reminded Rush, "because Alfred Bloomingdale was on Ronald Reagan's Kitchen Cabinet. So it was very political and Betsy Bloomingdale, Alfred's wife . . . thirty some years as Nancy Reagan's best friend. And Vicki the mistress for some twelve years. I could go on and on, you know. You have to just pick up the clippings that were in the file cabinet there. I did all the clippings for her. I worked for the William Morris Agency. I've got an agent who was going to handle—do the book, do a thing, they're very interested in it . . .

"All right—"

"And she went to bed this morning after I went and got the bagels. They went up, and she's fucking the writer. They fucked until about ten and then she slept until two. . . . Her mother and friend showed up, helped pack, but she wouldn't get out of bed. She didn't want to deal with anything. She didn't want to do anything at all today. And, anyway, she just went on about Vicki this, Vicki this, Vicki this, Vicki this. I couldn't take it anymore."

The last straw, Pancoast went on to claim, was that she'd told him that evening she didn't like the apartment he'd found and then kept him awake by fretting and whining about not knowing where she was going to go the next day, when the movers showed up.

"I just couldn't take it anymore," Pancoast repeated, ". . . [so] I hit her enough times on the head so that she would go to sleep."

Over the weekend, Marvin Pancoast showed no signs whatsoever of having second thoughts about his confession. He talked freely to reporters who visited him at the L.A. county jail.

He was especially forthcoming in the presence of *Los Angeles Herald-Examiner* reporter Andy Furillo, a freckle-faced redhead in his twenties. Pancoast gave Furillo a vivid account of how he had bashed Vicki's head in, though one that differed in a few key details from what he'd told Rush. He continued to insist, however, on his motive: "I wanted her to go to sleep."

And he went on to predict that he would be convicted of first-degree murder. "I expect to die in the gas chamber," he told Furillo.

It was a bizarre motive for homicide. When Furillo's story appeared in the Sunday *Herald-Examiner,* the headline compounded the confusion by announcing that Vicki Morgan had been killed "in her sleep." In fact, this wasn't true. But Pancoast did say that he'd spent an hour and forty-five minutes working up his nerve to do in Vicki Morgan, by which time she was lying quietly in her darkened bedroom, smoking a cigarette.

The argument was over. Vicki had stopped nagging. And there was nothing preventing Pancoast at that point from going to sleep in the spare bedroom if he wanted to. Or, for that matter, from simply getting into his car and going home to his mother and grandmother's house, where he'd lived until only three weeks before.

Not quite the usual pattern for a killing done in the heat of passion.

Monday, July 11, was the day that, in the words of the *Los Angeles Times,* the Vicki Morgan murder case began to "get complicated."

The day began with the appearance of Marvin Pancoast before Commissioner Robert L. Swasey in a Van Nuys courtroom. To no one's great surprise, given the absence of a completely rational motive, Pancoast's attorney Arthur Barens asked that arraignment be postponed until his client could undergo a psychiatric examination. Bail was set at $250,000.

Later that afternoon, Morgan's family gathered for a memorial service. Ironically, the service was being held at the Old North Church replica in Forest Lawn Cemetery. Vicki Morgan had, after a fashion, ended up in Burbank after all.

By the time the ceremony was ready to begin, the thermometer had already topped 105 degrees in the shade and was still climbing. Outside the chapel a team of policeman stood sweltering beside their squad car, waiting to fend off a media onslaught that never quite materialized.

Inside, the supercooled atmosphere was almost chilly and loudspeakers pumped out a Muzak medley of Simon and Garfunkel tunes: "Like a bridge over troubled waters I will lay me down. . . . I'd rather be a forest than a tree. Yes, I would. Yes, I would."

On the altar stood a replica of Houdon's bust of George Washington, and a plaque on the wall informed visitors of the historical significance of the *real* Old North Church in Boston. No one had thought to include a plaque explaining the significance of the replica in this, the Disneyland of death.

There were no flowers, no coffin—and, for that matter, no remains. Vicki Morgan's body was still being held pending the autopsy, after which the family had asked for cremation, the ashes to be scattered at sea in a private ceremony. For now, the deceased was represented only by a photographic enlargement resting on the altar. The portrait showed Vicki Morgan in profile looking achingly young and glamorous. It was fortunate that her gaze was not directed out toward the rows of empty pews in the sanctuary.

As eulogies go, the remarks delivered by Michael Dave, the deceased's attorney and personal friend, were strikingly candid and unsentimental. Dave spoke of Morgan as a child of the late 1960s and early 1970s, a young woman who came of age at a time when the most hallowed values of society were being questioned and openly flouted. Yet he resisted the temptation to portray Vicki Morgan as a hapless victim of her environment.

Vicki had a streak of materialism in her, said Dave, that was constantly at war with her better impulses. In the end, the materialism won.

"Vicki knew that the world was a difficult place," he concluded. "She certainly did some things she was not proud of and things that made her unhappy. . . . There is probably no one in this room who has not felt imposed on by Vicki recently.

"And yet, we all loved her."

Michael Dave's words were not only earnest and carefully considered but they were obviously true. For a self-announced mistress, excoriated in the press as a fortune hunter and worse, Vicki Morgan had certainly managed to inspire her share of love and loyalty in her private life. Among the mourners present were her two surviving ex-husbands and a half dozen or so woman friends, several of them married women with children who had been close to Vicki Morgan for more than a decade.

Nor could Vicki Morgan's "materialistic" life be blamed on rootlessness. The family that gathered to mourn the notorious

Vicki was not that different from any other American family of the 1980s in its strengths and weaknesses. True, Vicki had been the product of a fatherless home but of hardly an unsupportive one. Her sixty-two-year-old mother, seated now in the front pew, was a practicing Episcopalian who had lived in the same house for nearly twenty-five years, worked at one job steadily for seventeen years to support her children, and remained in almost daily contact with her troubled daughter right up to the last day of her life. There were also two younger half-brothers and a beautiful elder sister, an airline stewardess and a married woman who shunned publicity as assiduously as Vicki Morgan had sought it.

The only really exotic member of the assemblage was Vicki Morgan's own fourteen-year-old son Todd, who had appeared for his mother's funeral in full punk regalia—a dyed black Mohawk haircut, a diamond stud in his pierced nose, and a black T-shirt emblazoned with the word *Desire*. Yet even this image of rebellion was undercut somewhat by the presence at his side of a girlfriend wearing braces on her teeth and, in a neighboring pew, Sisters Lynn and Mary, nuns representing the Catholic school where Todd Morgan had recently been a student.

What was most striking about Vicki Morgan's funeral was the absence of the paparazzi; the Beverly Hills celebrities she had once considered her friends, and all but a few of the reporters who had once, ever so briefly, chronicled her campaign to win lifetime support from the family of the man she claimed to have served as mistress and "other wife" for a dozen years. Here was a woman who had been so frightened by her own notoriety that during the last months of her life she was afraid even to enter a supermarket for fear of being recognized. Now that she was dead, victim of a front-page murder, her funeral wasn't worth more than a passing footnote in the tabloid columns.

Vicki Morgan hadn't been forgotten, she'd merely been upstaged. At the very moment that Vicki's family was gathered at Forest Lawn to mourn her passing, Robert K. Steinberg, a forty-six-year-old criminal lawyer who had never even met the dead woman, was entertaining a room packed with print and TV journalists in downtown Beverly Hills, catapulting himself to national attention merely on the strength of his claim to have seen videotapes of Vicki Morgan having sex with prominent government officials and associates of the President.

A lot of observers were not terribly surprised when, a few days later, the alleged sex tapes disappeared as mysteriously as they had appeared. Shortly after Deputy District Attorney Mike Carroll let it be known that he planned to subpoena the tapes as possible evidence in the murder of Vicki Morgan, Steinberg filed a police report claiming that the tapes had been stolen from his office, presumably by a representative of the media.

But while the Steinberg tapes had turned out to be no more than a one-day sensation, they inspired other questions about the circumstances of Vicki Morgan's death among those who continued to follow the story. Had Robert Steinberg really been audacious enough or, more accurately, foolish enough to make up the story of the tapes out of whole cloth? And what, aside from a flurry of dubious publicity, might he have hoped to achieve? Was it possible that there was at least a kernel of truth in the tapes story after all? Or, conceivably, had Steinberg himself been conned into trying a public-relations flimflam?

During the week that the tapes rumor flourished and then expired, a lot of people recalled that Vicki Morgan had hinted that her forthcoming revenge memoir would reveal the details of high-level hijinks embarrassing to the Reagan administration. This was a woman who had boasted openly that the secrets she knew could "bring down the government." It was a reasonable guess that the targets of her revelations, whoever they might be, were not at all sorry that she had not survived to write her autobiography.

More unexpectedly, it developed that Morgan's accused killer, despite his confessions to the police and to the press, had his share of supporters. The initial press stories about the killing described Pancoast as a thirty-three-year-old unemployed male, presumably Morgan's lover, who was living off her at the time of her death. But those who knew Pancoast personally, and indeed anyone familiar with the contents of his statement to the LAPD, realized that this was not so. First of all, Marvin Pancoast was gay. Secondly, he had not been sponging financially off Morgan. If anything, the situation had been the reverse—he had given her a car and, just days before the murder, had arranged to borrow $3,500 from his family to provide a place for her to live after she was finally evicted from her Colfax Avenue condo.

Although the movie community normally gives celebrity hounds and hangers-on short shrift, it seemed especially eager to believe that this one was incapable of committing a violent crime. The consensus of the grapevine was summed up succinctly by

Vanity Fair contributing editor Dominick Dunne, who quoted an unnamed "movie star" of his acquaintance as telling him: "Oh no, darling. Marvin's not guilty. We knew Marvin. He worked for my ex-husband. Nutty as a fruitcake, yes. A murderer, no. You check his mother's bank account after this is all over, and you'll see she's been taken care of for life. They'll just put Marvin in the nuthouse for a few years. It's Marilyn all over again. Did you ever know that the CIA went to Marilyn's house afterward and cleaned out everything? I bet they did that at Vicki's place, too. I bet that's where those tapes went."

As the summer of 1983 wore on, it became apparent that the police case against Marvin Pancoast was going to do little to snuff out the smoldering rumors of conspiracy. During the course of pretrial hearings, the DA's office and the LAPD acknowledged that:

No fingerprint technician had ever been called to the scene of the crime.

No fingerprints had been found on the alleged murder weapon.

An autopsy performed on the victim had turned up no trace of drugs in her bloodstream, despite the reports of witnesses, including her mother, that she had been taking Valium on the day she died.

The crime scene had never been sealed.

The case against Marvin Pancoast, in short, was based on his own confession. And his attorneys claimed that he was mentally incompetent, with a history of confessing to crimes he had nothing to do with.

Even if there was no fire at all behind all the smoke of the conspiracy rumors, the death of Victoria Lynn Morgan posed certain mysteries.

How could it have happened that the central figure in one of the steamiest sex scandals of the decade had ended up being murdered by a gay buddy? And who *was* Vicki Morgan anyway?

In interviews with the press she had portrayed herself as the loyal and ill-served other woman, who had kept vigil by the bedside of her terminally ill lover Alfred Bloomingdale while his wife continued to party as usual.

In a sworn deposition given during the course of her palimony suit, Morgan had presented a somewhat different picture, describing herself as a reluctant but frequent participant in

Bloomingdale's sadomaschistic orgies, a victim of his flagellation fetish.

According to her mother, Vicki was nothing more than a poor girl "took up the creek," corrupted at seventeen by a wealthy and domineering older man.

According to others who knew her as an adult she had been, variously, a high-priced call girl, a frivolous party girl, or simply a fortune hunter who cultivated affairs with very wealthy men in the hope of tricking one of them into marriage.

Which was the real woman: Vicki the victim, or Vicki the victimizer?

Contrary to what cynical newspaper readers might have assumed at the time of the palimony trial, Morgan was telling the truth when she described her twelve-year relationship with Alfred Bloomingdale as a love affair. And she was telling the truth also when she described him as the pursuer—employing bribes, cajolery, and sometimes outright threats to defeat her numerous attempts to break off the affair. As one delved into her history, however, it also became apparent that Morgan was by no means the loyal, long-suffering Other Woman that she portrayed herself as being. She ran back to her wealthy lover as often as she tried to escape from him, and she filled the interstices in their affair with a series of adventures, marital and extramarital.

Vicki Morgan lived in the glamour capital of America, on the fringes of a society that was not so much evil or corrupt as just puffed up with fantasies of unearned wealth and unmerited celebrity. She wanted to grab a piece of the action for herself—she wanted to be rich and famous, but most of all to be loved unconditionally, and by someone who could fill her existence with the excitement and sense of purpose that she had been unable to find on her own.

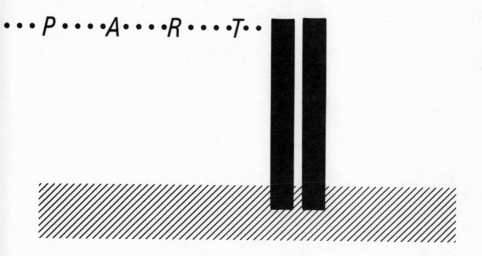

··· P ··· A ··· R ··· T ·· II

> *"It was only an average little conscience, a thing which represented the world, her past environment, habit, convention, in a confused way.*

THEODORE DREISER
SISTER CARRIE

A Girl of Average Conscience

///

Snapshot: *They make a handsome couple, tall, fair Connie Reid and her strapping Yankee soldier groom. In the wake of the global tragedy of World War II, it seems little enough to ask that a few couples like Connie and Delbert should be able to celebrate their own personal happy endings.*

Sergeant Delbert Morgan, an army air force corpsman, is about to be shipped stateside to Colorado Springs, assigned to recruit young men into the revamped peacetime U.S. Air Force. And Connie, despite the usual nervousness at leaving her family and the familiar scenes of her home town, Norfolk, England, is hardly sorry to be leaving a country still groaning over the restrictions of postwar rationing and shortages. Already in her mid-twenties, she is a slender woman with perfect posture that makes her seem taller than her claimed height five-feet-six, and her square jaw has a decisive set to it that makes her more likely to be described as striking or handsome than conventionally pretty. The war had put her life on hold long enough, and the prospect of getting out of England and settling with her new husband in the wide open spaces of the American West is an exciting one.

Quite soon, the couple will be starting a family. Barbara, their first child, joins the picture in 1946. Their second daughter, Victoria Lynn, was born six years later, on August 9, 1952.

By the time Vicki was born, this idyllic family portrait was already on the point of being shattered. Delbert Morgan had grown restless. He'd come to regret his match with a working-class woman who had no money of her own and no particular social aspirations, and he left when he found a woman who appeared to have more to offer.

One day when Vicki was just a few weeks old, Connie came across a crumpled letter in her husband's pocket, a love letter Delbert had written to another woman and forgotten to mail. Connie was convinced that the other woman's main attraction was that she was financially well fixed. "She wasn't *that* rich," recalls Connie, "but she had some money because that was the reason he split."

Delbert Morgan got a transfer to Texas where he remarried and remained in the air force until his twenty-year retirement came around in the latter half of the 1960s. After that, he became an executive with Foley's, the Houston department store. He continued to help out with child support, but his contact with his children was sporadic at best.

Her husband's desertion and particularly its timing, so soon after the birth of her second child, left Connie angry and embittered. A devout Episcopalian, she did not approve of divorce for others and was certainly unprepared for the fact that it was happening to her. For several years after that, she says "I hated the ground men walked on."

Everyone expected the divorce to be hard on Barbara, "the serious one," according to Connie, a typical eldest child who was just starting school. Vicki Lynn, only a baby, ought to have been too young to be seriously affected. Yet Connie, an observant mother, saw signs that told her otherwise.

"Vicki's relationships with men go back to a time when she couldn't hardly know what a man was," Connie said later. "She could be crying when she was six months old and have a male pick her up, and she'd stop crying."

After her divorce became final, Connie took her children and went back home to England. She was close to her family and needed their help to manage supporting and caring for two youngsters. In the early 1950s, however, England was not the easiest place for a young woman in her situation. Wages were low, class barriers still existed in a way that they didn't in the States, and opportunities for remarriage for a woman over thirty with two kids were few. After two years, with Barbara already in school and Vicki getting old enough to be left in the care of others, Connie decided to try America again.

Soon after her return to Colorado, Connie met Ralph Laney, a tool-and-diemaker. Laney was a steady man of few pretensions, but his skilled trade put him at the top of the blue-collar aristocracy. Vicky was four years old when Connie married Ralph and they all moved to California, where he felt, says Connie, "There were more prospects." The move paid off, as Ralph landed a job as foreman in a tool-making plant.

Connie was now thirty-six, and by the standards of time it was a bit late in the game for starting a second family. But Ralph wanted children of his own, and over the next three years, Connie gave birth to two boys, Patrick and John. In the late 1950s, not long after the first son was born, the Laneys purchased a modest one-story ranch house on Harvard Avenue in Montclair.

As an adult, Vicki Morgan, who felt a need to invent certain myths about her background and her identity, would choose to describe herself as "just a farm girl." In reality, she never lived on a farm and there was nothing even remotely bucolic about the neighborhood where she grew up. The Laney house with its attached garage was part of a typical postwar suburban community, a tract of working-class housing plunked down on the floor of the arid San Gabriel Valley, south of Pomona and north of Highway 60, less than an hour from downtown L.A.

It was one of those instant neighborhoods that seemed destined to grow, to flourish, and then to wane within a single generation. In the beginning were few amenities except for self-consciously anglophilic street names, such as Tudor Avenue and Surrey Avenue, names that appear to have been chosen in almost hostile defiance of the architecture, the climate, and the cultural origins of the place. Gradually, the dormitory community would begin to mature until there were new schools, a new library and post office, fast food places on the highway, and—most notably—a sprawling shopping plaza complete with enough asphalt-paved parking slots to accommodate every adult inhabitant of the town. But by the time these things were in place—before most of the owners had quite made the last payments on their mortagages—Harvard Avenue would already have become the kind of place that their teenagers would long to escape.

In the late fifties, however, the sidewalkless streets were still full of tricycles, and the neighborhood was full of couples just starting out. Connie and Ralph, like many of their neighbors, did not intend to stay around forever. "There would be other houses, better and bigger with more bedrooms." Harvard Avenue was to be just "a starter."

In the meantime, the acquisition of a stepfather and then two half-brothers required some emotional readjustments on the part of the girls. Barbara, still the "sensitive one" in the family, seemed to be the one who needed reassurance. One day not long after starting school in Montclair, Connie recalls, Barbara came home in tears.

"The teacher says my last name is Morgan, not Laney like yours. Why do we have to have different names?"

In fact, Ralph Laney had offered to adopt the two girls, only to have the plan vetoed by their natural father, Delbert Morgan. But Connie could see no reason why Barbara should feel set apart from her family because of a formality. "Don't worry," she told her. "Tomorrow I'm going up to the school to tell your teacher that your name is Barbara Laney. How will that be?"

Since there seemed no point in having Vicki be the only member of the family to use the name Morgan, Connie had her school papers changed as well, and she was known as Vicki Morgan Laney from then on. Unlike her sister, Vicki did not appear to need the emotional security of the name change. She showed no signs of feeling left out and loved having a new daddy to make a fuss over her and two baby brothers to play with.

Scrawny and long-legged, her fair baby hair already darkening to dishwater blond, she was the happy-go-lucky one of the two girls, the one who seemed to take changes in her stride. Vicki studied violin for a while and also played the accordion, but basically she wasn't the type of kid to get too serious about anything. She seemed content to be a tomboy, pedaling madly around on her bike and playing out-of-doors until that last possible moment in the evening.

During the summer of 1961, Ralph Laney received an offer to go to work for another company, at considerably higher wages and with prospects to move into the higher ranks of supervision. He decided to make the switch over Labor Day, allowing himself just a few days' vacation between his old job and the new one.

On September 2, however, Ralph suffered a massive and fatal heart attack.

Naturally, Connie was devastated, but she didn't have a great deal of leisure to spend mourning. Shortly after Ralph died, she discovered that the life insurance policy he'd carried, not to mention the family medical plan, had been fringe benefits of his previous job. The coverage was scheduled to be picked up by Ralph's new employer, but unfortunately, there was a thirty-six hour lapse in between when Ralph was not officially working for anyone and the insurance was not in effect. It was during that thirty-six hour hiatus that Ralph had died.

Things like this weren't supposed to happen, especially to the wife of a man who was the solid type, a good provider always with an eye out to do a little better for his family. Nevertheless, it had happened.

Connie, now just forty, hadn't worked in years, and she had four children this time around, the eldest fifteen and a half, the baby just one and a half. Fortunately, she now owned the house free and clear, thanks to a separate mortgage insurance policy, but otherwise she didn't have a dime to call her own.

Connie Laney prided herself in being able to tough out hard times. Shortly after her second husband's death, Connie went to work in the cafeteria of Montclair's Chaffee High School, a job she would hold steadily for the next seventeen years. "I did everything myself," she recalls. "My own yardwork, keeping up the house, the car, bringing up the kids. I did it all."

To everyone's surprise, the member of the family hit hardest by Ralph Laney's sudden death was Vicki, then just a few days short of her tenth birthday. "Vicki was just shattered through and through," says Connie. "She never did get over it." Although no one thought much about it at the time, the insurance mess drove home the lesson, for the second time in Vicki's short life, that the loss of a man meant financial calamity.

After her stepfather's death, Vicki became noticeably more quiet and withdrawn. But in spite of her despondency, she was also turning out to be quite a beauty. Barbara had always been a pretty girl, but Vicki seemed to have a special quality that attracted notice and made it easy to get the attention she craved from adults. Perhaps it was her big, lustrous eyes or her way of turning on a smile at the right moment, but Connie got used to hearing compliments on her daughter's looks: *She'll be a real beauty, that one. . . . Did you ever think of trying to get her into commercials. . . . Why, with her height, she could be a model.*

None of these predictions seemed entirely unreasonable, although Vicki in her preteen years had begun to show the usual symptoms of adolescent awkwardness.

Snapshot: Vicki Laney, as she is then called, in her 1968 high school yearbook, a baby-faced fifteen-year-old with a cute smile and the highest, most elaborately molded beehive hairdo in school—the type of girl who is naturally attractive but doesn't really believe it, who wouldn't dream of going anywhere without her oversize purse filled with lipsticks and mascara, an eyelash curler, her manicure kit, a complete armory of toiletries.

She is already tall—five-feet-ten and lanky—at an age when many of the boys in her class are just beginning to start grow into their adult bodies. Despite the fact that she is less mature and confident than many girls at sixteen and despite a chest she considers mortifyingly flat, Vicki is already too statuesque to get away with acting giggly and girlish, already the target of bewildering advances from older guys who expect her to be as grown-up as she looks.

Vicki's sister had attended Chaffee High, the same school where their mother worked in the cafeteria, but by the time Vicki was a sophomore there was a new school within walking distance of the house. Montclair High, built to handle the baby-boom overflow from Chaffee, was a no-frills version of the "open campus" plan school, its classrooms, gym, and library being housed in featureless, one-story rectangles arranged around an open-air courtyard and a covered walkway lined with students' lockers.

In 1968 Montclair High still belonged to that more innocent era when high school was a world unto itself, a world where students practiced the values of democracy and social adjustment. The hot issue on campus that year was the dress code and among the social highlights of the winter was Backwards Week, organized by the Girls' League, featuring such events as a "squirt-gun showdown" for boys only and "the traditional slave auction." The Glaive, the yearbook, is filled with photos of students chosen for school organizations. There were elections for class officers and club officers and Girls' League officers, for the cheerleading squad and "pep commissioners," for Homecoming Queen and her court, Band Queen and her court, Prom Queen and her court, Winter Sports Queen and her court, and so on.

Vicki, the future femme fatale, was not elected anything.

Of course, she was only a sophomore, but she was already a confirmed nonjoiner, lacking the essential ingredient for high school popularity—an "outgoing personality." An indifferent student—"She just didn't like to go into the classroom," recalls her mother—Vicki seldom cracked a book or spoke up in class, but at the same time she was not enough of an academic underachiever to attract notice. She was the kind of girl who would be remembered by her classmates, when remembered at all, for her "good grooming."

During the course of that year, Connie Laney managed to scrape together the money to enroll her daughter in a night-school modeling course in nearby Covina. At the very least, Connie hoped that the classes would build her daughter's confidence and ease her self-consciousness about being so tall. The Studio Seven Academy was a cut above the usual small-town charm school. For one thing, its director Leslie Stephenson, would only accept students who had at least the potential to put their training to use in modeling. Even to get into the night course Vicki signed up for, girls had to be over five-feet-six and attractive. Also, at the time, Studio Seven maintained a branch office in downtown L.A. that helped graduates get their portfolios together and could sometimes place them in their first jobs.

Though Vicki Laney was just one of hundreds of girls to pass through the school, she made enough of an impression that Leslie Stephenson would remember her fifteen years later as "a dedicated student, a very hard worker." Vicki had the looks, the dress size, and the carriage to make it in the modeling business, but above all she seemed to have the patience and desire to put up with the less glamorous aspects of the work.

"I have this image of her sitting alone at the makeup table while the other girls are busy socializing," says Stephenson. A loner, Vicki would spend hours studying photos and trying out new tricks for highlighting her cheekbones, for emphasizing her wide-set eyes, and for minimizing her slightly too prominent jawline.

Gradually she transformed herself from a gawky over-madeup teen to a young sophisticate.

When she was still fifteen, Vicki was chosen the school's Model of the Month for several months running, and she began to pick up weekend modeling jobs at Montclair Plaza. Connie, neither more nor less objective than any other proud mother, pronounced the change in her daughter "stunning." But then, Vicki "was always the star of our family," she later said.

In the meantime, like many attractive but shy girls, Vicki had solved her social dilemma by starting to go steady at an early age. Garry Haskell, her boyfriend, was Vicki's physical opposite, a stocky youth with dark wiry hair and dark eyes, and he was also more serious-minded, interested in science with ambitions to go into medicine. According to Connie, Vicki and Garry had already been going out for "several years" by the time she was a sophomore. At any rate, Vicki fit easily into the role of the confirmed steady, ready to let her social identity be defined by her boyfriend. The pair was inseparable and, as far as Vicki was concerned at least, very serious about each other.

Connie, who believes herself prone to flashes of psychic insight, says that the realization that something had gone wrong in her daughter's life came to her suddenly one day when she was on her way home from her job at Chaffee High.

"I'm driving home from school one day," she says, "and I stopped at a Stop sign, and there was this angel. And this angel told me that Vicki was pregnant. I swear on a stack of Bibles. . . .

"So I go right home and walk into the house. And she's there, and I say, "Vicki, are you pregnant?'

"And she says, 'Mom! How did you know!' "

Vicki was only in her second month. She hadn't started to show at all, and, as it turned out, she was somewhat less upset about her condition than she might have been. "Garry's going to marry me," she assured her mother. Why? "Well, because he's got to, doesn't he?" That was the way things were supposed to be.

Vicki continued to refuse to face reality even after the pregnancy began to show. Connie, for her part, realized that her daughter was "putting up a front," refusing to deal with the situation, but she, too, thought that marriage was not an unreasonable solution. "She would have married him," says Connie, "but he just walked out and left her standing. So that was three men now who'd more or less walked out on her. People she trusted."

Not at all surprisingly, Garry didn't see matters quite that way. He was still two years away from finishing high school, his own parents were divorced; and he and his mother couldn't see how a second mistake, a marriage for which neither partner was prepared, could set the first mistake right. Connie resented the idea that the boy involved could "walk away free" from the problem, but in reality it wasn't quite that easy. The Haskells left Montclair within the year, and later, when he was out of high school, Garry got in touch with Vicki and offered what help he could—help that by then, however, Vicki didn't need.

As for other alternatives, abortion was not even considered. On religious grounds alone, Connie found it abhorrent. And since her daughter wanted the baby, Connie was not about to push her into giving it up for adoption. Nor, in 1968, was it acceptable for a pregnant teenager to stay in school while she was awaiting delivery. Aside from quitting school and hiding in the house until her baby was born, the only real option for Vicki was to go away. So, that fall, she found herself being signed in as a resident at St. Anne's Maternity Home for unwed mothers.

Operated by the Franciscan Sisters of the Sacred Heart, St. Anne's is a pink stucco complex squatting in the midst of a rundown neighborhood in north central L.A. Despite its unprepossessing physical plant, St. Anne's had, and still has, an excellent reputation. St. Anne's girls today mostly live at home while attending the center's accredited high school and taking advantage of its prenatal health care, counseling, and social activities. Those who do live in have considerable freedom and are even allowed to go out on dates. However, even the school's own brochures concede that attitudes toward unwed mothers—its own and society's in general—have changed a good deal in the past two decades.

Vicki hated St. Anne's on sight.

It was a long, steep slide from being Model of the Month and the "star" of her family to a school where vocational training meant classes in operating a supermarket cash register. Nor did it help that Hollywood and Beverly Hills, the golden lands she'd dreamed of conquering, were only a few minutes away from the dormitory where she slept every night behind locked wrought-iron gates.

Vicki hated the rules and regulations, which made her feel that she'd been cast into prison at the very moment when her approaching motherhood entitled her to be treated as an adult. She hated the punitive attitudes of some of the nuns, hated being expected to feel guilty for something that she wasn't even particularly sorry about. But over the long run, her loathing focused in on the shabby surroundings—the pockmarked tile floors and the institutional furniture, the cheap posters that the girls stuck up on the dorm walls in a vain attempt to make their surroundings homey, the steam-table food and the cheap cutlery it was eaten with.

Vicki was naturally slender, perhaps even slightly anorectic, and extremely neat as well, at least where her personal appearance was concerned. She was appalled at the way the other girls could make self-deprecating jokes all day about their ballooning bellies and spreading backsides and then gorge on smuggled junk-food snacks at night. Determined not to let herself get sloppy, she made an effort to eat as little as possible. By her ninth month she'd gained only thirteen pounds and still looked like a tall, skinny kid who just happened to be carrying a soccer ball under her T-shirt.

There were other reasons, too, for feeling set apart. She was a little younger than most of the girls in the school—in the late 1960s, unwed motherhood was still something that, if it happened at all, seemed most likely to happen in a girl's senior year. Also Vicki was half-English and all WASP, not a Roman Catholic, and she was ill-at-ease surrounded by religious statues and nuns in habits, as well as the occasional appearance of Franciscan priests, who wore floor-length brown cassocks in the classrooms.

St. Anne's was a community of women and penitential poverty, and the lesson Vicki drew from her months there was that this was what happened to life's losers, to the girls who weren't either lovable enough or lucky enough to find men who would take care of them properly. She was angry with Garry and resentful of her mother for sending her away, but most of all—and most consciously at the time—she felt a desperate determination not to be poor ever again.

On January 7, she gave birth in the private hospital that was then attached to St. Anne's. She named her son Todd Morgan, having decided to take back the name of her real father. Although a lot of girls, particularly the younger ones, gave up their babies to be adopted, this was an option that Vicki didn't take seriously for herself. Her son was all hers, the first human being she had had to love who could neither walk out on her nor banish her.

Once she and Todd returned to Montclair, however, she discovered that motherhood hadn't made her an instant adult. There weren't many jobs around for a sixteen-year-old dropout with a baby at home and no car, and though her girlfriends dropped by to *ooh* and *ah* over the baby, it was soon painfully apparent that they and she no longer had much in common. Even Todd didn't seem to need her quite as much as she'd imagined. Connie, a veteran of four children with her youngest still in grade school, found it natural to take charge of this one as well, and Vicki was not sure enough of what she wanted to prevent her mother from assuming control.

It was obvious to both mother and daughter that there was not much future for Vicki in Montclair, where she could end up either waitressing for the minimum wage or getting involved with another boy not a whole lot better able to support her than the last. So when a friend named Emma, whom Vicki had met at Studio Seven, suggested that they move to L.A. together and look for modeling jobs, Vicki jumped at the chance.

Snapshot: On her own in L.A., Vicki begins making the rounds of photography studios and agencies and designers' showrooms, occupying an endless series of naugahyde waiting-room sofas under the glares of skeptical receptionists.

The girl from the sticks is finding out that being an L.A. model is a good deal less glamorous than she'd imagined. She's dreamed of doing print work or TV commercials, assignments that would give her a lot of exposure and might gradually move her into acting, but she has neither the right contacts nor the personality to make herself stand out from the horde of good-looking, inexperienced girls on the scene.

Even the unglamorous bread-and-butter jobs in runway modeling are not that easy to come by. Vicki is too big a girl, too sophisticated looking, to model teen clothes and not quite old enough to be the first choice for adult lines. Runway models have to put in long hours, to have stamina, and, at times, to be able to parry the advances of buyers who may be less interested in the clothes than in the girl wearing them. No one wants to be responsible for chaperoning an insecure sixteen-year-old.

Vicki learns to add two years to her age when it seems appropriate and necessary, but the white lies only make the process more agonizing. Never a good liar, always nervous when it comes to meeting strangers anyway, she finds that by the time she's called for an interview her palms are cold and clammy and, more often than not, she's actually shaking, her teeth chattering uncontrollably.

Then one day, an older girl who happens to be sharing one of those waiting room couches with her takes pity. "You look like you're in a bad way," she says. "Been doing this long?"

"Uh-uh. I've just been in town a couple of weeks." Vicki grins. "Guess it shows, huh?"

The other girl doesn't deny it. "Don't worry. You'll do okay."

"I sure hope so."

"Here, why don't you try one of these?" the girl offers. "It'll calm you down."

The small blue tablet Vicki swallowed didn't exactly turn out to be the key to success, but it did make her feel less like an impostor. One or two Valiums before going to an appointment, she discovered, left her floating in a mellow sea of indifference. Rather to her surprise, she usually made a better impression this way than she was capable of making when completely straight; strangers mistook the suppression of anxiety for composure.

With time and perseverance, Vicki Morgan might well have made a go of modeling. During her first few months in L.A., she got a few modeling assignments, but she never made enough to meet her expenses and to pay her share of the rent on the small studio she rented with Emma. She found herself taking a couple of very temporary hostessing jobs to eke out a living, and still she was just barely making it, never more than a few dollars ahead of disaster.

In the meantime, she also learned pretty quickly that, while good jobs were scarce, there was no shortage of men eager to rescue her from a life of penury. Oddly, the very qualities that had barred her from popularity in high school and that made job hunting so painful were especially attractive to older men. Unlike a lot of girls who are very young and gorgeous, she didn't spoil their nymphet fantasies by talking too much and reminding them that there was a teenage mind inside that teenage body.

Vicki was the kind of girl who was always meeting men who were going to do great things for her. But by far the most persistent of her older admirers was Earle Lamm, a clothing wholesaler with an office on Westwood Boulevard, who met Vicki during the weeks when she was making the showroom rounds. Unmarried and childless, Lamm was forty-seven, thirty years Vicki's senior. A slick dresser of the open-collar and gold-chains school, Earle wore a hairpiece to disguise his bald pate and fancied himself something of a swinger, but he had not had great success in putting his fantasies into action, at least until Vicki came along.

Earle took one look at Vicki and decided that this girl was too sweet and too vulnerable to survive in a tough business, much less to live on her own in Hollywood. There was no reason why she should, either, he told her, not when he was willing to take good care of her.

It was a classic let-me-take-you-away-from-all-this offer, but with a difference. Earle told Vicki that he wanted to marry her, and right away—no nonsense about living together for six months or a year first to see how things worked out. Earle was smart enough to see that he'd never win a girl like Vicki if the courtship dragged on for too long. Once Vicki had been in town for a while, she'd wise up and learn that she could do a lot better than him.

Vicki, for her part, was still smarting from what she saw as Garry's rejection of her and mistrustful of the intentions of men in general. Earle was not the greatest catch in the world, but he really did love her—she could see that he was sincere in that—and he was not even put off at learning that she had an infant living with her mother in Montclair. Unable to have children himself, Earle was delighted by the prospect of acquiring a tractable child bride, with a son into the bargain.

A few weeks after they met, Vicki got Earle to drive her out to Montclair to meet Connie and to see Todd. Connie recognized that Vicki was looking for a surrogate father, but she wasn't sure that her finding one in Earle would be entirely a bad thing. "Earle was older, but a very nice person," she thought, and he made a big fuss over Todd, which a lot of younger men might not have done.

Earle's friends were more skeptical.

Sally Talbert and her husband Arthur were old acquaintances of Earle's who ran a retail jewelry store in Reseda. One day, Earle, whom they hadn't seen in some time, dropped in with a very young girl, announced they were going to be married and bought Vicki a wedding ring.

A few months later, the newlyweds invited the Talberts to dinner. After being married in Vegas, Earle and Vicki had returned to live in Earle's apartment in Sierra Towers, a luxury

high-rise on Sunset and Doheny, near the border of West Hollywood and Beverly Hills. The two of them seemed to be getting
along, but the May–September relationship was obviously turning
out to be a bit lonelier than either had counted on. Vicki's friends
were kids, some of them still in high school, while Earle's were
middle-aged, uncomfortable about socializing with a girl who
wasn't even old enough to order a cocktail legally.

The Talberts figured that they occupied a middle ground as far
as age was concerned—Arthur was younger than Earle, and Sally,
then in her twenties with a son who was still a toddler, had more
in common with Vicki than most of the wives of Earle's friends.

Sally, an inveterate rescuer who could never close her heart to a
homeless puppy or a lost soul, liked Vicki and felt a little bit sorry
for her. Eventually, Sally and Vicki would become close friends,
and Sally learned that Earle and his teenage wife were already
having problems.

Some of Earle's and Vicki's spats were over her work. She still
had dreams of becoming a cover girl or an actress, and Earle
wanted none of that. He didn't mind if she got some kind of little
job for a while, but basically he was hoping she'd settle down to
being a housewife, to being there waiting for him when he came
home from his office.

As for Todd, Earle was fond of the *idea* of a son but less crazy
about having a squawling infant around the house, absorbing so
much of the attention he wanted for himself. The baby was
shuttled back and forth between Sierra Towers and his grandmother's house in Montclair, seldom remaining with Vicki and
Earle for more than a few days at a stretch.

Mostly, though, Vicki's and Earle's arguments had to do with
their differing ideas of a good time. What Earle really wanted to
do most evenings was to settle down in front of the TV or perhaps
to take in a movie. He didn't have a lot of party friends, and his
idea of a big time was to go to Vegas for a few days to see a floor
show or two and make the rounds of the casinos. But winning
Vicki had made middle-aged, balding Earle feel like a young
stallion again. He started poring over the personals columns,
pointing out invitations to wife-swapping parties and ads placed
by bisexual women looking to hitch up with an attractive couple.
He was fixated on the subject of wanting to watch Vicki make love
to another woman.

If Earle had been more successful at living up to his wild and
crazy self-image, the marriage might have actually turned out

better than it did. It can't be ruled out that Vicki went along with one or two experiments in acting out Earle's fantasies, but for the most part his fantasies were just that, just talk.

All the while, Vicki was living right on Sunset Boulevard during a summer that was widely being hailed as the dawning of the Age of Aquarius. Human beings over the age of thirty were irrelevant, and when Janis Joplin sang, "Get It While You Can," she certainly wasn't singing about getting married.

Vicki would run into the girlfriends she'd met during her first few weeks in town or get to talking to other kids her age on the street. They'd ask her to make the rounds of the clubs with them or to come to a party or just to drop by their apartments. It was tough for her to say that she couldn't go because she had a forty-seven-year-old husband who expected her home, and bringing Earle along was out of the question. Earle with his hairpiece and his lizard-skin loafers and his talk about the rag trade just didn't fit in.

So Vicki started going out on her own, throwing Earle into agonies of jealousy and insecurity. For the most part at least, Vicki's evenings on the town were innocent. But no doubt Earle was right in thinking that, if the situation went on much longer, Vicki was sure to get interested in some guy who would tempt her away from a marriage that was already starting to go flat after less than a year.

It was predictable that the marriage would soon be in trouble. It was less predictable that the cause of the trouble would be a man seven years older than Earle.

According to the story Vicki would give years later in a sworn legal desposition, her first meeting with Alfred Bloomingdale occurred quite by chance as she was strolling along Sunset Boulevard near the Old World Restaurant. She was alone, minding her own business, when a fiftyish man with a slight paunch and a toothy grin accosted her on the sidewalk.

"Pardon me, do you play tennis?" he asked. "You look like a tennis player."

"Well, not really," Vicki told him. "I mean, I don't play much."

Undeterred by her response, Vicki said, the man followed her right into the restaurant.

"I only asked because I thought you might be a good partner for my daughter," he went on. "She just came back from school in

England, and she's looking for someone to play with. In fact, you look like my daughter."

While Vicki may not have been the very brightest girl in town, she certainly knew a line when she heard one. What set Alfred apart, however, was his incredible self-assurance. He didn't bother to hold back on the information that he was married. In fact, during their brief conversation, he managed to get across the information that his wife had been in Europe, too, and that he'd been feeling lonely. He introduced himself and managed to get Vicki's phone number, still on the thin pretense that they might arrange a tennis date for her with his daughter.

If Alfred expected his name to make a big impression on Vicki, he was in for a major disappointment. Vicki had never been to New York, didn't read much, and in spite of having ambitions to become a model, didn't even follow fashion news. She'd never so much as heard of Bloomingdale's department store, much less of Betsy Bloomingdale, who was considered one the best-dressed women in the country. Alfred's Bel-Air address, combined with his talk of having a daughter in an English boarding school, did get across the idea that he had money, but still, Vicki would later say, she gave him her phone number on impulse and because she couldn't think of any other polite way to get rid of him. She figured he'd never get around to calling, or if he did, it would be easier to say a definite no over the phone.

As with a number of incidents in Vicki Morgan's life, the official account is not necessarily the only one.

Sheldon (Shelly) Davis, a friend and business associate of Bloomingdale's for many years, confirms that the encounter in the Old World Restaurant did, in fact, take place. Davis says that he and a third man were having lunch with Alfred that day, and they happened to seated at a table with a good view down Sunset Boulevard when Alfred spotted the tall, big-boned blonde coming up the street—just a kid, really, but a standout in the looks department.

Alfred jumped up from the table and was out on the sidewalk almost before either of his lunch companions had a chance to put down his fork. Then, says Davis, "He just took this girl by the elbow and led her into the restaurant. Just like that. It was the most amazing thing."

But a man who knew Vicki Morgan some years later heard a different anecdote from her: "All I know is, the restaurant story wasn't the one she told me at all," he says. "Vicki said the very first time she met Alfred was during the summer she was married to Earle. She had this job in a bank in Beverly Hills. Not as a teller— she was only seventeen—but some kind of little hostess job."

Vicki, he goes on, wore a little dress and pumps, and she was supposed to greet customers when they came in the door, to offer them a cup of coffee, and so on. One day, a man came in and made a beeline right for her. He wanted to know who she was. Was she married? Did she have ambitions to get into show business? Later, it turned out that the man had an appointment with the president of the bank, who wasn't particularly pleased that Alfred was showing more interest in picking up the bank hostess than in getting on with their meeting.

"I have no idea how this fits in with the thing about the restaurant," the friend says. "I'm not saying that never happened, but I think this [meeting in the bank] must have come first." Because, he adds, Vicki always said, "That was my first introduc-tion to Beverly Hills."—meaning, evidently, it was the first time she had a chance to meet the very wealthy and had a glimmer of recognition that at least some of them might be interested in her in return.

A third version of the story is that the meeting at the Old World happened much as Vicki recounted it in her deposition, except that, at some point during the conversation, Alfred stuffed a check into Vicki's hand. It was made out for a nice round sum— $8,000.

The check was for nothing, Alfred is said to have assured her. He was just the kind of guy got generous impulses in the presence of beautiful young women.

Vicki took it.

Possibly all these versions are true. If there had been a previous meeting in the bank, it would go a long way toward explaining why Vicki spoke so readily to Bloomingdale in front of the Old World. And if there was a check, this was a detail she would hardly have wanted to mention at the time of the deposition, when attorneys for the Bloomingdale family were hunting for evidence that her relationship with Alfred had been based from the beginning on sex for pay. Although it would have been difficult if not impossible to convince a judge, however, Vicki Morgan at seventeen may have been just naïve enough, and perhaps just greedy enough, to believe that the money had just dropped into her hand, with no strings attached.

At any rate, there is no disagreement on what happened next.

Alfred Bloomingdale not only called Vicki at home but he called between five and twenty times a day for several weeks. According to Vicki, she hung up on "many" occasions, but most of the time she stayed on the line as Alfred cajoled and wheedled her into agreeing to a lunch date. "No, I'm married," she said the first few dozen times he asked, but apparently not with enough vigor to discourage his calling again. Whether because she'd already taken the check or because she just didn't know what to do in the face of such persistence, she finally gave in. Alfred suggested they meet once again at the Old World.

A health-food restaurant and local landmark featured in tourist guides, the Old World, with its folk-art decor and a menu that extolls the benefits of wholesome soups and avocado-and-sprout sandwiches, was hardly a likely spot for plotting adultery. Vicki may have considered it safe, but she was unprepared for just how safe the lunch turned out to be. When she arrived, she was completely dumbfounded to discover that Alfred was not alone.

Vicki was so taken aback that she never did catch the name of Alfred's companion, a woman who qualified as "older" by her standards and who was perhaps in her thirties. She sat through the lunch in a mood of complete befuddlement. Was the woman some sort of secretary or a business associate who had latched on to Alfred that day and couldn't be gotten rid of? Or was she perhaps some sort of agent or talent scout who Alfred thought might be able to help Vicki launch a career? "I truly have no idea who this person was in relation to Alfred," she declared years later in her deposition.

Lunch was not a prolonged affair since Alfred was not a drinker, not the type to dawdle over cocktails even if the ambiance had encouraged such a thing. The meal was over, the check paid, and Vicki was on her way home to Sierra Towers before she'd had a chance to figure out exactly what was going on. She felt a little foolish but very curious, and she realized that despite Alfred's unorthodox and unromantic approach to their date, it had been tacitly agreed that they'd meet again—and under more intimate circumstances.

Since by this time she had taken the trouble to learn that Alfred Bloomingdale was indeed a very wealthy and apparently respectable businessman, she had no reason to suspect that she had anything to lose by pursuing the dalliance just one step further.

THE FATHER OF THE CREDIT CARD

//

The first thing Vicki heard when she mentioned the name of her persistent admirer to one of her girlfriends was: "I can't believe you've never heard of Bloomingdale's! Oh, Vicki—That's just like you! He just happens to be from the family that owns the most 'in' department store in New York."

It was common knowledge—to everyone except, for a while, Vicki Morgan—that Alfred Bloomingdale owned a department store. It also happened to be untrue. Alfred did not own the store; it hadn't been controlled by the family for decades, and he himself never worked there except for a very brief stint after he left college. Nevertheless, Alfred was very much a product of his family, a success-oriented dynasty that believed in the work ethic but somehow still managed to produce more than its share of black sheep playboys.

For the first thirty years of his life, Alfred Bloomingdale was, above all, the prototypical New Yorker, subspecies, Manhattanite.

The Bloomingdales, while perhaps not the most socially prominent of New York's old German Jewish families, had impeccable membership credentials in the elite portrayed by Stephen Birmingham in *Our Crowd.* The first Bloomingdale reached New York in the early years of the nineteenth century, and a Bloomingdale ancestor fought in the Civil War. Alfred's grandfather, Lyman Gustavus Bloomingdale, was a solid bourgeois who would no doubt be quite taken aback by the trendy image of the department store he founded. Bloomingdale's under Lyman Gustavas was a well stocked if slightly stodgy emporium run for the benefit of a well-heeled and slight stodgy clientele. It was only after the founder sold out his majority interest to the innovative marketing expert Freddie Lazarus that Bloomie's began to position itself on the cutting edge of fashion.

Although the store was no longer strictly speaking in the family, the Bloomingdales retained a financial interest—and owned, as well, the valuable parcel of Upper East Side real estate on which the store was built. In the next generation, Sam Bloomingdale devoted himself to the business, while his brother Hiram C. became the family wastrel. Leon Harris's *Merchant Princes,* a history of the families who founded America's major department stores, dismisses Hiram C. as an "unashamed playboy" who, according to Sam, was "usually just getting home in the morning as I was going to work." Hiram C., Harris goes on, "developed an interest in showgirls no less intense than Fred's (Lazarus's) interest in power and profits." Hiram C.'s love for theatrical affairs was transmitted to his son, Alfred.

Born in 1916, Alfred did not take long to go about proving that he was destined to follow in his father's footsteps. After attending private schools in New York, he entered Brown University, in that era a haven for nonachieving sons of wealthy families. Years later, Alfred told an interviewer that "academically, very little should be said of me. I majored in football, but did find time between games to study a little economics and geology." Even this is probably saying too much. It would be more correct to say that Alfred majored in social life and minored in football. Even in the relaxed atmosphere of Brown in those days, his studying on the side was not enough to qualify him for a degree. He left Brown in 1938 without graduating and, after a brief sojourn in France, returned to New York where he was set to work learning the retailing business.

Alfred was, if anything, less interested in retailing than he had been in academics. He cared nothing about fashion, noticing clothes only to the extent of appreciating the figures of the svelte

models who wore them and the clever, independent young sales-
women who worked behind the counters. These attractions paled
next to those of the night spots Alfred frequented in his nonwork-
ing hours.

Even without his father's example to inspire him, a young man
in Alfred's position—wealthy, bored, and immune to worrying
about the possibility of being drafted on account of a football
injury—would no doubt have found New York nightlife irresist-
ible. The late 1930s and early 1940s were the glory days of
Manhattan's café society, a time when Broadway still sparkled and
nightclubs were run for a magical circle of revelers whose latest
tastes in dance steps and dinner partners were dutifully chronicled by such gossip columnists as O. O. McIntyre, Walter Win-
chell, and Dorothy Kilgallen.

According to *Fortune* magazine, the origins of café society lay,
paradoxically, in the Depression. Given the mood of the country,
the very rich no longer cared, or dared, to draw attention to their
living circumstances by hosting lavish balls and parties in their
own homes. Those who felt the need to court the social spotlight
felt far more secure doing so in public establishments. Anyone
who could pay the tab was free to walk into the Stork Club, Fefe's
Monte Carlo, or La Conga.

On one level, the democracy of the clubs was merely theoretical. Every establishment had its Siberia to which social nonentities
were promptly banished. Nevertheless, café society bore little
resemblance to its stuffy progenitor. Social-Register types mixed
freely with the scions of the Jewish elite, "Our Crowd," as well as
with actors, musicians, and even the occasional writer. In a
surprisingly short time, the social distinctions between the various
types who met on the common ground of the nightclubs became
blurred—first in the understanding the public who read about all
their doings in the columns, next in the minds of the parvenus
who tended to forget their place rather easily, and last of all by the
true socialites who had more fun pelting each other with peanuts
ringside at the Aquacade than they had ever had at a Newport
lawn party.

Still in his early twenties, Alfred fit right in with the most
frivolous segment of this crowd, a clique of high-spirited young
Eastsiders who clubhopped in chauffered limos and whose party
manners more often than not upstaged the floor shows wherever
they alit. Alfred was an heir with an instantly recognizable last
name, tall and athletic enough to make up for his not-particu-

larly-handsome face and blessed with stamina that left him as charming and steady on his feet at four A.M. as at the beginning of the evening.

Most of his contemporaries accepted Alfred's description of himself as a playboy. But underneath the lounge-lizard façade, he was a driven young man. "My ambition," he later said, "was to make as much money on my own as my family left me." His ability to reach this goal, all the while projecting an image of himself has a genial but lazy rich boy, was just one manifestation of his complex personality. Torn between his attraction to the hedonistic indulgences of his father and to a family tradition that stressed hard work and sobriety, Alfred was determined to have it both ways. He intended to outplay his own father, and still vindicate him by making more money than any Bloomingdale so far.

Nor was it lost on Alfred that his family had managed to profit handsomely during the years of the Depression, while so much of the rest of the country was suffering. He followed family tradition by becoming a Tammany Democrat, active enough in politics to be elected a district leader, but privately, the only politics he truly had faith in was the politics of backroom deals and personal influence. The rich stuck together and looked out for their own interests.

While not the type to spread this insight around publicly—he did not claim to be a serious person, much less a reformer type—Alfred did believe that the rich had certain social obligations. All his life he would be a generous contributor, both to charities and to political campaigns. He had no use at all for what would later be called "radical chic." Wealthy individuals who were drawn to radical politics or who practiced conspicious nonconsumption by living in shabby gentility, wearing the same tweeds for decades, struck him as being equally stupid and hypocritical. The people who had the bucks had a positive obligation to enjoy it, spreading their wealth around a bit whenever possible.

This sounds like a healthy enough philosophy. But the obligation to have fun at all costs was not one that Alfred could pursue halfway.

By the age of twenty-four Alfred had set himself up as a Broadway producer, a phase of his career best remembered in a bon mot ascribed by legend to George S. Kaufman but really said by playwright Cy Howard. Having been called in during an out-of-town tryout to perform surgery on an ailing Bloomingdale production, Howard advised that the producer would do better to "close the show and keep the store open nights."

Howard's quip pretty well summed up the attitude of the professional theater folk towards Alfred Bloomingdale. He was viewed as a know-nothing rich kid dabbling in the theater, the better to chase girls and to spend his family's hard-earned money. A closer look at Alfred's record as a producer shows that this impression was at least partly accurate.

In the beginning of his producing venture, Alfred concentrated on light comedies, with less than notable success. A play titled *Your Loving Son*—the story of a precocious adolescent who reunites his "nitwit" parents—closed after three performances and a *New York Times* review complaining that the script exuded an aura of "squalid wholesomeness." *Sweet Charity,* a George Abbott farce lampooning women's clubs, lasted through eight shows; and a domestic comedy from the pen of mystery writer Charlotte Armstrong closed almost as promptly despite the presence of Barry Sullivan in the male lead.

Alfred had better luck with musical revues, notably his 1942 coproduction with George Jessel of *High Kickers.* Over his head when it came to evaluating and nursing along scripts, Alfred was equal to the task of judging chorus girls. Work and pleasure coincided to such a degree that, while the show was still running, Alfred found himself slipping across the Hudson to Fort Lee, New Jersey, to wed one of the chorines, Barbara Brewster. The marriage deterred Alfred only briefly from his pursuit of still other leggy show girls and ended with a Nevada divorce and a very quiet settlement after less than two years.

After *High Kickers,* another of Alfred's more successful productions was the 1943 musical *Early to Bed.* Alfred's partner at this time was Richard Kollmar, a baritone who had gone from playing juvenile leads in musical shows to producing them after his marriage to the doyenne of gossip Dorothy Kilgallen. Kollmar and Bloomingdale had much in common, including their obsessive interest in the female form and, apparently, a high tolerance for vulgarity.

According to Lee Israel in her biography *Kilgallen,* the book of this musical concerned the adventures of an aging bullfighter, played by Kollmar, who somehow mistakes a Caribbean whorehouse for a girl's boarding school. The songs included one whose lyrics rhymed *cobra* with *no bra* and *abdomen* with *roamin' the gloamin'*. The jokes ran to such clunkers as "We're not shaping their minds. We're shaping their shapes!"

While the critics were not slow to point out the defects of the book—one called it "downright dull and deliberately dirty"—the show had its positive aspects. The producers hired Fats Waller to compose the score—the first time a black composer had been employed to write songs for a musical performed and directed by whites. Nor did *Early to Bed* skimp on production values. In addition to the Fats Waller songs, it had sets by Jo Mielziner, costumes by Myles White, and, naturally, the best-looking chorines of any show in town. Most significantly, *Early to Bed* made money, running for nearly four hundred performances.

In the Kilgallen biography, Lee Israel complains that while Kollmar did most of the work on the coproduction, not only in the creative area but in lining up investment money, Alfred Bloomingdale came away with the lion's share of the credit. The phrase *Entire production under the supervision of Alfred Bloomingdale* appeared prominently in the play's credits. Israel's claim makes sense given that the major investors in the musical, aside from Bloomingdale himself, were the owners of the more popular Manhattan night spots—Sherman Billingsley of the Stork Club, Leon Enken and Eddie Davis of Leon & Eddie's, Lou Walters of the Latin Quarter—all individuals who might have found it difficult to turn down a solicitation from the husband of the "voice of Broadway."

During that same year, 1943, Alfred teamed with the Schubert brothers to bring forth the biggest hit of his career, a revival of the *Ziegfield Follies* starring the comedian Milton Berle. The show had all the hallmarks of the Bloomingdale approach: the best talent money could buy, mediocre material, and a bevy of New York's leggiest showgirls lovingly, almost fawningly showcased. A financial success, the show was received by the cognoscenti with the same sort of grudging respect that the early mammals might have extended towards a lumbering, herbivorean dinosaur who had somehow managed to defy the sentence of extinction. The musical revue, the stepchild of vaudeville, was already passé, and not long enough dead either to justify a nostalgic tribute.

With the help of Berle and the lingering magic of the Ziegfield name, the *Follies* was able to defy the times. Alfred's next venture could not. *Allah Be Praised,* by George Marion, Jr., who had written the book for *Early to Bed,* was set in the harem of a Persian emir and once again attempted to stretch a single dirty joke into three acts' worth of song, dance, and sniggering dialogue. The show had built-in problems—it was this production that defied even Cy Howard's redoutable talents as a script doctor and prompted his memorable quip. And by 1944, audiences were looking for sincerity, not glitter, and true romance, not bedroom farce. Theatregoers worried about family members overseas were no longer inclined to find exotic locales automatically hilarious, much less to laugh at a naïve American succumbing to a horde of lubricious foreign females. Generally speaking, audiences were looking for memorable love songs, down-home settings, and strong stories that would reawaken their faith in basic values. Formula escapism no longer worked.

After dumping $70,000 of his own money into a futile attempt to keep *Allah Be Praised* open into its second week, Alfred bowed to the verdict of the public.

Now he devoted himself to the war effort, becoming involved in the management of a Rye, New York, shipyard. When the war ended, Bloomingdale did not return to producing for the theater. He may have begun to recognize that his tastes were no longer in step with the times. Rodgers and Hammerstein's *Oklahoma!* had ushered in a new era in the history of American musical comedy, of productions with strong books and musical numbers well integrated with the story.

Now Bloomingdale moved on to the West Coast, where he attempted to shift to producing films under the aegis of Columbia's Harry Cohn. The movie studios weren't enthusiastic about musicals during the postwar years, and at any rate, Alfred sometimes seemed more interested in making starlets than in making pictures. The main reason Alfred moved to California, Shelly Davis says, was that "he wanted to meet girls."

Still, life as an underemployed producer did not satisfy Bloomingdale for long. In 1946 he married for a second time and set out to make some serious money.

Alfred's second wife was Betty Newling, the tall, coltish daughter of an Australian-born orthodontist living in L.A. Unlike Alfred's first venture into matrimony, this was no registry office ceremony. The Newlings had social aspirations, and Alfred's friends Buddy and Louise Adler honored the bridal couple with a large garden-party reception. Among the numerous guests, coincidentally, was a woman who would serve on the jury at the trial of Vicki Morgan's accused killer. "My husband and I didn't know the Bloomingdales and they wouldn't [have] known us," the woman said, explaining that she'd only been invited because a relative of hers happened to be Betty's gynecologist. It was an extensive guest list.

Betty Newling, who soon dropped her given name in favor of the more chic nickname Betsy, had briefly entertained ambitions of acting in films. But like Nancy Davis Reagan, who later became her best friend, she set aside all ideas of an independent career on the day of her wedding. A Roman Catholic, she intended to rear a Catholic family. Alfred went along with her plans to the extent that he not only converted but also proceeded to take an active role in Catholic laymen's activities, contributing generously to the charities his wife supported in her volunteer work.

During the five years of his marriage, Alfred experimented with a number of different ventures. For a time he set himself up as a business agent, managing the financial affairs of such performers as Judy Holliday and Frank Sinatra—folks who, as Alfred later boasted, "did pretty well" in the business. Indeed they did, though it's doubtful that Alfred had much of a role in their success. The agency allowed him to remain close to his first love, show business, but the work itself bored him and offered little scope for achieving his ambition of doubling his inherited fortune through his own efforts.

Alfred's image of himself in business was basically a romantic one. He had little interest in being a caretaker, coping with the grind of day-to-day administration. Rather, he dreamed of being a seat-of-the-pants entrepreneur, starting with nothing but a bright idea and building it into a financial empire. Among the ideas he toyed with for a while was a chemically treated "lint-free" dustcloth. Another venture, which lasted somewhat longer, was a plan to distribute a new type of popcorn and soda vending machine to movie theaters. The machines worked better than the distribution system.

It wasn't until the early 1950s that Alfred got into the credit card business, a service so identified with him that he would later be known as the "father of the credit card" and the "prophet of plastic."

The multiuse credit card—a single piece of plastic that could be used to purchase goods and services from many different vendors—was indeed a bright idea. It was not, however, Alfred's idea.

Honors in the social visionary category must go to the writer

Edward Bellamy, whose 1887 novel *Looking Backward* predicted a society in which cash would be totally replaced by a single cardboard "credit card." The novel's hero, Julian West, arrives in Boston as a time traveler in the year 2000 A.D. and discovers that the credit card system has become a method of instituting a universal socialist economy in which every individual receives an income equivalent to the value of his work.

As West's host in the world of the future, Dr. Leete, agreeably explains, "A credit corresponding to his share of the annual product of the nation is given to every citizen on the public books at the beginning of each year, and a credit card issued him with which he procures at the public storehouses, found in every community, whatever he desires whenever he desires it. This arrangement, you see, totally obviates the necessity for business transactions of any sort between individuals and consumers."

Imagine how horrified the utopian socialist Bellamy would be to discover that, well before the year his story took place, the credit card system would have evolved as a means of creating money rather than of eliminating it—and in the process shaping a generation of Americans more consumption minded and more debt-ridden than any in history.

In practical terms, the credit card idea started small. In the years following World War I, many large department stores began issuing metal charge plates as a method of identifying credit customers, whom its salespeople could no longer be expected to recognize in person. From there it was a small step to installment credit plans, which allowed the store to charge interest on certain forms of credit purchases. Anyone familiar with the department store business understood that the ability to extend credit increased sales. But the decision to give credit, and the accompanying risk, remained strictly in the hands of the store management itself.

During World War II, government restrictions on credit and consumer buying all but drove the single-vendor cards of the department stores and the gasoline companies out of existence. After the war, businesses eager to get back to normal resurrected their card systems in a flurry of publicity. The generation that had come of age during the war readily accepted the concept of credit buying, and the time was ripe for new variations on the old single-use card. The Bank of America began to investigate the feasibility of a bank-issued multiuse card as early as 1947. And in 1951, the late Franklin National Bank of New York became the first major financial institution to get into the game.

Most historians of the credit card agree that the first multiuse card to go into actual distribution was the brainchild of one Frank X. McNamara, a Brooklyn businessman who owned and operated a small savings and loan company. When one of his best and most reliable customers suddenly defaulted on payments, McNamara discovered that the customer had been making a tidy profit from lending out his personal department-store charge cards to friends and acquaintances. The man had then paid the bills promptly with loans from McNamara and charged the debtors an interest premium that went into his own pocket. Since the man had no capital, his brilliant idea worked only so long as all his friends paid up promptly. With the first default, his cottage brokerage business went crashing into bankruptcy and McNamara was stuck with a bad loan.

McNamara did what most distressed businessmen would do in such a situation. He repaired to a local watering hole with his attorney to discuss the prospects for taking action against his overreaching customer. Even before the main course was served, it was agreed that recovering the debt seemed unlikely.

But McNamara, so the story goes, could not help admiring his erstwhile customer's cleverness. Crude as the execution had been, his debtor had hit on a damned good idea. The average guy, or woman as the case might be, did not want to be bothered carrying around a wallet stuffed with charge cards from every store in New York. Still, even if a customer bought in a given store only once a year, charging was a great convenience.

But what would be in it for the stores, the attorney wondered. Most of the big department stores already had charge card systems of their own and were collecting tidy sums of interest from customers who bought on credit. True, McNamara agreed, but what about the little guys like the owner of the restaurant they were sitting in at that very moment. The ability to offer instant credit would bring in new customers and inspire ones to spend more.

A restaurant credit card!

By the time coffee and the check came, McNamara and his attorney, Ralph Schneider, were quite enamored of their idea. Neither of them, however, had any notion of its true potential. They both envisioned their restaurant card as a cardboard ID with limited uses, strictly a New York–based service for businessmen, who would appreciate the convenience of having their expense-account dining consolidated into a single monthly bill.

The business, originally called Hamilton Credit Co. and then Dine and Sign, started small with an $18,000 investment. At the end of 1950, its first full year in business, the club had signed up a total of twenty-two restaurants and one hotel, all in Manhattan.

By this time it was more than apparent that this "simple" concept was by no means simple to put into practice. The business was basically a straightforward factoring operation that purchased accounts and collected from card-holding customers. Cardholder fees helped pay for credit checks and overhead, but it was still necessary to ask for a percentage discount from the restaurants, a stipulation that met with considerable resistance in a business that normally dealt with cash customers. Advertising costs, too, were higher than anticipated.

Although the business had been Francis McNamara's brainstorm, he had little faith in it. In 1952 he decided that there was no future in credit cards and sold out his share in the business to Alfred Bloomingdale, who had recently joined the company as a vice-president to start up operations on the West Coast. Alfred became president of the reorganized Diner's Club, and Schneider remained as chairman of the board. McNamara, meanwhile, went into the construction business where he rapidly lost a lot of money; he went into bankruptcy and died several years later, by which time the "white elephant" he had unloaded was already turning record profits.

Alfred was an enthusiastic and talented salesman, and like most born salesmen he excelled as promoting his own image. By the mid-1960s, after the death of his partner and friend Schneider, Alfred developed a tendency to rewrite the Diner's Club legend in his speeches and interviews. In reminiscences worded to give the impression that he personally had been in on founding the business with Schneider in 1950, Francis McNamara was no longer even mentioned. Alfred also liked to take credit for using his café society friendships to sell the Diner's Club concept to such key New York clubs as El Morocco and the Colony, establishments whose names still had a clout that is almost unimaginable today. His technique, he said, was "to go after the biggies," realizing that eventually the less prestigious restaurants and clubs would be forced to fall into line. According to one story Alfred told journalists, he pursued Stork Club owner Sherman Billingsley for nine years, lunching and dining with him no fewer than fourteen times before Billingsley finally gave in and agreed to honor the card.

Matty Simmons, who later went on to become a producer and publisher of the *National Lampoon,* went to work for Diner's Club as public relations manager in 1950 and was the author of the club's very successful sales pitch predicting the cashless society of the future—a prediction that Alfred made himself, with minor variations, over the years.

In 1959, for example, Simmons told a skeptical "Talk of the Town" writer from *The New Yorker:* "All we're doing is consolidating a charge account nation. People who now sit down once a month for a couple of hours and write thirty or forty checks will eventually issue a single bank draft instead. Someday there won't be any money; there's really no need for cash. No money, and there'll be no robbery, no holdups, no worry about losing your money. Think of the billions of dollars that are destroyed in fires! Look at the economies that could be effected by a single credit card, single billing system! Look at the number of people who are hired just to guard money! . . . I honestly believe that someday money will be obsolete!"

The prediction that plastic credit cards would mean the end of crime turned out not to be true, of course. Within just a few years, Diner's Club would be having its own problems with criminals, including a well-organized ring that defrauded the club of many thousands of dollars in 1967. Nevertheless, Simmons' talk of a future when plastic would replace cash for many purposes, which *The New Yorker* treated with some amusement at the time, turned out to be anything but wildeyed.

By 1959, the smart money was betting that credit cards did indeed have a future. As *Business Week* noted that year, "Wall Street tended to look at credit cards as a gimmick, [but] the performance of Diner's Club made it clear that it was a pretty good gimmick."

Although Alfred later portrayed himself as a coast-to-coast commuter during the 1950s, corunning Diner's Club through its New York office while living in California, Matty Simmons' picture of the Diner's Club operation during its first decade gives a somewhat different view of Alfred's role in the club's success. Simmons says it was Schneider in New York who administered the day-to-day business of the club. Alfred, he says, was basically responsible for selling the Diner's Club concept on the West

Coast, and though he often came into New York for business meetings, he did not even have a desk there. As for the Stork Club, Simmons said, "I signed up Billingsley finally, and it took me three hours to do it."

Nevertheless, Simmons remembers Alfred Bloomingdale as a man with an appealing personality—genial, loyal to his friends, and unfailingly generous. "I loved him," says Simmons. "He was a sweet man. Just so generous. He had a very good heart. I can't think of a single bad thing to say about him. Not one."

Simmons' is by no means a minority opinion. To do business with Alfred was, apparently, to love him. In later years, when the Bloomingdales contributed thousands towards helping their friends the Reagans redecorate the White House, the gift would be seen by some as Betsy Bloomingdale's inspiration. But generosity was a lifelong habit with Alfred. In addition to his formal contributions to Catholic charities and to St. John's Hospital in Santa Monica, Alfred was always the first to reach for the check and to dip into his pocket to help out an acquaintance in need.

Even Alfred's flair for self-promotion and his tendency to fall short on the execution end of ideas seldom inspired any rancor. Alfred could be goodnatured about his own shortcomings and gave out at least the impression that he didn't take the competitive side of the business world all that seriously anyway. Since he also happened to be an amusing conversationalist and an agreeable dinner companion, he made many staunch friends.

Under the genial exterior, however, Alfred Bloomingdale was a very complex personality, with sides to his character that many who knew him for years never suspected.

All his life, Alfred felt robbed by sleep. He thought nothing of partying until the early hours of the morning then catching a brief nap and arriving at his desk again by six. It was almost as if he felt that by stretching the day at both ends he could manage to compete with and outperform both his successful uncle Sam and his bon vivant father Hiram.

Moderation was not a word in Alfred's vocabulary. Fortunately, hard liquor held little appeal for him or he might well have ended up as an alcoholic. As it was, he smoked four or five packs of cigarettes a day minimum and consumed iced coffee by the gallon. He loved good food and alternated periods of indulgence with stringent dieting. He was also something of a compulsive talker, addicted to the telephone. Alfred's five to twenty calls a day to Vicki Morgan were unusual but not out of character. Once he lit his first cigarette he could dispose of a pack at a sitting, and his phone jags could go on for hours.

All these habits were eventually fueled by the consumption of amphetamines. Since Alfred was never open about his drug use with friends, it is impossible to say just when he began to take pills, but his pattern of finding it difficult to change gears suggests that the pill habit came earlier rather than later.

Another of Alfred's addictions was to intrigue. He was fascinated by power, but he never had much desire to exercise it openly, preferring to luxuriate in the role of the easygoing good guy. His eventual role as a member of Ronald Reagan's so-called Kitchen Cabinet, shaping policy and appointments from behind the scenes, exactly suited him. Alfred cultivated friendships with colorful characters from all strata, Vegas high rollers and gangsters as well as conservative California Republicans, and there were many rumors over the years about his role as a liaison for purposes ranging from secret campaign contributions to negotiating alliances of the Mob and the politicos against Cesar Chavez. How much substance there was to these rumors and how much fantasy is impossible to say. Even Vicki Morgan, despite her later claim that Alfred confided in her fully, was never quite sure what truth lay behind Alfred's talk of backroom maneuverings and secret plots. She heard many hints, but few details.

Ironically, Alfred's mania for secrecy made him suspicious of the very credit system whose virtues he preached so eloquently to anyone who would listen. The Prophet of Plastic was among the first to appreciate that credit card records could be used to reconstruct the more intimate details of one's business dealings and private life. Accordingly, he perferred to deal in cash whenever possible.

One secret passion of Alfred's that was most definitely not just talk was his pursuit of sexual novelty. After his marriage, Alfred confined himself mostly, if not entirely, to casual relations with hookers; during the 1950s he was a steady customer of certain houses of pleasure operating in the hills above Sunset Boulevard. Alfred's preference for taking on hookers in pairs, as well as for administering beatings with his belt that sometimes became more realistic than the women had bargained for, made him a memorable and not always popular john.

Not surprisingly, Alfred was threatened with blackmail several times over the years. One such incident occurred in 1958, when a pimp managed to have photos taken of Alfred and a hooker with a camera hidden behind a two-way mirror.

Shelly Davis, who was West Coast public relations manager at the time, as well as Alfred's friend and sometimes companion in the pursuit of women, recalls that it fell to him to make the actual payoff. Alfred gave Davis $10,000 in cash, and Davis drove off to a prearranged meeting with the pimp, wondering if ten big ones was going to be enough to get the guy off Alfred's case. To Davis' surprise and glee, however, the pimp had gone to a lot of trouble to get the incriminating photos only to do a careless job of researching his mark. After some haggling, Davis managed to purchase the photos and the negatives for a mere $1,000 dollars.

Not one to moralize about such peccadillos, Davis admits that his friend's pursuit of sex was compulsive to the point of mania—and his tendency to think that any woman not entirely "pure" could be had for a price, occasionally embarrassing. Still, and despite some subsequent disillusionment in his business relationship with Alfred, Davis remained convinced that the generous, goodhearted Alfred was the "real" Alfred. The companionship of such a fascinating and basically well-intentioned man, Davis thought, was worth the price of occasionally having to clean up the messes he made.

Alfred made no connection between his sexual excursions and his marriage. He didn't regard them as cheating, strictly speaking, since the women involved were pros. His views on marriage, meanwhile, were rigidly traditional. His ideal wife was a combination of executive housekeeper, child rearer, and geisha. Alfred insisted on a well-run home, and he also preferred the effort needed to maintain his home that way to be discreetly invisible, his wife's competence hidden behind a doll-like facade.

Alfred liked to tease Betsy about her charming ignorance of business and political affairs, and he made it a rule never to discuss his own business affairs at home—a situation that no doubt made it easier for him to be absent from home for nonbusiness purposes without arousing suspicion. Alfred called his wife, affectionately, Nitwit—a nickname she did not object to.

Despite her later reputation as Nancy Reagan's frivolous best friend, "best-dressed Betsy," the leader of Beverly Hills most self-consciously chic circle of lunching ladies, Betsy Bloomingdale was, and is, by no stretch of the imagination a nitwit. She had no goals beyond the purely social, but she mounted her campaign for social acceptance with the tenacity of a field general and the flair of an actress.

In many respects, the Bloomingdale marriage was the time-honored match of inherited wealth and social ambition. Alfred provided the money and Betsy the panache. They both greatly enjoyed the rewards of their union, even though Alfred sometimes groused about Betsy's efforts to smooth over his more obvious rough edges. Having already transformed Alfred into a Catholic, Betsy supervised his metamorphosis from a Tammany Democrat to a California Republican.

She was also responsible for changing him from plain Al Bloomingdale into Alfred. When a New York gossip columnist who had known Alfred for years ran an item referring to her husband as Al, Betsy called up Sheldon Davis to complain bitterly. "PR is supposed to be your job," she reminded him. "Can't you *do* something about this! Can't you stop things like this!"

In 1958, about the same time Connie and Ralph Laney were purchasing their ranch house in Montclair, Betsy and Alfred and their three small children moved into a Palladian-style home on three acres in the Holmby Hills section of Bel-Air. The white-walled house, its floor plan arranged around an open-air atrium, and its grounds planted with lemon trees and camellias, was a natural showplace. An avid gardener, Betsy improved the grounds with a formal rose garden, its blooms an anthology of the latest and rarest hybrids. She had the interior redecorated several times, eventually settling on the cheerful citrus shades and bright paisleys of her favorite decorator Ted Graber.

Betsy's social ambitions went beyond the merely personal. She loved the California climate and the relaxed life-style, but, socially speaking, L.A. was a very small pond indeed as compared to New York. Not one to sit back and to do nothing about a situation that displeased her, Betsy set out to raise the tone of California society. Through an acquaintance she made when their children attended the same camp, Betsy got to know Nancy Reagan, whose husband was the rising star of California politics. Betsy used her influence to steer Nancy away from her provincial, middle-class housewife image and introduced her to chic clothes and "fun" friends.

By the end of the 1960s, Betsy and Nancy were firmly established as best friends, and Betsy had been accepted, however guardedly, by Nancy's former social circle, the wives of Ronald Reagan's wealthy supporters. For all his talk about his wife's frivolity, Alfred also liked to joke that the rising influence of California conservatives on national Republican politics was all part of his wife's plan to shift the center of the social whirl from the East Coast to the West, and into her home court.

For Diner's Club, meanwhile, the 1960s was a troubled decade. The club's billing revenues had been rising steadily, increasing by an average of 40 percent annually during the late 1950s. Then, quite suddenly, the company fell prey to the usual problems of success.

Diner's Club had done such a good job of selling the credit card concept that it had begun to inspire competition. The first heavy-weight challenger, the American Express card, appeared in October 1958, and after that Diner's Club was never quite the same. American Express could draw on its worldwide network of offices and the reputation of its universally accepted credit cards, an advantage that left Diner's Club, for all its decade of precedence in the field, struggling to keep abreast of its new rival.

While American Express had an unbeatable advantage in market acceptance, other newcomers in the business, including Hilton's Carte Blanche, attempted to undercut Diner's Club by offering restaurant owners better deals. Carte Blanche, for instance, took only 4 percent of the customer's gross tab instead of the 7 percent demanded by Diner's Club. The only way Diner's could pay for the heavy advertising and promotion necessary to maintain its position in the market was through continually issuing new cards in order to pump up charge volume. Of course, the competition was in the same position, but Diner's two major rivals, backed by resources of the Hilton chain and American Express, had more room to maneuver in the short run. And naturally, as Diner's reached deeper into the barrel, accepting less affluent card members, its problems with delinquent payment multiplied apace.

Diner's Club had to expand or die, and it nearly did both.

One of the first and most ambitious plays made by Ralph Schneider and Alfred turned out to be a near disaster. The Sheraton Hotel chain had initiated a paid-membership credit card club imitative of Diner's Club and known as Sheraton Central. Sheraton had also issued some eight hundred thousand free cards, good only at the chain's fifty-four hotels. In 1958, in exchange for 12½ percent of Diner's Club's existing stock, worth about $5.5 million on the market, Diner's agreed to take over both operations, with the additional promise that Sheraton would honor Diner's Club cards exclusively. Unfortunately, Sheraton's much vaunted list of eight hundred thousand new prospects proved to be just about worthless—one business reporter compared the list to the register of serfs in Gorki's *Dead Souls*, an apt parallel. It developed that some 40 percent of the Sheraton's list already held Diner's Club cards. A hefty percentage of the remainder could not even be located. Alfred Bloomingdale, of all people, should have been sophisticated enough to realize that all sorts of names get signed on hotel registers for all sorts of reasons. Yet, as Ralph Schneider later explained to reporters, the both men had allowed themselves to be "beguiled by numbers."

Even so, Ralph Schneider had generally been a moderating influence on his more flamboyant partner. He was the administrator with a grasp of the details of the operation, while Alfred was the idea man, salesman, and spokesperson—the one who delighted in mounting campaigns to open up new territory for the club abroad, as well as previously uncharted areas of the credit business such as car rentals and cruises. Schneider's long terminal illness during the early 1960s left Alfred free to expand at a faster pace—with heady but ultimately disastrous results.

In 1966 Diner's started a spinoff called the Wayfarer's Club, a travel-information service for automobile travelers modeled to some extent on AAA. A year later, it paid $5 million to acquire the Fugazy network of travel agencies. Then came Reservations World, a computerized reservations service that was touted as a centralized bureau for international hotel and transportation reservations.

The acquisitions were basically sound, but there was simply no way that they could do more than reinforce the loyalty of the club's more affluent customers. By the late 1960s, after many false starts, the banks were finally beginning to move in on the credit card business with MasterCharge and Visa. Many banks offered free cards to begin with, and when they did charge fees, their fees were less than a third of Diner's Club's annual "membership dues."

Alfred was much better at generating plans than at bringing them to fruition. A mediocre administrator at best, he had never been able to summon up much interest in such ongoing details as management structure, personnel, and customer relations. Balance sheets bored him. His attention flitted from one scheme to the next, without ever focusing on the problem of how this or that new acquisition might fit into the Diner's Club's overall profit structure.

Alfred's pet acquisition during 1968 was International Flotels, a scheme to crash the lucrative resort business through leasing "floating hotels." The houseboat-based flotels could be built wherever costs were favorable and then sold to franchise operators abroad, who would be able to avoid paying top dollar for beachfront real estate and local construction. Alfred was convinced that the plan had tremendous potential, particularly for creating instant resorts in picturesque but remote locales in underdeveloped countries.

While not, perhaps, as good an idea as the plastic credit card, the flotel had possibilities, and Alfred, who had taken Diner's Club into more than 130 different countries, had precisely the background needed to sell it. But the business also required capital, as well as managers capable of dealing with the infinite variety of problems involved in setting up and monitoring an international operation. Already overextended and constantly struggling to stay one step ahead of its competitors, Diner's Club was in no position to develop such a scheme.

In 1967 Diner's Club showed a profit of $2.5 million. By the second half of 1968 the company was in the red. In September 1969, the value of Diner's Club's shares plummeted from an annual high of 49 to a mere 15. Continental Insurance, which had been buying up shares in Diner's Club for two years—including Alfred's own—decided that the time had come to bring in new management. Alfred resigned his position as chairman of the board and CEO, announcing that he was leaving the company to "pursue other interests" and taking his favorite project of the moment, International Flotels, with him.

The slump in the fortunes of Diner's Club was not a financial calamity for Alfred. He'd already sold his ownership position to Continental before the slide. It was, however, a tremendous blow to his ego. Alfred had loved being identified as father of the credit card—loved the image and the work as well. His public failure was deeply embarrassing, and being ousted from the company left a huge gap in his life.

Within eight months of leaving his position as CEO, however, he had found a new passion that would preoccupy him for the rest of his life—the teenage wife of Earle Lamm.

PLAYING THE GAME

///

The meeting place chosen for Vicki's third date with Alfred was, of all places, the original Schwab's drugstore, the Sunset Boulevard landmark that for decades had been a magnet for would-be starlets looking to be discovered.

It is doubtful that Vicki had ever heard of the Schwab's legend. She knew as little about film lore as she did about fashion and, besides, considered anything that had happened before, say, 1955 to belong to the arcana of ancient history.

But Alfred certainly knew exactly what Schwab's was famous for. It was here, at least according to the apocryphal annals of press agentry, that the original sweater girl Lana Turner was innocently sipping a chocolate soda when a passing Hollywood mogul happened to recognize her unique, shall we say, characteristics and launched her on the road to stardom.

As Alfred no doubt also knew, this incident, like so many of the greatest moments in Hollywood history, never actually occurred—it was invented to hype Turner's debut as a sweater-clad schoolgirl in the movie *They Won't Forget.* Nevertheless, Schwab's was at one time a place where newcomers in filmland might actually find themselves standing at the magazine rack next to the very stars whose pictures graced the fanzine covers. It just happened to be next door to the Garden of Allah hotel, a California casbah with a roster of guests including, at one time or another, the Marx Brothers, John Barrymore, Katharine Hepburn, Greta Garbo, Humphrey Bogart, and just about every name New York writer who ever came west to do a stint with one of the major studios.

For years after the Garden of Allah's demise—it was replaced, originally, by a bank—Schwab's continued to be frequented by young hopefuls who felt that the spot just might be lucky for them. Even Marilyn Monroe, according to one of her biographers, used to go there for lunch during her starlet days, hoping to be recognized.

Although it also happened to be convenient to the final destination Alfred had in mind for the afternoon, it must have occurred to him that Schwab's would be humorously apropos for this particular rendevous. His nostalgia for the old Hollywood was all the keener for the fact that he'd arrived too late to be more than a fringe figure during the waning days of the studio system, and he was a man who loved quirky practical jokes. He couldn't help but be aware of the parallels—Vicki Morgan was about to be tapped for her first starring role, though the drama was being produced for his own private enjoyment.

Alfred was standing on the sidewalk when Vicki pulled up in the front of the drugstore, and in response to her wave, he approached her car and got into the front seat beside her.

"Pull around back into the parking lot," he directed her. "There's a young lady waiting there who's going to be riding with us."

"My heart sank to my feet," Vicki would say in her deposition a decade later. Here she had already more or less decided that she was going to have an affair with this enigmatic but clearly infatuated multimillionaire, and she couldn't even manage to get him alone.

Vicki pulled into the parking lot and a young woman who had been sitting in Alfred's Mercedes came over and got into her car. Vicki noticed that this woman was rather attractive and a good deal younger than Alfred's companion at their last meeting at the Old World, but once again she was too surprised to catch a name.

Following her companion's instructions, Vicki turned her car around and tailed Alfred's Mercedes, which headed across the boulevard and headed up Sunset Plaza Drive. The road was steep and winding, and Vicki, never a confident driver, found herself holding her breath, hoping that she won't meet a car on its way down.

Concentrating on the task at hand wasn't made any easier by the bizarre, one-sided conversation of the "young lady" who was riding with her. For that matter, the girl didn't look like much of a lady. She was heavily made up and hard looking, and she had a way of saying the most amazing things as if they were completely banal.

"Alfred wants you to know that he thinks you are very special," she said, for openers.

So why didn't he tell her that himself, Vicki wondered with annoyance. What was going on here?

"Alfred has a real interest in you," the girl continued in a washboard-flat voice, obviously delivering a prerehearsed message. "And I'm here to tell you that he's going to want to beat you when we get up to the house.

"Alfred will probably tie you up. He wants me to tell you this, but he also wants me to let you know that you're special to him and he will make special allowances."

Of course, Vicki could always have stopped the car, ordered her passenger out, and headed back down the hill to the safety of her apartment and doting husband. This is what any sensible woman with an ounce of self-protective instinct would have done, but then, a really sensible woman would not have put herself in this situation in the first place.

The two-car caravan snaked upward through the section of hills where bungalows are clustered together so thickly that they seem to be contesting with each other for standing room. They were up above the development line now, nearing Mulholland, when Alfred pulled into a parking space in front of modest cedar-shingled house. Led inside by her companion, Vicki found herself in a sparsely furnished living room that looked distinctly unlived in.

Already making himself comfortable on the couch, Alfred introduced a second woman who was apparently their hostess. Kaye, a bleached-blond, weathered-looking woman in her thirties, did not seem inclined to prolong the social amenities. "We'll just hop into the kitchen and fix you both some iced tea," she said, excusing herself and the younger girl.

"Come and sit by me on the couch, Vicki," Alfred directed her. "You'll be more comfortable."

Vicki numbly accepted, and there was an awkward silence until Kaye delivered two tall glasses of iced tea and disappeared upstairs with her companion.

"Do you know what this is all about, Vicki?" Alfred asked.

"Uh-huh." said Vicki, who by now certainly had the general idea, though she wasn't sure whether to be excited or scared by the prospect. After a year with Earle Lamm, she was no longer an innocent, but hers was the spotty sophistication of the very young. Earle had more or less told her that group scenes and kinky sex were what older men wanted. Still, it hadn't quite sunk in that the other women were pros, hired for the occasion. She suspected that they were. She just wasn't quite sure.

Alfred drank deeply of the iced tea and drew deeply on his cigarette.

"I think you're a very special girl," he said. "I knew it the minute I saw you. And I want you to become my mistress."

Vicki considered for a while. "Okay," she agreed. "But I'm married, y'know."

Alfred stubbed out his cigarette and immediately lit another. "Don't worry about that," he told her. "Just ask your husband what he wants. What it will take to get him to step out of the picture."

"But I'm married . . . like I said."

"Is that the only reason?"

"I don't know. But it's one reason."

"I told you. I'll take care of it. In fact, if you'll let me, I'll take care of everything for you from now on."

It was a brief, apparently straightforward conversation, but one that would lay the groundwork for twelve years of painful misunderstandings.

As far as Alfred Bloomingdale was concerned, there are only two categories of women, and Vicki, regardless of age or marital status, obviously belonged to the second. Otherwise she wouldn't have been sitting there on the couch with him, not after all that had happened so far. What he was proposing was essentially a business transaction, and no doubt he had come prepared for some serious negotiating. Vicki's blithe "Okay," her concern for nothing except how to ease her husband out of the picture, could have meant only that she was eager and none too bright.

Vicki, on her part, still half suspected that all this was some kind of an elaborate puton. If Alfred wanted to get into bed with her, fine. She was bored with her marriage and she'd come this far already, so why not? Besides, having come of age in the 1960s, she thought that *mistress* was a musty, old-fashioned synonym for a female lover.

For that matter, even the hints that the affair would involve group sex and S&M, didn't have quite the same connotations of decadence and evil that, for Alfred, were the entire point of indulging in them. Vicki Morgan belonged to a generation that believed that experimenting with kinky sex was just another form of self-liberation, perfectly fine as long as it was done in the right spirit and if everyone had agreed to the rules ahead of time.

"I promise you that you won't have to do anything you don't want to do," Alfred assured her. "Any time you want out, just say so."

Since Vicki apparently had nothing more on her mind, Alfred relaxed. Putting out his last cigarette, he took her by the arm. "How about it?" he said. "Let's you and me have some fun upstairs."

In the upstairs bedroom, Kaye and the other girl were waiting, seated on the bed, already nude. Nodding to Vicki to remove her clothes, too, Alfred undid his belt and took off his trousers. "Kaye, you get the apparatus ready," he ordered.

Although she had thought she was prepared for just about everything, Vicki was stunned by the total absence of preliminaries. It was as if she had stepped into a scene that the others had been rehearsing until the spontaneity was completely wrung out of their lines. And then there was that clinical-sounding word *apparatus,* whatever the hell that meant . . .

Numbly fingering the buttons on her blouse, she noticed that Kaye had fumbled around in the drawer of the nightstand and produced a phallus-shaped, battery operated vibrator and a tangle of neckties. Kaye set these on the bed and then deftly removed Alfred's belt from his discarded trousers.

With practiced assurance, Kaye knotted several of the ties together into a makeshift rope. With one end of the ties she secured her female companion's hands, and then, after positioning her against the bedroom door facing forward, looped the ties over the top of the door and fastened the free end to the outside doorknob. She then cooperated meekly as Alfred tied her up in the same position next to the other woman.

Alfred, however, put more enthusiasm into the task. When he had finished, Kaye's arms were stretched so tautly over her head that her heels could no longer quite touch the carpet. Seizing his belt, Alfred immediately started flailing away with gusto at the two women's buttocks. Both of them shrieked and cried and begged him to stop—not so much in genuine pain, Vicki thought, as because this was the response expected of them.

Then Alfred seemed suddenly to remember that Vicki was still in the room and turned to see how she was reacting. "Isn't this fun!" he demanded.

For the first time all day, Vicki was genuinely scared. The expression on Alfred's face, a peculiar mixture of rage and abandon, was one she'd never seen before. It was as if the gruff but basically genial middle-aged man she'd been talking to all these weeks had disappeared, his body taken over by another personality, malign and out of control. She noticed that a few nasty-looking pink stripes had blossomed on the women's backsides.

The two women's protestations still had a flat play-acting quality about them, but the acting was getting better by the second. Alfred was like a wild man, determined not to let up until he'd managed to get the women genuinely scared. Some of those strokes he was laying on must have really really stung.

"Come on, tell me. Say it!" Alfred demanded of her again. "It's fun! Isn't it!"

"Uh . . . sure. Okay. It's fun."

The novelty of Vicki's presence, of her genuine alarm and fear, seemed to push Alfred to a new plateau of excitement. He came over to the bed where she'd been sitting and pulled her across his lap, spanking her enthusiastically with his open palm. The spanking smarted but it didn't last long, and neither did the act of intercourse that followed.

When it was over, Alfred was quickly his old self again. He untied Kaye, who freed the other woman, and the two of them left the room. "Let's take a shower," Alfred suggested when they were alone. "Will you take a shower with me?" he wheedled, as if he were asking some sort of major favor of her.

That part of it was definitely bizarre. After all that had gone before, after Alfred's wild behavior just minutes previously, now he had shifted back to acting as if showering together were some sort of a big deal.

And, oddly enough, in a way it was. With Kaye and her friend off together, presumably cleaning up in the second bathroom, this was the first moment of real intimacy she and Alfred had ever had together. As they stood together under the hot jet of the shower, Alfred gently soaped her back and her still smarting ass and talked to her in soothing tones, telling her that she mustn't let today's little session give her the wrong impression.

He was just a jaded old man who needed a little fun and games to get him going. But she mustn't feel that this had anything to do with her or with the way he felt about her. He wanted to take care of her, to make her his special girl. They'd have lots of fun together, real fun. They'd go to Florida together and other places, too, places he knew Vicki would enjoy.

Vicki didn't say very much in reply to all this. She claimed she needed some time to think the matter over, but in reality, her mind was already made up. True, she didn't like the beating and the scary way Alfred had acted, but she wasn't as shocked as she might have been. The knowledge that Alfred was a powerful male with violent urges he couldn't control was titillating—and it was even more exciting to think that he had promised to make an exception for her alone, to hold himself in check because she was so very special to him . . .

Over the next three months, Vicki continued to play "the game," as Alfred called it.

Two, sometimes three times a week she'd meet him at the house on Sunset Plaza Drive, which by now she knew had been rented by Alfred to serve as his private playhouse. After his scare in the late 1950s, when he'd been photographed in bed with a prostitute without his knowledge, Alfred had become cautious about where he indulged in his fun.

Of course, Vicki also now knew now that the other women who participated in the afternoon sessions were hookers, though she never did see any money change hands or hear it discussed. Kaye, whom Alfred apparently trusted to manage his scenarios the way he wanted, was a regular, but the second hooker was seldom the same; it was apparently Kaye's job to select her partner and coach her on how to behave. Neither Kaye nor her partners ever had much to say to Vicki. They weren't there to socialize anyway, and perhaps they'd also been forewarned by Alfred not to get too chatty.

Vicki could never quite figure out the appeal of the game. It wasn't so much the kinkiness of it all that bothered her as the sameness. But it was the ritual, almost scripted quality of the games that seemed to turn Alfred on. The slight change in cast, the different looks and reactions of each new hooker, was all the innovation he needed or wanted.

And then, inevitably, there came the moment in the script when Alfred was totally consumed by the fantasy. Vicki called it his "Jekyll and Hyde" change, but it was no joke when it happened. In a matter of seconds, a glazed-over look would come into Alfred's eyes—"Like something you'd see in a hospital, or in a movie," she later said. She couldn't talk to Alfred when he was like that; he was a different person, and the transformation was always frightening to watch.

Then one day, after several weeks of adherence to the script, there came an afternoon when Alfred turned his glazed stare on her, and Vicki could see that he was no longer the same man who had promised never to beat her. Without a word, he took a spare tie and bound her hands in front of her body, turned her over on the bed, and proceeded to whale away. Vicki shrieked and started to struggle, but she soon realized that her resistance was only inspiring Alfred to hit harder.

"Alfred didn't know from sharp love taps," Vicki said later. He hit hard. "He was mentally ill during these scenes, or whatever you want to call them."

Alfred apologized abjectly. He just didn't know what had come over him to make him break the rules they'd agreed on. "I promise it won't happen again," he told her.

The promises that Alfred made when he was himself, however, didn't seem to apply to the "sick" Alfred who appeared in the playhouse bedroom. By the end of the three months, Vicki was getting tied up and beaten almost every time.

And she kept coming back.

Vicki's acquiescence in this affair was something she would have a great deal of difficulty explaining twelve years later, when, as the result of her lawsuit against Alfred, she would find herself having to describe the beginnings of the relationship to a team of skeptical and hostile Bloomingdale attorneys.

The only reason she would be able to give, in retrospect, for not breaking off the affair was that she found Alfred—the normal Alfred, that is—so "fascinating." Indeed, Alfred Bloomingdale was no doubt the most interesting and complex personality she had ever encountered.

Physically Alfred was no prize. He had a big-boned, naturally strong body that had gone to flab from careless posture and lack of exercise, and his voice was perpetually hoarse from chain-smoking. He cared not at all about clothes, frequently ordering his tailor to run up copies of the same nondescript suit he had been wearing rather than devote the time necessary to getting fitted for a new style. Added to all that, he was uncoordinated and physically clumsy, a failing, however, that Vicki found rather endearing since it gave her an area in which she could feel like the competent one.

Alfred could also be brusque and overbearing. Vicki described him as "a little arrogant, but not rude arrogant"—an evaluation others would say was too kind. Nevertheless, as many who knew Alfred more casually over the years would attest, he was a genuinely fascinating personality. In his late fifties, Alfred still had more energy than many men half his age. When he was enjoying himself, Alfred was a man who really did know how to savor life. He had an almost boyish passion for professional sports and, it seemed, an endless succession of enthusiasm and bright ideas—about politics, inventions, whatever.

He could also be a considerable raconteur, and in Vicki he had a fresh and impressionable audience of one. Although Vicki didn't guess it, some of Alfred's "insider" anecdotes were actually old chestnuts, completely apocryphal or at least highly exaggerated. Many, however, were true. Alfred had countless stories about his family's rise from immigrant poverty in the department-store business and about his days as a Broadway producer, as well as tales of his carousing in Hollywood and Vegas during the 1940s and 1950s.

He had known Howard Hughes, had flown and double dated with him. At a time when Hughes was still a mystery man, with the circumstances of his withdrawal from public life the subject of speculation, Alfred knew that Hughes was a junkie—that he'd become addicted to painkillers after being injured in a plane crash in 1946, when his personal quirk about cleanliness had begun escalating into genuine insanity. Alfred liked to talk about Hughes because the latter's sexual peculiarities made his own seem almost banal: At one point during the late 1950s, before he gave up sex altogether for fear of being contaminated, Hughes had slept only with a teenage mistress whom he kept stashed in an allegedly germfree place in Coldwater Canyon.

Alfred had also gambled with Johnny Roselli in Vegas. Well, a lot of people had done that, but he had known Roselli well enough to be able to hint broadly of certain connections between the Mafia and the CIA, and the Mafia and the Kennedy White House. He knew about the extramarital philanderings of JFK.

A lot of these secrets were known to scores, if not hundreds of others and would become widely written and talked about during the 1970s, but for a teenage girl from Montclair they were heady stuff.

No doubt Alfred's great wealth was one of the more "fascinating" things about him. Still, it couldn't have been the only attraction since Vicki was in no hurry to accept Alfred's offer to take care of her financially. Although she saw Alfred almost every weekday—meeting him for lunch or for a drive or for a few minutes' conversation in his office when there wasn't time to visit the playhouse—she was still going home every afternoon to Sierra Towers and Earle Lamm.

Vicki knew by now that she wasn't in love with Earle, but she dreaded having to face his reaction when and if she told him what was going on. Also, she was practical enough to be cautious about giving up a husband who adored her and provided for her rather well to become the kept woman of a man whose passion for her might cool in a month or two.

Alfred was turned on by anything that smacked of the clandestine. But Vicki was as bad at keeping secrets as he was practiced. She wasn't morally against deception, just not good at sustaining it for very long. The more important a lie became, the less good she was at telling it. Earle was more than a little suspicious of what was going on, but Vicki, out of cowardice, kept postponing the ultimate confrontation.

Finally, after a couple of months of daytime meetings, Alfred insisted that Vicki come with him on a four-day trip to Fort Lauderdale. Lauderdale, where Alfred had substantial real-estate holdings and where he and several coinvestors were building the posh Marina Bay Club, was also his favorite extramarital playground. Betsy Bloomingdale happened to detest the place; as far as she was concerned all of Florida south of Palm Beach could have been lopped off and allowed to sink into the ocean. Hence, in Betsy's absence, Lauderdale had become a sort of safe haven for Alfred's trips with other women. Naturally, Alfred couldn't wait to show off his latest conquest. Vicki wanted to go, too, so to pacify Earle she made up a thin excuse about going off with some girlfriends.

Alfred's womanizing was in some ways flagrant, but at the same time he observed certain strict precautions. His affairs might be widely known but they were not easily documentable, and he scarcely ever risked getting caught outright by his wife. In Fort Lauderdale, Vicki found herself being tutored in the rules. She was registered in a separate room and, in fact, almost invariably spent the night there. And when she and Alfred appeared in public, at poolside or in the hotel restaurant, there was usually one or more of his cronies around for the sake of appearances. The switchboard operators were under strict instructions never to put Alfred's calls through to Vicki's room, and she in turn knew never, ever to answer his phone.

Unfortunately, the procedures didn't work quite so well on Vicki's behalf. When Earle called Vicki at the hotel to check up on her, the confused switchboard operator for some reason connected the call to the room of Alfred's business partner Bill McComas.

Earle assumed McComas was the guy Vicki was fooling around with—he'd heard by now about Alfred's calls but couldn't quite believe that the very wealthy Alfred Bloomingdale was seriously pursuing his wife. So Earle laid into McComas, calling him every name in the book. Of course, when McComas denied everything, Earle didn't believe him and just berated him all the more.

When Alfred and Vicki learned of the mixup, they thought it was hilarious. Alfred's attitude was basically, "better you than me."

This, at least, was the story according to Vicki.

After Alfred's death, when asked about Vicki Morgan, McComas denied knowing anything about her. Vicki's friends say differently and, according to her mother, McComas and his wife actually entertained Vicki's son Todd as their guest in Florida for part of one summer. Since McComas never asked to be put in the awkward position of shielding Alfred from the consequences of his philandering, it's understandable that he preferred not to discuss the matter.

Alfred wasted no opportunity to tell Vicki that Earle wasn't good enough for her.

"He's just a two-bit guy," Alfred said constantly. "A born loser. You belong in a different league altogether."

After several months of this, Vicki still objected—but not very much. It was hard to deny that Earle was outclassed by Alfred and his friends, and she wanted very much to believe Alfred when he told her that leaving Earle wasn't something she should feel guilty about. It was just a matter of finding her own natural level.

When Vicki returned from California and had to face Earle alone, this insight no longer seemed quite so crystal clear. Earle demanded to know what had been going on in Florida, and she was forced to admit that she'd been there with Alfred, not with Bill McComas. Earle lost his temper all over again, but he had no intention of giving up on his marriage without a fight.

Several days later, Vicki happened to be in her bedroom when she overheard Earle in the living room take a call and then almost immediately get into what sounded like a one-sided shouting match. She picked up the bedroom extension and heard Alfred's voice trying to calm Earle down.

"There's no reason why we can't settle this between ourselves," Alfred was saying. "Just tell me how much you want."

"You heard that," Earle fumed to Vicki after he'd hung up. "What kind of a person would try to buy a human being? Anyone who would do something like that isn't human himself."

Vicki agreed that Alfred was acting outrageously, like an overgrown bully, but her disapproval was mixed with relief that the two men seemed ready to settle the matter between them. The corollary to Earle's question—what kind of a person would let herself be bought?—hardly seemed relevant. Neither Alfred nor Earle behaved as if she had any say in the situation.

Earle just couldn't bring himself to be angry with Vicki. His wife was just a sweet kid, naïve and maybe a little bit dumb, who sometimes acted irresponsibly but who didn't have a mean bone in her body. As for Alfred, he might have piles of money, but

Earle figured that he'd drop Vicki pretty quickly if it came to the threat of a scandal.

Earle took his problem to Paul Caruso, a Beverly Hills attorney who often handled tricky domestic relations cases involving prominent individuals.

"My wife is leaving me, and it's all the fault of Alfred Bloomingdale," he told Caruso. "Are you afraid to take him on?"

"I'm not afraid to take on anybody. Certainly not Al Bloomingdale," Caruso told him. But, he added, the California court system was unlikely to offer any remedy for Earle's problem. Alienation of affection was an outmoded complaint in 1970.

Caruso had no intention of threatening some sort of unwinnable, Mickey-Mouse action. The situation, he warned Earle, smelled of extortion, and he wanted no part of it.

Caruso had represented Earle in another matter some years earlier, and he basically liked the guy. Still he was struck by the man's odd attitude toward his wife's infidelity. Earle, Caruso says, aspired to be a "Svengali-like" figure in Vicki's life. He had wanted to make all her decisions for her, to mold her into his image of the perfect, ever-compliant wife.

And now that a more commanding Svengali had come along, he just didn't know how to compete.

Alfred kept calling Earle, and Earle kept talking back to him, but it soon became apparent that Alfred wanted Vicki in the worst way and wasn't going to be easily discouraged. Naturally, he didn't want any nasty publicity and didn't want his wife to find out, but he was either willing to take the risk or a good enough bluffer to convince Earle that this was so.

At any rate, Earle was overmatched when it came to a contest of intimidation. Alfred had taken the trouble to familiarize himself with Earle's background, which included a bad-check charge arising from a time when Earle had let himself get overextended financially. Alfred knew that a wholesaler needs credit to stay in business, and he wasn't above suggesting that bad word-of-mouth might become a problem for Earle in the near future. And at the same time, Alfred kept escalating his offers of a cash payoff.

Whether or not Earle Lamm did eventually accept money from Alfred Bloomingdale in exchange for getting out of Vicki's life is a matter of some dispute. Vicki swore that no such thing ever happened. Other sources in a position to know say that money definitely did change hands.

In the meantime, Vicki had already made her move. Alfred

installed her in a rented house on Sierra Mar Drive in the Hollywood Hills and provided her with an allowance that began at $1,000 per month and jumped in large increments to $5,000 as Vicki got better at figuring out ways to enhance her life-style. She acquired a leased Mercedes convertible, a cook, and a full-time housekeeper. The house didn't really require two servants, and except for brief stays with her, Todd was still being taken care of by Connie. But Vicki liked to have servants around for the companionship. She hated to be alone.

Alfred had been so eager to win Vicki away from Earle that he even gave up the playhouse and Kaye. For him, this was no doubt a temporary expedient, a bargaining chip that could be easily recouped once Vicki was financially dependent on him. She, not unreasonably, saw it as a sign that Alfred was willing to make major changes in his life for her sake. He was making an effort to renounce the game. Next, he might even give up his wife.

It was true that Alfred's feelings for Vicki were already getting more complicated than he wanted them to be, his straightforward sexual obsession modulated by feelings of tenderness and even guilt. For the first time in his life, perhaps, he was forced to acknowledge that he couldn't fit this woman neatly into his good girl/bad girl categories. Vicki was a lot nicer, even more innocent in some ways, than he'd thought at first, and she genuinely was in love with him.

Alfred's deeper feelings seemed to make him all the more determined to be in complete control. He had no intention of letting Vicki drift away from him as she had from Earle Lamm. Alfred's concept of a mistress's role may have been old-fashioned, but it bore little resemblance to the civilized Edwardian tradition of the once, twice, or thrice weekly "arrangement." The relation- ship Alfred had in mind was more medieval than anything else.

True, the time he had free to spend with Vicki was strictly limited, but he viewed mistressing as a full-time job, with no vacations and no days off. When he couldn't be with her, he wanted to know that she was docilely waiting for him, employing her time in making herself more attractive for his arrival.

Even their trips together, which he talked up as vacations, as her reward for being a good girl, usually ended with her spending most of her time alone while Alfred was off with cronies or conducting day-long business meetings. Vicki's role was to sit around the pool, chewing gum and perfecting her tan and, by her very existence, reflecting glory on Alfred's virility.

Vicki's first minor rebellion against these expectations led to a major blowup.

In October 1970, not long after she'd left Earle for good, Vicki and Alfred made a brief trip to Fort Lauderdale that was apparently even duller than usual. It happened, however, that Vicki overheard Alfred and some friends discussing the development of Paradise Island in the Bahamas.

"Alfred, I've never been to the Bahamas," she reminded him. "Y'know, I've never even been out of the country, except for England when I was a baby."

"Someday we'll go, Vicki, I promise," Alfred told her.

Both of them knew, though, that this was unlikely. Alfred's trips were almost invariably business connected. No business, no trip.

"Why can't I go now?" she suggested. "I mean, just for a couple of days. You'll be busy in L.A. when you go back anyway. I'd be home before you had a chance to miss me."

Alfred agreed, none too enthusiastically, and Vicki went on to the Bahamas alone. After two days she was enjoying herself so much that she decided to extend her stay for a third day . . . a fourth . . . and a fifth. As usual, she was in touch with Alfred several times a day by phone, keeping him up to date on how she was spending her time. By the fifth day, Alfred was starting to sound a bit plaintive, even irritated. He missed her. Wasn't it about time she came back home?

She had the idea by then that she'd drawn out the vacation too long, but she was completely unprepared when Alfred called, minutes after she got into her house from the airport, and announced that he was coming over right away. "We've got to talk about this," he told her. "It's something we'd better straighten out right now. For your own good."

In short order, Alfred pulled up in front of the house. "Come on," he growled, "let's go for a drive. We'll talk in the car."

Except for those times during sex parties when Alfred's Mr. Hyde personality took him over, Vicki had never seen him really angry. While he was taking out his frustration on the twisting curves of Mulholland Drive, she held on to her seat so hard that her knuckles turned white, trying to figure out what she'd done to bring all this on.

Alfred, it turned out, was not so much worried about what Vicki had been doing on Paradise Island—he was satisfied she hadn't been with another man—as irate that she hadn't been around when he wanted her.

For one thing, it seemed that Vicki had forgotten to pay her maid, and while she was away, the maid had called Alfred's office to ask about her check.

The major grievance, however, was that Alfred had been planning to bring Bill McComas up to Vicki's house for lunch. He'd wanted to show off Vicki and the house a little, and she hadn't been around. "How does it look," he fumed, "when I have to tell Bill that the plans are changed because my mistress can't make it? Because *she's* in the Bahamas having a good time while I'm here in L.A.!"

"Uh . . . I don't know. I guess he'd understand . . ."

"Of course, he won't understand! It's humiliating!"

"Well, I don't see *why* exactly," she ventured.

Alfred stopped the car at a pulloff, a considerable relief to Vicki since she didn't have a whole lot of faith in his ability to handle the car at high speeds—and not while arguing at the same time.

"Sometimes I forget how old you are, Vicki," he said. "But you obviously don't understand what a mistress is. So let me explain. It's like my other wife. You don't just call me every day from wherever you are and tell me how tan you're getting and how lovely this place is and that place is."

"Uh-huh."

"You're to be here for me."

"Uh-huh, fine. You're saying I'm your other wife. But the world is not necessarily saying that to me," she pointed out.

"Alfred, I'm insecure. You have another wife legally. I don't have a home of my own. I don't have a husband . . ."

"You know I want to marry you, Vicki. I'd love to marry you."

"Great. When?"

Now it was Alfred's turn to be on the defensive. "It's just too complicated right now. But if you want a house, fine. Before the lease runs out on this place you've got now, we'll start looking.

Meanwhile, during the period before and just after she left Earle, Vicki and Alfred spent a good deal of time with his old buddy Shelly Davis, by now a coinvestor and employee of International Flotels, as well as Alfred's favorite colleague in revelry.

A balding, heavy-bellied man who enjoyed gourmet meals and svelte women—and both in quantity—Davis admired

Bloomingdale's flair for excess. He didn't at all mind being included in some of Alfred's gamier exploits, though one thing he insisted on absolutely is that he never participated in Alfred's sexual scenarios. Alfred was, as far as he knew, strictly heterosexual and would never for a second have considered including another male in his bedroom activities.

Within this limitation, Davis probably knew as much about Alfred's offbeat sexual tastes as anyone in his life, with the exception of Vicki. Davis's comfortable home on a cul-de-sac off Coldwater Canyon was occasionally used by Alfred for his noontime assignations with hookers, and Davis saw who went into the bedroom and who came out and heard the shrieks and carryings-on that emanated from behind the closed door in between times.

Alfred started bringing Vicki around to Davis' house shortly after he met her, during the months when Vicki was still living with her husband, and Davis recognized early on that this relationship was something out of the ordinary. Alfred wasn't yet in love, he thought, but he was clearly infatuated, to the point that he and Vicki sometimes behaved like a pair of adolescent love-birds.

When Alfred and Vicki traveled together during this period, Davis occasionally came along to play the "beard," the putative escort. A philosophical amoralist, Davis didn't mind the role, but the job wasn't always an easy one. On one trip to New York, Davis recalls, Alfred asked Davis to give Vicki a tour of Bloomingdale's department store, which she had never seen. Davis agreed, but Alfred, it developed, couldn't quite bring himself to forgo the experience of being with Vicki to see her reactions. As Davis and Vicki were passing through the furniture department, Alfred "just happened" to run into them, and Davis had to go through the farce of pretending to introduce Alfred to his "date." Davis thought he played his own role pretty convincingly, but since Alfred and Vicki walked around exchanging moony-eyed glances for the rest of the tour, it was difficult to imagine that any of the store executives they encountered that day were truly fooled.

Davis was a man who liked to live well, and his house on Coldwater Canyon was particularly attractive. The kitchen was equipped for gourmet cooking, the small living room was dominated by a handsome floor-to-ceiling flagstone fireplace, and glass doors along the opposite living room wall provided a view of the tiny, but picturesquely secluded swimming pool. Vicki, Davis recalls, fell in love with the house on sight. It was her vision of the perfect love nest.

"I love this place," she'd tell Alfred. Completely unabashed by Davis's presence, she'd suggest, "Why don't you buy it for us?"

Vicki wasn't intentionally rude, but the notion that it was not quite polite to talk about buying a friend's home out from under him was already lost on her. She was starting to think like Alfred, that every whim could be satisfied for a price.

It was Alfred, however, who did the lion's share of the talking about how much he planned to give Vicki. According to Davis, Vicki was not exaggerating in the slightest when she claimed later that Alfred was constantly assuring her that he'd take care of her for the rest of her life.

What Davis knew, and Vicki didn't, was that such promises came rather easily to Alfred's lips. Alfred was a man governed by his impulses, and many of his impulses were extremely generous. His Christmas gifts were legendary, not just because they were expensive but because they were chosen with great wit and care. In moments of optimism about his business prospects, Alfred was quite prone to promise friends that he was about to make their fortunes for them.

Davis, who did not come from a wealthy background, says that over the years Alfred "promised me a thousand times, 'Stick with me, and I'll make you rich.'

"And he certainly made more promises to Vicki than he made to me," Davis adds. "He told her he would always support her."

Alfred was completely in earnest. He meant his promises to be taken seriously. Unfortunately, he often fell short when it came to keeping them.

Davis himself had "stuck with" Alfred for more than fifteen years. In 1971, however, Alfred suddenly came to him with a request that he forgo drawing a salary for a while. "I've got an expensive wife and an expensive mistress," Alfred complained. "I've got to draw the line somewhere."

"But Alfred," Davis objected. "I live on my salary. I can't afford to work for nothing."

Alfred, with the myopia born of congenital wealth, couldn't quite grasp this. "But you have stock," he countered. "You have a stake in the future of the business."

Davis couldn't see the logic of going into debt to work for nothing, while staking his future on his stock in International

Flotels. The difference of opinion was solved by his handing in his resignation.

The decision was for the best. Two years later, International Flotels was dissolved and Davis's sixty-five thousand shares turned out to be virtually worthless.

Davis was off Alfred's payroll, but Vicki soon replaced him—her monthly allowance checks disguised as payments for consulting work on the interior decoration of the Marina Bay complex.

Vicki said later in a sworn affidavit that her contribution to Marina Bay consisted of the following: At Alfred's request, she had attended "a few" zoning meetings in Florida and she had "helped Alfred research the Fort Lauderdale area, the life-style of the people there, et cetera, to decide how the Marina Bay ought to be decorated, the locations of the restaurants, et cetera."

By mid-1971 Vicki was already growing restive, and the subject of marriage came up more often. As far as she was concerned, the matter was pretty straightforward. "I left my husband for you," she'd remind him. "You say you love me. If that's true, then why can't we be together all the time?"

Alfred kept saying, "Okay, sure, if that's what you really want. But in the meantime, don't leave me. I need you."

Although she heard Alfred say the words, Vicki felt sure that any incentive Alfred might have to ask for a divorce was quickly slipping away.

For one thing, he'd been amazingly successful, Vicki thought, at hiding their affair from his wife. She had no talent for deception herself. Earle had sensed that there was something deeply wrong almost as soon as she started seeing Alfred, even if it took him a while to figure out all the facts. It seemed incredible that a man could keep a mistress right in town, walk down the streets with her, have her drop in at his office a couple of times a week, travel with her—and still not have his wife find out and call him on it. Yet Alfred seemed to have managed just fine. His secretary was incredibly loyal, his accountants apparently ingenious, his friends closemouthed.

Even more disturbing, Alfred had resumed playing the game. He had rented an apartment on La Cienega and was meeting hookers there, demanding that Vicki join in.

Vicki was adamant that she wasn't going back to getting flogged. It didn't matter that Alfred promised not to mark her up or that it only happened in certain specified situations. She told him flat out that his compulsion went beyond being just a sophisticated vice. It was an illness. She was scared to death that someday he was going to go too far and seriously hurt her or someone else.

It took considerable nerve to say all this since Alfred was not disposed to listen to what he didn't care to hear. Surprisingly, however, he agreed to a compromise. He wouldn't give up his little scenarios, but he agreed to change the script. From now on Vicki would be his surrogate, disciplining the other girls under his supervision.

The new scenario evolved with Vicki playing the dominatrix. "Darling, you beat them," Alfred would invite her. "Get them to call me 'master.'" The other girls, invariably a pair of hookers recruited for the occasion, would be ordered to get down on all fours, and Vicki would whomp them with Alfred's belt until he was satisfied that they sounded sincere. Often, Alfred would straddle one of the girl's back and sit there drooling as he urged Vicki, "Hit them harder! Harder!"

The last act of the drama remained unchanged. When he couldn't wait any longer, Alfred would hustle Vicki over to the bed and have sex with her. He never had intercourse with the other girls.

Vicki's rationalization for going along with this was that at least there was no danger of Alfred going bananas and really injuring someone. She always held back a little, relying on the other women to give convincing performances.

Aside from being plain scary, Alfred's sadistic bent played havoc with Vicki's dream of being Number One in his life. She didn't particularly care for playing queen of the hookers, and she was quite sure that as long as Alfred cast her in that light he wasn't thinking too seriously of her as a future wife.

Vicki would have been even more discouraged about the possibility of Alfred marrying her if she'd known his true views on divorce.

Once again, Alfred's buddy Shelly Davis had had occasion to hear these discussed somewhat more candidly than she ever did. According to Davis, some years earlier, when he was going through a divorce from his own wife, Alfred had lectured him sternly. "Divorce is a sin," Alfred had warned. "If you have to play around, fine. Do it. But stay married." Davis hadn't taken the advice, but he had no doubt that Alfred was completely serious. Alfred, he was sure, believed in sin.

Alfred's Roman Catholicism was a matter of public record. He and Betsy were very generous contributors to Catholic charities, in recognition of which Alfred had actually been inducted by the Pope into the honorary lay order of the Knights of St. Gregory. Many people who knew of Alfred's reputation as a womanizer assumed that his religious conversion was a facade adopted to please Betsy, who had wanted her children reared in a Catholic home.

No doubt this was the original motivation. Alfred joked about being a former Jew, which he considered a little bit ridiculous, like talking about being a former alcoholic. He never really put it behind him. Yet, even if his frame of mind may never have been quite 100 percent orthodox, Alfred was profoundly attracted to certain elements of Catholicism.

Although Vicki didn't know it, Alfred would often stop by the UCLA chapel after his assignations with her and before going back to his office or to his home. He had a personal chaplain and confessor there, a priest who was also the adviser of the campus Newman Club and, no doubt, a man with cast-iron ears.

Alfred Bloomingdale was a man who seemed to have no inner gauge to tell him when enough was enough, no innate sense of moderation. Whatever he enjoyed—tobacco, sex, work, telephone talk, practical jokes—he enjoyed to the point of self-destruction. The classic addictive personality, he needed to hedge his compulsions with prescriptions and rules and adherence to a few selected moral absolutes. It didn't matter a whole lot if his system of restraints was illogical or even hypocritical. At least it sufficed to hold some of his compulsions in check.

In the latter part of 1971, however, something happened that nudged Alfred into considering divorce seriously: Vicki discovered that she was pregnant.

Vicki had always wanted to have Alfred's child. She was delighted. And, initially, Alfred seemed to be even more thrilled than she was. For a couple of weeks Alfred talked as if he was on the point of confronting his wife about a separation. He even boasted in front of acquaintances that Vicki was carrying his baby.

Then, just when Vicki had begun to relax, assuming that the issue was settled, he started to express reservations. First, he balked on the marriage issue, and then he started saying that it wouldn't be fair to the child to bring it into the world illegitimate.

What Alfred seemed most worried about, however, was having to share Vicki's affections with another human being, even with his own offspring. He was pushing sixty, he reminded her, a little old to be starting a second family. Also, to tell the truth, he had never been overly fond of having children around. Nothing against the kids themselves, but once they came on the scene it would mean the end of Vicki's freedom to travel, to pick up and join him wherever he was going on a moment's notice.

Reluctantly, Vicki came to the conclusion that she could either hold on to her relationship with Alfred or she could have the baby and then try to figure out for herself how to get Alfred to support it. The latter didn't seem to be much of an option. She already had one child who she wasn't managing to do much for.

Vicki didn't consider that, if she just went ahead, Alfred might have a change of heart. By this time, she mostly did as she was told. In November 1971, she had an abortion at Beverly Glen Hospital. Alfred paid, but he didn't come along to hold her hand in the waiting room. He was married and a Catholic, after all.

Even after the abortion, there were many occasions when Alfred would bring up the subject of divorcing Betsy and marrying her. Vicki continued to fantasize that this might eventually happen, but the pendulum of hope and disappointment no longer swung in a very wide arc.

In 1972, even Vicki's search for a house to buy was abandoned temporarily when Alfred learned that he was suffering from cancer of the larynx and began to undergo a series of eighteen cobalt treatments to fight the tumor. No matter how unsatisfactory her relationship might be in some ways, Vicki couldn't just start issuing ultimatums when the man she loved was battling cancer. It just didn't seem right.

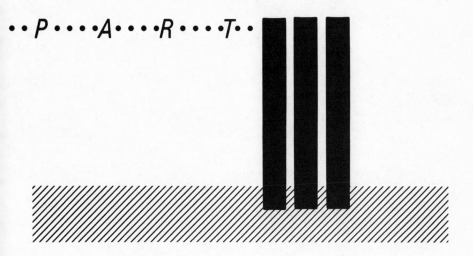

··P···A···R···T··

She said that any dream was better than no dream and beggars couldn't be choosers.

NATHANAEL WEST
THE DAY OF THE LOCUST

ANYBODY'S FANTASY

//

By the age of seventy-two, there came times when Mervyn LeRoy had to feel a certain empathy with the title in one of his classic films, The Wizard of Oz. He'd come out to have lunch at the Polo Lounge with his old friend Al Bloomingdale, but instead of a pleasant hour or so of reminiscing about the old days, he found himself being asked to perform an unlikely miracle.

Bloomingdale had brought along his latest girlfriend, a bottle blonde, beautiful but with nervous eyes that kept scanning the exits as if she were waiting for the cavalry to ride to her rescue. Naturally, the girl wanted to be a movie star, and Bloomingdale wanted him to do something to help her along.

The lunch with Mervyn LeRoy was the one of the first moves in Vicki's campaign to revive her dream of becoming an actress. With the marriage issue on the back burner for the time being, and Alfred not in the best of health, she had plenty of time on her hands. She was also painfully aware that even if Alfred did mean to take care of her "always," always for him might not be a very long time.

Vicki had never so much as acted in a school play, and there was no reason to suppose that she had the talent to become a star. Nevertheless, it was by no means unreasonable of her to think that she might be able to pick up a few roles and eventually eke out some sort of career. She was young, just approaching her twentieth birthday, and she radiated that quality of hazy seductiveness that the camera loves, a quality sometimes called vulnerability. She was sexy, but in an aggressive, undefined sort of way that suggested that she didn't know exactly what she wanted. She could fit into anybody's fantasy.

Vicki also had Alfred Bloomingdale, whose name could open doors for her.

Alfred had always said that he intended to do something about launching Vicki's career—another of his big promises—and after the abortion he could no longer think of any plausible excuse for putting off the effort.

If it had only been thirty, or even twenty years earlier, Mervyn LeRoy would have been the ideal person to see about getting Vicki started. Hollywood's legendary starmaker, LeRoy was the producer-director who had nurtured the careers of Jane Wyman, Loretta Young, Audrey Hepburn, and many others. Over a career that spanned from *Little Caesar* and *Gold Diggers of 1933* to *The Bad Seed* and *No Time For Sergeants*, he was renowned for his respect for a good script, for his uncanny ability to bring in films on time and at or under budget, and most of all, for casting inexperienced actresses in parts that made them look very good indeed.

Unfortunately, by the time Alfred sought him out on Vicki's behalf, LeRoy happened to be semiretired, and in any case, the studio system that once molded starlets into stars was long gone.

Alfred's idea was that Mervyn might be able to give Vicki some special coaching, a private tutorial on screen acting that would prepare her in case any actual parts turned up.

Fine, said LeRoy. He gave Vicki a three o'clock appointment in his office for a few days from then.

Vicki went dutifully to her appointments with LeRoy. Sometimes he reminisced about his career. Sometimes gave her some useful coaching, especially for her underpowered voice and sloppy diction.

Once, he told her, "My dear, you remind me of the young Vivien Leigh."

It was a lovely compliment, but Vicki soon got the impression that LeRoy didn't know why she was coming to him any more than she did. LeRoy, as she would say later, was "not a youngster," and he seemed to be spending time on her mostly as a favor to Alfred.

The only really interesting outcome of her tutorial with Mervyn LeRoy was that one day, sitting in the waiting room of his office, Vicki was approached by a distinguished looking, silver-haired man who plied her with questions. "Who *are* you? Are you an actress?" he wanted to know. "What have you done?"

"Not a whole lot," Vicki admitted. "In fact, nothing really."

"That's all right. We all start sometime," he said. "Maybe we could have a cup of coffee or lunch sometime and talk about it. What's your name?"

"Vicki Morgan."

The man's cleft chin and owlish intensity seemed vaguely familiar. Or were they? "And you're? . . ." she asked.

Cary Grant did not get asked that question very often, particularly by aspiring film actresses.

Later on, Vicki, who loved to tell wry stories about her own mental lapses, would have a grand time with this one. There she was, living out the dream of a million women—Cary Grant was trying to pick her up, and she hadn't even recognized him!

Once Vicki realized how others reacted to Cary Grant's interest in her—even Mervyn LeRoy told her this just wasn't the kind of thing a girl passed up—her own ardor warmed. The romance, however, was slow to get started.

Grant had just come through a protracted paternity battle with his ex-wife Dyan Cannon and was beginning what would turn out to be an intermittent but long-lasting affair with a young English gossip columnist. Also, a couple of years earlier, on the eve of being awarded a special Oscar from the Academy, which should have been the culmination of his unparalleled career, he'd been deeply embarrassed by a nuisance paternity suit. A young woman named Cynthia Bouron had announced that she was pregnant by Grant and planned to name her child, if a boy, Cary Grant, Jr.

Later, unfortunately too late to keep from casting a shadow over Grant's appearance at the ceremonies, it came out that Bouron had a criminal arrest record. There were also questions about her mental stability since she'd named her collie after Cary Grant as well, though with no suggestion that he was the dog's father. When the child was born, it appeared to be the offspring of a black father, and Bouron dropped her suit rather than take a blood test. (In a bizarre coincidence, Bouron was found bludgeoned to death in North Hollywood in 1973, in the same precinct where Vicki Morgan would die ten years later. Bouron's killing was never solved.)

All these problems, but particularly the Cynthia Bouron scandal, had made Grant extremely wary of rushing into affairs with unknown starlets and Hollywood hangers-on. Vicki, who did not understand caution, was somewhat bewildered when Grant invited her up to his house in Malibu for weekends; he even asked her to stay over in the guest room but never made a move to seduce her. She hated being nothing but a sex object, but now that she had met a man who did not assume that she wanted to jump into bed immediately, she felt rejected. Grant was in his early seventies at the time, even older than Alfred, but it was difficult for Vicki to convince herself that age was the problem since he was more fit and energetic than a lot of men two decades younger.

Eventually, Cary Grant relieved Vicki of her confusion. The two became lovers and dated off and on for several months, but with every meeting it became more clear that they had nothing in common apart from a passing mutual infatuation. Grant had been passionate about physical fitness all his life and, despite his suave screen persona, preferred to dress simply and live unpretentiously. Among the complaints of his ex-wife Dyan Cannon at the time of their acrimonious divorce were that Grant was so stingy he saved the buttons off discarded shirts, that he spanked her for wearing too much makeup and provocative clothes, and that his idea of a big evening was to settle down in front of the television with a warmed-up TV dinner.

Vicki encountered similar habits and was not enchanted. She was a heavy smoker, a habit Grant loathed, and at this stage in her life wouldn't think of going out on a date unless she was freshly coiffed, made up to the hilt, and loaded down with pounds of gold jewelry. And what was the point of getting herself up like that if all her date wanted to do was sit in front of the TV or take walks on the beach in the hopes of catching a glimpse of his daughter Jennifer, who lived with her mother in a house just up the road?

In her anecdotes to friends, however, the remembered affair took on a somewhat more romantic glow. Vicki told friends that Cary Grant had been sweet and terribly dashing but just not exciting enough for her tastes—not as exciting as Alfred.

A man who knew Vicki years later, with no apparent malice, offered a somewhat different viewpoint on Vicki's failure to fall in love with Grant, as she invariably did with charismatic older men whether they treated her badly or not. "It was just a few dates," he says. "Cary Grant never gave Vicki any money."

Whether or not money, or the absence of it, had anything to do with the tapering off of Vicki's interest in Grant, it was certainly true that the importance of wealth in her life was escalating out of control. Vicki had always wanted to find a wealthy man to take care of her, and she wanted a house from Alfred for security and as proof of his commitment to her. What had once been mere materialism, a desire to enjoy the good things in life, was beginning to turn into an unquenchable need for cash.

Alfred positively encouraged Vicki's spendthrift ways. As much as he might want to, he couldn't stop Vicki from at least trying to work and he couldn't keep her from meeting other men. The dalliance with Cary Grant was exceptional, but he could see that she was beginning to become more independent, to make friends of her own, and to get into situations where she'd be meeting other possible rivals. He recognized that as long as Vicki's tastes were sufficiently expensive, her efforts at breaking away gradually would be doomed to fail. She would never be able to afford to leave him.

In some respects, Alfred's behavior was less that of a lover than of a doting father intent on spoiling his daughter outrageously. If Vicki exceeded her allowance, he'd scold her and then reach for his checkbook. He had a hundred rules, all of them seemingly made to be broken, and when Vicki "misbehaved"—which could mean anything from arriving a few minutes late for lunch to sneaking off on a date with Cary Grant—he'd end up telling her how cute she was, his adorably naughty little girl.

Some of Alfred's more blatant attempts to play daddy bothered Vicki even more than his sexual demands. Practically the first words Alfred had ever said to her were "You remind me of my daughter." Vicki assumed there must be a strong physical resemblance and when, months later, she had occasion to see a picture of Lisa Bloomingdale, she was surprised to see that there wasn't.

She got even more upset with Alfred's behavior when they'd run into his acquaintances in restaurants or on the street in Beverly Hills. Instead of saying nothing about her at all or as passing her off as one of his secretaries, Alfred would often look his friends in the eye and bark, "You remember my daughter, don't you?" Vicki was mortified, sure that someday they'd run into someone who did remember all too well and had the nerve to call Alfred a liar on the spot.

"But I don't look like your daughter," she'd complain to him later. "How can you say that?"

She never did figure out why Alfred tried that ruse, whether it was his idea of a joke or whether he simply felt that none of the people he tried it on would be the wiser.

Sally Talbert, who had become close friends with Vicki after the divorce from Earle Lamm, had her own ideas about what Alfred was getting at. Alfred, she concluded, was a desperately "unfulfilled" man who wanted to live vicariously through someone who was younger and less jaded then he.

"Every time the three of us would have lunch together, which was very often," she said later, "he would want to know the smallest details of her life and what she had been doing since they last saw or talked to one another, even if their previous encounter had been only hours earlier. He just seemed to have a compelling need to know everything about her. He seemed to take a fatherly joy in her, and their relationship many times appeared to me to be that of father and daughter."

If Alfred encouraged Vicki's irresponsibility, he was at least as successful at sabotaging any attempts she made to become responsible and self-supporting. He just couldn't stand to see her grow up.

In the case of Vicki's acting ambitions, his strategy was fairly subtle. Instead of flatly forbidding her to work, he pretended to be encouraging. One minute he'd be her biggest booster and the next he'd expressing bemusement at the thought of little Vicki actually believing she could muster the discipline to get ahead in show business. "What makes you think you could get out of bed for a six A.M. makeup call?" he'd ask her. "You know you like to sleep late. What makes you think you could put in a twelve-hour day on the set? You never worked twelve hours straight at anything in your life!"

When Alfred's show business contacts did come up with the

occasional job for Vicki, however, it was Alfred who had problems with Vicki's work schedule. Just about the time Vicki had concluded that her coaching sessions with Mervyn LeRoy were leading nowhere, LeRoy did line up a small movie part for her, her first and, as it turned out, her last. The role was hardly a plum, just a bit part in a Zsa Zsa Gabor epic tentatively titled *Ring Around the Diamond.* Vicki couldn't have been more excited. But when she got her call for the shooting, it turned out that her scene was scheduled for a day when Alfred had other plans.

It was the old argument all over again. This time Vicki won, to the extent that she showed up on the set to work. She would have been nervous anyway, but the argument had left her so frazzled and distracted that she was barely able to pull herself together and follow instructions. The picture itself turned out to be a dud—never went into national distribution—and so Vicki was left wondering whether her victory had been worth the effort.

Alfred's other ventures in helping Vicki's career followed the same yo-yo pattern.

He arranged a meeting with Mike Frankovitch, who gave Vicki an introduction to Joyce Selznik. But when Selznick's office called asking Vicki to come in to the studio for a midday audition, Alfred objected to being deprived her company at lunch.

"Tell them you can't make it until four," Alfred instructed her.

"You can't do that," she said. "When the studio goes to the trouble of calling you up and *asks* you to come in, you can't just say, 'Well, gee, that isn't a convenient time for me.' "

"You goddamn well can, if I say so," he shot back.

And she did.

In the meantime, behind Vicki's back, Alfred made it clear that he was just trying to humor his demanding girlfriend. One agent and freelance producer who knew both Alfred and Vicki, recalled that Alfred once called to plead with her to find Vicki "one day's work in front of the cameras." The agent complied, as a personal favor. But again, when the job came through, it was Alfred who objected to the scheduling.

Ray Stark was another producer who found himself being invited to lunch with Alfred for the purpose of meeting Vicki and hearing about her ambitions to get into films. Stark had a project in the works with Barbara Streisand, and he sent Vicki to see the casting director—a polite brushoff, since if Stark had wanted to put Vicki in the picture, he could obviously have done so.

The casting director, a woman, said a few encouraging words to

Vicki and then suggested that she needed more training. Her recommendation was that Vicki take some classes with Lee Strasberg.

Alfred thought it was a terrific idea. He was always in favor of Vicki taking classes, particularly night classes, and the course at the Lee Strasberg Institute happened to be at night. Possibly, Alfred was sincere in thinking that the classes would do Vicki some good. In retrospect, however, they did nothing but destroy what shreds of confidence she had left.

Vicki's assets were youth and good looks. What she obviously needed was to garner some small, undemanding jobs that would give her experience, not to be thrust into situations that were far over her head. She'd never aspired to be a serious dramatic actress anyway, and she was agonizingly shy when it came to revealing her personal feelings in front of strangers. Workshop classes in the very citadel of Method acting, during which she was called upon to dredge up her most private emotions in front of students who all seemed infinitely more talented—not to mention, more at ease with the demands for self-revelation—were an agonizing experience.

Vicki attended the sessions dutifully, fortifying herself with Valium to get through the evening.

The classes accomplished little or nothing in the way of making her a better actress, but the knowledge that she was studying under none other than Lee Strasberg, who had been Marilyn Monroe's personal acting coach and guru, encouraged her unrealistic expectations. Strasberg, according to Vicki, was another top pro who claimed to see great "potential" in her, telling her at one point, "I see in you a lot of qualities I saw in the young Marilyn." He didn't elaborate on which particular qualities he thought the two women had in common.

Strasberg's comment was one that Vicki had plenty of time to brood over in later years, when she needed to cling to the belief that she could have done something more with her life under other circumstances. Vicki, and presumably Strasberg as well, was not completely off the mark in thinking that her appeal, a combination of overt sexuality and little girl hesitancy, was reminiscent of Monroe's.

And, indeed, over the years Vicki's life followed a course that in some ways strikingly paralleled Monroe's. Both were fatherless girls who grew up beautiful and desperately insecure. Both married three times and, finding it increasingly difficult to cope with the demands of everyday routines, became dependent on tranquilizers. Both had love affairs with prominent men and got paranoid about the consequences, then died under circumstances that led some people to believe that they had been silenced.

Of course, there was also one monumental, undeniable difference between the two of them: Marilyn Monroe had been a movie star. Vicki Morgan's career was an unrealized dream.

Vicki couldn't help but be achingly aware of this, but the recognition didn't stop her from building up a fantasy image of herself as a sort of movie star manquée, a clandestine celebrity, as if there could be such a thing.

L.A. is a place where it is all too easy to confuse the perks of success—the Mercedes convertible, the nice house, and the lunches at the Polo Lounge—with success itself. Vicki was only a little more self-deluded than most. She started thinking that maybe the world did recognize her status as Alfred's "other wife" after all.

In the early 1970s, *the* place to have your hair done in Beverly Hills happened to be an establishment called, appropriately enough, Ménage à Trois. Among the salon's regular customers were Nancy Reagan, whenever she was able to get into town from Sacramento; her by-then best friend, Betsy Bloomingdale; and— Vicki Morgan.

That Alfred would pay for his mistress to frequent the same hairdresser as his wife was courting disaster, but then he always got a tremendous kick out of doing just that. It also said a lot about the troublesome direction taken by Alfred's Pygmalion complex. Along with the many other roles he demanded that Vicki play from time to time, Alfred seemed determined to make her over into a carbon copy of his wife.

It might seem that this would be the last thing he'd want from a mistress. The portrait of his wife that emerged from Alfred's complaints about her to Vicki was certainly unrelievedly negative. Alfred groused constantly that his wife was self-absorbed and unsympathetic, too busy going to parties and fawning over Nancy and getting her face into the pages of *W* to spare him any attention. In short, it was the classic my-wife-doesn't-understand-me line, coming from a man who was no doubt fortunate not to be too thoroughly understood.

For all Alfred's complaints, Betsy was in many, if not most

respects, his ideal of femininity. Lawrence Leamer's *Make-Believe* quotes one of Betsy's friends as calling her "the too tall girl in class, precise, pristine, a cinnamon stick, the kind of woman who appeals to gays"—and the first and last parts of this description, at least, might also be applied to Vicki. Shelly Davis, who admired Betsy's panache and perfectionism even though he found her rather intimidating, summed up her style by saying, "Betsy doesn't sweat. And she doesn't like people who do"—an assessment that captured exactly the difference between Alfred's wife and his mistress. No doubt it was part of Vicki's fascination for Alfred that she was different from Betsy, a woman whose personal insecurities and fantasies were all out there on the surface. But this didn't stop him from playing the make-over game.

If Vicki went shopping in slacks, Alfred would remind her that Betsy never went downtown without putting on a dress and nylons. If she failed to have fresh flowers in her living room, he'd remark that this was an omission Betsy would never be guilty of. Much of what Betsy did or had was held up to Vicki as being worth emulating—Betsy's menus, her color schemes, her ability to handle servants, whatever. When Betsy acquired a pet shih-tzu puppy named Nu Nu, Alfred even gave Vicki a dog of the same breed.

The results of Vicki's attempts to follow Betsy's example were usually fairly disappointing. Even though Vicki had a cook, Alfred sent her to a gourmet cooking school in the hope that she'd learn to appreciate fine food and plan elegant lunches for him and his friends. Vicki picked up enough pointers to satisfy Alfred, but she went back to potato chips and take-out pizza as soon as he wasn't around. She had closets full of good clothes— one friend described her as "Gucci'd and initialed to death"—but felt most comfortable in hiphuggers and halters.

Ménage à Trois was exceptional in that Vicki liked that place just as much as Betsy did. By 1973, at least four of Vicki's close girlfriends were patronizing the salon as well. Since both groups of women liked to have their hair done several times a week, the Ménage à Trois receptionist must have been as harried as an air-traffic controller at a barnstormers convention. Amazingly, the salon's employees managed to keep their appointment books straight and their lips sealed, though on one occasion a woman who was Vicki's friend did find herself seated under the hair dryers next to Betsy and Nancy Reagan. "I must say [Betsy] was nice to me," the woman recalls. "She invited me to come pick flowers from her rose garden."

One day, however, Vicki's Mercedes happened to be in the shop for repairs and Alfred insisted on dropping her off right at the door of the salon. There was some nuzzling in the front seat, and then, when Alfred started to drive off, Vicki realized that she'd left a package in the car and called him back so that she could retrieve her parcel and give him one last little kiss. Betsy Bloomingdale and her daughter Lisa happened to be across the street and saw the whole thing.

Vicki knew something was wrong when Alfred didn't call that afternoon to make sure that she'd gotten back from her appointment promptly. Alfred called her so often, and always at the end of the business day before he left his office, that when the phone hadn't rung by six P.M., she was already sure that something terrible must have happened to him, a heart attack or an automobile accident. She was frantic all evening, but there was nothing to do but wait—the price of being the other woman.

Alfred called the next morning from a phone booth. "It's hit the fan," he told her. "She saw us. They both did."

Apparently, Betsy had confided in Nancy Reagan who then admitted that *she* had seen Alfred and Vicki together back in 1971 but had not wanted to be the bearer of bad news. According to Alfred, this had been the last straw. "She's threatening to file for divorce," Alfred said. "She told me, 'Not only have I and your daughter seen you; the whole town knows about you and this woman.' "

Vicki couldn't see why Alfred was quite as upset as he was. This was inevitable, wasn't it? The only mystery was why his wife hadn't issued an ultimatum before this. "Well, okay," she said. "I mean, what can happen?"

"You don't understand," Alfred warned. "This means she's going to start watching the money. Things could get tricky."

To Vicki's complete shock, Alfred completely caved in. Instead of telling his wife, "Okay, let's get a divorce," he was trying his best to placate her. Since Betsy would now be scrutinizing his expenses, Alfred told Vicki that there was no way he could continue her allowance. Sorry, but she'd have to give up the house.

Alfred had to go out of town for a couple of days—the trip had been planned before all this occurred—so Vicki had some time to think over the implications of his reactions. When he was due back and she tried to call him at his office, however, she discovered that Betsy had ordered all the phone numbers changed.

She couldn't believe this was happening, not after all Alfred's promises.

Vicki drove right down to Alfred's office and confronted him.

"I love you. Of course I love you," he told her. "But this is going to take time. It's going to take time to work out."

Vicki pointed out that she didn't have time. Her servants hadn't been paid. The rent was coming due. And, of course, she hadn't saved a penny. She couldn't just sit around running up bills.

"I can't tell her that. You tell her," he said.

"What does that mean . . . 'You tell her'?"

Alfred picked up the phone, dialed his home number, and asked the servant who answered to call Betsy to the phone. "Here," he said, shoving the receiver into Vicki's hand, "Tell her you're in my office. Tell her you need money."

"I can't do that!" She quickly hung up the phone before Betsy could come on the line.

"Okay, then. Tell you what, why don't you take a little vacation? Go to Europe for a while. Enjoy yourself. Just until things settle down here."

Somehow, though he couldn't come up with enough money to keep Vicki in town, Alfred managed to scrape together $20,000 to send Vicki to Europe. Whether this was intended as a sort of severance payment or just as the wherewithal for a temporary exile until Alfred could sort out his problems with his wife isn't clear. Vicki later claimed it was the latter. Alfred, she said, had tears in his eyes when he delivered the check, and he begged her not to forget him while she was away.

Vicki took Todd, who'd just started to get used to living with her again, and parked him back with her mother in Montclair. She lent some pieces of furniture to a friend who had an unfurnished apartment—she never did get them back—and broke the news to her servants that they were out of a job. Her dogs—by this time she'd acquired several strays as well as the shih-tzu and a white German shepherd from Alfred—were farmed out to various friends.

Alfred had encouraged Vicki to go to Paris where she could take a small apartment and and devote herself to learning the language and soaking up French culture, replicating more or less his own European sojourn during the 1930s. Vicki, however, had other ideas. She hated to be alone anywhere, anytime, and the prospect of spending more than a few hours in a city where she knew no one and couldn't speak the language appalled her.

Fortuitously, her good friend Leslie happened to be in Europe that summer with *her* great love, financier Bernie Cornfield. Vicki made arrangements to join them at Bernie's French chateau across the border from Geneva, and she later went along with them when they moved on to his London townhouse.

Since Bernie was a compulsive seducer, and Vicki a girl always ripe for seduction, it was inevitable that this arrangement would lead to trouble. Leslie, a petite, quiet girl, happened to be utterly devoted to Bernie, but she might have tolerated a brief fling between him and Vicki, if only because it was difficult to maintain a lasting relationship with Bernie unless you learned, at times, to ignore what couldn't be changed. It soon became clear, however, that Bernie's yen for Vicki was going to be more than transitory. Vicki was a tall, half-British shiksa with, at the time, long straight blond hair—the ultimate status symbol. Nor did it hurt that Vicki had been the girlfriend of Alfred Bloomingdale. Possessing her would be a coup.

Bernie's none-too-subtle courting of Vicki plunged Leslie into a sink of misery. Vicki, on her part, claimed to be disgusted by his behavior. In Bernie's presence, meanwhile, her manner of taking offense seemed more provocative than anything else.

When the three of them went shopping together, supposedly for Leslie, Vicki kept pointing out little items, dresses and jewelry and so on, and fussing over them until Bernie offered to buy them for her. Then, when Bernie acted on the assumption that he ought to get some affection in return for what he was spending, she'd haughtily remind him that Leslie was her dearest friend whom she'd never, ever think of betraying.

Vicki justified her behavior on the grounds that this was no better than Bernie deserved for acting like a sexist pig. It seemed that she hadn't learned the lesson of the $8,000 check—that no man doles out that kind of money for nothing. More likely, though, she had assimilated the lesson all too well.

Bernie went along with the charade to the tune of more than $25,000, buying her, among other things, the luscious red fox–trimmed coat that Vicki wore in the photograph widely published at the time of her palimony suit against Alfred in 1982. After several weeks, though, it became apparent that he wasn't going to remain patient indefinitely. His mood was turning foul, to say the least. Vicki was either going to have to give in and sleep with

Bernie, or think about giving back her presents and taking her leave.

In the meantime, Alfred had undergone a change of heart. Vicki hadn't been gone more than two or three weeks before he came to the conclusion that he couldn't live without her. He wanted her back at all costs, and when he couldn't locate her at any of the places he'd recommended in Paris, he started to get panicky. He began besieging Vicki's mother and sister and all her girlfriends with phone calls, often waking them at five A.M., to announce in a choked-up voice that he was "a dying man, *dying* for chrissakes!" and he desperately needed Vicki's address. Eventually, someone gave in and told him where to find her.

As if the situation with Bernie and Leslie weren't complicated enough, Vicki started receiving urgent transatlantic pleas from Alfred.

"I've had a lot of time to think things over since you've been gone," he said. "And for the first time I've had to come to terms with the fact that I'm not a young man anymore. My children are all grown up. My health is bad. You know, I've got a bad heart, too. I don't have that many years left to enjoy, and you're what makes me happy. I'm begging you to come back, Vick."

As usual, Alfred knew the right buttons to push. This time it was guilt—the argument that she'd taken his money and said she loved him, but now that he was getting old and had problems with his wife she was deserting him.

"I can't get a divorce," he added. "I can't afford to. But if you come back, I promise it will be different. I'll give up the other. No more girls. It will be just the two of us."

Still, she hesitated. "I need time to think it over," she told him. "Don't call me for a few days, okay? I'll be in touch."

The Valiums that Vicki was gobbling to handle the stress didn't exactly help her to put the situation in perspective, and soon she had worked herself up into a state of near hysteria. She was trapped! If she stayed in London, she'd end up giving in to Bernie, but if she gave in to Alfred, the whole messy affair would start all over again. As usual, the only solution she could think of was to turn to another man who would play the white knight, scooping her up in his arms and rescuing her from her perilous dilemma.

On the spur of the moment, the only white knight she could think of to call on was . . . Earle Lamm.

Earle responded exactly as Vicki had known he would, flying to

Europe immediately and playing the part of the outraged husband, insisting that Vicki return to the States with him whether she wanted to or not.

No doubt Earle believed that Vicki had had her fill of jet-set hijinks and was ready to come back to him, but when they got back to L.A., he was in for a major disappointment. Vicki moved in temporarily with Emma, her friend from modeling school, and Emma's then husband Alan Sachs, and within a matter of days she was in touch with Alfred again.

Alfred was still nervous about Betsy's wrath and still on a short leash financially, but he managed to come up with another, though much smaller gift of money for Vicki. Between that and what she had left over from the previous payment, Vicki was able to rent a house in the Hollywood Hills. The place was a good deal shabbier than her last home, and even so, she had to take in a paying roommate, a gay male, to make ends meet. The roommate soon became Vicki's great chum and confidant. Alternately amused and bedazzled by Vicki's aura of glamour and perpetual crisis, he tolerated her wide mood swings and her habit of treating him as a dear friend one day and a virtual lackey the next. It was a relationship that seemed to fill a deep need in Vicki and that she would try to duplicate years later when she developed a friendship with another gay man named Marvin Pancoast.

In spite of the unresolved money issue, Vicki and Alfred seemed to have effected a reconciliation. But just when they were settling down into a semblance of the old pattern, Alfred suffered a heart attack, his second in several years. As soon as he was well enough to travel, Alfred decided to go to Texas for a consultation with the renowned heart surgeon Dr. Denton Cooley, who eventually performed triple bypass surgery.

With Alfred out of town, Vicki began going out nearly every night, frequenting various nightclubs and after-hours joints on the Strip. For a time she dated a rock musician. During this period, she hung around for a while with Emma's boyfriend Joe Cocker and his band, and she also got to know the ex–football great Jim Brown. When he got back from his recuperation in Texas, Alfred was tremendously impressed that Vicki had met Brown and insisted that she set up an introduction, whereupon he bored the retired pro into a stupor with anecdotes of his own exploits playing varsity guard for Brown University.

In the meantime, Vicki's gay roommate had moved out and she'd given up the house in the hills to move into a tiny studio on

Doheny Drive near Wilshire Boulevard. Even though she was completely out of funds by now, she still couldn't stand the thought of living alone. Being by herself, even for a few hours, forced her to confront her deep conviction that she was unloved and unlovable, a worthless woman pursuing a trival mode of life. No doubt she would have been better off if she had confronted these feelings, but it was easier just to keep constantly in motion, all the while cultivating a buddy who was willing to hover in the background waiting to keep her company when her social friends couldn't be around.

This time, Vicki solved the buddy problem by inviting a young Thai woman, nicknamed Penny, to share the apartment with her. Penny was as petite as Vicki was statuesque, four-feet-eleven and weighing less than a hundred pounds. She'd worked for Vicki briefly when Vicki lived on Sierra Mar Drive and had lived in the house to take care of the dogs when Vicki traveled with Alfred. Now her status was more that of a nonpaying roommate and companion than a servant—Vicki was in no position to pay her a salary—but Vicki's friends invariably thought of her as "Vicki's little maid."

Vicki took Penny with her everywhere, except, perhaps, out on dates. Penny carried her packages when she went shopping and sat in waiting rooms when Vicki had a doctor's appointment. She rarely had much to say, though when she and Vicki were alone together, Penny heard plenty. She knew all about Alfred's sexual "problem" long before Vicki had confided a word on the subject to her other "straight" friends.

Since Vicki couldn't face living alone, much less doing her own housework, it was predictable that she was none too enthusiastic about another obvious solution to her problem—getting a job. She did, though, have a plan that was more realistic than anything Alfred managed to come up with. While he'd been ill, Betsy had taken an even firmer grip on the family finances—at least, so he claimed—and he was also preoccupied with the aftermath of the collapse of International Flotels, which soured his relationship with several of the major investors.

Even Vicki thought, at this point, that it was unlikely that he would be able to restore her generous allowance any time soon. As for the dream of his buying her a house, that had been abandoned, even as a talking proposition.

"Why don't you set me up in a little business?" she suggested when he came to see her at the new apartment. "You know, like a boutique. You could back me and call it a business investment. Eventually, I'd have an income, so I wouldn't be dependent on you."

"But who would run it?" Alfred asked blankly.

"I would. That's the whole point. And I'd have something to do."

Alfred thought the idea was laughable. Vicki! Run a business! "Be serious," he told her. "Anyway, I don't want you working. I need you to be with me."

As for Alfred's promise to give up "the other"—his hookers—that only lasted a few weeks. One day when Vicki was out, he left a message summoning her to meet him at the apartment on La Cienega.

The next day, Alfred was outside her apartment door at ten A.M., leaning on the doorbell. "How dare you stand me up?" he fumed, when Vicki finally let him in. "You can't do that."

"Why not?" she retorted. "I don't take orders from you. You aren't supporting me. You haven't helped my career like you said. And now you want me to get back into your orgy scene. You haven't done anything like you said you would."

In spite of the violent tendencies he showed during their S&M games, Alfred rarely so much as raised his voice in arguing with Vicki. No matter what happened, he usually just groused and sucked his teeth in disapproval and then gave in, whether or not he intended to keep his side of the bargain in the long run. This time was different. He let loose with an angry tirade, telling Vicki that she was a nothing, that she'd sucked him dry and almost ruined his marriage, and that she had no right in the world to stand him up now.

Vicki was unrepentant. "That doesn't change the fact that you don't do what you say you'll do," she taunted.

Having said his piece, Alfred seemed immediately contrite. "Well, you could always sue me," he reflected.

"I don't want to do that to you . . . Besides I can't."

"Sure you can."

"I can? Okay then, maybe I will."

"I dare you," he said.

Why Alfred would have planted the idea of a lawsuit in his mistress's head is anyone's guess. Perhaps he simply felt guilty and wanted to do his penance in the courts or, possibly, he thought that once Vicki consulted a lawyer she'd hear a discouraging appraisal of her position under the law. Perhaps he thought it was out of the question that any attorney would ever take the case, particularly since Vicki had no money, and she'd end up humbled into behaving herself.

In any event, Vicki didn't feel inclined to take Alfred up on his dare at the moment. She was preoccupied with still another new romance. For the one and only time in her life, she'd found a man who combined all the normally incompatible qualities of her ideal lover. He was wealthy and exciting, a playmate but also potential marriage material—at least so she thought.

Vicki had fallen in love.

Frank Allen, as we'll call him, is one of the movie business's most successful production executives. He remembers Vicki Morgan fondly, though, in view of her subsequent notoriety, prefers not to be identified by name.

Frank first saw Vicki by chance in a Beverly Hills restaurant, and he was "knocked out" by the sight of her. He didn't actually meet and talk with her until some weeks later, however, when she showed up on the lot of Twentieth-Century Fox to audition for a bit part in a film—not one of his. She arrived driving a Mercedes.

"I said to myself, 'What is this?' " Frank recalls. "A Mercedes?' " Unknown actresses arrived on the lot by various modes of transportation, but seldom driving Mercedes convertibles.

Attracted and more than a little curious, Frank invited Vicki into his office for a chat. "What's your story?" he asked her. "Are you *really* an actress? Come and talk to me."

It didn't take long to establish that Vicki's aspirations were real but her credentials inconsequential; still, Frank spent a few minutes giving her advice about acting schools. "Of course, I was attracted, but I didn't want to let on . . ." he says.

He was not at all unhappy when Vicki later took the initiative and called him to ask for more advice. "She seemed like a straight guy," he says. So the two of them started to date.

Soon he was more than a little infatuated. Vicki's attraction wasn't just that she was a beautiful girl, he acknowledges. L.A. was full of beautiful girls. But Vicki had something else. She was sexually "fantastic." Vicki had a sexual magic that went beyond just being good in bed, though she certainly was that. There was something about her that liberated all kinds of fantasies—suddenly men were doing things that up until then they'd just thought about.

"Plus," Frank recalls, "she had a lot of Alfred's paraphernalia. Whatever was interesting, we tried."

Vicki may have hated Alfred's deadly serious flogging scenes, but she had no objection to bondage games and the more playful varieties of S&M. Frank suggested some of these games, thinking he was being pretty daring, but found Vicki certainly eager and willing.

The surprising thing about her was that, in spite of having done just about everything, she also turned out to be so, well, nice. Vicki started spending a good deal of time at Frank's place in Malibu, and they got along fine. "For a while there," he says, "it was kind of my hope that she'd start eating bagels and lox and turn hamisch."

Whenever possible, the two of them would get out of L.A. on weekend trips to Big Sur, Aspen, or Santa Fe. They stayed at nice places, though nothing particularly out of the ordinary. But Vicki was charmed, like a kid savoring a new treat. She wasn't used to being with someone who would spend time alone with her, just relaxing and doing everyday things like taking long walks or sitting on the beach watching a sunset.

In the beginning, Vicki was cagey about discussing her background. She'd say that her mother was English, but nothing more, always hinting at a past filled with glamour and mystery. During the course of their weekends together, however, she began to pour out the real story. She talked about her war-bride mother and her enlisted-man father, and about how she'd come to L.A. from Montclair, and what a big shock *that* had been. Then, almost immediately, she'd met Earle Lamm. Earle had dazzled her. "He promised me the world," Vicki said. And then, soon after that, she had gotten involved with Alfred, who had in turn tried to give Lamm a quarter of a million dollars to disappear . . .

"The whole thing just keeps getting bigger and bigger," recalled Frank. "And crazier and crazier. Where's it all going to end?"

It occurred to Frank that Vicki was hoping it might end with marriage with him.

He was immediately wary. Recently divorced, he had lost his confidence that love could resolve all of life's problems. And sweet as Vicki was in many ways, she was definitely a girl with problems.

"Everyone used drugs in those days, 1974 and 1975," he recalls. Vicki, however, enjoyed the drugs a little too much. She had the beginnings of a problem. Then, too, there was the shadow of Bloomingdale hovering over the relationship. Though temporarily out of Vicki's life, Alfred was never quite out of mind.

Still, the first and major reason why he did not want to get too involved, Frank admits a bit ruefully, was his discovery that Vicki had a child. He had acquired an instant family with his first marriage and now, struggling with his new role as divorced father and stepfather, he was in no hurry to repeat the pattern. "I tried to avoid spending much time with the boy," Frank recalls. "I was afraid I'd get too fond of him."

Under all the designer clothes and the shell of Beverly Hills sophistication, Vicki had the personal style and daydreams of a Valley teenager.

Vicki had this "flip-flop" personality, Frank decided. Part of her was "street smart. But not New York street smart. Valley street smart . . . what they want is a lot less." Yet underneath there was always that disarming sweetness. "Married to the right man, she might have turned out completely different. Completely."

He took to calling Vicki his "gum moll" because she always seemed to have a wad of the stuff in her mouth. The ever-present gum symbolized all the reasons why he knew he didn't want to be the man to take on the job of rescuing her.

This distinction was lost on his own children. Vicki was sweet and endlessly patient with the kids, and the sticks of gum she dispensed at every meeting were, to them, the essence of glamour.

Frank watched his children's developing affection for his new girlfriend with a sense of foreboding. "I kept telling her, 'This is fine, as long as you realize it can't go anywhere.' " But it was hard to worry too much about the future when the present was so damn much fun.

One weekend after they'd been dating for several months, Frank took Vicki up to Sausalito, the artists' colony at the northern end of the Golden Gate Bridge, where they checked into a hotel bungalow with a bohemian ambiance and a gorgeous view of the bay. It was raining that evening, the rain coming down in sheets, and Vicki was inspired to suggest that they amuse themselves by staging a little drama. Frank, equipped with a plastic toy pistol, was to come in through the window and there she'd be, waiting in the room to be tied up and "raped."

Playing his part with gusto, Frank went outside and skulked around in the wet shrubbery for a while, giving Vicki time to prepare for her role. Unfortunately, as he crept slowly toward the open window to their room, a busboy carrying a heaping tray of dirty dishes happened along the path.

"I turned around and said, 'You get out of here,' " Frank recalls.

"And he saw a gun in my hand and [yelled] 'Stop! Police!! Security!!!'

"And I said, 'It's not *real*!'

"Then Vicki came to the window and she told him, 'Hey, it's not real. This guy's my friend. He's just crazy, that's all.' "

The busboy had a look on his face that said he was learning fast about the ways of hotel guests, but he took a while to be convinced that everything was okay. Finally, says Frank, "We got in the room and I said, 'God, I lost my hard-on because of this.' "

Frank hadn't quite figured out what to do about this bizarre relationship when he had to go out of the country for an extended period to work on project that was being filmed abroad. He and Vicki didn't break up exactly—she even made a brief visit to be with him on location—but it was unlikely that they'd being seeing much of each other for the next six months or so. Frank figured that by the time he returned, something would be resolved. No doubt by that time, even if he was still interested, Vicki would either be back with Al Bloomingdale or she'd have found somebody new.

Not long after Frank left the country there was a crisis in his family. His eldest daughter, a teenager, was in an accident and had to be rushed to the hospital. Since Frank couldn't be at his daughter's bedside, he called Vicki and asked her to go to the hospital and see the girl and find out whether his ex-wife needed any help.

"I felt very uncomfortable about having this girlfriend sent over, not because of jealousy but because it was a weird situation," says Frank's ex. "I'd heard reports from the kids that they were spending time with her, and then when I saw her I was surprised because to me she looked very common. I mean, she was not attractive at all. She had this mousy, dirty blond–type hair. I gave her a quick exam, and I just thought, 'My God, this is not up to Frank's standards.'

"But," she says, "she'd come tearing right over [to the emergency room] and she just seemed like a sweet girl. A little insecure. I think she was a little uncomfortable, facing the ex-wife . . . but she had an ability to talk to the kids. She spoke to [my daughter] and told her that her dad loved her and all that stuff . . . And I just got that polite, sweet feeling."

Frank's ex was grateful and at least half-charmed, but she also got the impression that Vicki was trouble waiting to happen. "I got the feeling there were drugs around . . . heavier drugs than, let's say, we'd been through. And, well, she had a hooker mentality. I think she loved Frank, but I don't think very much, because she had that kind of mentality that didn't really allow for her to even think [love] was feasible for her."

No
ORDINARY
GUY

//

With Frank gone, Vicki didn't quite know
what to do with herself.

Shortly before she and Alfred broke up, she'd had a breast
implant operation—Alfred's idea, though she agreed that her
small breasts made her figure too boyish and unerotic, and soon
after Frank left she started dating the plastic surgeon who'd
worked on her. Dr. Hal, as Vicki called him, was a nice Jewish
doctor, still youngish and doing quite well in his Beverly Hills
practice. A lot of her friends thought she'd be well off to grab him
and settle down, but Vicki just wasn't in love.

Nevertheless, Dr. Hal was shocked when Vicki suddenly announced in the middle of one of their dinner dates that she was
giving up her apartment and him as well. "I'm broke. So I've
decided to move into Bernie's place," she told him, as if that were
the most logical move in the world.

Hal knew of Bernie Cornfeld by reputation and thought he was
the last guy Vicki should be getting involved with. "Jesus, you
don't have to do that," he said. "Surely you have other places to
go. Come and live with me for a while if you want."

"No, no," Vicki said. "I've made up my mind. Anyway, I don't
want to impose, you know. I'll be better off there."

Of course, it was never a matter of having nowhere to go. For
one thing, Frank had left Vicki the key to the house he owned in
L.A., but Vicki didn't want to stay there because it was too lonely.
For another, her friend Sally Talbert had offered to put her up

temporarily, an invitation Vicki refused because, she said, she didn't want to be stuck way out in the Valley.

"I've got to be in Beverly Hills," Vicki said. "Have a Beverly Hills address. You can't expect me to live way out in the boonies."

Sally and Vicki's other friends from the Valley worked hard to afford their nice homes "in the boonies," and they were never too inclined to sympathize with Vicki's "need" to be in Beverly Hills. So they didn't bother arguing with her at length about the whole thing. It was a losing proposition.

No doubt there were other things about Bernie Cornfeld that attracted Vicki, aside from his possession of the right address.

Because she didn't enjoy getting beaten up, Vicki had managed to deny to herself that she was a masochist; the sexual "problem" in that relationship, as far as she was concerned, had been entirely Alfred's and none of hers. Nevertheless, Vicki's behavior when Alfred temporarily bowed out of her life, proved, if it needed proving, that she was indeed a *psychological* masochist of a very familiar type—a "love addict."

Substitute the female pronoun for the generic *he* in Karen Horney's classic description of the typical masochistc personality, and you can't have a better portrait of Vicki Morgan's tangled logic:

"There are several ways in which one can find reassurance against deep fears," writes Horney. "Being loved is the particular means of reassurance used by a masochistic person. As he has a rather free-floating anxiety, he needs constant signs of attention and affection, and as he never believes in these signs except momentarily, he has an excessive need for attention and affection. He is, therefore, generally speaking, very emotional in his relations with people; easily attached because he expects them to give him the necessary reassurance; easily disappointed because he never gets, and never can get, what he expects. The expectation or illusion of the "great love" plays and important role. Sexuality being one of the most common ways of getting affection, he also tends to overvalue it and clings to the illusion that it holds the solution to all life's problems. . . . his history shows a frequency of "unhappy loves"; he has been deserted, humiliated, badly treated. . . ."

Karen Horney argued against Freud's assumption that masochism was a feminine trait, a natural consequence of the female anatomy. But as she noted, the male "love addict," at least if he is heterosexual, is seen as a faintly ridiculous character. A love-addicted woman, on the other hand, gets plenty of social rein-forcement. Men often flock to her because she seems so feminine and romantic, so concentrated on her own sensuality and un-threatening in her need for affection and her desire to please at all costs. Other women tend to develop deep, emotionally sup-portive friendships with her; since she's always the victim, always the loser in love, her attractiveness to men seldom is the cause for envy.

But the need to have a "great love" constantly on the scene can become a heavy burden. Abandoned by Alfred, something she never dreamed could happen, and then rejected—at least as a potential wife—by Frank, Vicki was desperate to fill up the gaping hole in her life. For the moment at least, an ordinary guy, even a socially desirable and moderately wealthy doctor, wouldn't do. She was looking to be swept off her feet by someone whose charisma was powerful enough to mesmerize her—and, in the process, make the men who had rejected her crazy with jealousy.

Financier Bernie Cornfeld was certainly no ordinary guy.

Like Alfred Bloomingdale, Bernie was wealthy and flamboyant, an Easterner who transplanted himself in Southern California to enjoy the pursuit of wealth and of women—no one could be sure in what order of priority. But while Alfred was a born-and-bred Manhattanite, scion of one of the old families of New York's German Jewish aristocracy, Bernie was pure Brooklyn. Corn-feld's father, a Rumanian actor and theatrical impresario who had worked in the nascent Central European film industry, was hardly the typical Eastern European immigrant, but his death when Bernie was still a boy left the family in much reduced circum-stances. Bernie grew up on Farragut Road and attended Brook-lyn College, where he devoted most of his energies to leading the YIPSELS, the youth branch of the Norman Thomas Socialists, in their factional wars against the Trotskyist Socialist Youth League.

The unlikely leap from cafeteria debater and socialist organizer to investment salesman came about when Bernie was introduced to Walter and Ruth Benedick, a German-born couple who were part of the group that founded the Three Arrows Camp in upstate New York, a socialist-oriented summer community. In the early 1950s the Benedicks were among those who had become convinced that mutual funds would be not only a safe and profitable investment vehicle but also a means by which the ordinary working person might acquire an ownership interest in the capitalist system.

The concept of "people's capitalism" encouraged Bernie to channel his energies into a business career. After a brief stint as a B'nai B'rith youth counselor in Philadelphia, he decamped for Paris, where he became a sales agent for the Dreyfus Fund and eventually founded his own company, Investors Overseas Services.

IOS moved energetically into untapped markets, selling investments to American servicemen and expatriates and later to foreign nationals. A student of Adlerian psychology since his Brooklyn College days, Bernie was a creative manager who knew how to recruit and to hold talent—for a while, he ran ads in the Paris *Herald Tribune* seeking salesmen "with a sense of humor." But the real secret of IOS's success was that it operated "offshore," selling investments in American business but free of regulation by the SEC and American law.

Perhaps the best known offspring of IOS was the highly touted Fund of Funds—as the name suggests, a mutual fund engaged in buying other mutual funds. Although cooler heads realized that this concept offered investors little except the opportunity to pay double management fees, the Fund of Funds posted spectacular paper profits during the bull market of the 1960s. Wall Street loves nothing so much as success; for many, Bernie Cornfeld became a hero, the flashy entrepreneur/evangelist who thumbed his nose at the stodgy regulations of the SEC and managed to make a fortune, while bringing the benefits of capitalism to small investors all over the world.

As long as IOS funds kept raking in new investment dollars, few people worried unduly about the fact that a good deal of the money was going into schemes that ranged from the speculative to the harebrained—the development of Paradise Island in the Bahamas; a plan to drill for natural gas in the Arctic; and a company, owned by one of Bernie's chief lieutenants, that manufactured battery-operated pencil sharpeners. Still other funds were diverted to pay for executive perks, such as Bernie's French chateau, and into something called the IOS Foundation; it sponsored a peace convocation in cooperation with the Center for Democratic Studies and gave out a lot of dubious grants, including one to buy wool so that German women could knit mittens for African lepers.

By 1970, a declining market and a dearth of new investors willing to throw their money into the maw of the monster had caught up with IOS. But Bernie Cornfeld was lucky even in defeat. Ousted from control by a disorganized board of directors, he was allowed to sell his shares in IOS for an amount that still left him with a tidy fortune. The board then brought in their own man to "rescue" IOS—a fast-talking financier named Robert Vesco.

Vesco promptly absconded with what was left in the coffers, and reeling from this new betrayal, a lot of people found it hard to be as angry with Bernie as they might have been. At least he had sold a dream.

Bernie eventually served eleven months in a Swiss jail, although the charges were eventually dropped. After the IOS debacle, he promptly settled down in Beverly Hills where he purchased Grayhall, a palatial establishment that had once belonged to Douglas Fairbanks, Jr.

In addition to the obligatory pool, steam room, and basement screening room, the house boasted an eighty-foot-long ballroom, parking facilities for thirty cars, a private zoo, and thirty-nine telephones. Bernie furnished his wood-paneled living room with massive antiques, the upper floors with velvet wall hangings and mirrors, and the whole place, top to bottom, with gorgeous, long-legged women.

Those who judged the Grayhall scene by appearances tended to assume that the women who decorated Bernie's house were mostly, if not all, pros—an impression not contradicted by Bernies habit of boasting openly that he could "supply [his friends] with the greatest women in the world." But this assumption missed the point. The man who could sell the Fund of Funds to some of the shrewdest minds on Wall Street was easily able to sell his scene to impressionable young women. He didn't need pros.

Bernie had a number of inventive stratagems for keeping up a steady supply of girls into Grayhall. Back in the 1960s, before the IOS collapse, he had purchased an interest in a New York modeling agency known as Talent Modeling International—no connection with several currently established businesses of the same and similar names—which, as of 1974, was operating in California out of Grayhall, representing a smattering of legitimate clients but also offering a lure to prospective bed partners who believed that Bernie could set them up in a lucrative modeling career.

There was also a drama coach—an eminently respectable lady in her sixties—who had been recruited in England from the Royal Academy of Dramatic Arts to give acting lessons. "We used to laugh," says a woman who once worked for Cornfeld's talent agency, "and say, if only she knew that at the age of sixty-three she was really nothing more than a pimp for Bernie Cornfeld. [The agency] brought her over in order to give classes to the girls, acting classes, cold reading, and stuff like that. She had a room there. I think she was out in the pool house. Every day, rain or shine, we'd have lessons and the girls would all show up, and she'd either do Shakespeare or something, and all the girls that couldn't afford to go to acting class would start showing up at the house taking these free classes. And all they had to do was fuck Bernie in order to take the classes. So I used to laugh . . ."

In addition, Bernie simply encouraged his friends, male and female, to invite any good-looking girls they happened to know up to the house. Sometimes after dinner, a few of the male guests would even make the rounds of local night spots, inviting any likely young ladies they might encounter back to the house to party. So many stayed on that it became necessary to convert part of the third floor of Grayhall into a warren of partitioned-off cubicles known as the barracks.

The women, in turn, sometimes asked over *their* friends. "He'd say, 'Don't you have any friends you can invite over?' It would get so boring after a while that you *would* start inviting people over. Then he'd run through all your girlfriends."

Over this scene, Bernie presided like a pasha over his harem, regaling journalists and friends with descriptions of his sexual prowess and, at times, entertaining guests while snuggling under the covers with a female companion. Of course, the image of no-holds-barred hedonism was never quite lived up to in reality. Bernie always had all the girls he wanted, though frequently he was devoting himself to a particular Number One lady. And in the meantime, a good many of the other women who were around the house regularly were actually paid staff—Bernie's European secretaries and so on. Other young women managed to stay at Grayhall for some time without ever sleeping with anybody—it was possible if they just kept your wits about them.

A young woman we'll call Lorna Matlin (not her real name), who was living at Grayhall when Vicki moved there in the spring of 1974 and who later became her close friend, recalls that Bernie's role as sexual master of ceremonies was basically a feat of salesmanship, another testimony to his mastery of Adlerian psychology: "Money never changed hands," says Lorna, "but favors, yeah. . . . [He'd say] this guy really likes you and you should go out with him because he'll be able to do good things for your career. That kind of putting the bug in the girl's ear to make her greedy so that she would go after the guy. . . .

"He got pissed at me a few times about that because there were these men he was positive would be great matches. And I said he was disgusting. And he said I was disgusting, and that I didn't know where reality was at."

Vicki didn't have to deal with that aspect of the Grayhall scene because she came into the house as Bernie's personal girlfriend, a role she inherited from Leslie, who was by now happily and very respectably married to a Swiss banker.

Bernie hadn't seen Vicki since her ill-fated visit with him and Leslie in Europe, but in April 1974, after he returned to California from his brief stay in a Swiss prison, Vicki took the initiative and paid him a welcome-home visit. Bernie, it developed, didn't begrudge all the money he spent on Vicki in London with no reward. He was inclined to be philosophical about such things. Appalled to learn that Vicki was living in a shabby studio apartment, he immediately suggested that she move in with him.

He didn't have to do a lot of convincing.

In some ways, Vicki and Bernie were a natural match. Like her, he'd started out as "ordinary people." He'd worked and hustled his way to the top, and Vicki admired his ability to do as he pleased and thumb his nose at anyone who didn't like it. It was an attitude she shared but seldom managed to bring off with the same degree of insouciance.

Also, though obsessed with performance in bed and his image as a cocksman, Bernie was at least a Dionysian. He had the idea that sex was supposed to be fun, a pleasant change for Vicki from Alfred's endless guilt trips.

As for Bernie's philosophy about women, it was summed up in a comment he made years earlier to his former employee and biographer Alan Cantor. Accounting for his preference for German girls, he told Cantor, "They may not be the most exciting girls in the world, but they are easy to have around and used to taking orders. It's part of their national psychology." This, at least, was what Bernie said. In reality, the women who had played important roles in Bernie Cornfeld's life over the years tended to be notably strongminded—from his mother, with whom he remained very close until his death, to actress Victoria Principal, who was his steady girlfriend for a number of years in the 1960s.

The problem for Vicki, oddly enough, was that she was too

conventional for Bernie, at least at this stage of his life. Although always attracted to the fastest men in the fastest crowds, Vicki's daydreams were decidedly bourgeois. She wanted monogamy, if not marriage. Bernie was infatuated with Vicki to the extent of installing a bedroom for her, connected to his own by a private passageway, and to letting her play queen of the manor at Grayhall, but he had no intention whatsoever of giving up the party scene he was enjoying so much.

And the house party at Grayhall ran twenty-four hours a day. Aside from the thirty or forty people who were likely to be in residence at any one time, there was a constant flow of casual visitors. Bernie liked to get up very late and then station himself at the desk at one end of his oversize den, doing paperwork and conducting his business over the phone while groups of guests amused themselves at the other end of the room, watching TV or · chatting or engaging in marathon backgammon sessions. And that would be just a normal day.

Bernie also gave elaborate parties and social dinners at which the guests included corporate CEOs, politicos, and some of the top names in Hollywood. Depending on the guests and the size of the party, the atmosphere could be elegantly formal—though Bernie himself invariably passed up the vintage wines to sip Coca-Cola—or somewhat more free swinging.

Vicki knew exactly what the party scene was at Grayhall because she'd been there a number of times over the last few years; it was where she'd gotten to know with Bernie's then girlfriend Leslie. By mid-1974, when Vicki moved into the house, the pace was, if anything, more stimulating. Bernie's gospel of "sexual anarchy," as he called it—though, in fact, in practice he ran his own house as a semibenevolent despot—was in vogue, and a lot of people who might have hesitated to be part of such a scene in more conservative times were eager to check it out. Grayhall was also a great place to make contacts, particularly for a young, would-be actresses interested in meeting producers, directors, scriptwriters, and so on. Among the long-term guests at the house that summer was the late Howard Sackler, author of *The Great White Hope* and the screenplay for *Jaws,* who also happened to be an old Brooklyn buddy of Bernie's.

Although she continued to talk vaguely about her dream of an acting career, Vicki had no idea how to use the contacts she made at Grayhall to promote herself. She was surrounded by people who affected hedonism while, more often than not, using the party-time atmosphere as a setting for trying to advance their own ambitions. Vicki lacked the self-assurance to play power and influence games, and for that matter, she was too conventional at heart to enjoy the party scene for its own sake.

"Vicki wasn't promiscuous," says a young man who was part of the household staff the summer that she was there. "Some of the girls, if you gave them a couple of joints, a couple of drinks, that was it. They were ready to party. But not her. She was never like that."

When Vicki did talk, it was usually to the other women, several of whom became her lifelong friends. Judy (not her real name) was an aspiring singer from the Pacific Northwest who had come to L.A. hoping to break into the music business. Judy had a reputation as a wit—as one of her friends noted, she "gave good conversation," a skill she employed to avoid having to do anything else to justify Bernie's hospitality. Judy had first noticed Vicki hovering on the sidelines of a Grayhall screening party in the summer of 1973, before the break with Alfred and almost a year before Vicki moved into the house as Bernie's girlfriend. It was out of sympathy more than anything that Judy set herself the task of drawing Vicki out of her shell.

"I was fascinated by her silence," recalls Judy. "She was very quiet . . . very shy. Shy to the point of sweaty palms when meeting someone new. But when she opened up she had this incredible humor. . . . It must have been something I said to her . . . we just hit it off. . . . She had a magnetic personality. You just couldn't help but like her."

It's striking that, while men were likely to dismiss Vicki as just another dumb blonde, other women tended to see her as fairly intelligent. A high-school dropout or not, Vicki read books—mostly popular romantic novels and books on the occult, to be sure, but reading at all was by no means de rigueur in the crowd she ran with. Judy, who appreciated wit, discovered that, once Vicki felt at ease, she had a sardonic sense of humor and some sharp opinions on the pretentiousness of the Grayhall scene. Vicki's problem wasn't that she lacked brains but that she had no self-confidence, no idea of how to relate to men except as a plaything, which made her the perfect patsy for any line.

"She was open about her life," says Judy. She had "insight into people. But it was not always right. It sometimes led her down the wrong path. I mean, she trusted sometimes more than she should have. . . . She did have Alfred to protect her, but not always. . . .

He told her who to see. Who not to see. Whether this was a good area to get into. Whether it was not a good area to get into. He was very protective. Very. . . . [But] you know, the two of them never really were in touch with the ground. Their feet weren't on the ground. . . . Alfred was never, I mean, he was probably good in some of the areas he was into. He founded the Diner's Club, and he could do things. But. . . ."

Over time, the two women had many conversations about getting away from the "major flakiness" of the Hollywood scene. "Her dream—'cause she knew who she was—was to go off and live way up in the mountains somewhere with her animals," recalls Judy. "Every time there was a real problem, the two of us would talk of this wonderful cabin and self-sufficiency, away from it all. [But] eight years can be eaten up very quickly in a town like that. . . ."

Daily life at Grayhall was about as far from the dream of self-sufficiency in a little cabin in the woods as could be imagined. Another woman who happened to be living at Grayhall during the summer of 1974 remembers one day in particular when she and Vicki happened to be sitting on Vicki's bed, reading and chatting. Bernie came into the room looking for Vicki, and he was in the mood, and pretty soon the two of them were fucking right there on the other side of the bed. "I didn't even look up from my book," the other woman recalls. "I just kept on reading."

Vicki's problem with this wasn't so much prudishness. It was just that in the long run Bernie didn't make her feel, well, special enough.

The longer Vicki stayed at Bernie's, the more nostalgic she became for Alfred's controlling love. If only he had kept his word, had taken care of her financially, and given up the hookers, she thought, being with Alfred wouldn't have been so bad. If only . . .

The two of them had never been entirely out of touch since she returned from Europe. They continued to talk on the phone and even arranged brief, covert meetings from time to time. Perhaps Vicki had thought that her moving into Grayhall would make Alfred jealous enough to risk his marriage by resuming their old arrangement. If so, it hadn't worked, and she was soon ready to try another strategy for getting his full attention. She would take Alfred up on his dare—she'd sue!

Bernie Cornfeld, he says, did not encourage this idea. Even if he approved of discarded girlfriends dragging their ex-lovers into court, which he didn't, he had no reason to want to support

Vicki's lingering obsession with Al Bloomingdale. Vicki got plenty of encouragement, however, from another source—her ex-husband Earle. Delighted when Vicki called him up to say that she was on the outs with Alfred and thinking about suing him, he had enthusiastically recommended that she see Paul Caruso, the attorney who had once turned him down when he wanted to go after Alfred.

Paul Caruso's first impression of Vicki Morgan was that she was "a stunning woman . . . one of the most stunning, most attractive women I've seen. And I've met many of them in my lifetime because of my profession and because I live in Beverly Hills."

His second was that she was a schemer. A cold fish.

Vicki had this clipped, laconic manner of speaking. It might have been a way of putting on a front, of trying to appear tougher than she actually was—or, it might in fact have been borrowed from Alfred's habit of talking in short, staccato bursts—but Caruso didn't think it was an act. He just felt that it revealed a personality that was unattractively brittle, an "adding machine type" of mentality. When he greeted his would-be client at their first meeting in his office, his impression was instantly confirmed. Shaking hands with this beautiful woman was "like plunging your hand into a bowlful of ice cubes."

Vicki got this first interview off to a bad beginning by expressing some qualms that Caruso would have the guts to oppose Bloomingdale in court. "Alfred is a *very* powerful man," she observed. "I trust you won't be afraid to take him on."

This was the second time Caruso had heard it suggested that he might be scared of Alfred, and he was exasperated. The suggestion of intimidation by an opponent is never flattering to an attorney's ego, and less so to Caruso, who had represented his share of big names, from Audie Murphy and Fernando Lamas to Evil Knievel.

Caruso had run into Al Bloomingdale once or twice in social situations and considered him a pleasant enough fellow, though "not the attention-getter in his family." "Of course we [were] not in the same circles," he clarifies. "I [was] way below him. Well, I think it's way above, but that's a point of view."

What he heard from Vicki Morgan about her situation, however, did not exactly leave him in awe of the "rich and powerful" Mr. Bloomingdale. If what his potential client said was true, and

Alfred had allowed his wife to take over the family purse strings, then he could only be a "complete weakling."

Vicki complained that Alfred had driven away her husband, sabotaged her chances for an acting career, and then reneged on his promise to take care of her. As he listened to the litany of troubles it struck Caruso that this bitter woman couldn't be more than twenty-two years old, yet she already felt used up and worn out.

"She was spiteful," Caruso recalls. "But she went on and on about Alfred. "I think she was very fond of [him] and she was incensed that he wasn't being given more attention by members of his own family."

She also went into detail about her sex life with Alfred. "She told me that Alfred had made her the 'queen bee,' " he says. "I got the impression that she more or less organized and supervised these other women but that she never participated. Never actually participated. Then, at a certain point, there would just be the two of them alone together. She was very proud of that."

As far as Vicki was concerned, her grievance was pretty straightforward. Alfred had promised to keep her "always," then gone back on his word. Caruso did his best to explain that the courts weren't going to see matters quite that way. The law did not guarantee the rights of a discarded mistress to support. He did think, though, that Vicki might have an action based on Alfred's claiming to promote her career while in fact doing his best to keep her from working at all. The grounds would be "interference with a business right."

Caruso thought the prospects for the suit were good enough to take the case on contingency, since Vicki said she was broke and had nothing to pay up front.

"I did do this, though," he says. "To avoid being called an extortionist or a blackmailer, I wrote his lawyer a letter beforehand and I wrote him a letter saying, 'Go to your lawyer. I want to discuss this.' I didn't rush pellmell to the courts and get a lot of publicity out of it. There was a lot of legal arguing back and forth as to whether we had a good lawsuit or we didn't have a good lawsuit."

Curiously enough, Alfred wasn't angry at all when he learned from his attorney, Jacques Leslie, that Vicki was suing him. Everything Vicki did was cute. Even her suing him was kind of cute. Imagine her having the nerve to pull a number like that! It just went to show what a feisty little piece she really was!

Alfred was so impressed by Vicki's spunky maneuver that he dropped in at Grayhall to tell her so, naturally at a time when he would not run into Bernie. He was already feeling guilty about abandoning Vicki, and what he saw of the place where she was now living only appalled him further. Grayhall was a temple to nouveau riche vulgarity, and quite unapologetically so. The wood-paneled living room was lined with seventeenth- and eighteenth-century portraits, whose subjects Bernie flippantly referred to as "my ancestors." There were acres of velvet everywhere—curtains, upholstery, wall hangings, what have you. There was even a mirror on the ceiling of Bernie's bedroom. He'd made Vicki into a whore, and now she was living in a place that even looked like a high-class whorehouse.

Vicki was already dying to be rescued, but Alfred didn't quite go that far. He still kept saying he wanted Vicki back eventually, but his answer to the question *When?* was always the same. "It's going to take time."

In the meantime, Vicki spent the early part of the summer hanging around the pool and the endless marathon backgammon games in the den, more or less playing the role of the Beverly Hills flower child. When she felt intimidated by the more sophisticated company, felt that she was in over her head, she always reached for the same excuse. "I'm just a country girl. A farm girl. A barefoot-in-the-grass type." Albeit one who couldn't survive without her twice-weekly manicures and pedicures, or her thrice-weekly hair-dressing appointments.

Since Bernie was usually occupied with business or with backgammon or with the guests, Vicki spent a lot of time with the other women who worked and/or lived in the house. One of the women she was getting to know rather well was Rebecca Borland, a fresh-faced twenty-four-year-old with a freckled complexion and a lustrous mane of dark hair that hung loose to her waist. Rebecca was the Grayhall housekeeper, whose duties included supervising the servants, keeping track of the estate's two dozen–odd cars, and taking care of the household bills, for which she received the not exactly princely salary of $100 a week plus room and board. She'd only been working at Grayhall since January.

One of the things about her job that disturbed Rebecca was the presence in the house of two gizmos known as "blue boxes." Technically called multifrequency signal generators, the gadgets were designed to replicate the frequencies produced by Touchtone telephones, making it possible to place long-distance calls without paying for them. The boxes were, naturally, totally illegal, although the underground salesmen who peddled them were quite successful at appealing to the notion that ripping off Ma Bell was not only an all-American sport but a sort of guerrilla protest against a greedy monopoly. Bernie Cornfeld, the one-time apostle of "people's captalism," had apparently bought this argument along with the boxes themselves.

Because of the transatlantic time difference, Bernie did most of · his phoning to Switzerland late at night, and frequently he'd ask Rebecca to stay up so that she could place calls for him at two or three A.M. Rebecca was smart enough to realize that since she was also handling the household accounts—Bernie merely signed the checks—she might be liable if there were ever any repercussions over the boxes. And there was some reason to think there might be. A number of individuals who'd purchased similar devices in the early 1970s, thinking of them as harmless scams and virtually untraceable, at that, had learned to their dismay that the phone company not only had ways of discovering box locations but was determined to prosecute users for violating federal fraud-by-wire statues. Among the celebrities who'd been recently caught with blue boxes in their homes, to their considerable embarrassment, were Ike and Tina Turner.

According to Rebecca, she communicated her nervousness about the situation to Bernie several times that summer, only to be told that it was essentially none of her business.

Vicki had known about the presence of the first blue box at least since early 1972, when her friend Leslie, then Bernie's girlfriend, had called her with the good news that she had a way to place free long-distance calls. Later that year, visiting Leslie at Grayhall, she had been in Leslie's bedroom and watched while Leslie used the box to make a call to Bernie, who was in Switzerland.

Vicki, who wasn't the least bit good with gadgets, never did learn to use the blue boxes herself; but she later said when she moved into Grayhall she was told to go through Bernie's German secretary Monika Hallmeyer, who would use the blue box to place her long-distance calls for her.

During the early part of August, Vicki and Bernie were part of a group invited to fly to New York with Hugh Hefner on his private plane. Hef and Bernie were up in the front of the cabin playing backgammon while Vicki sat in the rear lounge with Clare (not her real name), a blond ex–Playboy bunny and model who had been hired by Bernie to run his agency, Talent Modeling

International. Both women were leafing aimlessly through a stack of magazines and newspapers when Clare spotted an article detailing the phone company's latest campaign to track down and to vigorously prosecute the users of blue boxes.

"What do you think of this?" Clare commented, passing the article on to Vicki. "Bernie had better watch his step."

On August 22, not long after the New York trip, Clare was involved in another disturbing incident. Bernie, normally a genial gnome type, had a nasty temper when crossed, and he and Clare got into a violent quarrel.

According to sources who were living at Grayhall at the time, what happened was that Clare knew a very wealthy and perpetually randy elderly man who had a big house in one of the canyons. Although past physically participating in sex himself, the old geezer enjoyed ogling young women, particularly unclothed or partially clothed ones. Clare occasionally brought a girl up from Grayhall to the man's house for what they thought was going to be a casual visit and a dip in his pool. Clare would then disappear, leaving the man and her friend alone together. On several occasions the man made lewd suggestions and used obscene language. The incidents were reported back to Bernie, who was furious.

Clare's version of the quarrel was completely different. She later claimed that Bernie was merely angry with her because she was trying to run the modeling agency as a legitimate business, refusing to give contracts to several girls who would never be models and were only on the agency's roster because Bernie wanted to seduce them.

At any rate, the argument got started in the Grayhall kitchen that evening, with Bernie loudly accusing Clare, in front of witnesses, of "pimping for other men, pimping girls right out from *his* house." Clare fled upstairs to get away from him but he followed, and they got into a tussle. Bernie got so incensed—so Clare later charged—that he punched in the neck, held her down, and seemed about to throttle her when Jerry Laba, one of Bernie's accountants, pulled him off.

Laba called a doctor, but when Clare made the mistake of saying she intended to go straight to the police to file a complaint, Bernie refused to let her leave the house, haranguing her for hours and eventually locking her into one of the upstairs bedrooms until morning.

Somehow Bernie managed to talk Clare out of going to the cops with her story, but she was so steamed when she left the house the next morning that she filled the trunk of her car with linens, blankets, and several paintings. Clare denied ever taking anything from the house; however, the incident was later described in detail by two eyewitnesses in an unrelated federal court trial in which Clare was called to testify.

Vicki had already taken to complaining that she felt like a prisoner in the big house because Bernie didn't like for her to go off on her own, particularly for the purpose of seeing other men. After witnessing his display of temper, she had more reason than ever to feel uneasy about her situation.

She was not so upset, however, as to refuse to go along on the three-week European tour that Bernie had been planning. The two of them, accompanied by Bernie's friends Jim Weber, Curt Franks, and Maria Quee, left California at the end of August, stopping in Geneva and in Paris before going on to St. Tropez, where Bernie had rented a houseboat that he planned to pilot down to Monte Carlo.

Bernie had promised Vicki that the trip would be a fantastic experience, a chance for the two of them to spend time together away from the distractions of the house and the constant partying and the other women. From the first day, however, there was trouble.

To begin with, Vicki later told friends, as they were about to go through customs in Switzerland, Bernie handed her his small traveling case, which, she later learned, had an amount of undisclosed cash sewn into the lining. She felt used and she was seething, particularly since Bernie hadn't had the nerve to ask her to take the case through beforehand but had just thrust the thing into her hand when it was too late for her to protest without attracting the attention of the customs agents.

There was also some question about the provenance of the airline tickets that the group had used. Vicki suspected that they were hot, though it isn't clear that this was true or, if true, that Bernie and the others knew about it.

But the serious bickering didn't start until they got to St. Tropez. Vicki's idea of a Riviera vacation was to stay in a luxury hotel, or perhaps a rented villa, dress up every night and head out to do the town. She just couldn't believe that anyone who could afford to travel in style would voluntarily want to be cooped up on a houseboat, eating galley food and staring at the faces of the same little group he'd brought from California.

Less than charmed to begin with, Vicki got hysterical when they started the coastal journey and Captain Bernie turned about to be something of an amateur as a pilot. For Bernie, the fact that he didn't have a clue as to what he was doing was the essence of the adventure; he was having a good time and so, apparently, were the other guests.

After hours of aimless meandering and hysterical laughter, the boat ended up crashed against a rock, and the passengers were forced to abandon ship and row to shore in the dory. In the final act of the comedy of errors, they were rescued by a group of bizarrely dressed Amazons and learned that they'd beached at the site of a lesbian bistro, where they had to spend nearly twelve hours waiting for transportation into Monte Carlo.

Vicki was the only member of the group who failed to see the humor in all this, and her sulking was not at all appreciated by the others, who were doing their best to be good sports.

On top of everything else, Vicki's luggage never made it to Monte Carlo, a major disaster since she traveled with an extensive wardrobe including furs and valuable jewelry. Bernie offered to replace everything she'd lost and more, and the ensuing orgy of shopping somewhat lightened Vicki's spirits. She shopped, as she had with Alfred, as an outlet for aggression, a means of revenging herself on the male sex in general. Still, when the shopping spree was over and she felt a lot more cheerful, her resentment of Bernie hadn't quite abated.

Perhaps the last straw was that, in the course of the trip, Bernie had acquired a stack of pamphlets explaining how to use the blue boxes for a more sophisticated scam that involved making connections through toll-free WATS lines. Vicki knew that Rebecca, who'd been ill and in the hospital recently, would be anything but happy over this latest sign of Bernie's determination to continue using the boxes, and after her scare with customs, she was inclined to sympathize.

Vicki got back to L.A. a few days ahead of Bernie, who'd stayed behind in London to handle some personal business. She used the opportunity to move her things out of Grayhall and into the apartment of a girl who had also formerly lived there. After a few days, the girlfriend got so nervous that she insisted that Vicki leave. The reason: Vicki had driven away from the mansion in Bernie's Maserati—which, she felt, served him right, considering how badly she'd been used.

Vicki went from the girlfriend's to the Westwood Holiday Inn, which happened to be owned by a friend of Alfred's. She checked in under an assumed name and then called Alfred's office.

"I've escaped. I'm out of that house for good," she announced.

She told Alfred that she was sure Bernie was going to come looking for her, and if he found her there'd be trouble. Apparently, she didn't say why. So Alfred somehow managed to arrange a way of paying Vicki's hotel bill without his own wife finding out.

He also had some news. While Vicki was away, Paul Caruso had filed his suit. Also, Alfred's lawyer Jacques Leslie had died of a heart attack. Alfred claimed that the two events had been directly related, that Leslie had been served the papers and immediately gone into a state of cardiac arrest and died on the spot of shock— not a likely story since Paul Caruso had discussed the suit with Leslie on several occasions, so the actual service of the papers was hardly a surprise. Nevertheless, it made a good Alfred-style story.

"You killed my goddamn lawyer!" he groused.

But of course, he forgave her.

Vicki was still pursuing the suit, and Alfred was still too worried about his wife to be seen with her in public. He had managed to drop in on her at the hotel, where they spent their visits arguing. When Alfred left, he'd frequently give her whatever used bills he had in his wallet. Alfred, who was anything but a hypochondriac, had a quirk about well-circulated paper money; he considered it unclean. Occasionally, the bills he passed on to Vicki were fifties, even hundreds. She took them, but not without mentally registering the implied putdown.

After nearly four weeks, Bernie found out where Vicki was staying. Even in Beverly Hills, it isn't easy to drive a hot Maserati without being noticed. He sent someone to pick up the car but didn't press charges. As for getting Vicki back, he didn't even try.

Instead of being grateful that Bernie didn't have her arrested, Vicki was halfway insulted. She'd expected Bernie to treat her defection as a lover's quarrel and to do his best to reclaim her, thus, no doubt, inspiring Alfred to charge to her rescue. Instead, Bernie was petty enough to make the car the issue, for which she never forgave him.

Paul Caruso saw Vicki perhaps a dozen times during the course of 1974.

"I was never that attracted to her," he recalls, "but my associates, the people in the office, and in the restaurants we went to [for lunch], they all were saying, 'Look at that!'. . . But over time, she really degenerated. Deteriorated. She was starting to look in a bad way."

At one point, after the suit was already in motion, Vicki told him over lunch that she was flat broke. She had no car, and she needed to lease one but had no credit and no one to cosign for her.

"I was confident we'd win," Caruso recalls, "so I agreed to guarantee the payments."

It was a few months after that, he recalls, that Vicki dropped out of sight. His secretary called to set up an appointment and discovered that the number Vicki had left was no longer good. "She just disappeared," says Caruso. "She never called me. And I couldn't find her. That was it."

FRINGE CITY

//

The lovers' assignation that took place every Saturday morning at the Palm Car Wash, then located on the corner of Palm Drive and Wilshire Boulevard, provided an endless source of gossip for its employees. The guy was big and more than a little stoop-shouldered, his athlete's body gone paunchy, but his horsy face bore the sun lines that advertised their owner as a man who could afford to spend time beside a swimming pool. The girl was a looker with beauty-parlor-blond hair, all too obviously hiding from the world behind oversized sunglasses. Both of them drove new Mercedeses. Invariably, the man arrived first, pulled over just down the street, and sat behind the wheel chainsmoking. When the girl showed up, they'd send their cars through the wash in tandem while they met by the vending machines, exchanging fur-tive kisses—and a slim envelope that no doubt contained cash.

The car-wash employees would have been even more amused to learn that the male participant in this weekly drama was none other than Alfred Bloomingdale, the man from Diner's Club who had once enthusiastically prophesied the obsolescence of cash. Now, his own cash flow cut off by his wife, Alfred was reduced to a mere $500 a week in pocket money, half of which he tried to save to give Vicki when she showed up at the car wash on Saturdays.

Not much had changed for Alfred over the past year. As crazy about Vicki as ever, he was still too chary of his wife's wrath to see his lover more than occasionally, and even then he was always looking over his shoulder, nervous that he might be spotted with Vicki by one of Betsy's friends.

Vicki had finally left Bernie Cornfeld's bed and board for good. The question was, What now? She'd been doing a lot of drugs, downers and coke, mostly, which meant that she needed more money than ever and was even less in shape to do anything about earning it. The only solution she could see was to find a new man, a nice uncomplicated guy this time, who would love her and take care of her.

The search quickly took on a desperate quality. She had no trouble at all finding guys to date, guys who were more than willing to spend money on her, but for one reason or another none of them were right. And the real ringer in the situation was Frank, who'd come back from his location-work abroad while she was still living with Bernie. Frank was the man she loved, the only man she felt she could be truly happy with. That he didn't think she was good enough to marry hurt a lot, but she was too hooked on him to give up. She kept thinking that if she just held on long enough, something would happen to make him change his mind.

When Frank got back to L.A. and decided to call the new phone number Vicki had given him, he had no idea that he was ringing Vicki's private line at Bernie Cornfeld's. He'd been out of circulation for quite a while and had no one else whom he was seeing seriously, and he'd thought it would be nice if Vicki were free to come up to Aspen with him for a few days.

"I'd love to go," Vicki said, "but I don't think I can."

"Why the hell not?"

"I don't think Bernie will let me out of the compound."

"What!!"

Frank knew who Bernie was and knew the general situation at Grayhall, but he was half-appalled, half-exasperated with Vicki for getting herself into a mess like that.

"What do you mean, he won't let you out?" he said. "If you want to come with me, then he can't stop you. I'm coming over there with a couple of limousines and a tank. I'll bust you out!"

Vicki giggled. "We don't have to go that far." It wasn't all that desperate a situation, she allowed; she'd just have to leave without letting on to Bernie where she was going. "Let me handle it," she said. "Maybe I can think of a way."

Frank hired one limousine, dispensed with the tanks, and the next morning at six had the car waiting near Grayhall, out of sight of the main gate. Vicki slipped out of the house practically on tiptoe—the mood was very cloak and dagger—and sprinted to the limo, and they drove straight to the airport where they caught an early morning flight to Aspen.

After all that, when the trip was over, Vicki headed straight back to Bernie and his enchanted castle. Frank decided to sit this particular dance out.

A month or two later, though, Vicki called with a big announcement. "I'm through with Bernie," she told him, "for good. I'm staying with some friends in the Valley and it's boring out here. Why don't you drop in and visit me?"

Frank went to see Vicki, who was at the house of her friends Lorraine and Michael Dave, but soon after he arrived, another visitor showed up—Alfred Bloomingdale. Frank had never met Alfred before, though naturally he'd heard plenty. Somewhat to his surprise, the meeting was anticlimactic—"Just a casual hello and that's all," he recalls. Alfred, he decided, had sized him up and figured out that he wasn't going to try to marry Vicki. So he couldn't care less.

Though upset with Bernie for a variety of reasons, Vicki was brimming over with stories about the European trip he'd taken her on. She told Frank that she'd especially loved Rome. Vicki's evaluation of cities, it developed, had a lot to do with the quality of the shops, and in Rome she'd gone on a shopping spree, spending more than $50,000 dollars on souvenirs for herself and for friends. Frank's gift was an ivory statuette. "It was exquisite, really," he says.

"Where's this girl going to go from here?" Frank found himself wondering. "After blowing fifty grand on one shopping trip, what's she going to do? Get a job as a salesgirl at Von's?"

In the short run, he had to admit, Vicki seemed to be managing quite well. From the Daves', Vicki found another studio apartment on Doheny Drive. The building was full service, more like a residential hotel, with a central switchboard in addition to uniformed doormen. Vicki also seemed to be swimming in cash. Frank figured that the money was probably coming from Alfred.

Gradually, though, he became aware that Vicki was seeing several other men. One of the guys he knew about was a retired bookmaker named Allen Smiley, a Vegas type said to be well connected with the underworld, who lived in the same building as Vicki, on another floor. Smiley was paying at least part of Vicki's rent. Vicki tried to say, not at all convincingly, that he was "just a friend" with a fatherly interest in her welfare.

"Smiley was about sixty-five," says Frank. "I think he wanted to marry her. I kept telling her that was a good thing." But Vicki was doing an awful lot of drugs by now, coke and downers. Her habit was completely out of control. "She was the type of person who couldn't deal with what was out there, so she was running away from it. Ran away from everything. . . . It was Fringe City, really. You could call your book that, Fringe City.

"In the beginning, that might have been the attraction," concedes Frank. "[But] I respected a lot of things about her, and I kept thinking I didn't ever want to be the one who had the guilt. . . . I didn't want it to be me who was fucking her up."

After only a few weeks at the Doheny Drive apartment, Vicki's life had become more complicated than even Frank could guess. Rick DePaul (not his real name) was the switchboard operator at the building at the time Vicki lived there, and for a three-month period he became her confidant, with a unique perspective on the tangled web of intrigues and fantasies that Vicki had managed to weave around herself.

Like Frank, DePaul first spotted Vicki in a Beverly Hills eatery. Apparently she had a way of getting noticed in restaurants. "We got to talking," he remembers, "and she told me that she was going to be moving into the Doheny Drive apartment. I said, 'Great. I'm studying at UCLA, and I work the switchboard there. We'll be friends.' "

Fielding Vicki Morgan's calls soon turned out to be a job in itself. "When you work the switchboard," Rick says, "you get to know everything. I got to hear a lot of the conversations, and she [started to] confide in me about her life. . . . We used to talk for hours."

Before long, he took to dropping in to see Vicki in the afternoons before he went on duty. Twenty-eight at the time, Rick never dreamed that Vicki was a couple of years younger than he was. He saw her as a glamorous older woman, not that much his senior in years, perhaps, but infinitely more experienced, and he soon became caught up in the seductive craziness of her way of life.

You just had to take one look at her apartment to know that her scene was really bizarre. Although she had no real furniture and was making do with pillows on the floor, a secondhand table, and a few chairs, Vicki once again had her full-time "maid," Penny, living with her. And the place was stuffed full of gifts from men— expensive clothing with the price tags still attached, jewelry, gift-wrapped boxes she'd never even bothered to open.

Also, Rick couldn't help noticing that Vicki always seemed to have plenty of cash around. Really breathtaking quantities. Three or four thousand dollars at least.

One noontime, Rick stopped by after he went off duty, and, with Penny hovering discreetly in the background, the two of them managed to pass the entire afternoon coking up and talking. Just when he was thinking it was time to get out of there, Vicki suddenly pepped up. "I'm starving," she announced. "I've got a great idea. Let's go out for hamburgers."

Okay, thought Rick. Fine.

He was about to name a couple of places within walking distance when Vicki, cool as anything, picked up the phone and ordered a chauffeured limo to take them to McDonald's.

Later he learned that this was Vicki's idea of a casual afternoon excursion. After a stop at McDonald's for burgers and fries, they'd get the driver to cruise down the coast, where he would wait while they stopped off at the beach to have a quick swim and to do some more coke.

Rick had smoked grass and tried coke before, but it was Vicki, he says, who turned him on to Valium, her favorite high. One night they had stayed up very late talking and doing coke and he got really worried about his job. "I said, 'Shit, I've got to get up at six A.M. tomorrow, and I'm never going to get to sleep.' She had these ten-milligram Valiums, and she said, 'Here, this will do the trick.' " After that, she began to give him the pills regularly.

By the time he went on duty, Rick's head would be swimming, but Vicki never seemed the worse for her afternoon jaunts. Vicki had a date almost every night—if not with Frank, with someone else. There always seemed to be a limo or a Rolls or a Bentley waiting outside, and she'd would come down to the lobby dressed in a different evening gown, topped off with her red fox or her mink. "She'd stop to talk to me, and she'd say, 'Guess where I'm going?' It was usually a banquet somewhere. Or dinner at La Scala. Something like that."

After a few weeks of this, Rick says, he began to suspect that some of the "banquets" existed only in Vicki's fantasies and that many of Vicki's evenings on the town took her nowhere except the inside of yet another hotel room. Besides Frank and Smiley, the retired bookmaker, Vicki had six to ten other "steady dates." Nor was Frank the only producer in the group. Rick knew of at least one other very well-known and successful studio executive who was among Vicki's steady admirers.

While Rick suspected that Vicki might have been meeting some of these men by working through some sort of very classy escort service, he was never sure of this. Vicki, he says, was very friendly at the time with Claudia Jennings (now deceased) who had been a Playboy centerfold and a steady girlfriend of Hugh Hefner. "I knew that Vicki was involved with . . . that whole crowd," he says. Vicki and Claudia used to drop in at the Playboy mansion, where there was plenty of opportunity to meet wealthy guys.

During their afternoon drives, Vicki often talked about her crush on Frank. He was the "romantic" interest in her life, and she was deeply hurt that he didn't care enough to want to introduce her to his friends and business associates. Vicki was convinced that Frank considered her too dumb, not educated or high class enough for the circles he moved in. It didn't quite sink in that her whole way of life, the drugs and all the other men, weren't exactly helping her chances of changing his mind.

"I used to ask her," says Rick, " 'How come you go out with so many people? Why don't you stick with one? Why don't you just go out with Frank? He's a really nice guy.' I think he really liked her, too, but he quickly found out she was . . . all over town."

Strangely enough, Rick recalls, with the exception of Frank, each of the men in Vicki's life seemed to block out the existence of the others. Each had managed in one way or another to rationalize that he knew the "real" Vicki, that their relationship was the one that counted.

Even Rick, who was fielding the messages for all the others, found himself falling prey to the syndrome. There were certain implications to be drawn from Vicki's behavior and from all the money, but "I blanked that out with her because I really liked her."

"Blanking out" the negatives was easy enough to do because Vicki was already doing the same thing. The hooker with a heart of gold is a cliché, but Vicki seemed close to the real life embodiment. She didn't consider herself a hooker and technically, perhaps, she wasn't one. Vicki wasn't just having sex for money, she was *loving* all these men who just happened to give her things—in the undiscriminating way that a child loves Santa Claus. Once, Rick says, Vicki returned from an evening out flashing an enormous diamond ring. "Look what I got," she exulted. Within a few days, the ring was forgotten, stuck away in a drawer somewhere with all the other jewelry she never wore.

Vicki gave presents in the same spirit as she took them. When Christmas came, she summoned Rick to her apartment and presented him with a magnificent full-length man's fur coat. "I can't take this," he protested, "It's too expensive. Besides, I'm not going to wear this. There's nowhere in California where I can wear this."

"Oh, come on. Take it," Vicki said. "I bought it for Bernie, but now I'm mad at him. You might as well have it."

Another night during the holidays, Vicki took Rick with her to a celebrity party at a beach house in Malibu. Vicki, who could charm just about anyone on a one-to-one basis, was terrible in crowds. Just the sight of the packed room turned her mouth dry and palms sweaty. So she and DePaul spent most of the evening outside, drinking champagne in the back seat of the limo. His tongue thickened by the mixture of bubbly and downers, Rick once again found himself in the rather absurd position of trying to play big brother. "How do you know all these people?" he asked her. "How'd you ever get into a mess like this? Can't ya see you're fucking around with too many guys? Don't you see they're all using you?"

Vicki just laughed.

By this time, Rick himself had become one of Vicki's lovers. One evening he'd dropped in to say goodbye after his shift ended, and they started doing coke and he just never left. Knowing that he'd lose his job if the management found out what was going on, he was careful to get up before dawn and sneak out of the building through the service entrance to avoid being seen by the doorman.

The doorman, however, didn't worry him half as much as Mr. Smiley, Vicki's admirer on the ninth floor. Rick had heard some heavy rumors about Smiley's past—supposedly, he'd been an associate of Bugsy Siegel's. Smiley was said to have been present when Siegel was assassinated. No one was sure in precisely what capacity, and no one had the nerve to ask him. Rick was scared of getting in the man's way.

Smiley, Rick recalls, had decided that Vicki was a real lady, a good girl at heart who was being victimized by predatory males, a category from which he excluded himself. One day Rick was in the lobby when Smiley happened to overhear Ida, another switchboard operator, mention Vicki Morgan's name in a disparaging tone of voice. Smiley just exploded. "Don't you ever say anything bad about her!" he thundered. "You treat that girl with respect!"

"Vicki was, like, a high-class call girl," says Rick. "But it was never a cheap thing. She was never a cheap date." All these men kept talking about how much respect they had for her—Smiley, and Frank, too. "And they were very protective."

Rick figured that if Smiley ever decided to eliminate some of the bad influences from Vicki's life, he would be the first to go.

He was not the only one feeling nervous. Some time around the end of December, the aura of mystery that Vicki liked to surround herself with began to sour into paranoia. When Rick showed up at Vicki's door unexpectedly, she'd fly into a panic. "Never come up here without calling first," she told him. "Don't scare me like that."

Rick suspected that the problem was Alfred Bloomingdale, who had suddenly begun calling as often as four or five times a day. At first, Vicki was very secretive about the identity of the persistent caller, but it was impossible to keep secrets from the switchboard crew. "Come on, Vicki," Rick coaxed her, "I know it's Bloomingdale. I know who he is."

"You can't tell a soul about it," Vicki warned. "You can't discuss *that* with anybody."

Rick was unimpressed. "Oh, come off it. I don't give a fuck about Bloomingdale. I only care about you."

Since he knew the truth anyway, Vicki enlisted him to begin screening Alfred's calls. "Bloomingdale would be on the line," Rick says, "and I'd call up and ask Vicki, 'Do you want to talk to him?' She'd say, 'No, no. Tell him I'm not here. Tell him I've gone out of town.' So I'd lie and say she was out of town for three days. She'd gone to Palm Springs for three days."

Finally, Vicki told Rick that she had to get away from her apartment altogether. He was housesitting in Malibu at the time and gave her a key to the place so she could stay there with him for a couple of days. "People would ask, 'Have you seen Vicki? Where is she?' And I'd say, 'No, I haven't seen her.' Meanwhile, she was at my house."

While sympathetic, Rick also thought that Vicki's fears were largely the product of her overactive imagination. "It was paranoia from the coke," he says. "[She thought] somebody was trying to get her."

Vicki hid out in Malibu for a while, then came back to her apartment. It seemed that whatever she'd been scared of was no longer bothering her. Then, one day, she simply vanished—walked out of the apartment house and never returned, even to collect her belongings.

Rick was fired shortly thereafter—the result of a complaint lodged with the management by Smiley. He never learned what became of Vicki or if anyone had come around to collect her things.

About a year later, Rick was working in New York when he ran into Vicki on Third Avenue in Manhattan. She was with her son Todd and she looked great, completely transformed: "Very elegant. Very New York. Very . . . Park Avenue."

Vicki told Rick that she was seeing Bloomingdale again and had come to New York to be with him.

"She told me, also, that she had been dating somebody in Washington who was very powerful," Rick recalls. But she was very closemouthed about that. It was top secret.

"And I said, 'Come on, why don't you tell me the name?' She

said, "I can't!' " But she said she was traveling periodically, going on these little trips with the man. Clandestine trips.

Rick heard nothing more from or about Vicki Morgan until 1982, when the story of her palimony suit against Bloomingdale hit the papers. In the intervening years, he'd joined Alcoholics Anonymous, given up drugs and alcohol completely, and opened a small but successful boutique in Beverly Hills.

Although, or perhaps because, he had known Vicki well enough to have some unexpurgated insights into her life-style, Rick found it impossible to believe the stories he read about Vicki's sadomasochistic affair with Bloomingdale. He thought he'd known *all* the faces of Vicki Morgan, and none of them resembled the woman he was reading about in the paper. "I truly believe she made it all up," he says. "I think it was all . . . exaggerated. I wouldn't say Vicki was tough. Vicki was like—she could be the little all-American girl sometimes. And that's the kind of feeling I had about her. She made me feel good."

After the palimony suit was thrown out, Rick figured that Vicki might be in need of some friendly support, and he gave her a call. "But there was no way [to help her]," he says. "She was so out of it. Just so out of it."

THE KING AND I

Vicki's flight from Doheny Drive was triggered neither by Alfred nor by Smiley. Nor, as Rick DePaul half-suspected, was it caused by free-floating pillhead paranoia. She was hiding out from the FBI.

The FBI's interest in Vicki Morgan began on a morning in December 1974, when one William Chaney sat down at his desk to review a thick stack of computer printouts. A consumer fraud investigator with twenty-six years of experience, Chaney was employed by Pacific Telephone to uncover instances of customer cheating, including misuse of INWATS 800 numbers.

Computer analysis was Chaney's first line of investigation. As Rebecca Borland, who had once worked in computers, had predicted in her warnings to Cornfeld, those INWATS 800 numbers were by no means as anonymous as they might seem to the user. True, a hotel chain's reservation number might receive thousands of calls a day, from private and public phones all over the country. But a properly designed computer dragnet could make short work out of separating the legitimate calls from the phonies.

Chaney began with a statistical survey that showed him that the average caller needed approximately three minutes on the line with a Sheraton reservations clerk to complete his business. From there, all he had to do to pinpoint potential fraud cases was to select out customers who ran significantly over the limit.

On this particular day, Chaney hit the jackpot. His printouts showed that during a ten-day period, beginning on October 29 and ending on November 7, no fewer than twelve "800" calls were made from telephone number 274-8698. Seven of the twelve calls, lasting a total of 89 minutes, were to the Sheraton reservation service—an average of 12.7 minutes per call.

By January 8, Chaney had received permission to attach a device known as a Hekemian 51A to the customer's phone line. Triggered by a 2,600-cycle tone, the characteristic frequency emitted by illegal blue boxes, the Hekemian 51A automatically activates a tape that records the first two minutes of the call in question. By January 22, Chaney felt that he had enough evidence to take to the Federal Bureau of Investigation.

On January 28, six days later, an FBI team led by Special Agent Willie White descended on Grayhall with a search warrant. In a locked third-floor bedroom they recovered two illegal blue boxes, as well as several index cards containing a handwritten list of 800 numbers and instructions for using them to make free long-distance calls. The writing was that of Rebecca Borland.

Rebecca, who had resigned from her job at Grayhall in mid-October, was living quietly in a modest apartment in Manhattan Beach. At four o'clock on the morning after the search, she awakened to the sound of someone banging on her door so hard it seemed that it might collapse at any moment.

"What's going on?" she cried out groggily. "Who's there?"

"FBI, ma'am," a voice answered. "Open up."

Only minimally comforted by this assurance, she opened her door cautiously.

"Are you the Rebecca Borland who formerly resided at 1100 Carolyn Way?. . . . Is this your handwriting?"

"Yes, I worked there," she admitted. "Yes, that is my writing."

Wanly trying to explain to the FBI that she had only been following her boss's orders, Rebecca kept having flashbacks to Bernie's flip reassurance, "They won't arrest you." Her visitors were unimpressed by this logic. They reminded Rebecca that the use of a blue box constituted fraud by wire, a felony and a federal offense. They discussed the possibility that she might go to jail if she refused to cooperate.

"I'll never get rid of this guy," she recalls thinking at the time.

Before leaving, the agents handed her a federal grand jury subpoena.

In retrospect, the immediate issuance of the subpoena suggests that from the first the FBI saw Rebecca as a witness, not as a target for indictment. She did not have any way of knowing this, and even if she had, there would have been little reason to feel comforted. She had no desire to get Bernie into trouble and knew that he'd be furious if she did testify against him, yet the agents made it clear that if she didn't, she would be liable for a contempt citation, a perjury charge—or, possibly, even wind up taking the rap herself.

Unable to get through to Bernie at Grayhall, she called Vicki and warned her about what had happened. Vicki had better luck getting past the Bernie's secretaries. "What's going on?" she asked him. "Some FBI agents woke Rebecca up in the middle of the night, and she's completely freaked out."

"I don't know anything about it," Bernie barked into the phone. The FBI had swooped down on him with a search warrant, he told her, and he was completely flabbergasted by their claim to have found what they were looking for. "I don't know how that box got there," he insisted. "I don't know who brought it in." Complaining that he couldn't talk about the situation now, that it would be stupid to trust his phones at this point, he brought the conversation to an abrupt end.

Vicki tried to get back to Bernie at eight o'clock the next morning. She felt that if she were going to try to help him out, Bernie ought to at least provide her with a lawyer. The secretary who answered the phone, however, was informing all callers that Mr. Cornfeld had left for a vacation in Europe.

Vicki had placed numerous personal calls through the blue box over the years, particularly in the summer of 1974 and that October, when she was at the mansion briefly after coming home from Europe. She had a pretty good idea that if the phone company started tracing numbers, some of them could be connected with her. In any event, as Bernie's former girlfriend and his presumed confidante, she was naturally a potential witness.

Vicki hadn't a clue as to what she was going to say when the FBI finally caught up with her; that was why she hid out for several days in the Malibu beach house where Rick DePaul was housesitting. And after she became too bored to hang around there any longer, she went off to a Palm Springs spa for another week—or, at least, so she told Rick.

She came back because she was afraid to stay out of touch with Frank for too long. Even when on the run, she had a little trouble with priorities. She was still clinging to the unrealistic notion that Frank might eventually marry her, but she also knew that Frank was just waiting for an excuse to end the affair with a minimum of grief on both sides. She didn't want to provide him with a pretext.

As it happened, Frank had already figured out a strategy of his own.

A number of Frank's friends had been extolling Werner Erhard's EST training. EST seminars were grueling affairs where initiates, having paid dearly for the privilege, sat in meeting rooms on folding chairs for up to twelve hours at a stretch, harangued by trainers who denied requests for bathroom breaks by accusing their audience of being "nothing but tubes"—machines for eating and elimination who lacked the superior mental control vouchsafed to those who had assimilated the lessons of EST. Critics compared EST techniques to brainwashing, but many who survived the training emerged full of evangelistic fervor, convinced that they'd finally found the key to bringing their lives under control.

Frank was curious to experience for himself what all his friends were talking about, and when a friend invited him to sign up for a seminar program in New York City, he saw that going along might have other advantages. The training program, combined with other commitments in the East, would keep him out of town and fully occupied for two weekends running. If nothing else, he reasoned, the commitment would keep him apart from Vicki for that long.

Two weeks was a long time in the context of Vicki's revved-up emotional life, he figured. A lot could happen.

And he was right.

Frank was gone for his two weekends. By the third, when he was back in town and wondering how Vicki might be doing, she was off in Las Vegas marrying her second husband.

Vicki didn't even meet John David Carson, her second husband, until after Frank left town. She was shopping at Nick's Fish Market on Sunset Boulevard when they were introduced by mutual friends Ann and Ben Gage. Ben (now deceased) was a former husband of swimming-star Esther Williams and had known Alfred Bloomingdale for decades. His wife Ann had met Vicki separately before knowing her through Alfred. The Gages could never have dreamed that their introduction would result in an instant match.

John David was an attractive young man but, for all sorts of reasons, the last person anyone who knew Vicki would expect her to elope with. For one thing, he was Vicki's age, a boyishly handsome man whose all-American face erupted in deep longitudinal dimples when he smiled. For another, he was an aspiring actor whose career was just beginning to take off, and like every other aspiring actor in L.A., he was broke.

For her, of course, the marriage was pure escapism, but she did try for a while to make a success of it. Leaving quite a few of her possessions behind in the abandoned Doheny Drive apartment, she set up housekeeping with John David in a small converted carriagehouse in West Hollywood. For the first time in her adult life, she was doing her own housework and cooking, efforts that were more sincere than successful.

With John David temporarily surviving on unemployment checks, she even went out and got a job of her own, working in a public relations office in the Valley. Somehow, on the occasions when Vicki did try to do the right thing, fate always seemed to work against her. She'd been on the job only three weeks when she awoke one morning with a knifelike pain in her abdomen— appendicitis. She was rushed to the hospital for emergency surgery, and by the time she recovered, her job was gone.

At the end of February, John David got a part in a film being made on location in Oklahoma. Vicki went along, in part because she wanted to be with her husband and dreaded sitting home by herself in their cramped little house. Coincidentally, though, she wasn't sorry to be getting out of town. Several women who had lived and/or worked at Grayhall during the time she lived there had just received subpoenas to testify before a federal grand jury.

She was fairly sure that she'd covered her tracks pretty well. She had left no forwarding address at her old apartment, no one there knew where she was, and she and John David had been married out of state. Still, Oklahoma was remote, but not that remote. The FBI had learned of Vicki's marriage and her whereabouts—it isn't clear from whom—and she was served with a subpoena on the set. When she returned to L.A., Vicki called up Paul Caruso, and as a courtesy to his nonpaying client, he arranged for her to be interviewed in his presence by assistant U.S. attorneys Paul Flynn and Tom Nolan. At the interview, as in her actual testimony before the grand jury several weeks later, Vicki waffled. There were gaping chasms in her memory, particularly involving anything to do with communications at Grayhall. The phrase *I don't recall* more or less summed up her contribution.

Vicki thought she'd managed to avoid implicating herself or anyone else, but her testimony was contradicted by that of other witnesses—there was, for example, that conversation aboard Hugh Hefner's airplane to indicate that she did indeed have some inkling that a blue box was being used at Grayhall. For a time, the prosecutors did nothing, preferring to wait until the right psychological moment before planting the suggestion that she might be facing a choice between a perjury charge and cooperation.

Paul Caruso, meanwhile, heard nothing else from Vicki after that March 5 meeting. The lawsuit against Bloomingdale had been filed and was still proceeding, but his client dropped out of sight again, this time not to reappear.

Vicki's involvement in the Cornfeld prosecution gave her an excuse to get back in touch with Alfred. She always turned to him for advice when she was in trouble, and this time was no exception. Alfred was the first to tell her that she could get herself in big trouble by trying to outsmart the U.S. attorney and the FBI. She was in way over her head.

No doubt Vicki had reasons for calling Alfred beyond the court case. After only a few months, she was bored with married life and with her second husband as well. Vicki had little idea of how to amuse herself without spending money, and it was always difficult for her to take a man seriously if he was too nice to her.

Alfred contributed to her doubts with his machine-gun sarcasm. "Wake up," he told her. "Stop kidding yourself. You're used to the best. You deserve it. What are you doing married to some snot-nosed kid? Look what you're doing to yourself. You'll end up as a Valley housewife in pedal pushers for chrissakes!"

Nothing forced Vicki to listen to all this, but she was mesmerized because Alfred had a way of reinforcing all of her own fears and snobbish prejudices. No fate held more terrors for her than ordinariness. Better to end up sleeping in the gutter or hopelessly mad than as a suburban housewife with a stack of bills on the kitchen table and a squawling kid under each arm, because if she were just like everybody else she'd be . . . nobody.

Once he had her new phone number and realized she was in a mood to be persuaded, Alfred stepped up his calls to his old pace. He started shortly after eight A.M. and called perhaps five, ten, even fifteen times during the day. And the theme was always more or less the same: "How can you do this to yourself? To me?" he'd cajole. "My marriage is on the rocks because of you. And you're living in a dream." On one hand, he kept telling Vicki she was "special," too good to waste herself on a semiemployed actor. On the other hand, he'd remind her that she was a born loser, beautiful but fucked up, and far too incompetent to survive without his full-time protection.

By this time, at least, Alfred's manic energy and nonstop verbosity were getting a boost from "diet pills"—amphetamines. Most likely, he'd been using them for years, since it seems doubtful that he would start the habit after surviving heart surgery. Alfred, a high-intensity personality to begin with, was always up, and Vicki, by now using Quaaludes as well as Valium when she could get them, was always down. The energy flow was strictly one way, and Alfred's marathon harangues worked Vicki into a state of desperation. She felt she had to get out of the house, to get her hands on some really significant money—to do something, anything, to break herself out of the rut she was in.

According to Connie Laney, John David became aware of Alfred's calls and their unsettling effect on his wife, and when she wouldn't take his advice and simply cut them off by refusing to listen, he decided to take matters into his own hands. John David went down to Alfred's office, pushed his way past the receptionist, and confronted the older but larger man face-to-face. "You son of a bitch!" he fumed. "You leave my wife alone!" Alfred's reaction was, in effect, Who is this nobody? "You can't threaten me," he told John David. "I'll see that you never work again."

On April 14, 1975, about the same time that Alfred's telephone campaign to get Vicki to leave John David Carson was gearing up, "best-dressed" Betsy Bloomingdale, returning from a trip to Europe, was arrested at Los Angeles International Airport. A customs official refused to accept Betsy's claim that the French couturier clothes in her suitcase had not been purchased during the course of her trip, and a search of her belongings turned up the invoices, hidden elsewhere in her luggage.

Mrs. Bloomingdale was charged with knowingly and willfully concealing an invoice from a customs inspector for two Christian Dior dresses valued at $3,880—not "tens of thousands of dollars" worth of clothes, as claimed in a widely quoted article in Britain's *New Statesman*, but a felony nonetheless. Betsy eventually pleaded guilty, was fined $5,000, and was placed on probation for one year.

It was certainly ironic that Betsy Bloomingdale should end up with a felony conviction while her husband, who consorted with prostitutes and gambled thousands with bookies, among other indiscretions, managed to sail through life without a criminal record. Mrs. Bloomingdale could certainly afford to pay her way, but along with her friend Nancy Reagan, she was known to be very tight with a dollar. Apparently, it just didn't occur to her that slipping her purchases past customs was anything but an excusable exercise in domestic thrift.

Betsy's arrest could not have come at a more embarrassing time for her or for her good friends, the Reagans. Ronald Reagan had just decided to challenge Gerald Ford for the Republican presidential nomination, and the news that Mrs. Reagan's closest friend had been caught smuggling Dior dresses into the country was not precisely the ideal kickoff gift for the campaign.

No doubt the incident also made it somewhat awkward for Betsy to continue to lecture her husband about his profligate ways. Coincidentally or not, within a few months after his wife's arrest, Alfred sweetened his inducements to Vicki, telling her that if she came back to him he would once again be able to afford to put her up in a nice house. She could have her generous allowance back. Travel. All the luxuries she had enjoyed during the earlier phase of their relationship and more.

The case against Bernie Cornfeld came before the United States District Court for the Central District of California in August 1976. Vicki was extremely nervous about the trial. In spite of her protecting him before the grand jury, Bernie was still uncommunicative on the subject of his plans for his defense. Vicki thought that Bernie ought to be willing to pay for her to retain her own lawyer—a request he turned down for the obvious reason that an independent attorney would no doubt advise her to tell the truth, which would hardly be in his own best interests.

On March 26, 1976, Vicki had been interviewed by FBI special agent Loran McKee in the office of her lawyer friend Michael Dave. By this time she knew that Bernie's secretary, Monika Hallmeyer, who had been back home in Europe when the grand jury met, had been indicted along with him on a federal charge of fraud by wire. Rebecca Borland, meanwhile, had been forced to agree to testify as the key prosecution witness. Belatedly, it dawned on Vicki that the women who'd lived in the house were being used as pawns. The government was basically only interested in convicting Bernie but was ready to play hardball to get the womens' cooperation. Bernie, meanwhile, was busily lining up his still loyal friends to testify as character witnesses for him and against the women.

Once she finally realized the situation, Vicki's memory improved dramatically. Vicki gave McKee a full statement and agreed to appear for the prosecution. Once the prosecution had its star witnesses lined up, the indictment against Monika was dropped.

When the trial got under way, it became obvious that Vicki had made the only possible choice. The U.S. attorney argued that the blue boxes had been all Bernie's idea, with the women more or less innocently doing what they were told. Cornfeld's lawyers turned the argument on its head, claiming that it was Bernie who had been duped.

Defense attorney Roger Cossack of the prominent firm Cossack & Artz (later Kirschner & Greenberg, Cossack & Artz) told the jury that his client had instructed his household manager, Rebecca Borland, that the phone bills were getting out of control, presumably inflated by the excessive long-distance charges run up by various Grayhall employees and guests. Rather than try to limit access to the phones, the defense claimed, Borland had resorted to using the blue boxes.

There was no proof, said Cossack, that Cornfeld himself had any contact with the illegal devices. Further, it was Borland who processed and paid the monthly accounts. Cornfeld merely signed the checks.

The defense produced a number of character witnesses, including the writer Howard Sackler. Most had little to add aside from describing the chaotic comings and goings of the house guests and suggesting that it was entirely possible for the owner to have been unaware that the blue-box scam was going on under his roof. One witness, William Masse, went further, recalling that he had seen the blue box on Rebecca Borland's desk. When he drew her attention to it, Masse said, Rebecca had begged him, "Don't tell Bernie about it. It's mine."

Of course Rebecca Borland told a completely different story. She testified that her responsibility for placing calls had increased after Monika Hallmeyer left for Europe in early July 1974, and that part of her duties had been to be home and available to place late-night calls to Europe. It was her employer who insisted that she use the blue boxes, over her objections.

In addition to Borland, the chief prosecution witnesses were

Clare, who had worked for Cornfeld's agency, Talent Modeling International, and Vicki, who testified as Vicki Carson.

Vicki's testimony was particularly damaging to the defense's scenario. She said that she had learned of the existence of the first blue box as early as 1972, when her friend Leslie took her into her third-floor Grayhall bedroom and showed her how the box worked. The device had been in the house long before Rebecca came to work there, so it couldn't possibly have been hers.

Vicki was also able to back up Borland's contention that Cornfeld knew very well that the devices existed and that they were his. Among other conversations, she told of how she'd warned Cornfeld that "50 percent of the people in the house" knew about the boxes and that the situation was getting out of control. She also said that Cornfeld had specifically told her not to use the private line she'd had installed for her use for toll calls, but to have Monika place them for her on one of the blue boxes.

Vicki's testimony was devastating, but her demeanor was a good deal less impressive. Obviously ill at ease, she frequently garbled her answers and lapsed into tongue-tied confusion when asked to explain why she hadn't told all this to the grand jury a year earlier.

On her way out of the courtroom, she was confronted by Jim Weber, the interior decorator friend of Bernie's who had gone along on the ill-starred European tour in August of 1974.

"Did you say anything in there to hurt Bernie?" Weber demanded.

"I don't know if I hurt him or helped him," Vicki mumbled. "It seems to me I walked out looking like a complete idiot."

Weber reported the conversation to the defense attorneys. According to his account, Vicki had also added, "The jury could tell I was lying."

Vicki took the stand a second time to deny this allegation. She had never said she lied, only that she had been unable to give any good reason for why she had failed to mention certain incidents when she talked to the grand jury.

As prosecutor Tom Nolan noted in his summation, there was a built-in illogic in the defense's story. On the one hand, Cornfeld was supposedly so concerned about the phone bills that his employee had resorted to breaking the law. On the other hand, it was claimed that his concern was so minimal that he never noticed that the charges on his later bills were completely out of line with actual usage. During the month of July 1974, for example, the Grayhall phone bill had shown only $190.67 in long-distance charges—an unrealistically low amount considering Cornfeld's frequent transatlantic communications and the number of guests and employees who had occasion to use the phones. Properly billed, long-distance charges for this month alone would have come to $2,969.68.

It would seem, Nolan went on, that Cornfeld had arranged matters all along so that his secretaries and girlfriends would be vulnerable if the blue boxes were discovered. "In this particular case," he said, "you have a clever individual who used people to insulate himself from criminal responsibility . . . in a very clever way, by keeping quiet about the blue boxes."

The jury agreed, convicting the defendant Bernard Cornfeld of three counts of fraud by wire. So did the Ninth Circuit Court of Appeals, which upheld the conviction a year later.

The striking characteristic of Vicki Morgan Carson's trial testimony was the total absence of any display of indignation. Since this was the same woman who'd driven off in Bernie's Maserati in a fit of pique, it would seem that she had to be capable of malice, yet her demeanor in the courtroom was apologetic, almost submissive—and this in a trial that had all the earmarks of a family feud, with Bernie's loyal supporters doing their damnedest to blacken the characters of the defectors.

Vicki's behavior during the trial makes it possible to begin to understand the otherwise incomprehensible web of forgiveness that surrounded her almost to the last day of her life: She never talked back. No matter what she might do, how irresponsible she might be in her actions, she seldom or never stood her ground in a face-to-face conversation.

She was supposedly very angry with Bernie. She'd told FBI agent McKee that she was ready to "get" him for setting her up. Yet even supported by the entire apparatus of a federal court proceeding, she couldn't bear to come out and confront him. Her demeanor was that of a puppy dog who rolls on its back and makes little fawning gestures to placate a more powerful animal.

Her lovers, her ex-husbands, her friends—everyone kept forgiving her and forgiving her. Even Bernie Cornfeld: "She testified against me, but I forgave her for that," he said when asked about Vicki's role in the case some years later. So when Vicki finally did run into someone who had no forgiveness, no guilt, no empathy for any victim except himself, she was going to be in big trouble.

Vicki's ambivalence about testifying against her former lover at his trial may have been deepened by her fear that Alfred Bloomingdale had somehow instigated the case against him. Whether or not this was true, the curious circumstance cannot pass unremarked that the two individuals who had come between Alfred and Vicki in 1974, before her marriage, were by 1975 both under indictment for federal crimes.

Bernie Cornfeld had his share of ill wishers. He had emerged from the IOS collapse legally unscathed, at least in the United States, and still relatively wealthy, much to the embarrassment of the SEC and the Justice Department. There was no lack of enthusiasm for prosecuting Cornfeld on other charges, and given the size of Grayhall's phone bills and semipublic nature of the social life there, it is hardly surprising that the existence of the blue boxes eventually came to light. Still, it was a remarkable coincidence that the use of the Sheraton reservations center number, only one of several 800 numbers being used by callers from the house at the time, proved to be Cornfeld's downfall.

Diner's Club, in Alfred's day, had established an exclusive relationship with Sheraton's reservation network; for some time, Sheraton accepted no other credit card, and the hotel chain had shared its mailing list with the club. Although Alfred was no longer running Diner's Club and the exclusive arrangement no longer existed, Alfred still had close connections with individuals in Sheraton's management, as well as with high executives at Pacific Telephone. Vicki had talked to him about what was going on in the house during her stay there—he had even visited the place—and he might well have found it interesting that Sheraton's 800 number was being touted in underground newsletters as an easy mark for phone cheats.

According to his longtime friend Shelly Davis, Alfred might offer to buy out his rivals, even threaten them, but to get them into trouble with the law would have been "not his style." Perhaps this is so, though given Bloomingdale's complex and often contradictory personality and his love of the clandestine, the temptation to plant a hint about the Grayhall situation in the right ear must have been nearly overwhelming. And some suspicion that Alfred had a role in the arrest might also go far toward explaining why Vicki seemed so guiltridden during her courtroom appearance.

Betsy's arrest a few months later was almost certainly coincidental. The publicity over the incident was almost as embarrassing to Alfred as it was to his wife, and in the long run it would prove even more damaging—upsetting his hopes for an ambassadorial appointment from the Reagan administration.

While there's no proof that Alfred Bloomingdale had anything to do with Bernie Cornfeld's legal problems, and no proof that he ever acted on any of his threats to "do in" the various individuals who stood between him and Vicki at one time or another, Vicki herself certainly suspected him. To some extent this may have been unfounded paranoia, the product of her tendency to promote herself to a starring role in every drama. Yet she did know better than anyone else the lengths Alfred would go to in his passion for behind-the-scenes maneuvering and intrigue. Interestingly, she never doubted that the man she said she loved would be morally capable of taking petty revenge. She just could never quite figure out whether he would have taken the trouble to set such schemes in motion.

To Alfred's surprise and disgust, Vicki stuck with John David Carson a lot longer than he dreamed she would. In the early autumn of 1976, however, John David was cast in another movie part that required him to go out of state on location, and Vicki was left behind to vegetate.

While her husband was gone, Vicki happened to hear from her friend Clare, who mentioned that she'd just turned down a modeling assignment that would have paid $3,000 for two weeks work in Morocco. Supposedly, the work involved posing for tourist brochures and an appearance in a publicity film that was being made in conjunction with an international golf tournament—all part of a campaign to lure back upscale, and particularly Jewish, American tourists who had been discouraged from visiting Morocco by that country's alliance with Egypt against Israel.

To Vicki, the job sounded wonderful. She could enjoy an all-expense paid trip and come back with several thousand dollars—money she'd actually earned!

There may actually have been such a film being made, but Vicki Morgan never got to appear in it. She flew to Rabat and then on to Marrakesh with a group of L.A. models and their official escort, Abdeselam Jaidi of the Moroccan consulate in New York City.

According to stories she told later, on her first night in Morocco she was introduced at an official reception to a short, slightly jowly man in an impeccably tailored business suit. Although she didn't realize it at the time, she was meeting none other than King Hassan II himself. After that, she never saw the other women in her group again. She was whisked off to a royal villa on the outskirts of town, where she was the one and only guest.

The accommodations were unsurpassed, combining Moorish opulence with the most modern conveniences and ranks of obsequious servants, none of whom happened to speak English. But when Jaidi disappeared, leaving no one behind who could explain to her what was going on, she began to get nervous. She'd heard stories about white slavery and young women disappearing into Middle Eastern harems, never to be heard from again. What's more, she realized that she was a virtual prisoner in the villa. Even if she were allowed to walk out the front gates, which she doubted she would be if she tried, she had no local currency, no notion of the language, and no idea of her specific location. For that matter, she didn't even know how to use the phones.

Vicki spent a sleepless night alone in what she was gradually coming to believe was nothing more than an especially sumptuous prison. The next day, she managed to get the idea across to one of the servants that she wanted to make a phone call to the States, and he helped her raise the international operator. Naturally, she used the opportunity to call Alfred.

"Guess what?" she told him. "I'm over here in Morocco, and I'm supposed to be making this movie. But I don't like the setup. It doesn't smell right."

Alfred was even more upset than she and promised to get in touch with the American embassy right away.

Whether he ever did so is a moot point. Apparently Jaidi found out about her phone call and appeared just minutes later to question her about it. And some time after that, a group of business-suited functionaries descended on the mansion. "Please get ready," Jaidi told her. "Your car is leaving very soon."

"What's happening?" she protested. "Where am I supposed to be going?"

"Anywhere you want," was the answer.

Vicki said she just wanted to go home, and Jaidi stuffed $3,000 into her hand and hustled her into a limo that, he said, had orders to deposit her at the Rabat airport.

Belatedly, she realized that she was getting the bum's rush. A royal version of the bum's rush, but still, that's what it was.

This was the story Vicki told about her introduction to Morocco, and maybe it was even true. It was her way to wander blindly into compromising, even potentially dangerous situations, then panic and claim that, well, she had no idea what she was getting into. Still, it's difficult to believe that she could have been quite as naïve, not to say uninformed, as she pretended to be.

Once she was safely back in L.A., Vicki certainly held no grudges. King Hassan sent her a gift of champagne, which she accepted. And when Jaidi showed up in town to explain that the king wanted a chance to get to know her better, perhaps in some more neutral setting such as Paris, she wasn't at all offended.

In November, shortly after she returned from her aborted Moroccan journey, Vicki called up Lorna Matlin, a girlfriend from Grayhall days, and suggested that she might like to come along on a free jaunt to Paris.

"I have a date with someone there," she explained. "Someone very special. But, the thing is, he's an important man. Just extremely important, and he's going to be busy a lot of the time. So I need someone to keep me company. Please come. I don't want to be in Paris all by myself."

What's the big mystery? Lorna wondered. She was a bit wary, but not at all reluctant to accept a free trip abroad, and knowing Vicki, the offer was not as surprising as it might have been.

It turned out exactly as Vicki had promised. There were prepaid tickets to Paris on Air France awaiting them in New York and reservations for them at the Paris Ritz. Lorna settled in for an enjoyable few days window-shopping. "Do you know the Place de la Rouge?" reminisces Lorna. "It has some of the best jewelry stores in the world. To me, that was like going into a candy store. It was *the* most fascinating place to be."

It happened to be Thanksgiving weekend, and Lorna was invited along with Vicki to join the king for dinner at his villa outside the city. By now, she knew that Vicki's mystery lover was a Middle Eastern monarch, but having heard the story of their meeting, she was surprised to find that Hassan in no way resembled the rough-hewn sheik that this description brought to mind.

In Vicki's anecdotes about the trip, Hassan's villa became a dazzling fairytale palace and the party he held that night a royal ball, where she as Cinderella was wooed by her Prince Charming. Lorna had a somewhat more down-to-earth view of that evening. The mood was informal, and most of the other guests were unaccompanied Moroccan men. "The king cooked us a Thanksgiving dinner," she recalls. "Then we all went back to the hotel."

One thing both women agreed on was that King Hassan was a charming conversationalist and possessed unparalleled good manners.

Hassan, then in his mid-forties, was enjoying a playboy phase that he has since repudiated. He was highly educated, well versed in French history and culture; fond of L.A., a city he knew well; and an avid follower of Grand Prix automobile races. Lorna felt instantly at ease. "The king and I hit it off conversationally," she recalls.

Whatever his true attitude may have been, Hassan was too much of a gentleman ever to let on. He courted Vicki as if she were a princess, and she was utterly charmed.

Lorna also "hit it off" with Mr. Jaidi over the course of the Paris stay, and the two of them eventually made several trips together, one to Europe and a few to Morocco. At the onset of the European trip, Jaidi made a great show of "forgetting" Lorna's rented fur coat by leaving it behind in the limo. When they got on the plane, he presented her with a full-length mink. "I didn't feel right about accepting it," Lorna recalls. "After all, he wasn't a king. He was just a working man."

In Morocco, she was entertained by Jaidi's family. Lorna could never quite forget that somewhere Jaidi had a wife and children, whom she never saw. "I asked one of his brothers about it. . . . and he said, 'Well, they understand because he travels so much and he's hardly ever home.' And it's accepted down there in Morocco. I tried to accept it. But I couldn't. I'm too American, and I can't share."

Vicki continued her own liaison with the king. She also met him once more in Europe and perhaps twice in Morocco, though not on the same trips that Lorna went on. As for the realization that there was a queen somewhere, whom in fact Hassan talked about frankly and often, it didn't bother her in the slightest. But she vacillated between the illusion of high romance and a preoccupation with Alfred's reactions to the affair. "I think the king wanted a sort of girlfriend on the side," Lorna says. "Vicki could have been it. But she was [only] worried about making Alfred jealous."

Hassan plied Vicki with gifts.

On one occasion, he made the Napoleonic gesture of having a necklace placed on Vicki's dinner plate, under her napkin, so that she would discover it when she sat down at the table. According to Vicki's mother, the necklace contained gemstone emeralds. But

Lorna Matlin, who once kept Vicki's jewelry at a time when Vicki thought that Betsy Bloomingdale might try to seize her possessions, says the green stones in the pendant were malachite, not emeralds. Nevertheless, it was a fine piece of jewelry, suspended on a heavy gold chain.

Other gifts from the king included a sapphire-and-emerald ring, a gold bracelet, and an expensive wristwatch. Vicki was enthralled that she, the high-school dropout from Montclair, was receiving presents from a royal admirer, but in spite of the fact that she was always broke and had scads of unpaid bills, her attitude toward these gifts was almost aggressively careless.

The gemstone ring she considered too showy, not at all her style. She seldom wore it, didn't bother to have it insured, and one day some time later, she offered on impulse to trade it for a small and much less valuable diamond that her friend Lorna wore.

Lorna was appalled. "Those are gem quality stones," she told Vicki. "It's a valuable ring."

"Oh well, then. Since you like it, it must be good," was Vicki's reaction.

As for the watch, it was soon stolen when she left it lying in plain sight on the bureau of her Fort Lauderdale hotel room during a trip she made with Alfred. No one knows for sure what became of the necklace.

Vicki had talked to Hassan about her son, who was still being cared for most of the time by her mother. She wanted to have the boy with her, she told the king, but somehow that never worked out. If she was working or traveling, she had no one at home to care for him.

Hassan was concerned. Nothing could be more painful for a mother than to be apart from her only child. He saw that Vicki was given money—a $25,000 check, tactfully presented as being a gift to be used toward the upbringing of her child. He also promised that he would see that she would never have to worry about the boy's care again. He would provide her with a maid—for life.

When Vicki told her friends back in L.A. about this promise, they found it hard to take seriously. No one has a maid "for life"—not in America. How gullible could Vicki be?

Shortly thereafter, the maid arrived. Her name was Fatima, and she was a small, rather inscrutable woman who quickly took charge of domestic arrangements in Vicki's modest West Hollywood house.

Vicki was still married at the time, so Fatima's presence in the household was a bit awkward. "I was wondering, 'How's John David going to take this?' Sally Talbert recalls. "So I went down to the house, and we're sitting around the kitchen table and he [starts] telling me about this new maid who turns down the bed at night and puts rose petals between the sheets."

If Carson had any other thoughts on the matter, he wasn't saying. By this time the marriage was already under so much strain that the end was in sight regardless, and he had drawn his own conclusions about who was to blame. "I never loved anyone like I loved Vic," he told a friend years later. "I know it sounds crazy, but Alfred Bloomingdale ruined her."

Not long after Fatima moved in, Vicki and John David split up for good. Vicki retreated to her mother's house in Montclair until she could figure out her next move. Practically her first words when she came in the door, her mother Connie recalls, were, "Mom, if anyone calls me, I'm not around. I'm walking the dog, or I'm asleep or whatever. I'm not available to take phone calls."

It went without saying that "anyone" meant Alfred Bloomingdale.

Alfred started calling at 6:15 the next morning. Connie knew as soon as the phone rang who it must be. No one else in her acquaintance ever called that early. Picking up the phone, she said automatically, "She's still asleep."

"Can't you wake her? It's important," Alfred barked.

"No, I won't wake her."

The phone continued to ring, at least six times a day for the next week. It was no use refusing to answer because Alfred would just keep ringing until the noise practically drove you nuts.

"Alfred knew how I felt about him," Connie recalls. "He was ruining my girl. She was like a babe taken up the creek. . . . Well, not the creek, but you know what I mean."

At the moment, however, she was even more frustrated with her daughter. "Why don't you just flat out tell him to go to hell?" she asked Vicki.

Vicki couldn't think of an answer. Alfred hadn't supported her now for several years, so the attraction couldn't have been purely mercenary. He was the possessive daddy always hovering in the background, ever around to predict disaster for Vicki's attempts to go it alone and to hold up the safety net when his predictions inevitably proved correct.

Guardedly at first, she began negotiating a reconciliation.

One thing she was adamant about was that this time she wanted to have Todd living with her. The boy had been just coming to think of John David as a father figure, and Vicki thought the divorce would be hard enough on him. She herself had never been a full-time mother, and she decided that with Todd already eight years old, if she didn't make the effort now, it might soon be too late.

Alfred, who liked Todd in particular but not children in general, agreed reluctantly. Fatima was still in town, and Alfred had no objections to Vicki keeping her on as a nursemaid and all-purpose servant. At first, the housekeeper's salary was paid through an arrangement made by the Moroccan consulate in New York, no matter what. Later, when it became apparent that Vicki wasn't going to be seeing Hassan again, the salary must have been cut off because Fatima eventually claimed that Vicki owed her for back wages.

Vicki's second condition was that Alfred agree to seek psychiatric help for what she called his "problem." She'd been given the name of a Beverly Hills psychiatrist, Dr. Victor Monke. "I'll come with you," she promised. "We'll go together."

Alfred did go to see Monke, but it was Vicki who ended up as his long-term patient—a not uncommon outcome.

Alfred knew very well that he was a driven man. At the age of sixty-two, he was less worried about his sexual excesses, though, than about his continued chainsmoking. After a bout with cancer, and then heart surgery, he had still been unable to cut his five-pack-a-day habit. He went dutifully to his therapy appointments for a while, hoping to placate Vicki, but his faith in psychiatry was limited. It wasn't that he was ignorant or unaware of Freudian concepts—he'd lived through the era when intense self-revelation was in fashion and discussions of one's progress in analysis were the stuff of cocktail party chatter. None of this shook his conviction that his problems were the result of an untreatable condition: congenital wealth.

The very wealthy, Alfred liked to say, were the "freaks of the world." They weren't subject to the limits imposed on the average Jack and Jill. They were driven to do everything on a bigger scale—the measures of success, and of depravity, that the rest of the world accepted did not apply.

Alfred also briefly saw Dr. Kroger, the well-known Beverly Hills shrink who treated comedian Freddie Prinze before his suicide.

Alfred complained to Vicki, however, that his wife had come across a bill for a $100 treatment session and called the doctor's office to complain about the size of the fee. Another example, he said, of Betsy's absurd miserliness. The story may or may not have been true; maybe it was a good excuse for Alfred to give up his therapy. Betsy's interference frequently was cited as the reason why Alfred couldn't do things he didn't much care to do anyway—and Vicki invariably took these excuses at face value.

Vicki herself continued to see Dr. Monke for some years. He wasn't the first psychiatrist in her life and not the first, either, to point out to her that she was living with a lot of suppressed anger. One reason that therapy never seemed to do Vicki any appreciable good may have been that no one ever focused sufficiently on her drug problem—understandably so, since Vicki herself denied that it existed and was fairly good at disguising the effects. More importantly, there was a double-bind operating: She could only afford therapy because Alfred was paying the bills, and Alfred's paying for everything was part and parcel of the problem.

Dependency was a sickness, but there were also certain economic realities. Vicki had been around wealthy men for a long time, and she saw no reason why she shouldn't live as well as they did. She wasn't either smart enough or tenacious enough to become one of the minority of women who could make it on her own. On the other hand, she'd met an awful lot of people, men and women, who seemed to be doing damned well without anything going for them but dumb luck, and she was resentful that she wasn't one of them. Holding on to Alfred, at least until he came through and gave her the house she'd always wanted, was her only chance to grow old in comfort, and no shrink was going to be allowed to threaten that.

Pills made the double bind more or less bearable, and Vicki boasted to friends of her ability to wheedle and deceive various doctors into writing prescriptions for her.

Vicki's third condition for a reconciliation was that there would be no more hookers and no more group scenes. Whether Alfred succeeded in renouncing his "games" this time around is a matter of debate. Five years later, in the deposition given during her palimony lawsuit, Vicki claimed that he had or at least that she was no longer involved. Other sources who were close to her suspect that the scenarios still continued, but by no means as often as before. Alfred still believed that a real man was obligated to prove his virility by having sexual intercourse as often as possible, but he was in poor health and increasingly obsessed with his advancing age.

Alfred found Vicki a house on Basil Lane up near the Stone Canyon Reservoir. The house was part of a new development, and its advantage was supposedly that the neighbors were mostly young couples with children who would be playmates for Todd.

More to the point, the real advantage of the house's location, as far as Alfred was concerned, was that he could drive straight up Beverly Glen from his house in Bel-Air and be at Vicki's in a matter of a few minutes.

"I can come up here and see you after *she's* asleep," he told Vicki. "And get back before anyone's the wiser."

Actually, Alfred rarely did this, but Vicki got the message. Even though he had made his last checkup call of the day and was supposed to be at home for the night, Vicki could never be sure that he wouldn't turn up unexpectedly on her doorstep.

Vicki did not find this arrangement as happily convenient as Alfred did. She'd gotten used to her freedom, but Alfred's ideas of the proper way to supervise a mistress hadn't changed a whit. She was hardly moved in before she began to have second thoughts about the new arrangement.

In the meantime, the lawsuit Paul Caruso had initiated on Vicki's behalf had been technically alive, though going nowhere thanks to various delays, including the death of Alfred's lawyer and Vicki's complete inattention. Vicki never even bothered to call Caruso to tell him that she and Alfred had reconciled on their own. He only learned of this development when he called up Alfred's new attorney to discuss their lack of response and was told that the whole issue had been resolved.

"You know, if she'd come to me later and said, 'Paul, I made a deal with Al and here's a thousand or two thousand or whatever it is I owe you,' I'd have great respect for her. Not for the money alone but for the sensitivity. I thought she showed extreme bad faith and a lack of any sense of loyalty or dependability," Caruso groused.

Caruso already had another reason to be irritated with his sometime client. Earlier that same year, 1977, he'd been informed that Vicki had stopped making payments on her leased Mercedes, the one he'd guaranteed the payments on. The car was repos-

sessed and sold at auction for just over $13,000, but Caruso was
being held liable for an unreimbursed balance of $3,600.

Since he couldn't even locate Vicki at the time, much less get
her to agree to pay the money owed, Caruso began civil proceedings to recover his loss. He won in court but couldn't collect. Vicki
Morgan had no listed phone number, no property in her name,
no assets that could be located. If she received any notices in the
mail, she ignored them, and the asset searchers and investigators
he hired drew a total blank.

"That was when I started to realize just how well protected she
was. How very clandestine her life was," he recalls. "I made the
assumption that the whole thing was about guilt. Alfred felt
guilty, and then he'd overcompensate. And it got out of hand."

THE HALLS OF TARA

///

Among the Marilyn Monroe parallels that inevitably make their way into the conversation when those who knew Vicki Morgan discuss her life, none is more striking than the description of her third husband. Invariably, Bob Schulman is dubbed her Joe DiMaggio.

Vicki met Schulman through her friends Lorraine and Michael Dave, people who, along with Sally Talbert, counted among the stabilizing influences in her life. The Daves were family people, a happily married couple of the sort who are not shy about introducing phrases like "spiritual values" into their conversation.

Lorraine Dave, an attractive, curvaceous champagne blonde whose preference for bouffant hairdos and three-inch spike heels hardly suggest New Age bohemianism, had nevertheless been a professional astrologer during the early 1970s. Vicki, who frequented an occult bookstore on Sunset at the time and was looking for someone to do the horoscopes of herself and her son, was referred to Lorraine by the shop manager. Vicki was more than pleased with the results. The charts, she thought, were right "on target." She stayed in touch with Lorraine, and eventually the two of them became personal friends.

Some years later, after her falling out with Paul Caruso, Vicki also became a client of Lorraine's husband Michael. An attorney with numerous clients in the music business, Michael Dave wears a dapper mustache, three-piece suits—and a large onyx ring that symbolizes his spiritual allegiance to the Indian guru, Sai Baba.

"Vicki," reminisces Dave, "was a very complex person. . . . She was not misguided or lost. In a generalized metaphysical way . . . she was interested in seeking a higher way of life. . . . She had a charisma about her. She had a magnetic electric quality about her. . . . [And] she had many goals and aspirations—the majority of which remained unfulfilled."

Dave knew none of the details about Vicki's falling out with Paul Caruso; he had no idea that Caruso was pursuing Vicki with a judgment. But when he learned that Vicki had no legal representation, he had agreed, out of friendship, to advise her during her appearances at Cornfeld's trial. In addition, his brother and law associate Jamiel handled her divorce from John David Carson.

Since Vicki was frequently broke, could seldom pay for the legal help she needed, and often without a place to live during the hiatuses in her affair with Bloomingdale, the Daves—and all her friends, for that matter—had plenty of opportunities to do favors for her. Friendship with Vicki meant supporting her, emotionally and sometimes in more practical ways, as she drifted from one crisis to the next. Obviously, the charisma was there, since so many of her friends were willing to go the extra mile.

Robert Schulman fell in love with Vicki. A fortyish real-estate developer who worked out of Agoura, Schulman had first met Vicki in 1975 when she was staying temporarily at the Daves' house after fleeing Grayhall. When they met again, it was nearly two and a half years later. Vicki was in the process of divorcing Carson and, though reunited with Alfred for only a short while, was already beginning to have second thoughts.

Both she and Alfred had changed since their last episode in playing house five years earlier. Advancing age made Alfred more paternalistic than ever, and Vicki less disposed to accept his constant phone calls and his determination to make her over into his image of the perfect mistress.

In addition to his phone calls and occasional surprise nighttime visits, Alfred had taken to dropping by, usually on Saturday mornings, to do Vicki's grocery shopping and to see if there were any little chores around the house that needed attention.

Alfred was exasperated with her spendthriftness. It was one thing for him to drop a few thousand betting on a game, but it was a woman's role, he thought, to practice domestic economy, to set a standard.

Saving money wasn't quite the point. Alfred did much of his shopping for Vicki and Todd in Beverly Hills' most expensive gourmet outlets and delis, and he was constantly showing up with exotic, overripe cheeses and the like, which he considered treats and Vicki could easily have done without. But Alfred did object to pointless waste. Vicki's method of shopping was to go to the market without a list and come home with scads of food she didn't need, whatever caught her eye. What didn't get pilfered by the household help was allowed to spoil. And, more often than not, when he wanted to stop by for lunch, Vicki would complain that there was nothing in the house to make a decent meal out of.

After several weeks of monitoring the grocery outlays, Alfred went out and ordered a deep-freeze unit. This, he explained, would encourage Vicki to shop ahead, to buy at the supermarket instead of constantly running out to the deli for last-minute supplies, and to take advantage of sales.

It seemed that what being the "other wife" really meant was that, like any married couple, she and Alfred now argued about the grocery bills and the goddamned freezer when the real problem was something else entirely.

Another source of Vicki's unhappiness was that Todd's move to Basil Lane was not quite an unmitigated success. As any eight-year-old might, Todd was having problems adjusting to leaving Connie, who had always been more like a mother to him than a grandmother, and to the separation from the familiar surroundings of Montclair.

Not surprisingly, Todd developed a strong bond with Fatima. The Moroccan housemaid came from a culture where a son, particularly an only son, was virtually an object of adoration. She'd been dispatched to work for Vicki in the first place on the understanding that there'd be a child to take care of, and now that the boy was actually living in the house she enveloped him with attention. Feeling that she was becoming drawn into a humiliating competition with the maid for her son's attention, Vicki accused Fatima of spoiling the boy, of overindulging him. She herself had good intentions of setting standards and of imposing discipline, but she resented being cast in the role of the demanding mommy whose rules the maid immediately set out to subvert.

Vicki in a Monroe-esque pose. Lee Strasberg had once told Vicki, "I see in you many of the qualities I saw in the young Marilyn," a comparison she took to heart. (Chas Gerretson)

Vicki's choice of props for these shots taken for her portfolio was revealing. She was becoming increasingly reclusive, depending on marathon telephone calls for contact with friends and the ever-present wine glass to prop her failing self-confidence. (Chas Gerretson)

Vicki took up painting and perused art books in part to please Alfred, who considered himself a connoisseur. Only after his death did she discover that a number of supposedly "collectible" painti he had given her were of no particular value.
(Chas Gerretson)

Alfred Bloomingdale in 1940, when he was Broadway's youngest producer and an ornament of New York café society. His companion is socialite "Honeychile" Wilder. (AP/ Wide World Photos)

Alfred Bloomingdale was thirty and his bride Betty, as she was then called, was twenty-two when they married in September 1946. Alfred later quipped, "One day I was a Democrat and a Jew, and the next day I was a Republican and Catholic." (AP/ Wide World Photos)

"The Father of the Credit Card" as he appeared in 1958. Diner's Club was riding high, but about to come under pressure from the newly launched American Express card. (Wide World Photos)

In May 1974, a month after his release from a Swiss jail, Bernie Cornfeld posed arm-in-arm with V to celebrate his return to the sybaritic life at his Beverly Hills mansion, Grayhall. The small investor who had lost their savings in the collapse of Cornfeld's brainchild, IOS, were not smiling with him. (AP/Wide World Photos)

:ki looking glamorous in her fox-trimmed coat, a gift from her former lover, financier manqué Bernie
rnfeld. This was the picture of Vicki released to the press at the time her attorney, Marvin
chelson, filed a suit asking for a multi-million-dollar palimony settlement; it attracted attention, but
little to generate sympathy for her cause.
/Wide World Photos)

*J*ohn David Carson, Vicki's second husband.
(Contemporary-Corman Artists, Ltd.)

*K*ing Hassan of Morrocco (right) welcomes
King Faisal of Saudi Arabia to Rabat on the
occasion of the 1969 Arab Summit Conference.
Vicki Morgan's brief affair with Hassan was
followed by her liaison with one of King Faisal's
daughters. (AP/Wide World Photos)

o, sue me," was Alfred's dare when Vicki complained about his failure to keep his promises of
time support. Vicki did sue twice, but her relations with her attorneys were stormy. Paul Caruso
t) (photo © 1983 by Basia Kenton) handled the first suit discreetly, but Vicki never bothered to
orm him when she and Bloomingdale had settled their differences privately. Palimony attorney
rvin Mitchelson (right) was fired for getting too much publicity.

Michael Dave, Vicki's last attorney and executor, won a judgment
against the Bloomingdale estate in 1984. (Jimmy Townes)

Vicki and Alfred, poolside, at Marina Bay in Fort Lauderdale. At one time, Vicki was on the resort's payroll as an interior design consultant. (Bart Bartholomew/Black Star)

...i, Alfred, and her son Todd in 1978. (Bart Bartholomew/Black Star)

Alfred and Betsy in 1981, enjoying the social whirl of the early days of the Reagan administration. (Wide World Photos)

A solitary red rose, Vicki Morgan's calling card, and a newspaper photo bearing her handwritten protestation of love were the only tributes left on Alfred Bloomingdale's unmarked grave in Holy Cr cemetery. His family had buried him hastily in a wooden coffin, before the news of his death becar public knowledge. (AP/Wide World Photos)

Studio City condominium where Vicki Morgan was murdered, hours before she was scheduled to evicted for nonpayment of rent. (AP/Wide World Photos)

ew of the condo living room shows stacked packing boxes as well as two custom-upholstered e couches that Vicki had purchased in better days, when she was redecorating her house on Tower ve Drive in Beverly Hills. An Associated Press photographer was able to take this picture through a dow opening onto the condo's courtyard on the morning after the murder. The crime scene had not n sealed. (AP/Wide World Photos)

Gordon Basichis, Vicki's ghost writer. Eight months of collaboration gave rise to a love affair but, as he later testified, only six hours of taped reminiscences.

Marvin Pancoast, Vicki's self-described "little slave," appears for his arraignment on homicide charges, flanked by his attorneys Ted Mathews (left) and Arthur Barens. (AP/Wide World Photos)

Vicki's attempts to fit into the maternal role all too often ended in smothering the boy with affection and then leaving him alone with Fatima while she flew off on short notice to spend a few days with Alfred in Florida. She'd envisioned Todd as a sort of playmate and companion, someone to keep her company during the long boring evenings when she had nothing to do and nowhere to go, but the reality of motherhood was less fulfilling than she'd imagined.

Vicki did make an effort to fill her appointment book, to keep busy. She was an avid believer in self-improvement, taking lessons in tennis and aerobics and ballet, and at home she worked at sketching and painting. Artistic talent ran in the family; both her stepbrothers were craftsmen, and drawing had been the one school subject for which she showed more than average aptitude. At one point, Vicki had purchased for herself an easel and a professional-caliber set of acrylics, but her sporadic efforts to paint never got beyond the daubing stage.

As with so many of her other efforts at self-betterment, painting put her into indirect competition with Betsy, who'd been an art major in college and whose flair for design and fashion savvy were uncontestable.

The one hobby that Vicki continued to find truly absorbing was spending money. To call what Vicki did "shopping" would be a misnomer. Betsy Bloomingdale and her set were shoppers, women who set trends and whose patronage of the shops on Rodeo Drive accounted for the street's transformation from an ordinary upper-middle-class ex-urban shopping neighborhood into the ultimate in chic. But if Betsy and her friends made Rodeo Drive famous, Vicki was the sort of impulse shopper and pseudo-celeb who was fast turning the neighborhood into an overpriced tourist attraction.

Although by now she had another Mercedes, Vicki still preferred to hire a limo that would deposit her on the doorstep of Neiman Marcus or I. Magnin's and wait while she made a foray inside. She was getting an average allowance of $10,000 a month from Alfred at this point, and for all the talk of saving on household expenses, she had no trouble disposing of the money in shops where a single handbag could cost $1,000 and a set of luggage run into thousands.

There was always some way to be found to fill the daytime hours, but the evenings seemed to stretch out endlessly. "I'm getting older and I'm getting lonelier, and I'm going to bed earlier," Vicki said, summing up this period of her life. "TV is boring . . ."

When she couldn't put up with the stay-at-home routine any longer, Vicki would talk Alfred into tolerating her making an occasional early dinner date with a "safe" escort. One such escort was her hairdresser of the moment, and Alfred would occasionally suggest that Vicki and her friend show up at the same restaurant where he and Betsy were dining out.

She and Alfred, she later said, "would meet in the men's room and the ladies' room and talk or chat for a minute or so and kind of, you know, blow things [presumably kisses] across the tables. Because he would be over here, and I would be over there."

Alfred took a never-ending adolescent delight in these arrangements, but for Vicki the thrill of fooling Betsy had worn awfully thin.

It was as another of these supposedly "safe" escorts that Bob Schulman came into the picture.

Sitting around the Daves' listening to Vicki complain that she never got to dress up and go out, Schulman couldn't see any reason for a woman who looked like Vicki to hang around being bored. He offered to take her out to dinner any time she liked.

Vicki cleared the first few dates with Alfred, promising him that she wasn't interested in him in any serious way. Vicki may also have told Alfred that Schulman was gay, a ploy she had used in the past in comparable situations. This was not a particularly plausible excuse in Schulman's case, but then, Alfred didn't know the man.

More importantly, Alfred had always found it difficult to take any man of lesser wealth than, say, Bernie Cornfeld or Hassan seriously as a rival. Vicki was a money junkie, he figured, and would never be happy for long without the patronage of a man who was both extremely wealthy and extremely indulgent.

As it turned out, Bob Schulman was anything but a "safe" escort, as Alfred defined safe. His interest in Vicki was not only sexual, it was matrimonial. "You don't have to settle for this kind of life," he told her. "You could have a husband, a family life."

In fact, when Vicki mentioned that she'd never had a real wedding, in front of family and friends, Schulman saw no reason why she shouldn't have that either.

Finally, she couldn't put off telling Alfred any longer. When she broke the news over the phone, she was expecting him to blow his stack and start shouting at her. Instead, uncharacteristically, he started to weep.

"Vicki, I'm begging you," he sobbed. "I'm begging you not to marry him."

"You know, I'm not a young man," he went on. "And I love you. You're the only person I've ever loved in my life. If you can possibly understand that."

"It's too late," she told Alfred. "I've made up my mind."

"Vicki, no," he pleaded. "I'll divorce my wife. We'll do it together. We'll do it, and then we'll be married."

Vicki said thanks but no thanks and hung up. If, even at this point, Alfred had talked about facing Betsy himself, the conversation might have ended differently. But the we'll-do-it-together ploy was one she'd heard too often before. Alfred returned to L.A. to find that the wedding talk was indeed serious.

Schulman had taken over the Vicki's lease payments and household expenses, and she had the phone number changed. Alfred frantically began calling Vicki's family, her friends, everyone he could think of, demanding to know the new number. He'd call at six in the morning, sometimes at five, and he'd say, "Please, I'm dying. I've got to talk to Vicki. At least give her a message. Tell her I love her. Tell her not to do this."

When Vicki still refused to talk to him, Alfred took to parking his Mercedes in front of the house, just sitting there in the driver's seat staring straight ahead, while she tried her best to ignore his presence. Or he'd pick Todd up at school, drive the boy home, and send him into the house with messages. "Alfred's parked down by the corner," the boy would say. "He's waiting for you to come talk to him."

Finally, Alfred went directly to Schulman. "If you want to marry this woman," he fumed, "then you'll have to pay her bills! And you might as well start with these."

Schulman took exception to hearing his fiancée discussed as if she were chattel, and the two men exchanged a few shoves. When they calmed down enough to continue the conversation, Schulman learned that among the items Alfred wanted to be reimbursed for was the freezer. Alfred mentioned a figure of $10,000 for everything.

"Fine," said Schulman. "I'll write you a check."

This was not the response Alfred had been expecting. His bluff had been called.

He did take the money, however.

Seemingly, the way had been cleared for the wedding to go on as scheduled.

Vicki ordered a floor-length formal wedding gown—not white, but cream colored. She ordered engraved invitations and booked the Hotel Bel-Air for the reception.

Now, the Hotel Bel-Air is a very nice place indeed, but it's difficult to imagine that the choice of location was not in some degree calculated to irk Alfred. Also, Vicki placed her order for flowers with David Jones, Betsy Bloomingdale's florist. Betsy was not only Jones' steady customer; she missed no opportunity to promote his talents and later boasted in *W* that Jones, impressed by her gardening and flower-arranging talents, "once offered me a job."

Vicki, it seems, was unnerved by Alfred's threats that her this time her desertion was going to be the death of him for sure. Also, she'd concluded on her own that the marriage to Schulman was pure escapism and would never work.

She and Alfred met to discuss the situation, and Vicki allowed as how she might consider changing her mind and reconciling with him for $1 million, an amount she figured would enable her to buy a house and to provide for her son's future.

Vicki saw nothing extortionate about this. It was Alfred's idea that she should be his "other wife," and she felt that if she were going to give up her chance for a real marriage, she at least ought to be able to negotiate some security for herself and her child.

Alfred's response was: Fine. Okay. I'll give you the million. But just not right now.

And Vicki, who either never learned or hadn't been serious about the ultimatum in the first place, canceled the wedding. Bob Schulman departed from her life in disgust, and Alfred and Vicki and the freezer continued on as before. The $1 million was never paid, at least not in a lump sum, and the subject didn't come up again.

During this period, Vicki received one of the few letters that Alfred Bloomingdale ever wrote, begging her to spend the weekend away with him at his favorite resort, La Costa.

Dearest Vick:
I planned and fought for this trip for weeks against all odds. . . . It was so we could be together and straighten out a few things. This trip is the most important thing in my life at this

time. I only live for you. . . . I'm old and I need you. I will come
by tomorrow at 10:00. . . . Don't disappoint me. I love you and
it's our only chance to be together for any length of time. Last
week I only saw you about 1 hour all told. It's always a rush. It's
my fault but please forgive me. And forgive me for yesterday.
I'll explain more in La Costa. Please, please love me and go with
me.

I love you,
Alfred

P.S. This is the 1st letter I've written in 25 years.

This time Alfred and Vicki were together for nearly a year.
Nothing had changed except that Vicki, deeply depressed, once
again increased her daily ration of downers. She had been addicted to pills on and off since she was a teenager, and this was
definitely an "on" period. The difference was that before she'd
been able to dry out, or at least bring her habit under control, at
will. Now, at the age of twenty-six, she could no longer count on
the fog lifting on command.

In December 1978, Vicki ran into Bob Schulman once again.
According to the account she gave in her 1982 deposition,
Schulman told her during their first conversation since the
breakup that he was still willing to marry her. This time she
jumped at the chance, and the wedding took place that same day.

Schulman rented a splendid house in Benedict Canyon for
himself and his bride. The house, which had once belonged to
Max Baer, was the most luxurious Vicki had ever lived in, with the
obvious exception of Grayhall. It's name, announced in bold
letters on the wrought-iron entrance gate, was Tara.

It isn't clear whether the house was named originally after
Scarlett O'Hara's homestead in *Gone With the Wind* or after the
legendary castle of the high kings of Ireland. Certainly, the
gabled, flagstone house, which had an artificial grotto in addition
to its own tennis court and pool, bore no resemblance to a
antebellum plantation house.

For Vicki, however, there was only one Tara. And she, of
course, was Scarlett O'Hara, tempestuous belle caught between
two men—one suitable but boring, the other troublesome and oh,
so exciting.

Alfred, alas, seemed undecided about whether he was playing
Rhett Butler or General Sherman. Still unwilling to accept Vicki's

defection as a fait accompli, he continued to telephone and to haunt the house, parking his Mercedes down the road in the hopes of spotting Vicki on her way out. One day, in a fit of pique, he simply put his car in gear and rammed it through the driveway gates. Bob Schulman happened to be home at the time, and he and Vicki watched openmouthed with astonishment as Alfred strode into the dining room and plopped a thick folder down on the table—a folder that he said contained a record of Vicki's expenses for the previous year.

"Do you really think you can afford this woman?" he taunted the husband. "If you do, think again."

Schulman kicked him out of the house.

Although Alfred's actions obviously didn't help, they weren't the only problems in the marriage.

"Bob," says a friend, "wanted to be the husband, lock, stock, and barrel." He had provided Vicki with a lovely home, and now his idea was that the two of them would settle down to enjoy it together. But Vicki, for all her talk about wanting a normal, quiet, domestic life, began to lose interest once the romance of being swept away from Alfred had played itself out. Schulman was a plainspoken, direct man, athletic and an avid sports fan, who had at one time owned the contracts of several professional boxers. He also happened to be genuinely in love with Vicki.

What he couldn't provide was the continual round of crises, the oscillation between rejection and reconciliation, necessary to convince Vicki that she was in the midst of a great love affair.

For obvious reasons, Fatima was part of the baggage from the past that Bob Schulman wanted to unload. He was hardly about to keep a housekeeper whose services were a gift from a former lover, even a royal one, and Fatima's dislike of him and strong influence over Todd gave him additional arguments for getting rid of her expeditiously.

When she was finally convinced that she would have to fire Fatima to placate Bob, Vicki felt responsible for finding the woman a new position. The housekeeper had no desire to return to the cold winters of New York and even less to be shipped back to Morocco, since she had relatives there who depended on the dollars she sent back home. One of Fatima's friends, another Arabic-speaking maid, suggested that she might be taken on by her own employer, a very wealthy Saudi woman who lived just up the canyon. Perhaps motivated by unselfish concern for Fatima's future—and perhaps in part by the report that the Saudi woman was an honest-to-God-princess—Vicki decided to check the situation out personally.

Vicki dropped in on the Princess, expecting a middle-aged matron who would invite her for tea and a chat about the servant problem. Instead, she was ushered into the Princess's living room and found herself in one of the most wildly decadent environments she's seen in her entire life—which was saying something. The Princess's favorite colors were black and white, and she'd chosen them to decorate her living room—black leather on the walls, lots of mirrors, low Moorish-style tables and banquettes, and for the touch of white, gobs of cocaine and smack very much in evidence.

As for the princess herself, her full name was Jawaharal Bessima Bint Saud, and she was a daughter of the late Saudian Arabian King Faisal—an exceedingly wealthy woman with a powerful, incandescent personality. She also happened to be a lesbian and a heroin addict with a very heavy habit. The Princess was also called The Spider, an appropriate nickname considering how easily Vicki Morgan became caught in her web.

As she later confessed to a friend, Vicki was dazzled at first sight. Here was this small woman with this "incredible black hair and this incredible . . . presence. She was just magnetic."

Others less under the spell of the Princess have described her as a woman who bears a distinct resemblance to Yoko Ono as she looked during the early days of her marriage to John Lennon. Not conventionally beautiful but certainly highly dramatic, the Princess was a thin, very short woman with a flyaway mane of waist-length hair and a fondness for man-tailored pants suits— perferably all white to match her white Jaguar.

Like Vicki, the Princess seemed to be escaping hellbent from a reality she found it impossible to cope with, and in her case, as a lesbian born into a patriarchal Islamic society, she had a good deal to escape from. However the rebellion may have started, by the time Vicki came on the scene, it had been distorted into a painful caricature by the presence of too, too many drugs. The Princess was wealthy enough to be able to afford to destroy herself without restraint, and she'd tried just about every chemical means available, starting with coke and heroin and continuing on through the more exotic designer drugs. Along the way, she'd developed a raging paranoia and the habit of carrying a small pistol, which she brandished often and occasionally discharged at random during fits of temper.

The ceiling of the Princess's house was pockmarked with bulletholes, and her propensity for gunplay had been demonstrated often enough in public to become the talk of Hollywood. One acquaintance of the Princess who hadn't seen her for some time recalls running into actor Jack Nicholson, who remarked, "That girlfriend of yours sure does like to shoot 'em up." The woman thought Nicholson was referring to the Princess's drug habit until he explained that he'd been at a party that Jay, as she was called, considerably energized by whipping out her gun and firing it into the air to emphasize her side of an argument.

Vicki learned about the more erratic side of Jay's personality the first day they met. She'd hardly returned to Tara from the Princess's house when Jay called to suggest they get together later that same night. Apparently the excuse for the meeting was that the Princess had some pills for Vicki, but there really didn't have to be an excuse. Vicki was already fascinated. The two of them arranged to meet at Tower Records.

Vicki, as usual, was late for the rendezvous, and the Princess, not used to being kept waiting, had plenty of time to get suspicious that she was being set up. When Vicki finally pulled into the parking lot and approached the Princess's Jag ready to apologize for being late, she found herself staring down the barrel of a gun.

Vicki was terrified enough of firearms to stay away from the Princess for a few days after that, but unquestionably, the aura of menace that emanated from the Princess was also a turnon. Characteristically, what bothered Vicki about the Princess was not so much the drugs and the guns, not that fact that she herself was married and had supposedly given up extracurricular attachments, but the fact that she was feeling a sexual attraction to a woman.

Fatima, meanwhile, had gone to work for the Princess part time, not very happily. One day while she was working there, the Princess nodded out from an apparent overdose, and Fatima—who didn't dare call the police, knowing her employer's fear of them—phoned up Vicki to ask for help. By the time Vicki arrived, Jay had already begun to recover, but Vicki, on the excuse that she couldn't walk out on a friend in need, stayed around to comfort Jay through the night.

During the course of the evening, Vicki learned enough of the Princess's history to begin to see her as a fellow victim of male tyranny—an insight that made it easier for her to accept their becoming lovers. The Princess confided that her cousin Princess

Misha'il had been publicly stoned to death in Riyadh two years earlier for the crime of adultery. The Saud family had recently learned that British filmmaker Antony Thomas was in Cairo, making a semidocumentary reconstruction of the incident, later released as *Death of a Princess*, and it was up in arms over what it viewed as an unwarranted, culturally biased intrusion into a family scandal. The stoning itself had been frightening enough, but the family's collective sensitivity about its international image on the eve of the film's release was enough to give black sheep members in exile, such as the Princess, some concrete grounds for worry.

Vicki's night with the Princess delivered the coup de grâce to her already moribund marriage. Jay promised to buy Vicki a Ferrari and to celebrate their getting together with a luxury cruise to Hawaii by chartered yacht, an offer Vicki was not disposed to pass up.

The Ferrari was deferred for the time being, but the Princess did proceed to hire a yacht and crew for the voyage. Four other women, including Vicki, were invited along.

The yacht was hardly out of its home berth in San Pedro before the drugs came out of the suitcases and the Princess and her guests settled down to some serious partying. Everyone was having too good a time to notice that the captain was extremely upset about finding himself in charge of a floating narcotics cache. ("All the drugs on board were for personal use," explains a friend who was not among those on board. "But the Princess never did things halfway.")

The captain was particularly upset because the passengers were freebasing in their cabins—mixing cocaine and ether was a definite fire hazard. When he told the princess that he couldn't allow such a dangerous practice on board his vessel, she produced her ubiquitous pistol and ordered him to mind his own fucking business.

There was nothing the captain could do as long as he was on the high seas except grit his teeth and hope for the best, but as soon as he got into Hawaiian territorial waters he radioed the coast guard and asked for help. The passengers, still too out of it to realize that the captain was taking all this *seriously,* didn't come to their senses until they saw the coast guard cutter actually steaming its way toward them, bearing a crew of uniformed seamen armed with rifles and looking distinctly humorless.

The guests—excepting the Princess herself, who was merely

outraged by this intrusion on her privacy—immediately ransacked their cabins and started dumping the stash overboard. It was the closest thing to a blizzard ever seen in Hawaii, drifts of white powder rising in a cloud about the boat while the women tried frantically to figure out what to do with the damned Baggies, which they'd precipitously emptied and now, of course, wouldn't sink.

By the time the coast guard pulled alongside the yacht, the drugs were gone, except for a small amount of heroin someone had hidden in a Kleenex box belowdecks. The captain was not in a forgive-and-forget mood, however. He wanted his passengers off the boat, and one by one, the women were spreadeagled face down on the deck, body searched, handcuffed, and removed to the coast guard cutter.

On shore, Vicki made her usual phone call to Alfred, begging to be rescued. For once, though, it seems that Alfred's intervention was not necessary. The Princess was able to use her status as the member of the royal family of an important U.S. ally to get them all released without charges.

As soon as she was released from detention and had checked into a hotel in Honolulu, Vicki called home with the news of her "safe" arrival, only to learn that her first husband, Earle Lamm, had just died of a heart attack.

Earle had come back into Vicki's life in the late 1970s after being out of touch for several years, and when he reappeared he had taken up smuggling marijuana into California from Mexico.

Earle had been arrested in L.A. on a drug charge in the mid-1970s, and by 1977, he was imprisoned again, this time in Mexico. When Vicki learned of his troubles, she immediately went down to visit Earle in jail. Bob Schulman, who was not yet married to Vicki at the time, went along to watch out for her and to keep her company. This time, Vicki learned, the problem was not drugs. Earle had been arrested on a charge of trafficking in prostitutes.

"It was a total frameup," Earle told Vicki. "Someone's got it in for me."

It does seem difficult to understand what commercial motive Earle might have had for smuggling hookers into Mexico, which was the charge. Vicki and Earle both toyed with the suspicion that perhaps Alfred Bloomingdale was getting his revenge for Earle's refusal to stay away from Vicki. People who crossed Alfred did seem to have extraordinarily bad luck when it came to getting into trouble with federal authorities and customs officials, though in

Earle's case it would seem that his drug activities would give the Federales plenty of reason to look for a reason to detain him.

At any rate, Earle was released and back in L.A. within the year, and he had been in sporadic touch with Vicki during the last few months of his life. The news of his death at a relatively young age—he was only in his late fifties—plunged Vicki into a miasma of guilt. She'd ruined the last ten years of Earle's life, driven him to crime and, finally, into a premature grave. And, well, it was odd how many of the men in her life developed heart trouble at a relatively young age—her stepfather Ralph Laney; Alfred, who'd suffered two attacks after she met him; and now Earle.

Vicki flew back to California for the funeral. Those of Earle's friends who knew her were shocked by her appearance. She looked emaciated and sallow. Exhaustion showed in her eyes. Vicki did her best to transform her encounter with the coast guard into another of her wry little anecdotes, describing how wild and crazy it had been with all those drugs going over the side and the Princess halfway prepared to take on the entire boarding party. For once, however, her friends were not amused.

Several of Vicki's friends tried to talk her into signing herself into a hospital to dry out from the drugs. Bob Schulman, who was still legally her husband, was even willing to have his insurance pay for the treatment.

But Vicki's mind was still on the Princess, and she took the first available flight back to Honolulu, where she found that the lost stash had been replaced, and then some. The Princess, in a rotten mood after the run-in with the coast guard, seemed disinclined to do anything except sit around in her air-conditioned hotel room getting high, and the other members of the group were starting to get restless. They'd been promised a fantastic trip, a once-in-a-lifetime cruise around the islands, and now they were stuck trying to humor Jay into coming out of her room.

Once Vicki returned to the group, the Princess's bad mood seemed to find its focus. There was a terrific row, which ended with the Princess accusing Vicki of stealing from her. The real problem, it would seem, was that the Princess was upset that Vicki had walked out on her. She'd spent a lot of money on the trip, only to have Vicki blithely take off for the States immediately after the harrowing experience with the coast guard. The Princess was not fond of men in general, and she couldn't see why Vicki thought the funeral of a husband she'd abandoned a decade ago justified the inconvenience to her.

When she got back to L.A. for the second time, Vicki could no longer deny that she needed to dry out. In late October 1979, she checked into the Thalians Community Mental Health Center at Cedars-Sinai Hospital in Beverly Hills, where she was treated for drug abuse and depression.

Once she was weaned off drugs, Vicki rebounded quickly—perhaps too quickly for her own good. She was never able to admit that she had a continuing problem with drug abuse, and even this time around she persisted in thinking that she'd just let herself get carried away temporarily by Jay's influence. As soon as she was straightened out, she'd be fine.

Thalians was an elite facility, but Vicki still didn't feel that she belonged in the company of the other patients who, unlike her, supposedly, were seriously troubled. Within a few days after checking in she had managed to strike up a friendship with another patient who also felt that he was out of place.

Twenty-nine-year-old Marvin Pancoast had worked off and on in public relations since dropping out of a journalism program at the University of California at Santa Barbara a decade earlier. He had an address book overflowing with the names of celebrity acquaintances and a stock of anecdotes about his homosexual encounters with well-known personalities in the business. Some of the stories may have been the product of an overactive imagination or at least greatly exaggerated, but by no means all of them. Vicki had been around enough to know the difference between hot gossip and fantasy, and she was impressed by some of the inside stories that Marvin knew. He, in turn, was mesmerized her account of life in the fast lane.

Marvin did not seem mentally ill. He was well-spoken and somewhat self-effacing, gay but not flamboyantly so in his mannerisms. He told Vicki that he'd been hospitalized for depression after a failed suicide attempt, which was accurate, though not the full picture.

Marvin's medical records showed that he had been hospitalized repeatedly since 1969, and always for the most serious mental disorders. A number of his commitments had followed suicide attempts, but he also told his doctors repeatedly about his struggle to control his feelings of aggression toward women, feelings that focused primarily on his own mother and on an imaginary "woman in a red coat" who, he thought, was persecuting him. His most recent diagnosis, made at the time he entered Thalians, was psychotic depression.

On November 26, 1979, one of Marvin's doctors at Thalians made the observation in his notes that Marvin appeared to have improved rather dramatically over the past month. He no longer expressed homicidal feelings toward his mother, his aggressive fantasies seemed under control, and his delusions about the "woman in the red coat" appeared to have abated. "The patient," the doctor also remarked, with apparent approval, "seems to be involving himself in a symbiotic relationship with a female patient to escape his troubles."

Marvin Pancoast himself recalls what was going on during that month a bit differently. "Vicki and I just sat in the corner and laughed at everybody else," he says.

··P····A····R····T·· IV

*These violent delights
have violent ends.*

ROMEO AND JULIET
ACT III, SCENE VI

VIOLENT DELIGHTS

///

The whole time she was in Thalians, Vicki was preoccupied with getting in touch with Jay. Whatever it was exactly that had happened back in Honolulu, she was convinced that she could get the Princess to forgive her and to take her back, if only they had a chance to talk. Jay was supposed to be back in L.A. by now, but she was never an easy person to get in touch with, even under the best of circumstances.

"Look," she said to Marvin, "There's this woman named Mary who works as the Princess's secretary. Maybe I could get a message to Jay through her."

Marvin had a pass on a day when Vicki didn't, and so he made the call.

By the time Marvin was released from the hospital in January, Vicki had already been out for some weeks. She hadn't wanted to go back with Schulman. She simply didn't feel up to it or to taking care of Todd, for that matter. So Bob and her son were living in a condo he owned up Beverly Glen, near her former home on Basil Lane. Vicki, meanwhile, had moved into a hotel.

Marvin knew all this, and one of his first moves when he got out on the street was to look up Vicki.

"She was staying at this very fancy place on Burton Way," Marvin recalls. "I want to say La Mirada, or La Mirage, but that's *Dynasty.*"

Actually, the name was L'Hermitage. And when Marvin arrived, he discovered that Vicki was not alone. Mary had come by to see her, and the two women had hit it off, and so Mary just moved in. Marvin was not particularly happy with this development. Mary never liked me," he says. "I don't know why. She was very anti-men. Maybe that's why."

There were no doubt other reasons for Mary's disapproval, starting with the fact that Vicki had met Marvin on a psychiatric ward. Also, he happened to be carrying a major torch for Vicki, which couldn't have helped. Marvin was homosexual but not particularly happy about it, and his most important emotional relationships were with women. Friendships formed inside psychiatric hospitals can get intense very fast anyway, and Marvin already considered Vicki very important to him.

Vicki returned the feeling, but not so strongly and not in the same way. She had numerous confidants in her life already.

When the bills from the hotel began to come in, Bob Schulman was aghast at the charges Vicki was running up in his name. L'Hermitage was expensive to begin with, and Vicki, it seems, had been celebrating her freedom, ordering vintage champagne from room service and inviting in various girlfriends to party on her tab. Bob insisted that Vicki move to Le Parc, which was cheaper. She did, taking Mary with her. Later, for a brief period, Vicki moved back to Tara, which Schulman still had under lease.

One day during the time Vicki was at Tara, she and Mary called Marvin and suggested that he come down and cook up some of that great chili he knew how to make. When he arrived, the two of them were sitting around talking about how the Princess had borrowed Vicki's vacuum cleaner and never returned it. Since Jay was upset with both of them at the moment, they weren't sure how to go about getting it back.

"You go over there," Mary suggested to Marvin. "Take the Jeep and go pick it up."

So Marvin took the gray Jeep Cherokee that belonged to Schulman and drove to the Princess's. When he arrived, he rang the bell down by the foot of the driveway. No one asked who he was. The electronically controlled gates swung open, and he drove on up to the house—but no one came to the door. He rang and rang for nearly half an hour without getting an answer. The gates had closed behind him automatically. He couldn't drive out. There was nothing to do but keep trying.

He could tell that someone was moving around inside the house, so he pounded hard on the door. He heard the Princess inside, shouting that she had a gun and he'd better get out.

"But I can't get out!" he yelled.

Eventually, it dawned on the Princess that this was the God's truth, and she opened the door to him. She said she was sorry, but she'd lost her head. She'd been expecting someone else, and when she realized she'd opened the gate for a man in a Jeep she just panicked.

Marvin didn't know what to make of the incident. Sometimes the people outside the loony bins acted a lot crazier than the ones inside. He figured that maybe the Princess was worried about getting busted for drugs. Jay had huge quantities of drugs around her house, and her ideas of interior decoration were definitely bizarre. Sort of S&M Roccoco. He was particularly struck by the leather walls.

Marvin thought the princess was scary but, in a way, impressive too. She was one more piece of evidence of Vicki's incredibly exotic past.

Vicki's affair with Jay had been too bizarre even for Alfred. When Vicki entered Thalians, however, he'd come to visit and, naturally, made a plea for the two of them to get back together again. The whole business with Bob had been a mistake, Alfred pointed out, as if that needed to be said. He, Alfred, was the only man who had ever been able to take care of her and keep her out of trouble, to love her in spite of all her faults.

For once, Vicki was ready to agree. For years now, she'd been running away from Alfred only to run back to him immediately.

The routine had been going on so long that even the two of them couldn't take it entirely seriously. Both of them were getting a little tired of riding the old love/hate seesaw.

This time, Alfred agreed that Vicki should definitely have a house. They could start looking right away, but in the meantime, until they found just the right place, he'd found her another rental in the canyons. The house at 1611 Tower Grove Drive was an eagle's next, perched above the road so as to provide both privacy and a glorious view. It had a swimming pool, naturally, and rented for $2,700 a month.

Vicki's monthly allowance was originally supposed to be $10,000 a month, the same as she'd had when she lived on Basil Lane. But that soon turned out to be inadequate, so Alfred increased the checks until they leveled off at $18,000.

Vicki's half-brother John, a skilled carpenter, happened to be visiting from Texas, and she got him to come stay at the house and do some work. John put new cabinets in the kitchen, rebuilt a damaged wall, and did some work on the floors.

Then Vicki started buying: appliances, new furniture, draperies. She chose a white couch and double-pile gray carpet for the living room, augmented a chrome-and-glass tables and occasional pieces. For her bedroom, she purchased a black lacquer bedroom set with an elaborate vanity.

"Everything she picked out was exquisite," one friend recalls, "in the best of taste." But perhaps the tastefulness of it all was a bit too self-conscious. The house was decorated throughout in black, silver, and gray. Vicki claimed these were her favorite colors, but she may well have been wary of venturing into the color spectrum for fear her taste would be revealed as tacky. Anyway, the spare effect was soon undone by her habit of packing the house with accessories—Chinese lacquer bowls, statuettes, hand-blown glass bud vases, marble ashtrays, oversize house plants in decorative containers. All the little odds and ends Vicki picked up were expensive, and some of them were indeed exquisite. There were just too many of them, and the house began to take on the appearance of a very discreet gift shop.

In no time at all, she'd spent $70,000.

Alfred viewed the renovation with a certain bemusement. He could never deny Vicki her whims, but even he wasn't happy about shelling out $70,000 over and above Vicki's allowance. Mary, meanwhile, had moved into the house and taken over the

role of Vicki's confidante and general factotum, managing all
those details of life that Vicki could never quite bring herself to
deal with. She supervised the renovation, paid the bills, and more
often than not, chauffered Vicki around town. None of her
managing could keep Vicki solvent, however. In addition to the
bills for remodeling work and new furnishings, there was the
monthly rent and the lease payments on a new Mercedes.

Also, there were Todd's school fees to pay. Oddly, considering
her own negative experience at St. Anne's, Vicki was very anxious
for Todd to have a Catholic education. When Todd's grades
weren't good enough to get him into Good Shepherd, the elite
Catholic school in Beverly Hills, Alfred had pulled strings to have
him admitted. Later, Todd moved on to a Catholic high school.
Vicki, eager to be accepted by the other parents contributed to
fund-raising drives as well as paying the required tuition.

And then there were the servants. Vicki always managed to
have live-in help, even in her first studio on Doheny. When she
wanted to hire a maid for the Tower Grove house she called a
friend for a recommendation who happened to know of not one
but two women recently arrived from Mexico who were looking
for maid's jobs. "That's okay. Send me both of them," was Vicki's
response. Never good at coping with loneliness herself, Vicki
thought that a single Spanish-speaking maid would feel the want
of company. So what if the house wasn't exactly big enough to
require live-in servants?

Vicki had no trouble disposing of what remained of her
$18,000 a month after her fixed expenses were taken care of. It
was nothing for her to spend several thousand dollars on a
shopping spree. Her monogrammed Pratesi sheets alone, cost
$500 a set. As for clothes, if she got bored with her purchases
after a few wearings—or after they had aged in her closet for a
while unused—she would pass the items on to one of the maids.

Gifts to friends were on a similar scale. Having decided to give a
cigarette lighter, she chose one from Cartier's. It cost $1,400.

Not all her generous impulses were impractical. Vicki helped
her mother with payments on a new car and took care of various
medical and other expenses for her half-brothers. When Penny,
her maid and companion during the Doheny Drive days, wanted
to take courses to become a dental hygienist, Vicki gave her
money toward tuition. Often, though, the help went beyond what
the recipients either needed or wanted to accept. Relatives ar-

rived from England to visit her mother, and Vicki insisted on putting them up at the posh Westwood Marquis and giving them a grand tour of Beverly Hills' more expensive eateries.

"Vicki wanted so badly to show her family that she'd made good," says Marvin Pancoast, "and she felt guilty." On meeting strangers, she would invariably find some excuse to mention that her mother was English, that she herself had lived in England as an infant. "But the details," says Marvin, "were always left mysterious. She was ashamed that her mother was only a war bride, that she came from Montclair. And she was ashamed of being ashamed."

Despite the fact that Mary did not particularly approve of him, for reasons he found arbitrary and baffling, Marvin continued to drop in at Tower Grove, drawn there by the magnetic pull of Vicki's personality.

On one occasion, he says, Vicki invited him to come along on a trip she and Bloomingdale took to Marina Bay in Fort Lauderdale. Vicki frequently asked friends to accompany her on such trips to keep her company while Alfred was otherwise occupied. Although they may not have been aware of it, such companions also filled Shelly Davis's old role as the "beard"—the putative escort whose presence made it less obvious that Vicki and Alfred were traveling as a couple.

Marvin took to the role with alacrity. The Bloomingdale charm and charisma, which had won the loyalty of the far more sophisticated companions, had a predictable impact on the impressionable and celebrity-awed Pancoast. At Marina Bay, Alfred took Marvin and Todd deep-sea fishing while, Marvin recalls, "Vicki stayed on shore sunbathing and looking beautiful." Marvin provided a fresh and eager audience for Alfred's well-worn collection of insider anecdotes. While Todd was busy fishing, Alfred regaled the younger man with reminiscences of his days as a pal of Harry Cohn and Frank Sinatra and Johnny Roselli and tales of his high-rolling exploits in Vegas.

Out of the hearing of Vicki's son, Alfred laced his conversation with personal remarks that managed to be self-deprecating and boastful simultaneously. "You'd never believe it," he told Marvin. "But I used to be Jew. I started out as a Jew and a Democrat, and in one day I became a Catholic and a Republican. My wedding day."

A favorite plaint of Alfred's was that he was henpecked. He talked of having been madly in love with Betsy, the perfect woman in his estimation, but groused that "the honeymoon only lasted one day." He seemed, however, to regard this as a rather typical duration for marital happiness, and the theme of wifely domination took on a certain ritualized quality. In the next breath, he would be complaining, "I spent a million dollars on hookers last year. A million."

Coming from anyone else that last statement could be dismissed as hyperbole, but Marvin, knowing that Vicki alone was getting close to a quarter of a million, figured that it was close to the truth.

Also, according to Marvin, it was not quite true as Vicki would later claim in her palimony deposition that she had managed to wean Alfred away from his taste for S&M scenarios. On occasion, Alfred still insisted on indulging in the game. During the early part of 1980, says Marvin, he was invited on another trip, this time to La Costa, the exclusive coeducational spa north of San Diego. Also along on the jaunt was young woman named Evelyn, whom he had never seen before and whose last name he never learned.

"We didn't take part in the social life down there at all," Marvin says. "Only Alfred and Vicki went out. Evelyn and I just stayed in our room. Alfred had this, like, fantasy, that we were a family. He was the daddy and Vicki was the mommy. Evelyn and I were brother and sister, and he got us to dress up in diapers. When we were 'naughty' he spanked us.

"Alfred gave me money and he gave Evelyn money," he adds.

Vicki and Alfred had tried just about every sexual twist they could think of over the years. It wasn't so much that Alfred had given up the game as that Vicki had encouraged him to change the rules, substituting novelty for intensity. On one occasion, reportedly, she hired a dozen streetwalkers of various shapes and sizes as "surprise" for Alfred. So it wasn't all that unpredictable that Marvin, readily available and eager to participate, should eventually become the novelty of the month.

And in the meantime, Vicki was also mothering Marvin in more conventional ways. She listened to his problems and gave solace and advice. And in the latter part of 1980, when Marvin was arrested for lewd conduct while crusing in Hollywood Park, it was Vicki he called to pay his bail and to come get him out of the slammer.

What neither Vicki nor Alfred may have realized was how neatly Marvin's role as baby in the fantasy family fit into his own psychological needs. While 1978 and 1979 had been bad years for Marvin, after he met Vicki, his mental state seemed to improve considerably. His various doctors noticed that he no longer seemed quite so preoccupied with his relationship with his mother, one that had formerly vacillated between a deep longing for acceptance and homicidal fantasies.

Vicki, it appeared, was a steadying influence.

BEST FRIEND BETSY

//

What eventually did cause Alfred to give up the game was a combination of failing health and his growing preoccupation with a more public form of gamesmanship— electoral politics.

During the autumn of 1979, while Vicki was a patient at Cedars-Sinai, Alfred had been taking part in a series of strategy meeting with the group of longtime supporters who constituted Ronald Reagan's Kitchen Cabinet. Ever since 1976, when their man had suffered the humiliation of being outmaneuvered by Gerald Ford, the Reaganauts had been looking forward to this second chance at the presidential nomination. At the time, their candidate's success was anything but a forgone conclusion. The age factor was still an issue of unknown potency, and Reagan's paid staff often seemed to be expending more energy on infighting than on organizing. In his first significant test of electoral appeal, the Iowa caucuses of January 1980, Reagan narrowly trailed George Bush, an opponent his staff had previously regarded as an unthreatening lightweight.

Nevertheless, the mood in the Kitchen Cabinet was close to euphoric. The members of Reagan's inner circle were also his contemporaries or slightly older, in their late sixties and early seventies. Not only were they looking forward to the long deferred triumph of their conservative, probusiness philosophy,

but there was an element of personal rejuvenation as well. At an
age when most of their friends were retired or at least far past the
peak successes of their careers, the veteran Reagan boosters were
looking forward to taking over the reins of government. Several
of the senior members of the circle, including Jack Wrather,
Justin Dart, and Henry Salvatori, were realistically resigned to
staying in the background roles as influential but unofficial advis-
ers.

Alfred had no intention of settling for a behind-the-scenes role.
He wanted, indeed expected, that if Reagan won the election he
would be appointed to a major ambassadorship. He even had the
specific post picked out. He wanted Paris, the city where he had
lived during his sojourn abroad after dropping out of Brown
University and for which he had a nostalgic attachment.

In some respects, Alfred's ambition was not unrealistic. He was
an internationally known businessman and a prominent Catholic
layman, a member of the Order of St. Gregory. He had contributed generously and over a sustained period of time to furthering
Ronald Reagan's political ambitions. Besides his personal financial support, he had acted as a link to numerous potential givers—
contacts in the travel and entertainment fields, Sunbelt real-estate
developers, and even, reportedly certain casino and underworld
figures who might want to make very discreet contributions to the
Republican war chest.

But Alfred's hopes rested primarily on the influence of his wife.

It was no secret to California political insiders that the Kitchen
Cabinet as a whole was Nancy Reagan's creation. Over the years,
her contribution toward keeping the group together had gone far
beyond socializing with the members' wives. Mrs. Reagan never,
ever paraded her influence over her husband in public, but it was
she who had the flair for in-group maneuvering and for building
personal loyalties that is the necessary component of any political
career. An inveterate telephone user, one of the few characteristics she had in common with Alfred Bloomingdale, Nancy did the
lion's share of the work in pulling the Kitchen Cabinet together,
and her frequent phone calls were responsible for keeping the
members informed and enthusiastic.

But more than any other member of the inner circle, Alfred
was linked to the Reagans through his wife. Betsy Bloomingdale
was Nancy Reagan's closest and dearest friend, a position quietly
resented by some of the women who had known Mrs. Reagan
even longer than Betsy had.

Betsy's special place in the inner circle went beyond the matter of seniority. It was a question of style. She was not so much society as café society and comfortable in the public eye. Five times on the best-dressed list, she had been a fixture of the *Women's Wear Daily* social notices for over a decade. Her friends included the influential gossip writer Aileen "Suzy" Mehle. For years now, she had conducted a social life quite separate from her husband's. Her most frequent escorts at parties and luncheons were her interior decorator Ted Graber and Jerome Zipkin, the self-appointed doyen of the New York party scene.

The very characteristics that made the other women of Mrs. Reagan's group a bit uneasy were the essence of Betsy Bloomingdale's appeal for the would-be First Lady. Betsy was not just a wealthy matron who had spent her way onto the best-dressed lists. Tall and slender and amazingly youthful looking, she also had an unerring nose for fashion. During the years between Sacramento and the 1980 campaign, her influence had remolded Nancy Reagan's image from California conservative to elegant woman of the world. From Betsy, Nancy had learned to deal with being constantly in the public eye and continually photographed. And for better or for worse, Betsy had instilled the confidence that would enable Mrs. Reagan to risk making "fashion statements," as during the 1982 European summit meeting when Nancy set tongues wagging by appearing at a dinner for heads of state in a Galanos creation consisting of black satin knickers under a tunic top.

Loyal to her most amusing friend and fashion mentor, Mrs. Reagan had absolutely no interest in hearing reasons why Betsy Bloomingdale might not be the most suitable best friend for the wife of a United States President. She had even less interest in hearing hints about Alfred's undesirable habits. Although Alfred's compulsive womanizing and relations with hookers were common gossip in certain Hollywood circles, the Reagans may possibly have managed to remain oblivious. Even though she had seen Alfred and Vicki Morgan together years before, even though she must have known of the affair, in another sense she didn't know about it at all. Both Nancy Reagan and Betsy Bloomingdale had been brought up to believe that there were certain areas of human experience that were never discussed—period. They carried on in spite of them. They blotted them out of the public consciousness, the only level of consciousness that truly mattered anyway.

Even Mrs. Bloomingdale's 1975 arrest belonged to the category of nonhappening. It was in bad taste even to remember it.

If Nancy Reagan saw her friend Betsy in the role of the wife of the Reagan administration's ambassador to France, there was no reason to doubt that the appointment would come about in due course.

Their common interest in electing Ronald Reagan to the presidency brought the Bloomingdales closer together than they had been in years. The campaign was challenging, it was fun, and it gave Alfred plenty of occasions to refresh his admiration for his wife's elegance and drive to achieve. Vicki saw all this clearly enough to feel threatened. Just when she'd been cured of her taste for rebellion and was ready to settle down in style as Alfred's *mistresse en titre,* suddenly all he could talk about was going to Paris with his wife.

"But what about me?" she demanded.

"Don't worry," Alfred told her. "We'll still find time to be together. I can probably get you some kind of consular appointment. Maybe something in the Bahamas."

Although patronage plums in the consular service are not unknown, Vicki Morgan's chances of receiving one of them were exactly zero. Even if Alfred had the influence necessary to promote such an unlikely appointment, neither Mrs. Reagan nor Mrs. Bloomingdale would have tolerated it for an instant. Vicki, nonetheless, saw nothing unrealistic about the promise. In all of Southern California, perhaps in the entire fifty states, there was no one more passionately pro-Reagan than Vicki Morgan.

At Alfred's suggestion, Vicki went to work as a volunteer at Reagan's campaign headquarters. Most of her work was of the envelope stuffing and mailing-list-checking variety, but on a number of occasions she was deputized to pick up dignitaries arriving at L.A. International Airport and to bring them to headquarters. Vicki would brag to her friends that her contribution to the campaign had included acting as "chauffeur" to vice-presidential candidate George Bush. In reality, though, the distances she drove anyone, let alone Bush, were short, and her responsibility was considerably less than what is implied by the title of chauffeur. Furthermore, she was an odd choice for the duty of driving anyone anywhere. A notoriously inept and accident-prone driver, Vicki never took the wheel of her own car if there was anyone around willing to drive for her. Also, after a brief period of being off pills entirely, she had begun to drop several Valium, and when she could get them, a Quaalude or two.

After one "chauffering" stint, Vicki confided to Marvin that Alfred had given her a plain white envelope containing $10,000 dollars in cash. Her instructions were to hand the envelope to the arriving dignitary, whom she named. Not say anything, just to hand it over.

Alfred, as Marvin himself noted, "was very careful." He realized that Vicki would never betray him, she couldn't afford to. For that matter, if for some reason she did talk, her accusations could be passed off as the lies of discarded mistress bent on petty revenge.

Vicki grasped the first half of this equation, but not the second. Naïvely, she believed the old saw that knowledge is power.

Ronald Reagan's election victory was as much a social coup as a political one. Come January, his California friends descended on the capital en masse, like courtiers whose black-sheep patron had just been elevated to the throne. None seemed more determined to enjoy themselves than the Bloomingdales, who took a suite at the Watergate and settled in for the social season.

Vicki Morgan went to Washington, too. She had received an engraved invitation to one of the inaugural balls but did not make an appearance. Instead, she stayed holed up in a hotel room, getting reports from Alfred whenever he could slip away from the festivities long enough to get to a phone.

Being stashed away incommunicado while Alfred appeared publicly at his wife's side was not exactly a new experience, but the thrill of participating in Alfred's clandestine naughtiness had worn off. Betsy was enjoying the triumph of a lifetime, getting reams of publicity and being dubbed by the press the new First Lady's quasi-official "First Friend." Not unsurprisingly, there was little talk of Vicki's getting a government post in the Bahamas.

As it turned out, even Alfred was snubbed when it came time to hand out appointments in the new administration.

Immediately following the November election, Alfred had been named along with Justin Dart, Holmes Tuttle, Jack Wrather, and others to Reagan's Transitional Advisory Committee, a group that met periodically in the law offices of William French Smith to screen candidates for political jobs. The committee's list of nominees, top-heavy with millionaire cronies and, particularly, former Bechtel Corporation executives, was accepted almost in toto by the President-elect. William French Smith became attorney general. James Watt and Anne Burford, protégés of the conservative brewery owner Joseph Coors, got the Department of the Interior and the Environmental Protection Agency. Helene van Damm, formerly Reagan's administrative assistant in Sacramento, got the embassy in Vienna. And William Wilson, the other Catholic in the Reagan inner circle, became a special envoy to the Vatican.

Alfred Bloomingdale had the negative distinction of being the only Kitchen Cabinet member who wanted an appointment for himself and was turned down flat. The rejection was all the more devastating because his ambition to go to Paris had been the worst-kept secret of the transition process, discussed by both himself and Betsy as if it were a fait accompli.

The official excuse for his being passed over, Alfred told Vicki and the one he himself claimed to believe, was Betsy's 1975 felony arrest for customs evasion. While an ambassador's wife known to be a devoted patron of French couture would normally have been most welcome in Paris, it was a bit awkward to contemplate one quite so devoted as Betsy had shown herself to be.

Whether Betsy's arrest record was the only reason, or even the primary reason, why Alfred was denied a chance to go to Paris is a moot point. Vicki herself told friends that a background check had turned up information about Alfred's relations with prostitutes and that "the CIA [had] found out about our relationship."

At any rate, Alfred Bloomingdale was handed the consolation prize of an appointment to the Foreign Intelligence Advisory Review Board, a group whose responsibilities include overseeing the CIA's covert operations abroad. The appointment was a rather odd one for a man as exposed to the possibility of blackmail as Alfred was, but it went a small way toward easing his disappointment. In his own life, Alfred got a tremendous kick out of the subterfuge necessary to maintain his multiple relationships with women. Fascinated with clandestine activities in all their aspects, he was also an amateur espionage buff.

Perhaps the appointment was gratuitous from the beginning, because it was obvious to anyone who knew him in early 1981 that Alfred Bloomingdale was not a well man. Once a tireless coast-to-coast commuter, contemptuous of people who complained of nonproblems like jet lag, he was now worn out by the strain of travel. He was coughing and even more short of breath than usual, and he was experiencing stomach pains that at first he blamed on indigestion.

Vicki, for one, kept begging him to see a doctor, but her pleas got nowhere. "Alfred didn't trust doctors," says Marvin, who was present during some arguments between Vicki and Alfred on the subject. His attitude was that doctors would always find some excuse to get him on the operating table and earn themselves a fat fee. He avoided them as long as possible.

Alfred, says Marvin, was brooding over his failure to be sent to Paris. "He wanted that so bad. To get the ambassadorship, or whatever you call it. To be made an ambassador." Vicki kept trying to get his mind off the subject by suggesting that there were certain advantages to the situation. Now they could be together, and there was no reason to put off househunting any longer.

Over the years, Vicki had probably inspected at least a hundred houses in Beverly Hills. Her househunting forays had been fitful, but intense while they lasted, and she probably knew as much about residential property in the area as a lot of full-time salesmen. Vicki had given out various stories to the agencies she frequented. Sometimes she hinted that she was the daughter of a Texas oil millionaire or, an idea she no doubt picked up during her stay at Bernie's, that her father had been associated with the fugitive financier Robert Vesco. All the stories, of course, were intended to reassure realtors in case it came out that their potential customer happened to have no job, no visible means of support, and no credit rating.

On several occasions, it had seemed that Vicki was on the verge of getting her house, when one of the recurring crises in their relationship intervened. Other bouts of househunting fizzled for less obvious reasons. Sometimes it was Alfred who changed his mind, either because he was ambivalent about spending so much money on his mistress or because he suspected that she would not be responsible enough to hold on to the property once she had it.

Just as often, though, it was Vicki who scotched deals at the last minute. A house she had seemed quite satisfied with would be rejected because it was too small, or needed too much work, or was simply in the wrong location. Partly Vicki's objections were inspired by petulance and greed.

By 1981, however, Alfred seemed to be on the point of changing his mind. Both he and Vicki sensed that he had not long to live—though neither acknowledged it openly—and the talk of a financial settlement took a serious turn.

In March of that year, Vicki's friend Sally Talbert spent four days at La Costa with Vicki and Alfred, keeping Vicki company in exercise classes and around the pool. According to an affidavit Sally Talbert later made in connection with Vicki's suit against the Bloomingdale estate, she and Vicki joined Alfred for lunch and dinner during this trip, and the conversation at mealtimes revolved around the plan to get Vicki a house. Alfred, said Talbert, authorized Vicki to look for a house in the $500,000 to $600,000 range and promised that, when she found a suitable property, he'd contribute $150,000 toward a mortgage. According to Talbert's affidavit, the mortgage payments, property taxes, and other expenses were to be paid by Vicki out of her allowance.

Over the next several months Vicki located and made offers on at least seven houses. In April 1981, for example, she entered a bid on a house at 1764 Clearview Drive, for which the owner was asking $550,000, including a $250,000 down payment.

Since the down payment on this particular property happened to exceed what Alfred had promised to advance by the small matter of $100,000, perhaps it is not surprising that he refused to close the deal. Why *none* of the proposed purchases ever went through is more difficult to figure out.

One reason may have been that Alfred simply had his mind on other things. He'd been deprived of France, but he was determined not to be deprived of the chance to savor the social rewards of Ronald Reagan's election victory. No sooner had Vicki stopped fighting Alfred than his attention became focused elsewhere. Most unexpectedly, at least from her point of view, Vicki found herself having to compete for Alfred's attention. And her rival was none other than Betsy Bloomingdale.

In Washington, the California contingent's arrival on the social scene was enjoying mixed reviews. The new President and Mrs. Reagan were the most glamorous couple to occupy the White House since the Kennedys, and Washington society, not to mention large segments of the media, welcomed the infusion of California chic after the drabness of the Carter years.

But, initially at least, there was also a strong dissenting minority. Lawrence Leamer's book *Make-Believe* (Harper & Row, 1983) portrays in scathing detail the negative reactions to the Reagans within established D.C. social circles. In a city where high-powered political talk had long been considered the only party game worth playing, White House dinner guests smirked and yawned behind their napkins as the President reeled off one pointless Hollywood anecdote after another. The wives in the new administration, known collectively as the "helmet heads," were dismissed as so many Galanos-gowned Barbie dolls—overaged, over-dressed, and virtually impossible to tell apart.

Nancy and her "First Friend" Betsy Bloomingdale came in for especially heavy criticism.

Again according to Lawrence Leamer, Nancy's habit of promoting freebies for herself was well established. Even in the mid-1970s, he writes, "Nancy wasn't beyond accepting her own alms for the rich. . . . Her friends were always giving her gifts. Her birthday was a day of tribute." Reportedly, Nancy even went so far as to leave magazines around her home, laid open to illustrations of Bulgari necklaces or other baubles she particularly coveted.

As First Lady, Nancy soon found that the same habits her loyal friends had found charming and entirely justifiable in the wife of a struggling politician—not a rich man, at least in comparison to some of his key supporters—made her an easy target. Gossips were tempted to note that a First Lady who claimed to be a defender of old-fashioned values seemed most devoted to the old-fashioned right of tribute. The cartoonists and pundits had a field day with Nancy's "china policy," and she was forced to donate part of her designer wardrobe to museums after being forcefully reminded that there were laws governing the acceptance of gifts by officeholders and their wives.

Although Mrs. Reagan's views on the morality of accepting freebies never fundamentally changed, she was eventually able to project a more acceptable public image by devoting her time and efforts to the campaign against drug abuse—and, no small factor, by displaying a certain sense of humor about her own foibles as she danced and sang a paean to "Secondhand Clothes" during the annual Gridiron Dinner, a political roast sponsored by the elite of the Washington press corps.

Initially, however, the criticism was no joke. Nancy Reagan was hurt and bewildered. She had hired Betsy Bloomingdale's friend, the "in" decorator of the moment, Ted Graber, to redo the upstairs rooms of the White House and arranged for the work to be supported by contributions from friends; among them were Alfred and Betsy Bloomingdale, who gave $20,000. Nancy felt that she had done the country a service, that the remodeling was a gift to "all Americans." She was appalled when reporters pointed out that the contributions were tax deductible and that the only way the public could even see pictures of this gift to them was by plunking down $4.50 for the tony magazine *Architectural Digest,* which had been given exclusive rights to run photos of Graber's handiwork.

As anyone might have predicted, Betsy Bloomingdale's other frequent male escort Jerry Zipkin came in for more than his share of sniping. *New York* magazine's Marie Brenner reported delightedly that Zipkin answered the phone at his Park Avenue digs by saying, *"Je suis ici,"* and went on to quote him as saying *"Au fond,* I am a businessman. I am not just a dilettante with nothing to do." Mrs. Reagan only compounded the fun when she rushed to Zipkin's defense, describing him as a sort of "modern-day Oscar Wilde"—except, of course, that Zipkin had never written anything. But then, who reads anymore?

Betsy, who had been the darling of *WWD* for more than a decade and who imagined herself an expert at managing the press, also came in for her share of hard knocks. For example, Diana McLellan, the *Washington Post*'s "Ear" columnist, quoted Betsy as saying, in all seriousness, that "one of the ways I save energy is by asking my servants not to turn on the self-cleaning oven until after seven in the evening." Confronted with the difference between the real press and the vanity press—which would either not have reported the remark or found it charming—Betsy was furious. Journalists who insisted on taking such a negative attitude toward "nice" people, who pried into matters that did not concern them, were simply irresponsible.

A good deal more thickskinned when it came to the press, Alfred basically agreed that criticisms of the California rich lifestyle were so much sour grapes. The envy of the have-nots was, in his view, just one of the unfair burdens borne by the wealthy. He could still afford to derive a certain amount of amusement from the flustered reactions of the women.

One of Alfred's favorite themes during this period, according to Marvin, was that despite a few teapot tempests in the gossip columns, Nancy Reagan was still the most powerful person in Washington. And Betsy, by extrapolation, was not far behind.

"Do you know who runs this country?" Alfred would snort. "It isn't Reagan. It isn't Baker. It isn't those clowns in the White House. It's the girls!"

For all his sarcasm, Alfred appeared to find this development thoroughly enjoyable.

On February 6, the Bloomingdales came to Washington for

Ronnie's surprise birthday party and dinner dance at the White House.

In March they were back in town to join an intime "fun group" assembled in the upstairs rooms of the White House to entertain Prince Charles, who was making his last visit to the States as a bachelor. Among the other guests were Cary Grant, Audrey Hepburn, Bobby Short, model and TV actress Shelley Hack, and, of course, Ted Graber and Jerry Zipkin.

On July 4, Alfred and Betsy were among seventy-six guests bused down from the Watergate to Woodlawn Plantation in Virginia to attend a gala birthday celebration, Tex-Mex barbecue style, in honor of Nancy Reagan (whose birthday is actually July 6). Alfred appeared to be in especially good spirits that day. Reporters noted that when Frank Sinatra donned an apron to play waiter, Alfred playfully rewarded him with a fifty-cent tip.

The culmination of the social season was to be Prince Charles's wedding to Lady Diana Spencer on July 31.

The President, busy and still recovering from the assassination attempt by John Hinckley at the end of March, had sent his regrets. Nancy, however, was going as his representative, and aside from her hairdresser, she had invited only two friends to accompany her—Alfred and Betsy Bloomingdale. The women were agog. The festivities were going to be *the* highlight of their lifetimes. Alfred, claiming to be unimpressed by all the brouhaha, was perhaps no less excited. He might never be an ambassador, but for this occasion at least, he was going to be the President's quasi-official representative.

Vicki was not entirely enjoying being upstaged by Betsy and Lady Di. Not only had the subject of the house been shelved once again but Alfred's health was continuing to deteriorate. Vicki put the blame on Betsy for dragging Alfred off on an exhausting trip when he obviously should have been resting under a doctor's care. This was a lot easier than acknowledging that Alfred preferred to spend his last remaining good weeks partying with Betsy instead of staying home in L.A. with her.

PALIMONY

‖‖‖

The royal wedding was indeed a fairytale, marred for Nancy and Betsy only by the insistence of the British press on treating them as if they were the evil fairies who had shown up uninvited at the palace to cause trouble. Fleet Street's reaction to Mrs. Reagan's style was far more negative than anything she had ever encountered, or was likely to encounter, back in America. From the tabloids to the staid Times, *all the British papers found something to criticize: Her overelaborate wardrobe; the pushy rudeness of the secret service; even Mrs. Reagan's own manners in scheduling so many parties for herself that she was forced to walk out on a polo match attended by the queen before Prince Charles's team took the field.*

The height of the furor came when not only Mrs. Reagan but also Betsy Bloomingdale landed invitations to the queen's ball—an event supposedly limited to royalty and their aristocratic kin. Even some heads of state, among them François Mitterand, had been excluded. When Betsy showed up at the gala, so tall and hovering constantly at Mrs. Reagan's elbow, some of the scribes covering the event pretended to mistake her for a female body-guard. After the ball, a reporter quoted Betsy as gushing that the affair was "beautiful, stunning and divine. . . . All the kings and people had their decorations on!"

Alfred's presence in London was scarcely noticed.

Vicki had followed the extensive coverage of the trip in the papers, and she doted on the negative criticisms, which confirmed exactly what she wanted to believe about Alfred's wife.

In August, just days after his return home, Alfred finally agreed to see his doctor. The news was what he had feared all along. Diagnosis: cancer. Prognosis: terminal. He was rushed to UCLA Medical Center where he underwent immediate surgery to remove part of his esophagus. The cancer was already more advanced than initial tests had indicated, and the doctors were forced to do a partial gastrectomy as well.

Even at the best of times, Alfred was by no means an easy patient. He believed, perhaps not inaccurately, that he had survived his previous bouts with death through sheer orneriness. He was suspicious of his doctors and of hospital personnel, resistant to following orders, and highly demanding. This time, however, even his determined bullheadedness could not slow down the rapid collapse of his bodily systems. Although the initial operation went as well as could be suspected, he was plagued over the next several months with a host of complications—kidney failure, requiring dialysis; bleeding ulcers; and the gradual loss of his hearing.

Alfred's normal distrust of physicians was deepening into an almost childlike paranoia. The only person he seemed to respond to was Vicki, and he wanted her at his side every possible moment. On the evening before his surgery, he refused to let her leave his room, insisting that she spend the night at his bedside. *Don't leave me here alone,* he kept pleading. *You're the only one I trust. I'll never be able to sleep without knowing you're here.*

Vicki, who had parked in a lot for short-term visitors, emerged bleary-eyed from the hospital the next day to find her Mercedes gone. Being Vicki, it took her hours to figure out that the car wasn't stolen, just towed for illegal parking. Still, she managed to recover it from the pound and be back at the hospital waiting when Alfred came out of the recovery room.

The switch from rebellious daughter to dutiful one was made with amazing rapidity. Flighty, disorganized Vicki managed to get to the hospital every day and to handle Alfred's moods more effectively than anyone else when she was there.

Betsy Bloomingdale, meanwhile, was also visiting her husband regularly, though she normally stayed only for brief periods. Alfred's wife had endured a lot over the years, loyally maintaining the image of a happy marriage without uttering a single word of complaint or criticism—at least not where it might be heard by anyone who would repeat it as common gossip. She kept up appearances throughout Alfred's last illness, but for whatever reasons and whatever her private feelings may have been, it was not she who was keeping the deathbed vigil. It was Vicki who was on hand to wipe Alfred's brow, to cope with his frustrations, and to witness his pain and humiliation over being unable to eat, drink, vacate his bowels, or even communicate normally.

"Alfred frequently told me about the fights he had with his wife because of his phone calls to me," she later said. "[He] told me that his wife was too occupied with her social life, her shopping, her lunches with designers and lady friends, to give him the support he needed. . . . He said he wanted me to promise him that I would help him get well, no matter how long it took, and to supervise the nurses whom he said he did not trust. He said he was afraid of the nurses. . . . On his deathbed, he's afraid of his wife, not me."

Vicki's friend Mary, who accompanied her to the hospital at least half a dozen times, later swore in a deposition that Alfred "on each one of these occasions, said that Vicki would never have anything to worry about and if anything should happen to him she would always be supported and taken care of. In my presence he was always seeking to reassure [Vicki] that she would always be provided for. . . . It appeared to me, that at this point [Vicki] was his primary reason for remaining alive."

A somewhat more objective gauge of the situation is that Alfred's nurses accepted Vicki's constant presence, keeping quiet about it in front of his wife and even protecting her from discovery. At the suggestion of one of them, Vicki bought a nurse's uniform and changed her hairstyle, the better to slip into the background should Mrs. Bloomingdale arrive unexpectedly.

On February 12, Alfred at last put something in writing to back up the promises he'd been making for so long. From his hospital bed, Alfred signed a pair of letters to his longtime business associate Bill McComas concerning Vicki's financial future.

The first of these says simply:

> As per our conversation, if we finalize Showbiz Pizza, then Vicki Morgan, now residing at 1611 Tower Grove, Beverly Hills, is entitled to ½ (one-half) of my interest in the above. Her name should be included in all contracts so that this cannot be taken away from her, in the event of my incapacitation or absence.

The second mandates:

> I have made an agreement with Vicki Morgan that she get $10,000 a month for two years beginning March 1, 1982. This money should be paid to her by the 28th of each month from the proceeds of my profit from Marina Bay, etc.
> Should my lawyers, business managers, heirs, or anyone else object to his agreement, this letter will serve as your authorization to follow through on the above.

The language of the letters is certainly straightforward. Alfred obviously anticipated that whatever he bestowed on Vicki, his heirs might later try to take away. The logic of the two letters was, theoretically, that two years of guaranteed income would sustain Vicki until the profits from the Showbiz Pizza venture began to come in, after which she would be more than adequately provided for.

Reading between the lines, however, it seems that Alfred was still ambivalent. Alfred owned a lot of real estate, in addition to investments and, presumably, a healthy bank balance. Why make Vicki's future dependent on a business deal that had yet to be "finalized"? Why drop the whole messy business in the lap of Bill McComas? Surely Alfred realized that, after he died, the bulk of his estate was going to his widow, who would become McComas's new partner.

Surely it would have been much more secure simply to transfer existing property to Vicki outright. Or, if he didn't trust Vicki to manage property on her own, he could no doubt have arranged for some form of trust.

The obvious explanation, and surely the correct one to some

extent, is that even now, or especially now, he couldn't bring himself to choose between cheating his wife and children and cheating Vicki. He didn't wish to give Vicki existing property that, by rights, ought to be part of his legacy to his family. He didn't want to cheat her, either. So he left her a lien on wealth as yet unearned.

A harsher explanation is that, no doubt subconsciously, Alfred was writing the script for his final scenario. The letters he had signed made it virtually certain that the two women in his life would end up in a humiliating and painful legal catfight over his estate. Even when he was in his grave, a certain highly formalized version of the game would still be being played out.

Marvin Pancoast was also driving Vicki to UCLA hospital during the period when she was visiting Alfred daily. Unlike Mary, says Pancoast, he never went inside but waited out in the parking lot. "Alfred was in the hospital and he was signing things like mad," Marvin recalls. "He had some warning that Betsy was going to, you know, fire the accountants. Get rid of people." One day, Vicki returned to the car and said that Alfred had given her some advice: Sue me.

"So you know whose idea that palimony suit was," says Panocast. "It was Alfred's. It had been done before."

In late spring, the doctors having done all they could, Alfred Bloomingdale was allowed to leave UCLA hospital and return to his home on Delfern Drive in Bel-Air, where he was attended by a staff of private-duty nurses. Although she had curtailed her appearances at White House events and other semipublic functions, Betsy continued to travel and to pursue an active social life. She was absent so frequently that Vicki managed to visit Alfred at his home at least two dozen times.

On the last of these occasions she brought Todd, now thirteen years old.

The next day, Alfred called Vicki, with the help of an aide, to report that there had been a terrible row when Betsy got home. One of the servants had tipped off his wife. Betsy, he said, was incensed to learn from a servant that Vicki's Mercedes was newer than the car she herself drove and that "there was a child involved."

"There's no point in trying to come over to see me," the message continued. "She's given orders that you're not to be allowed in."

This account, though secondhand, has the ring of truth, if only because it inadvertently calls into question the view of his marriage that Alfred had been feeding to Vicki. All these years he had been telling her that his wife was aware that their relationship had continued, that it had been the subject of constant arguments. According to Alfred, Betsy had frequently threatened to file for divorce. And, he reported to Vicki, he invariably told her, "Go ahead. Divorce me. That would be fine with me."

If, however, Betsy Bloomingdale did not know by this point that Vicki Morgan had a child and that the child was not Alfred's, then how much *can* she have known?

On June 16, Alfred managed to get away from his sickbed to come to Tower Grove Drive for one last visit. The outing was arranged with the cooperation of Jan, the Danish male nurse who was Alfred's private-duty attendant and sympathetic to Vicki.

Vicki went to great lengths to make the visit a memorable occasion. She bought new clothes, choosing a proper daytime dress over the pants and hostess gowns she herself preferred, and spent over $1,000 on floral arrangements that filled the house. The food, which Alfred could hardly do more than admire and taste tentatively, was carefully chosen and prepared by a hired chef. The table was set with her best crystal and china, an arrangement Vicki called, tellingly, her "Betsy table."

Alfred, by this time, could not walk unaided and was reduced to communicating in scrawled notes. Overwhelmed with emotion, he broke down weeping in the middle of the carefully planned luncheon and had to be taken home by his concerned aides.

The next morning, when Vicki called Delfern Drive to check with Jan on Alfred's condition, the person on the other end of the line hung up on her.

And when the end of the month came, there was no check.

On calling Alfred's office, she learned that the not-unexpected coup had occurred. Betsy Bloomingdale had taken over handling her husband's finances.

Vicki might well have ended up filing a lawsuit in any case, but she would never have gone ahead and done so while Alfred was still alive without at least his tacit permission. Alfred, in her mind, was never intended to be the real target. He *wanted* her to be taken care of, or he never would have signed those letters.

A good indication that she expected this lawsuit to be more or less a replay of the 1974 action—that is, discreet and unpublicized—is that Vicki's first move was to call Paul Caruso.

Caruso, who had not heard from Vicki Morgan since she stiffed him for the lease payments on her car, was curious enough to agree to see Vicki when she asked for an appointment. But when she launched into a lengthy recital of her latest grievances without even making a token excuse about the Mercedes incident, he lost patience.

"*Wait a second,*" he said, interrupting her in midcomplaint. "*What about this judgment I have against you?*"

"But that car was repossessed!" Vicki protested. "I don't have it anymore."

Vicki went on to claim that she'd had *no idea* that Caruso had finally been required to make good on the defaulted payments. As far as she knew, when the company took back the vehicle that had wiped the slate clean.

Caruso found all this incredible, yet no doubt it was all true as far as it went. Vicki would be highly oblivious to reality at times, especially unpleasant realities. If she had thought twice about the car and about Caruso's commitment, she would most likely have lacked the nerve to face him.

"Fool me once, shame on you. Fool me twice, shame on me," said Caruso, bringing the interview to a close.

Vicki contacted several other lawyers, all of whom turned her down for one reason or another, before she finally linked up with Marvin Mitchelson, the man responsible for putting the word *palimony* into the dictionary. One way or another, it was inevitable that Vicki Morgan and Marvin Mitchelson would get together. A man with an impish grin that belies his high-pressure personality, Marvin Mitchelson gravitates toward high-profile cases and celebrity clients, plaintiffs with star quality.

Coincidentally, one of Mitchelson's first celebrity clients was Pamela Mason, who came to him on a referral from Paul Caruso's office while the latter was out of town on vacation. Subsequently he handled divorces for the wives of Bob Dylan, Marlon Brando, and multibillionaire Adnan Khashoggi. Mitchelson's national recognition, however, came with the suit of Michelle Triola Marvin against actor Lee Marvin, the case establishing that, in California at least, it is possible to have divorce without marriage.

Mitchelson's target in pursuing *Marvin* vs. *Marvin* and related cases has been the legal principle of the "meretricious spouse," a doctrine holding that any woman who lives with a man outside of marriage is, in effect, engaging in prostitution. Since contracts made for purposes of prostitution are legally unenforceable, the "meretricious spouse" is left with no legal recourse in any dispute with a lover or cohabitant.

In practice, there have been certain exceptions to the meretricious spouse doctrine. One traditional exception, common-law marriage, was widely recognized in the United States until the turn of the century, when all but fourteen state legislatures decided, in their wisdom, that the custom of forming a marital relationship without benefit of license had no place in the modern world. Even in jurisdictions where the meretricious spouse rule held sway, unmarried couples frequently found themselves in court over contract disputes. Live-togethers bought houses jointly, invested in each other's businesses, and so on. Sometimes the complaining party might even win such a suit, provided that the sexual relationship between the parties could be shown to be a side issue, irrelevant to the agreement in dispute.

Even suits by mistresses against their erstwhile patrons were by no means unknown, as evidenced by Vicki's earlier action against Alfred Bloomingdale. The point is, they did not become too well known either, precisely because the plaintiff's attorneys took care to avoid basing their cases on what may or may not have happened in the bedroom.

Where other attorneys trod lightly through the minefield of the meretricious spouse doctrine, Marvin Mitchelson attacked it head on. His not-unreasonable contention was that the doctrine had been made outdated by changing social mores. Quite respectable people no longer considered a marriage license a necessary precondition to setting up housekeeping. Sexual liberation would turn out to be a cruel joke on the female sex if the law made no distinction between the female half of a live-together couple and a prostitute.

What all this had to do with Vicki Morgan is not immediately obvious. Alfred Bloomingdale had been a married man for the duration of her relationship with him. They had never lived together. They had never even registered together at a hotel. Alfred had continued to reside with his wife while being more or less careful to keep his liaison with Vicki Morgan a secret.

As Mitchelson knew, however, *Marvin* vs. *Marvin* had gone beyond the straightforward question of a right to palimony. Michelle Triola had met Lee Marvin on the set of the movie *Ship of Fools,* in which he was the star player and she was an extra. She had moved into his Malibu beach house even though he was still married to another woman and remained so for three years. During the six years they remained together, Marvin had prospered in his career, but the property he acquired was all in his name. Triola had nothing on paper, but she considered herself as good as married. Marvin, she would claim, had continually told her, "What I have is yours and what you have is mine." He had assured her that she had no need to worry about continuing her career because he would always take care of her.

When the relationship ended abruptly in 1967, Triola felt that she'd been a passenger on a ship of fools for the past six years. Lee Marvin contended in court that he had only said those things because he wanted Triola "in bed." His attorneys took the position that "pillow-talk promises"—those foolish things that get said in the act of seduction—were not and never had been legally enforceable.

To the surprise of an awful lot of previously carefree lovers, the California Supreme Court disagreed.

Triola did not get the division of community property she had asked for, but she was awarded a settlement to enable her to "rehabilitate" herself economically—$1,000 a week for two years.

In some respects, Vicki Morgan's legal position was stronger than Triola's had been. Not only did she have witnesses to Alfred's promises over the years, she had signed and witnessed documents—documents created at a time when Bloomingdale had been pronounced terminally ill and could hardly have been motivated by a desire to get Vicki into bed.

Even the fact that Alfred and Vicki had never cohabited might not turn out to be an insurmountable legal obstacle to a palimony-type case. Mitchelson was encouraged by a precedent in which a man who had shuttled between a wife and a girlfriend had been forced to pay support to both of them. And Mitchelson was already representing another mistress in a palimony-type suit.

Still, Vicki could not realistically claim that she had provided Alfred with wifely services. Alfred had kept no belongings at her houses, had never even spent the night. In any case, she certainly hadn't been doing housework. What, besides sexual pleasure, had been the basis of the relationship?

After hearing the details of Alfred's tormented sexual life, Mitchelson decided to address the issue directly. Vicki had tried continually over the years to curb Alfred's sadomasochistic excesses. Couldn't it be said, then, that she had acted as a sort of sexual therapist?

On July 8, Mitchelson filed suit on Vicki's behalf in Los Angeles Superior Court. She was asking for $5 million.

On July 25, Alfred Bloomingdale signed a new will, leaving the bulk of his assets to a family trust—a change providing that details about the value of the estate would not have to be disclosed at the time of probate and that the bulk of the money would be virtually, if not totally, beyond the reach of any potential challenge in the courts. Vicki Morgan's name was not even mentioned in the document. Of course, it is not really known if it was in the earlier one either.

Vicki was convinced that Alfred had been browbeaten into changing his will. Hadn't he warned her all along that this was exactly what would happen?

Perhaps she was right, though a skeptic would have to wonder. What wife of thirty-six years wouldn't be extremely distressed to learn that her husband on his deathbed was signing letters of intent giving away money to his mistress? What wife wouldn't want to take action to protect the interests of herself and her children?

A week later, on August 2, Alfred reentered the hospital. This time, however, he did not go to UCLA but to St. John's in Santa Monica, an institution he had supported through large charitable gifts over the years. He was signed in by family members under a false name. This time there were no leaks from sympathetic staff members. Vicki could not get up-to-date reports on his condition, much less manage to breach security for a visit.

In the meantime, Vicki had put her trust in Mitchelson, who told her she had an excellent chance of winning her suit.

"I liked Vicki very much," Mitchelson later said. "I felt she was a young girl who was, at a very young age, taken on by this older man. I think she truly loved him. I really do. I think she was totally dependent on him and was utterly lost when he was no longer able to support her. . . . Suddenly, all the money was cut off. She was extremely upset. She hated to get involved in litigation, but there was no other way because they made it very clear that she should get lost. . . .

"She wasn't a book intellectual, but she had a basic, simplistic approach, which was kind of refreshing. . . . She was mysterious."

On another occasion, Mitchelson described Vicki's approach in somewhat harsher terms: "She had a certain mentality. This is hard to relate to other people, because you'd have to know her. She was not very bright. Not very bright. But scheming and kind of cunning. . . . She had some nicer qualities, too. But not [when it came to] conscience things, really. She fucked Paul Caruso out of a car [metaphorically speaking]. She'd leave you in a minute."

Mitchelson had good reason to be less than infatuated with Vicki Morgan as a person. He was handling her case on a contingency basis, yet she showed absolutely no consideration when it came to wasting his time. She was late for every appointment, sometimes hours late.

On the other hand, he had to admire her determination. "It wasn't a pleasant case. It wasn't pleasant giving a deposition. But she never backed down. She did what she had to do."

On Friday, August 13, Vicki Morgan gave her deposition to Bloomingdale lawyer Hillel Chodos. Often rambling on in response to Chodos's queries, Morgan talked all too candidly about the seamier aspects of her affair with Alfred—her initiation into sadomasochism at the playhouse on Sunset Plaza Drive, Alfred's attempts to buy off her three husbands, his lectures to her on the duties of a mistress, the decade-long barrage of phone calls, the explicit financial arrangements—all the while insisting on her love for him.

Reading her comments about Alfred calls to mind the insistence of Madeira headmistress Jean Harris that her lover Herman Tarnower was a wonderful man, even as she testified to all the rejections and humiliations she suffered at his hands. In background, education, and sensibility, Vicki Morgan and Jean Harris could not have been more different. Their psychological makeups, however, were remarkably alike. For both women, the more time they had invested in an unhappy affair, the less they could afford to admit that they felt exploited. The compromises, once made, had to be justified.

Vicki claimed that Alfred's wife had forced him to change his will and interfered with the payments promised to her in Alfred's signed letter of intent. At her deposition, Vicki stated, "Betsy Bloomingdale eventually locked herself in the room with him and made the nurses leave and was in there for over four hours with that [man] he's not strong. . . . Betsy did say to someone that she'd make him mentally incompetent by the time she was through with him."

Mrs. Bloomingdale, in a subsequent deposition, denied that her husband acted under duress.

After a long day of questioning, made longer by Vicki's tendency to transform questions that might be answered in two words into cues for monologues, the interview finally came around to the suit's contention that, during the period when she lived on Tower Grove Drive, Vicki acted in part as Alfred's business confidante and aide.

"Now I'm looking for houses," Vicki recalled, "and it's something that we're really trying to do and I'm getting more into real estate. I'm learning a little bit more. I'm learning about offers and counteroffers, and it's—it's sort of interesting. And that's what Alfred is doing."

This description of her expertise may not be very impressive, but the specific deals Vicki "got into" were. Among the properties Vicki claims to have located and researched for Alfred was a plot of undeveloped land at the end of Tower Grove Drive owned by the sister of the late shah of Iran. Also, she said, she went with Alfred to look at a certain Rexall Drugstore on La Cienega and Beverly Boulevard—better known to the locals as Rexall Square— "where Justin Dart is going to be selling out."

When it came to explaining her role as a sex therapist, helping Alfred to overcome what she called his "Marquis de Sade complex," Morgan was less than persuasive:

> HILLEL CHODOS: "First of all, do you know anything about the Marquis de Sade?"
>
> MORGAN: "It's a masochist."
>
> "Okay. Do you know what the Marquis de Sade was, or when he lived, or . . ."
>
> "I think it was the eighteenth century or something, wasn't it?"
>
> "Do you know who Justine and Juliette are?"
>
> (No response.)
>
> "Do you know?"
>
> MR. RHODEN (Mitchelson's associate): "That's assuming that they are people. I object to the question on the grounds that it assumes facts not in evidence."
>
> CHODOS: "Do you know who they are?"
>
> MORGAN: "No."
>
> "Have you ever read any of the books of the Marquis de Sade?"
>
> "No, but I know about them."
>
> "Okay. What do you understand a 'Marquis de Sade complex' to mean?"
>
> "Someone that enjoys and believes that the other person enjoys getting pleasure out of hurting another person."

"All right. And part of the deal, the original deal, was that you would act as a therapist to help Alfred over his Marquis de Sade complex?"

"Because he had a serious one. Yes."

"And how were you to help him overcome it?"

"To watch him. It started off to watch him—not—when I say 'watch him,' meaning how seriously he gets involved when he starts some of his actions and there were times when it was serious, and I mean it with all my heart; it was serious. Now, I told you I was scared for myself. So I wasn't about to say, 'Alfred, I don't do that?' because I probably would have been dead. But I see a lot."

"Right."

"And I would give him the look, because I could see that he was hurting. . . . I mean, seriously hurting somebody and he would calm down. He would calm down but he wouldn't calm down unless I—he didn't do this for anyone. I mean, he didn't care. He got mentally ill when he had these scenes, or whatever you want to call them."

". . . What I'm trying to do . . . you understand what I'm here to do is to find out what your claims are [that] you're acting as a therapist. You're continuing on in the relationship with Alfred, as you have described it, so that he wouldn't need emotionally to do these things with other women?"

"And to talk to him about it—which we had numerous amounts of discussion about it, you know. . . .

"Did he?"

"I'm not sure he ever totally stopped it. But to my knowledge he has."

". . . All right. Now Miss Morgan. You never had a license to practice psychotherapy from the state, have you?"

"No."

Aside from Hillel Chodos, who was conducting the questioning, did anyone present realize how disastrous this was?

Apparently not.

Since the contents of the deposition were at least as embarrassing to the Bloomingdale family as to Vicki, Mitchelson figured that their attorneys would file the document away in a drawer somewhere and begin thinking about an out-of-court settlement.

Said Mitchelson later, "Chodos asked the questions. He didn't have to file that deposition [with the court]. But he did. . . . Believe me, I would have loved to settle it. I've settled a half a dozen suits where no one's read a word about anything, and they involved people who are just as high and just as involved in high places. I don't mean the government. But it happens all the time. Do 'em every day.

"The case was publicized, and it's still being publicized, because it was a sensational-type case. [But] it never would have been publicized that much had the attorney for Mrs. Bloomingdale not decided to file a deposition—make it public, mind you—and file a motion on it."

A ROSE AND A CALLING CARD

///

Exactly one week after Vicki gave her deposition, at five minutes past ten o'clock on a Friday evening, Alfred Bloomingdale died at St. John's Hospital.

The man who so feared solitude that he had lived with a telephone receiver all but glued to his ear had been not only deaf but virtually unable to speak for the last weeks of his life, communicating with his attendants through laboriously scrawled notes. And he died alone. Betsy Bloomingdale had stopped by the hospital earlier in the day and then left to attend a dinner party. It was after one A.M. when she returned home and found the message from the hospital.

She and the family wasted no time making funeral arrangements. By noon the next day Alfred's body had been consigned to the ground. He was buried in a $200 coffin, and the brief gravesite ceremony was attended only by the widow, his children, and his grandchildren. There were no flowers, and if there were tears, they were considerably diluted by feelings of shock and outrage.

The family withheld the announcement of the death until the following Monday, but on Saturday afternoon following the funeral, a few of Bloomingdale's relatives and close friends were discreetly informed of his passing. Inevitably, one of them decided that he had better break the news to Vicki.

While hardly unprepared for the news, Vicki had not expected the end to come quite so soon. And she was indignant to hear how he had been buried. Alfred, the dominant personality in her life, had been disposed of as if he were of no account whatsoever.

Vicki spent the weekend at home, refusing to take any phone calls, but by Tuesday she had decided to have her say. That afternoon, she made a pilgrimage to Alfred's grave in Holy Cross Cemetery and left her own tribute—a single, perfect red rose and her engraved calling card. It was a gesture both elegant and brutal. The woman who had lived clandestinely for so many years, was emerging from hiding.

When she returned home, Vicki picked up the phone and dialed David Israel, a *Los Angeles Herald-Examiner* columnist, and volunteered an interview.

"I went to the cemetery and I found there was not one flower on the grave except what I put there," she told Israel. "When I saw that I was shocked. I still am in a state of shock. . . . That was, believe me, all done because of Vicki Morgan.

"She buried him—and excuse my expression—like a dog. This woman only thinks of one person, and I'm excluding her children, and it's Betsy, Betsy, Betsy."

It was all done because of Vicki. But it was all Betsy's fault. And why, in the context of this denunciation, give Betsy credit for being a concerned mother? A certain confusion of identities was taking place.

At any rate, the battle lines had been drawn, the weapons chosen by the combatants.

Following the funeral, Betsy Bloomingdale maintained a total silence about the suit and its revelations. Not only would she not discuss the issue publicly, she had nothing to say off the record, and she cut dead anyone who had the temerity to raise it with her or anyone else. When she did finally give an interview after two years, for a feature in a *W* issue devoted to the California scene, she went out of her way to talk about what a wonderful husband

Alfred had been—never once alluding to the fact that the world might have any reason to think otherwise.

Ironically, Alfred's sterling character was the one subject the two women agreed on.

In conversations with Carole Hemingway, a journalist who had befriended her after doing a short piece on the palimony suit, Vicki launched into a lengthy defense of Alfred's virility—as if that were the issue. Alfred, she said, had been a more active and a more tender lover than most men half his age. Dismissing his sadistic tendencies as an aberration that had been overcome relatively early on in the relationship, she said that during the latter years of the affair she and Alfred had developed a love that was both tender and satisfying. They were the best years of Alfred's life, and of hers as well.

It sounded idyllic.

In the meantime, the juggernaut of the palimony suit was rolling on.

During the week after Bloomingdale's death, Mitchelson amended the suit, demanding in addition to monies from Bloomingdale's estate an additional $5 million from Betsy Bloomingdale on the grounds that she had interfered with the contractual agreement between Alfred and Vicki.

Mrs. Bloomingdale, who was named as executor in her husband's will along with attorney James Carroll III, filed a petition asking that probate be delayed. In the interim, she asked to be appointed special administrator of the estate with full powers to defend against the Morgan lawsuit.

Attorney Hillel Chodos followed up this action with a motion for dismissal of the suit. Arguing the motion before Judge Christian E. Markey during the first week of September, Chodos noted that the case had now developed into a case of mistress suing her lover's widow. He ridiculed the size of Morgan's claim. Nowadays, he pointed out, even divorcing wives could not necessarily expect to be taken care of for life. The plaintiff, he said, "is asking for larger amounts over a longer period of time than a wife would get. It's absurd."

Further, argued Chodos, "Mrs. Bloomingdale has a right to tell her husband not to leave money to his mistress."

Mitchelson, with unbeatable chutzpah, disagreed. "That may violate the contract. It may sting us. It may shock us. It may not sit well with the Judeo-Christian system of ethics. But that is not really the point here."

What was really the point, though it was never mentioned in the courtroom arguments, was which side had the most to lose through full disclosure. Chodos had, in effect, called the plaintiff's bluff by filing Vicki's deposition in support of his dismissal motion. This meant that, while not yet public, the papers would become part of the open record once the motion was decided.

Mitchelson countered by hinting to reporters that his side had a lot more to say about Alfred Bloomingdale's conduct that was not in the deposition.

Mitchelson's associate Harold Rhoden then speculated aloud, "What would it be like if we had a trial of this case and Vicki Morgan took the stand? All of the details would come out."

Morgan herself was beginning to get an idea of what it would be like, and she was not happy. The press had gone wild over the story of the suit, and the reaction toward her was much more negative than she'd dreamed possible. It was unbelievable to her that the world could sympathize with Betsy over poor Vicki, but that was exactly what was happening.

A week later, while Judge Markey was still considering the motion to dismiss, Mitchelson went public to confirm a rumor that he had discussed the palimony suit in the White House itself, during a two-hour conversation with Reagan aide Morgan Mason. Mitchelson had known Morgan Mason for eighteen years, ever since he handled his mother Pamela's divorce from James Mason, and he told the press that he had received Mason's unofficial permission to confirm that a discussion had indeed taken place, centering on the White House's concern over the unfavorable publicity the suit was generating.

Although Mitchelson blandly insisted that he considered the conversation nothing out of the ordinary, no one else was surprised when it made the front pages of the tabloids, some of which claimed that Mitchelson had been "summoned" to Washington for the conference. The exaggeration was fueled by Mitchelson's refusal to specify who in addition to Mason had been present, or exactly what the White House's concerns were.

Mason, in turn, was forced to issue a limp rebuttal, denying that Mitchelson had been "summoned" anywhere. Anyway, he added, the conversation was "not really about Bloomingdale"—a formulation that was something less than a convincing denial. Mason's days as a presidential special assistant were numbered.

It was this, Mitchelson's "umpteenth unauthorized press conference," says Marvin Pancoast, that made Vicki push the panic button. She felt that the situation was way out of control, that Alfred's name was being dragged through the mud, and that the only way she could stop it was to fire her attorney.

One of the reasons Vicki was so upset was that the publicity was having a traumatic effect on her remaining friends and her family, and on her son in particular. "Bloomingdale had always been Uncle Alfred to Todd," says Marvin. Not that the boy, now thirteen, was totally naïve about the nature of the relationship, but the facts that were emerging now had a devastating impact.

When she stared to talk about getting rid of Mitchelson, Pancoast suggested that she go to see Arthur Barens, a successful Beverly Hills attorney who had been a friend of his family for twenty years. Barens's practice was largely PI, personal injury cases, but he was the sort of colorful, audacious personality who might be able to take over the case and win it. He certainly wouldn't be scared off by the publicity.

Vicki went to see Barens in his office, a small stucco structure on Santa Monica Boulevard with a plaque out front that grandly announced it as the Barens Law Building. There are varying accounts of what happened.

According to Barens, he saw pretty quickly that he didn't want to touch the case. It was a can of worms. Mitchelson had already set his strategy, gotten boatloads of publicity, not all of it good, and now the client was unhappy and looking for a miracle worker. He also didn't trust his would-be client. She was a very expensive lady, but with no education or culture. Her mind was "a raft of prejudices."

"Put it this way," he said later, "if you walked into a bar and saw five girls, Vicki Morgan was the last one you'd think about picking up. She was good looking all right. But was also just the type who'd call your wife up." As for getting involved on her behalf in a contingency case, with no retainer up front, his answer was "Thanks but no thanks."

Vicki later claimed that Barens *was* intrigued by the case and had even offered to advance her money to live on while it was in the courts, but that she didn't trust him.

Her friend Mary, who was present during the interview, gave a friend a third version of what went on. "He was running at 78 rpms and Vicki was doing about 33 ⅓." They were talking right past each other.

Vicki walked out of the office and her head was spinning. Mary said, "Whew, she couldn't handle that."

At any rate, Marvin Pancoast confirmed Barens's account of the meeting. "After Arthur saw Vicki," he says, "He got back to me, and he said, 'Marvin, you stay away from that woman. She's trouble.'"

Pancoast paid no attention to the warning. Fascinated by Vicki Morgan since their meeting at Thalians, he was more drawn to her than ever since the lawsuit. He was making her a scrapbook of all the news clippings the case had generated, as well as a videotape, collecting all the segments that had been on the TV news.

Vicki's search for a new attorney soon led her back to her longtime friend Michael Dave. He, too, was somewhat hesitant to pick up the reins from Mitchelson.

"I don't want to make this a lifetime case," he told Vicki. He explained that, while he thought she had a legitimate claim on Bloomingdale's estate, he wasn't prepared to go for millions of dollars and lifelong support.

Unhappy as she was with Mitchelson, Vicki was deflated by Dave's prediction that the case might take some time to settle and, in any case, wouldn't net her the $10 million or so she'd begun to hope for. But she was nervous enough to go along with his more sober counsel on the subject.

The next day, September 15, she called Mitchelson at his Century City office.

According to Mitchelson, the conversation was spacy. "Marvin, what's your sign?" Vicki asked as soon as he got on the line.

He told her.

"Uh, that's not so good," Vicki said. Then she told him he was fired.

A press release issued by Vicki later that day through Dave was a good deal more articulate. It cited "continuous and fundamental differences" as a parting of the ways.

Michael Dave immediately proceeded to get a new affidavits from Vicki and two of her friends and to prepare papers for a more limited action.

But it was too late to squelch the deposition. On September 26, Judge Markey ruled in favor of Hillel Chodos's motion to dismiss the case, noting in his opinion that Morgan was "no more than a well-paid mistress." He did leave open her right to sue on two causes of action, based on Alfred's specific promises from his hospital bed—the very basis of the suit Dave wanted to pursue in the first place. However, the deposition, part of the record of the

Chodos motion, became publicly available on the next day.

As reporters began poring over the transcript, culling the accounts of the late Alfred Bloomingdale's sexual hijinks, even those sympathetic to his family couldn't help wondering why the Bloomingdale side had moved so fast in allowing these things to become part of the public record. Surely, an out-of-court settlement would have saved them a lot of embarrassment. Even if, from the family's point of view, Morgan's demands for money were outrageous and extortionate, it was no time to stand on principle.

There were several reasons why the Bloomingdale attorneys might not have seen it that way. According to a source close to the case, women claiming to have been Alfred's mistresses were "coming out of the woodwork." A woman in New York City, in particular, said she had known about Morgan all along, but she had been her East Coast counterpart. True or not, such claims would only be encouraged if Morgan's suit came to trial.

Nor can it have been clear that a settlement would be possible. Morgan had been asking for a lot of money and had been in no mood to scale down her demands. Her then attorney Marvin Mitchelson, aside from being a flamboyant, controversial personality whose remarks irritated a lot of people, also happened to be well heeled and persistent. He'd hung on with the Marvin case for ten years before finally winning in court.

But above all, the dispute had already gone beyond money, beyond any practical considerations of damage control. Vicki Morgan wanted revenge. She had already gone to the newspapers, making personal accusations against Betsy Bloomingdale. There were rumors that she was going to write a book.

Vicki was already running out of money.

Her views on personal finances had always been surreal, at best. Now, the disparity between her image and expectations, on the one hand, and reality on the other, had become insane. Throughout September, when her $10 million suit had been before the court, pictures of Vicki looking glamorous and witchy in her full-length fox coat had been splashed across the front pages. But her income was exactly zero. What was she supposed to do, go down to Hamburger Haven and apply for a job waiting tables? In fact, people in similar situations have done precisely that sort of thing. But Alfred had told Vicki for years that she was beyond such nickel and diming, and this was one lesson that she had learned well.

The walls of the Tower Grove house were hung with contemporary paintings that had been given to her by Alfred at a time when he was having his Century City offices redecorated with antiques. "Alfred had said the paintings were good. Were worth something, or at least would be someday," says Marvin Pancoast. He had given them to Vicki as a kind of investment. "Well, what did we know about it? Nothing."

But Alfred supposedly did. One of Alfred's favorite anecdotes was about how, in Paris after dropping out of Brown, he'd befriended a scruffy, down-and-out painter whose studio happened to be near his rented room on the Left Bank. Seeing that the artist, a fellow named Raoul, was hardpressed, Alfred had made a habit of treating him to meals at the local cafés. In gratitude, Raoul had sold him more than a dozen canvases for peanuts. Later, it turned out that Raoul was Raoul Dufy. Alfred liked to tell the story as a joke on himself, the rich kid who'd been too much of a boor to know that the damn paintings were actually any good. Nevertheless, he also gave the impression that he'd gotten a lot smarter since. He'd held onto the Dufys and continued to buy art for the rest of his life.

Hard up for cash, Vicki decided that, much as she hated to do it, the paintings would have to be sold. She got Marvin to help her load them into the car and take them down to a gallery on Rodeo Drive. "The guy there took one look at them and said, 'This is junk.' " Marvin recalls. "It was one of those boy-were-our-faces-red type of experiences. Really embarrassing. We couldn't wait to get out of there."

Discovering that the paintings were worthless had no particular impact on Vicki's opinion of Alfred, but it did make the prospect of doing a book all the more alluring.

At least since Alfred's death, Vicki had been saying that if she ever went public with the scandal she knew about, it would "bring down the government." Aside from the story about acting as a go-between for unreported campaign funds, she claimed that two prominent members of the administration had been silent investors in the Showbiz Pizza deal—an arrangement which, even assuming it existed, would not necessarily be illegal unless it covered an attempt to evade disclosure laws. She also indicated that she had arranged assignations between various women she recruited and certain friends of Alfred's, not necessarily political figures.

Vicki was simply wrong, though, in thinking that any of these charges—even if true, and even if provable—were likely to destroy the administration. None of them involved Ronald Reagan personally. For that matter, they might not even have done permanent damage to the careers of the individuals named, aside from causing some moments of acute embarrassment. The scandal she claimed to know about that touched on illegality and possible malfeasance had to do with violations of campaign funding laws—and in this case, even if she could come up with the accurate details, which was problematical—the person most implicated by her charges was Alfred.

What she had discovered was hypocrisy. She had seen the undercarriage of the California establishment—and there were cracks there! Millionaire businessmen, supposedly respectable, supposedly defenders of conservative, all-American values, were quite willing to use the Vicki Morgans of the world. When Alfred was alive she'd been worth $18,000 a month and been plenty good enough to go to lunch with his friends. Now she was dirt, sleaze, and even some individuals she considered personal friends of hers, people she'd known for years, looked the other way when she passed on the street.

Vicki was outraged. So outraged that the idea did not glimmer very brightly that exposing the hypocrisy, vindicating her affair with Alfred, and making millions for herself in the bargain might be mutually incompatible. She wanted her revenge, she wanted to bring down the goddamn administration. And yet, she expected to become rich and celebrated and loved at the same time. After all, this was Beverly Hills! This was America!

No one told her this was a crazy notion. In fact, she got a lot of encouragement.

Marvin Pancoast had been working in the offices of the William Morris Agency since early in the year. When the palimony suit was all over the papers and it came out that he was a friend of Vicki Morgan, he says, there was a certain ripple of interest. Kim Brussa, who was then secretary to William Morris agent Steven Weiss, went up to Tower Grove and talked to Vicki about her plans for the book. She thought Vicki's story had the makings of a book and arranged a Friday appointment for her with Weiss.

"First off," says Marvin, "Vicki was late. You had to know her. She was always at least an hour late for everything."

Eventually, Vicki did show up, accompanied by her friend Sally Talbert. Weiss seemed interested in what Vicki had to say—there was nothing on paper—and toward the end of the meeting, William Morris executive Larry Auerbach showed up. No definite agreement was made, no one had said yes in so many words, but the mood was very up, says Marvin. "Larry Auerbach patted me on the back. He actually put his arm around my shoulder. Before that, he didn't even know who I was. I'd been around, but I was, like, invisible."

When Pancoast showed up for work the next Monday morning, one of the first people he passed in the halls was Auerbach. "And he looked right through me," he says. "No eye contact at all. So I know something had changed." Later, he heard that Norman Brokaw, the head of William Morris, had talked to the agency's client Gerald Ford over the weekend, and Ford had been livid. Supposedly, he'd threatened to quit the agency. He'd even fumed that if Morgan became a William Morris client, the IRS would never give them a moment's peace again. As a result, Vicki had become a nonperson.

When Sally Talbert called that morning expecting good news, she heard much the same story from the secretary who took her call. She couldn't remember the woman's name.

Both Brokaw and Auerbach eventually denied this account. Not only was there no Ford phone call, there was no book deal. Vicki who?

But the story certainly did circulate around the office. A year later, after Vicki's death, it surfaced in the British press, where it was cited in support of the theory that Vicki Morgan had been silenced by agents of the Reagan adminstration.

While the much-gossiped-about story is all too believable, at least in its general outlines, it says less about a possible conspiracy than about Vicki's naïveté. Knowledgeable persons might have anticipated that the powers behind William Morris, which represented Henry Kissinger as well as Ford, would have had second thoughts about a project that was sure to alienate some of their most lucrative clients. If Ford did discuss the project on the phone with Brokaw, what would he have said? Would he have been pleased by the news? And if he wasn't, and he went on to throw in some mumblings about the IRS, so what? Gerald Ford, in the fall of 1982, was not even in the government.

It takes a good deal of imagination to believe that threats were necessary to discourage Brokaw from taking on the project. Was the revenge memoir of a discarded mistress worth all the grief? Vicki Morgan was not some civic-minded whistleblower. There was every reason to think she'd be a problem client—difficult to work with, litigation prone, and tricky to promote.

The point is, there was a certain lack of realism on Vicki Morgan's part. She expected to walk into the establishment's favorite talent agency and say, "I have a story that will really put the screws on the establishment." And everyone there would say, "Hey, that's great. Here's a writer who'll do the work for you. Here's a contract worth millions. Sign on the dotted line."

When it didn't work out, instead of chalking the narrow miss up to experience, Vicki started wondering if she was the victim of a conspiracy. It was paranoia time.

Freelance writer Wendy Leigh met Vicki on October 20 at the home of Michael Dave. The subject: the possibility that Leigh might ghostwrite Vicki's memoir.

Instead of the tough, hard-as-nails vamp she'd been expecting, Vicki Morgan impressed her as shy and vulnerable. Vicki appeared for the interview wearing casual clothes—all black, she explained, because that she was still in mourning for Alfred—and no makeup. Her hair, now reverted to its natural dark brown shade, was hastily drawn back into a ponytail. She arrived after Leigh and entered the living room clutching an unopened bottle of white wine. "I hope you don't mind," she said, pointing to the wine. "I stopped on the way to get it because I was really nervous about meeting you."

There was as yet no contract, and no agent willing to handle the book. Leigh returned to New York with nothing resolved. Calls from Vicki came sporadically. At first she seemed friendly, even reasonably cheerful. Then, gradually, her voice took on a hunted quality. Speaking in a hoarse whisper, she confided that she was afraid of an IRS investigation, or worse.

During one of their last conversations, which Leigh subsequently described in an article coauthored for *US* magazine, Vicki confided, "I wanted to tell everyone that we had a deep relationship, not a sleazy affair. I was like a second wife to Alfred. I miss him dreadfully; I think about him every day. But at least I had one thing. I had Alfred. That's the one thing I'll always hold on to."

She also told Leigh that she was considering taking her story, her knowledge of incidents that could discredit the Republican administration, to Ted Kennedy—no doubt the last person who would have been interested in identifying himself with an exposé of sexual hijinks.

With another friend, Vicki discussed the possibility of going to Alexander Haig—who had been forced that June to resign his post as secretary of state as the result of factional battles with White House staffers. Haig, she reasoned, must be steaming for revenge and might be willing to pay her a lot of money for information embarrassing to certain of his enemies.

None of these ideas got past the talking stage, but there was a lot of talk. "Vicki was the kind of person who kept everything," says Marvin Pancoast. "I knew she had all kinds of records. All of Alfred's canceled checks. Everything. And Alfred wrote a lot of checks. And he was always saying that she had records of everything. All of it."

ALFRED'S MISTRESS

//

It wasn't just the William Morris Agency that was unwilling to gamble on Vicki Morgan's as yet unwritten story. Several agents she contacted that fall expressed interest but explained that there would be no possibility of striking a deal—and certainly not the kind of a big-money deal Vicki had in mind—unless some pages of actual manuscript existed. At the very least, they would want to see a sample chapter and a detailed outline.

Although she was already in touch with Wendy Leigh, Vicki began calling around town, asking for recommendations from just about everyone she'd ever met who was in the business. Among the names mentioned to her was that of a freelance scriptwriter named Gordon Basichis.

Philadelphia-born and educated, Basichis had worked during the late 1960s as a reporter for the Philadelphia *Bulletin.* A few years later, he moved to Santa Fe, New Mexico, where he did journalism for a while and began work on a novel, *The Constant Traveller,* described by those who've read it as a hallucinatory and mystical odyssey heavily influenced by Carlos Castaneda's Don Juan series. Despite some good contacts, including a cousin who was a well-established New York literary agent, Basichis's authorial career never quite took off.

In L.A. he'd had somewhat better luck. Though none of his full-length film scripts had so far been produced, by 1982 he had several projects in various stages of development, including a contract to adapt his own novel for the screen. The project was what is called a "step deal," meaning that there was no major financial commitment up front, but it offered the possibility of working with some of the currently hot talents.

In the meantime, he had been married for nearly ten years to a woman with a promising career in television. Marcia Basichis, a pale, intense blonde, was at that point an executive with ABC, where her job involved overseeing the production of ongoing prime-time series. Gordon had done several scripts for *Fantasy Island,* one of the series his wife was responsible for, though to avoid the appearance of nepotism he had used the pseudonym G. Bass.

Although he had no particular experience in ghosting autobiographies, Gordon Basichis had the most important qualification for the job: He was willing to take a chance on working with a problem client, on a project that was as yet uncontracted.

In mid-November, when Vicki first got in touch with him, she was still living in the house on Tower Grove Drive. The two of them hit it off immediately. Although she had no source of income and was living on the proceeds of her recently sold Mercedes, Vicki was still a glamorous woman, whose feisty sense of humor had still not been entirely overwhelmed by the rising tide of depression and self-doubts.

Gordon, aside from being male, which did not hurt, was able to project a vision of the book that Vicki found intriguing and flattering to her ego. She had always seen herself as an outsider, a naïf adrift in the playground of the rich and powerful, with only her wits to survive on. Gordon, whose persona was part streetwise Philadelphian and part ex-hippie philosopher, encouraged her to feel that her failure to belong was something to be proud of. She was an all-American girl among the decadents, a grassroots rebel against social hypocrisy. It was a very 1960s concept, applied to a woman who was a product of that generation without ever having been a part of it. What Gordon was saying was not necessarily untrue, it just happened to be the truth fused with the glow of romanticism. What it missed was that Vicki, while exploited, was also a natural-born exploiter. She just didn't happen to be very good at it.

Gordon also told Vicki that she was smart—not book smart maybe, but a person of great "native intelligence." Again, this was not quite the case.

"It was instant karma between me and Gordon," Vicki told friends.

Michael Dave drew up the collaboration agreement that Vicki and Gordon eventually signed in the spring of 1983 calling for a fifty-fifty split in proceeds from the book. It also named August 8 as the deadline for Basichis to come up with an outline and the first chapter of the manuscript. Vicki then had an option to accept or reject the material for any reason at all. If she rejected it, she would be free to terminate the relationship and to find another collaborator. And Basichis would get nothing for his ten months of work.

This was a rather large commitment of time to make on speculation, but such arrangements are by no means unheard of, particularly when there is a potentially commercial story involved and the writer is inexperienced and has no impressive credits. It did, however, put the collaboration under certain built-in pressures.

Like many who set out to turn their first-person stories into books, Vicki failed to realize that there was a lot more involved than simply hiring a writer. There is a widespread delusion that one's "story," fully formed and framed in the most empathic humanly appealing terms, exists somewhere out there in the ether, requiring only a writing technician to translate it into words. Doing an autobiography is a feat of hard work, discipline, and sometimes agonizing self-revelation.

Vicki had always possessed a wry sense of humor and a certain flair for storytelling. This side of her personality must have still been evident when Basichis met her in November, but as the dismal exercise of dredging up the past continued, Vicki became mired in self-pity. Vicki insisted on portraying herself as a "country girl" and described her months at St. Anne's, actually one of the better institutions of its kind, in terms reminiscent of Jane Eyre's sufferings at Lowood School for Orphans.

Basichis also had reason to be distracted. The nighttime collaboration sessions—Basichis always preferred to work at night—had become increasingly personal. By the end of December, he and Vicki had become lovers.

As Gordon Basichis became more important in Vicki's life, other close relationships waned. Mary moved out. Vicki's attorney Michael Dave, who had been on the receiving end of frequent and lengthy phone calls from Vicki, asking for progress reports on the lawsuit as well as advice on the book and her problems in general, found that he was being left in peace. He assumed that this was a good sign, that Vicki was putting her energies into the book instead of into fretting about problems she could not control.

One friend who continued to come around, despite that fact that Gordon liked him even less than Mary had, was Marvin Pancoast. As far as Marvin was concerned, he was Vicki's only true friend—excepting, of course, Vicki's mother Connie, whom he liked. All the others wanted to use her in one way or another, wanted money or sex or to make a reputation by plugging into her celebrity. He, meanwhile, had extended himself to help Vicki through her troubles. He'd tried to help her find an attorney by sending her to Arthur Barens and had brought her to William Morris, an introduction that had backfired by making him quite unpopular around the office. But it was the very motivelessness of his devotion, its affectless, spacy quality that seemed hardly related to Vicki's feelings for Marvin, that made others uneasy.

Connie Laney had been in England visiting relatives in August. She returned just at the height of the palimony suit furor and, seeing that Vicki and Todd were in need of moral support, began coming in from Montclair to spend the day several times a week. On the occasion of one of her first visits, she found a wan, fey-seeming young man seated at the kitchen table, chainsmoking and toying with a tepid cup of coffee.

At first, Connie had thought that Marvin was coming around

because of his interest in promoting the William Morris deal. When that fizzled and he continued to show up at the house on a regular basis, Connie was perplexed. She tried not to let her prejudices against homosexuality influence her judgment, but there was a sickly aura around Marvin Pancoast that disturbed her. "Marvin never looked healthy," she said later. "I assumed it was because he'd been drinking and doing drugs for years."

Finally, unable to contain her curiosity about the source of his attraction to Vicki, she asked him straight out, "Marvin, aren't you gay?"

"Well . . . yeah," he admitted.

"So why do you keep coming around here?"

The question seemed uncork an emotional dam. "Because I love her," he told Connie tearfully. "I love Vicki like a sister."

Embarrassed, Connie changed the subject. Marvin, she decided, was just another of the lost souls that Vicki had taken up with over the years. A sad case, but harmless.

Marvin and Gordon were, as the cliché has it, as different as day and night. And it was only this difference and the hours they kept that made it possible for Vicki to see both men.

Gordon was a fast talker, a man who prided himself on being able to dominate any situation he got into. Tall and large boned, slightly hatchet-faced with a lower jaw that tended to go slack when his face was in repose, Gordon bore a certain resemblance to—well, Alfred Bloomingdale.

Marvin, very thin and pale, with dishwater-blond hair and blue eyes, had the opposite personal style; he strove to ingratiate himself even, occasionally, at the cost being thought a wimp. People who relied on first impressions sometimes failed to notice that Marvin was a lot sharper, both more intelligent and alert, then he seemed. And, in his way, he was every bit as ambitious as Gordon. He had big plans.

"Gordon's style of dealing with people was by intimidation," says Marvin. "He had this idea that he could 'take a reading' on people, size them up on first meeting and decide whether they were worth bothering with or not.

"But, of course, you can't do that."

Gordon's reading on Marvin was that he was inconsequential. Marvin reacted by staying out of Gordon's way. He was just biding his time.

As it turned out, work on the book was progressing a lot slower than Michael Dave thought. At the end of the year, Gordon's wife Marcia gave birth to her first child. Also during December, Vicki had to face the fact that she could no longer afford the house on Tower Grove Drive.

Surviving on the proceeds of the sale of the Mercedes and some of her better jewelry, Vicki was a poor risk as a tenant. However, her friend Mary helped her find a contemporary townhouse condo in Studio City in North Hollywood, and her ex-husband Bob Schulman helped her out by arranging the lease in his name.

The duplex had three bedrooms and two baths upstairs, a raised dining nook and a den downstairs in addition to the living room and the kitchen, and a basement-level two-car garage and laundry room. Sublet from the owners, a *Los Angeles Times* editor and his wife, at $1,000 a month, the condo was hardly in the slum category, but Vicki considered it a humiliating comedown. She hated giving up the swimming pool and the spacious rooms she had spent so much to fix up. She hated having party-wall neighbors, and she especially hated the neighborhood. Instead of shopping on Rodeo Drive in her Mercedes, suddenly she was driving a mere Jeep Cherokee, a vehicle that didn't even belong to her—it was Schulman's—and bargain hunting along Ventura Boulevard.

When not worrying about money and her financial future, Vicki was preoccupied with the change in her son. Todd had transferred to Notre Dame High School in the Valley, only to clash immediately with the school authorities over the disparity between the Catholic school dress code and the punk style he'd recently adopted. Sleeveless T-shirts and motorcycle-chain belts, worn with a single earring and a Mohawk, were not the sisters' idea of proper school attire.

Everyone who knew Todd during this period agrees that he was basically a good kid, just having trouble coping with the scandal of the palimony suit and its revelations about his mother's way of life—which had come just as he was entering his teens and starting to date himself. Oddly enough, considering, Vicki's ideas about parenting were highly conventional, almost Victorian. And since Alfred had never spent the night at her house, showing up mostly when Todd was in school, it had been relatively easy to shield him from the realities. But now that, too, had changed. Vicki hadn't a clue of how to deal with her son's rebelliousness.

As Basichis later testified in court, Vicki's reaction to her problems was "histrionic" rather than practical. *I can't work like this,* she kept complaining, *not with all these problems hanging over me.*

As the months went by, Gordon found himself investing more and more energy in just keeping Vicki afloat, financially and psychologically. He began by lending her a few dollars for groceries now and then, until eventually his outlays amounted to several thousand dollars. But these were stopgap measures at best. The only hope of reassuring Vicki and of keeping her solvent was to raise some money by selling a share in the book's future earnings. Since he had no legal rights to borrow against Vicki's percentage, it was part of his share that would have to be put up.

By this time, more than six months had passed since the suit was dismissed and there were still no sample manuscript pages, so Basichis's prospects for getting a large advance were even less than Vicki's had been the previous fall. The one thing the two of them had settled on was a title, *Alfred's Mistress*—Vicki's idea.

One reputable and prominent Beverly Hills attorney/businessman who saw Basichis in the late spring of 1983 recalls that Bashicis arrived in his office dressed in "beige patent-leather shoes, slacks, a silky or satin-looking shirt that was unbuttoned, [and] wearing a gold necklace . . . that sort of Hollywood slick look."

Basichis, the attorney recalls, explained that "he was the ghostwriter and she [Vicki Morgan] was the writer. I got the impression that he was interviewing her on tape," and he was asking for $50,000 in exchange for "a piece of *his* action . . . whatever his deal was with Vicki Morgan. He never showed me any contract between him and her . . . but my sense of it was that he did have a contract with her and that he was required to make certain payments to her under it. [Not, in fact, the case.] He said the contract was running out. He definitely said that he needed the money in order to give her the money, and it was his responsibility to kind of keep her going . . . 'and she really doesn't have a farthing left.' "

Basichis stayed in the attorney's office "for roughly an hour and a half," says the attorney, but "what he ultimately said in substance could have been said in five minutes. He kept repeating himself, and he talked so fast I literally couldn't get a word in."

To convince the attorney of the potential of the book, Basichis produced a small pocket tape recorder and played a tape of Vicki talking—"He said there were many more tapes"—describing "her unhappy childhood, her mother, and then this home she was put in . . . the pregnancy and how she felt really bad about it. The theme of it was what a shitty life she led . . . a girl who had nothing and then was later destined to go all the way to the height of power."

"I said, 'This is fine, but what the world wants to know is about Bloomingdale.' "

Basichis's reply was "a lot of leading stuff . . . like there were other people besides Bloomingdale and that this goes right to the White House, and that what people knew now was 'only the tip of the iceberg.' He called it 'the book of the twentieth century,' which would 'rip the lid off things.' . . . The book would be bigger than Watergate."

Pressed by the attorney, however, for specifics, Basichis could only remind him that Betsy Bloomingdale was Nancy Reagan's best friend.

Either Basichis was attempting a snow job or else he didn't see fit to disclose the details of what he had. Either way, the attorney wasn't interested. "It must have taken fifteen minutes to say goodbye to him, you know, shaking hands, standing up, edging toward the door."

At one point during the spring of 1983, Basichis even took Vicki to Las Vegas, where the two of them tried—unsuccessfully—to win enough money in the casinos to keep her going for a few more months. Basichis had come into Vicki's life to write her life story and had ended up becoming part of it, the latest in a long line of men whom she had counted on to rescue her from herself.

Worried about her daughter's depression and its effects on Todd, Vicki's mother had also begun to spend a good deal of time around the Studio City condo. Since Gordon's visits, working and otherwise, occurred mostly at night, she and the ghostwriter did not see a great deal of each other. She had seen enough, however, to convince her that Gordon was not a good influence on her daughter.

One day early in the spring, Connie was attempting to straighten up Vicki's bedroom when she noticed a greeting card propped against the lamp on the nightstand. "On the front of the card," Connie would recall, "was a gal laying back on a couch with some pillows behind her. There was a brassiere laying on the pillows. She had her clothes on, but the male had his hand right in her crotch. And [inside] it said, 'Vickie, a little something to remember the occasion, for what I know will be better days ahead.' And it was signed, 'Gordon.' . . . I swear to God, I wrote it down so I would not forget the words. . . . So I figured from that, it had to have been the first time he had got to her."

Although the card may well have been the expression of a private joke, Connie could see nothing humorous about it. What kind of a man would send a dirty greeting card to commemorate the beginning of an extramarital affair? The knowledge that her daughter's new lover had a young, attractive wife and an infant child at home especially offended her sense of proprieties. Gordon, she felt, should be spending his nights at home, not hanging around Vicki's place.

Yet, increasingly, Vicki seemed to look to Gordon as not just a lover but as a confidant and adviser. Her conversation was salted with references to Gordon's opinions. He had convinced her to make him a cosigner of the safe-deposit box she opened at a nearby bank. He was, so Connie felt, "monopolizing" Vicki's mind.

It was no use trying to discuss any of this with Vicki. One day after she found the greeting card, Connie tried to sit her daughter down and warn her that the affair could only lead to another thudding disillusionment. "Gordon's no friend of yours," she said.

Like a petulant child, Vicki dismissed the advice as so much empty moralizing. "Oh, Mom, you're so out of it," Connie remembers her saying. "You just don't understand."

In one way, Connie was wrong about Gordon.

She blamed Gordon, a whiskey drinker, for influencing Vicki— long a pill abuser and white wine drinker—for introducing Vicki to hard booze. And worse, for getting her involved with cocaine.

Although later at the trial, Connie would deny knowing anything about her daughter's use of cocaine, she told a reporter shortly after Vicki's death that "during the last six, seven, eight months [Gordon] was with her . . . I think he drove her down the toilet. That was where all the cocaine was coming from." Connie made similar charges to the investigator from the DA's office— charges Gordon flatly denied, though other witnesses confirmed Connie's impression.

Whatever Gordon's influence had to do with it, Vicki did not need his example to get her into trouble with drugs and drink. What had changed was that she was no longer able to hide the effects of her habit from her mother and others who might disapprove. She'd traveled the long looping curve of addiction past its apogee and had begun the downward slide. Once able to swallow ten or fifteen pills a day and still function, she found her tolerance slipping away from her. Her best friend, Valium, was failing her. She couldn't get started, couldn't get organized, couldn't make the smallest decisions without getting bogged down in pointless, circular dissections of the pros and cons of each individual option.

Vicki seldom went out of the condo. She'd lived a clandestine life for years, and now that she no longer had any practical reason to be in hiding, irrational fears, a rampant case of agoraphobia, kept her more secluded than ever. Connie had taken to coming to Colfax Avenue several days a week to do errands and to keep her daughter company, and Vicki, reluctant to drive, often asked Connie to chauffeur her. When Connie drove her to the supermarket, she would sit trembling in the passenger seat, afraid to go inside.

Connie would pick up the groceries on her way to the condo, only to find that she was asked to run out time and again for items that Vicki had forgotten to ask for over the phone. Then she would straigthen up the apartment, clearing away the dirty ashtrays and unwashed glasses that had accumulated since her last visit, and try to convince her daughter to eat something sensible. Connie suspected at times that she had replaced the maid that Vicki could no longer afford.

Vicki's self-pity had reached the stage where she resented anyone who made demands. In her nighttime taping sessions with Gordon, Vicki spun out a long list of grievances against her mother. Connie, she complained, was too fond of her gin, had been too strict with her and too lax with Todd, and was now making her life hell with her constant nagging. These complaints were just plain untrue, unfair, or simply myopic. Connie had stood by her daughter a lot longer and more staunchly than a lot of mothers would.

Within a very few weeks, the three-bedroom condo, crowded with the superfluous possessions of a lifetime of shopping binges, the air thick with resentments, had become a very claustrophobic place indeed. Everyone was irritated with everyone else. And at the center of the miasma was Vicki, her famous charm used up and her wry, seductive sense of humor distorted into a whine whose single theme was "Poor Me."

Even Vicki's longtime friends were at a loss to deal with this new personality. If they kept their distance, they were accused of deserting her now that she was broke and in exile from Beverly Hills. If they tried to maintain contact they found themselves trapped inside the psychodrama.

One of the first friendships to crack was Vicki's decade-long relationship with Leslie, the former girlfriend of Bernie Cornfeld who was now divorced from her banker husband and living quietly in the Los Angeles area. Leslie had invited Vicki and her friend Mary to dinner, and when they arrived they found another guest present, a man who mentioned in the course of the conversation that he knew of a very wealthy individual who might be interested in setting Vicki up as his mistress.

The proposition was tasteless, but hardly the sort of thing that a woman with Vicki's history should have found completely unexpected. Vicki reacted with tears of outrage and humiliation, accusing her friend alternately of playing the pimp and having arranged the whole evening to insult her and drag the memory of her love for Alfred down into the mud. Leslie, who swore she'd meant nothing of the kind, couldn't see anyway what Vicki had to be insulted about and she had a few choice words to say about the invocation of Alfred's sacred memory. End of evening. End of friendship.

Sally Talbert, by nature a "rescuer" of lost souls, was more patient than most. By the early spring of 1983 Lorna Matlin had concluded that no purpose was served by listening to Vicki's telephone monologues, calls that came in the small hours of the morning and could go on for hours. Afraid of abandonment, Vicki soon found a more effective way of holding on to her friends' attention.

On March 5, Sally, Lorna Matlin, and Karen (not her real name), another friend of Vicki's who was visiting from out of town, had invited Vicki to have lunch with them.

Knowing that Vicki might not have transportation, Sally called before leaving for the restaurant and offered her a lift. Vicki sounded sleepy. She had only just then awakened, and Gordon was still in the house. "You guys go ahead and I'll meet you there," she told Sally. "I've been down the last few days, really depressed. But I'll pull myself together and join you."

Vicki never showed up.

Used to their friend's perpetual lateness, the women went ahead and ate without her and then went on to Lorna's apartment, as planned. They were just settling down to continuing their conversation when the phone rang. Karen answered. It was

Vicki on the line, slurring her words and sounding very groggy.

Fortunately, or perhaps deliberately, Vicki had not downed enough pills to knock herself out. When her friends arrived, she was just barely conscious and insisting hysterically that she didn't want them to call an ambulance. The last thing she needed was to have the newspapers pick up the story of the palimony mistress's suicide attempt.

There were two empty liquor bottles in the bedroom and two empty pill bottles, one of them labeled Valium. While Sally did her best to get Vicki on her feet and keep her moving, Karen tried to call Dr. Monke. When she couldn't get through to him immediately, she phoned the hospital emergency center, which advised that if they couldn't bring the victim in immediately they should try to induce vomiting. Lorna, who had some knowledge of first aid, ran out to a nearby drugstore for syrup of ipecac, which did the trick.

In retrospect, there was some doubt that the scene was quite what it appeared to be. "It's a debate as to whether it was a suicide attempt or not," Lorna said later. "I think she just drank too much and took too many Valiums." At any rate, the "attempt" had occurred on an afternoon when Vicki knew that the chances of someone finding her before it was too late were extremely good. Not only did she have a date with three close friends, who would be sure to answer her call for help, but Gordon Basichis was expected back at the condo later in the day—and, indeed, had arrived just after the crisis ended.

Suicide attempt or overdose, the incident was a classic "cry for help." Still, Vicki refused to admit she had a problem. She'd stopped seeing Dr. Monke and was not in a bad enough way for involuntary commitment, even if her friends and family had been desperate enough to take the step.

As her friends knew very well when they decided not to call the ambulance, there was nothing that terrified Vicki quite so much as the word *hospital*. The reason was not at all irrational. She had no health insurance—Alfred or her husbands had always taken care of that before. So, if it came to hospitalization, she wouldn't be returning to Thalians or its ilk. She'd be headed for the wards of Camarillo State.

D - *D A Y*

///

Curiously enough, the man who lived in Condo C, directly adjacent to Vicki's, was an ex-FBI agent, a fact that would have fed her already rampant paranoia had she known of it.

Joel Graydon, who also had a degree in law, had been retired from the bureau for some years and now managed clients in the movie business. He was well known in the neighborhood, however, having lived there for nearly nine years, and his career had been the subject of a *Los Angeles Times* profile that March.

According to Graydon, he had lived next door to Apartment D for more than five months without ever so much as suspecting that the woman in the neighboring condo was the notorious palimony mistress.

"I don't believe I saw her more than four times," Graydon recalls. "She rarely came out of the townhouse." And then, it was usually in the early evenings, around six or seven o'clock to walk her dog—"a very sweet Doberman."

Once and only once, Graydon passed his elusive neighbor on the sidewalk out front on Colfax Avenue and went out of his way to say hello. But, he recalls, he didn't attempt to introduce himself. "I didn't say, "My name's Joel Graydon because it's obvious when somebody wants to be alone and she obviously wanted to be alone. In retrospect, it's obvious that she wanted to remain incognito. . . .

"She always wore slacks . . . a sweatshirt and a pair of slacks. She did nothing to make herself attractive. She didn't wear makeup.

Her hair was just hanging down. . . . And she was extremely thin. Extremely. I had the feeling as I would watch her walk the dog, those few moments when I did see her, that she must have been . . . I could imagine her as being almost emaciated under her clothes."

Besides the woman, whom Graydon had pegged as a "Greta Garbo–type" minus the glamour, the only other resident of the condo was her teenage son, whose Mohawk haircut, dyed a fluorescent green, was by far his most noticeable characteristic. Initially alarmed by the boy's appearance, the neighbors were relieved to discover that he was hardly ever around and caused no problems at all when he was. The consensus was that, despite his bizarre looks, he was just your average good kid.

Some time around the beginning of June, Graydon became aware of the fact that there was a new addition to the rather eccentric household next door. A slender young man, unremarkable looking but friendly, had largely taken over the job of walking the Doberman, Katy. Unlike Vicki, he frequently stopped to exchange greetings and to chat with other dogwalkers and with neighbors on their way out to the street.

One Sunday afternoon in late June, just a few days after Joe Graydon's wife had mentioned having a conversation with the new neighbor, Graydon answered his doorbell and found Marvin standing there with Todd and a teenage girl who, says Graydon, was obviously Todd's "little girlfriend." One of the wires that held the girl's braces in place had snapped—it was protruding out between her front teeth—and Marvin wanted to know if Graydon had a wire clippers for an emergency repair.

Graydon rummaged through his closet and found a pair of clippers delicate enough to to the job. All the time he was looking, Pancoast talked a blue streak, telling Graydon how "they" were going to be moving soon into a new place, a house with a yard. It was as if Pancoast had somehow not only become part of the family but had taken over responsibility for its welfare. He was particularly concerned about Katy. Katy wasn't happy in the condo. The rooms were too small and she needed a yard where she could run for exercise.

Graydon couldn't help wondering idly just how this fellow, who was apparently gay, fit into the picture. But the guy was so meek and colorless that it was difficult to work up any great interest. "It's a funny thing," Graydon says, "in all my years at the bureau we were very careful about observing people and giving descriptions of them." But Pancoast was so completely average that he almost defied categorization. "I know fifty thousand guys like that . . . just very usual. Not an especially attractive guy. Not an especially bright guy. Not especially anything. Just there. He obviously wasn't doing anything because he didn't have anything to do."

Graydon did notice, however, that the boy, Todd, showed no enthusiasm whatsoever about the new house that Marvin was extolling with pride. "Through it all," Graydon recalls, "he didn't say three words."

Dismaying as the prospect was to Todd, Marvin's plan that the three of them—he and Todd and Vicki—become a family was almost a fait accompli.

This was an amazing turnabout, not just for Vicki but for Marvin, who had begun the year with a run of bad luck. In January he had been booted from his job at the William Morris Agency at least partly, he believed, in retaliation for his role in the embarrassing flap over Vicki's noncontract. Almost immediately, he found a job with a would-be producer who was trying to develop a network TV series, only to discover too late that the producer was bankrupt and would neither pay Marvin's back salary nor reimburse him for research expenses he had advanced out of pocket. Depressed and drinking again, he spent a bad few weeks before deciding, in early April, to sign himself in as a voluntary patient at St. John's in Santa Monica—the same hospital where Alfred Bloomingdale had died the previous year.

Judging by Marvin's records at St. John's, his mental health had undergone a dramatic improvement since his hospitalization at Cedars-Sinai more than three years earlier. Always before, the psychiatrists who examined him during his hospitalizations had labeled him psychotic, though the category of illness was specified variously as schizophrenia, manic-depressive psychosis, or psychotic depression. At St. John's the diagnosis was "borderline personality with paranoid features."

In laymen's terms, this meant that while Marvin might have a tremendous amount of difficulty adjusting to the demands of normal life, he was no longer—and most likely never had been—suffering from one of the biochemical diseases known as psychoses. Any hallucinations, delusions, or other extreme symptoms he might have manifested in the past might be dismissed as temporary manifestations of depression and/or drug abuse.

Marvin remained at St. John's as a voluntary patient from April

9 until May 1, then signed himself in for another four-day stint between the fifth and the ninth of May. During this second admission, Dr. Paul Cantalupo interviewed Pancoast and further refined the original St. John's diagnosis, describing the patient as suffering from a "depressive neurosis" and noting that he did not appear to be delusional at the present time.

Dr. Cantalupo, who also had a private practice in Beverly Hills, decided that Marvin could best be treated by analysis. At least three days a week, and more often if he could manage it, Marvin visited Cantalupo for therapy sessions to talk through his problems. In the meantime, he had moved back to his mother's home in Thousand Oaks, promising as a condition of his therapy to give up using street drugs and alcohol, as well as to attend Alcoholics Anonymous meetings regularly.

Arthur Barens, the attorney who was a friend of the Pancoast family, was a staunch advocate of AA, and he helped get Marvin started in the program. Although none too pleased that Marvin had ignored his advice to drop Vicki, Barens considered it a good sign that Marvin was very concerned about Vicki's pill habit and her drinking.

Since Vicki had stopped seeing Dr. Monke a few months earlier, Marvin wanted in the worst way to get Vicki to come with him to AA, as well as to get her hooked up with another shrink, possibly even Dr. Cantalupo. But Vicki couldn't acknowledge to herself that drugs were her problem, and even if she could have, the idea of talking about herself in front of a room full of strangers was terrifying. By now, her agoraphobia was so bad that she broke out in a sweat over going up to the newsstand to buy a paper.

But others who met Marvin through AA suspected that his interest in getting Vicki on the program was not 100 percent unselfish. Marvin, several of them recall, would often take the floor at meetings and invariably end up straying from the subject at hand to brag about this beautiful woman he was involved with.

Coincidentally, one of the people who happened to hear these monologues was Rick DePaul, Vicki's buddy from her Doheny Drive apartment days. This guy Marvin was going on about this fantastic, beautiful female, talking about her as if they were lovers, Rick recalled, and gradually it dawned on him that the woman being described had to be Vicki. Rick just couldn't put the two individuals together. It was beyond imagining. Vicki had always had her pick of men, and this guy was "so strange. He was like—a psychopath."

"I told him, 'Tell her Rick says hi.' " He adds, "But I'm sure she never got the message."

For the first time in his adult life, Marvin was being told by his doctors that he wasn't psychotic, just suffering from common-garden variety depression. The kicker to this good news was that the physicians at St. Johns had also given him plenty of reason to stay depressed. At the outpatient clinic where he'd gone for a routine physical checkup, a medical doctor had taken one look at him—underweight, his body a sink of intractable infections and a history of homosexual promiscuity—and pronounced a tentative diagnosis: AIDS.

The findings of AIDS was never officially confirmed at the time, but Dr. Cantalupo considered it "probable." So did Marvin, and the knowledge that he might have only a few years, or even a few months, to live made him feel all that much closer to Vicki.

None too eager to spend his days hanging around his mother's house, brooding over his future or lack of it, Marvin signed up with temp agency in late may. Coincidentally, the agency found him a job with a clinical psychologist who ran a phobia clinic in the same building in Beverly Hills where Dr. Cantalupo had his offices.

"I had an immediate rapport with him," a young woman who worked in the same office recalls. "He seemed like a very sweet person. Quiet and gentle. Real sensitive." Marvin, who had been hired with the idea that he would be around only long enough to oversee the preparation of a special mailing for a forthcoming seminar, also impressed his employer. He put in long hours and seemed very dedicated to doing the best possible job. After he'd been in the office only a few days, the psychologist brought up the possibility of offering him a permanent position doing public-relations work for the clinic.

Almost immediately, his co-worker remembers, Marvin seemed overwhelmed by his heady success. "He hedged about accepting the PR job," the woman says, "saying things like, 'I don't think this is going to be worth the time I'm putting into it.' And 'They can't afford me.' " He demanded special privileges, an expense account, and a percentage of whatever business he generated. And he wanted to be allowed to smoke in the office, despite the existence of a strict no-smoking policy.

On June 5, Marvin confided to his co-worker that the job "just wasn't working out." "Money was the big issue," according to him, she recalls; Marvin told her that he was being underappreciated, undervalued. But the real problem was that "he was just panicked by responsibility. He was real good at carrying out tasks, but couldn't take initiative."

After giving up this job, Marvin was even more reluctant to face the disapproval at home. He began sleeping in the spare bedroom at Colfax Avenue, and though he never brought over any clothes or personal possessions, it was more or less accepted by Vicki that he'd moved in. Although, obviously, he had nowhere else he wanted to be and nothing much to do with his time, the reason he gave for sticking around was that he was her only loyal friend.

Bored and eager to please, Marvin slipped easily into the role of Vicki's unpaid go-fer. "Vicki," says a longtime acquaintance, "was very indulged. . . . And she always had someone like Marvin Pancoast around. Someone to get her gum. Someone to get her tea." In the past, this tendency to use people had been balanced by Vicki's innate sense of humor and generosity.

Marvin had no idea of where to draw the line. If Vicki wanted a bottle of wine, he went out for it. If five minutes after he returned, she wanted some candy as well, he'd pick up the car keys and go out a second time. He shopped and emptied ashtrays and did the dishes. And he performed more intimate services as well—brushing Vicki's hair, doing her nails, massaging her back. Vicki thought nothing of chatting with Marvin while she was in the shower. She even invited him to sleep in the bed beside her, since it was less lonely that way.

Vicki was, by now, sure that her phone was tapped. When she called Marvin at his mother's house in Thousand Oaks, they would inevitably joke about the "bugs" on the line. Sometime they'd make up dialogue calculated to burn the ears off their anonymous eavesdropper.

In the privacy of her bedroom, seated on the king-size bed where she spent a good part of her days, they daydreamed about various plans for getting revenge on Betsy Bloomingdale. Vicki was particularly taken with the idea of blackmail and had thought up a very complicated scheme involving compromising allegations—totally false—about a young friend of Bloomingdale's daughter who happened to be living in the gatehouse of the Bel-Air mansion.

According to Marvin, Vicki also bragged of having arranged a one-night stand with then presidential advisor Edwin Meese. The motive, so the story goes, was spite. Allegedly, the idea came into her head during the period when Alfred was in the hospital, his condition rapidly deteriorating. Betsy Bloomingdale, who liked Meese and wanted to promote his career—as did Alfred—had arranged for him to be the honored guest at a formal party in Bel-Air. Vicki, however, was miffed that Betsy was busying herself playing hostess while her husband was suffering through the final stages of his terminal illness. Besides, she huffed, *she* could do a better job of entertaining a man than Betsy Bloomingdale! Thus inspired, says Marvin, Vicki managed to arrange through a third party to get Meese to meet her after Betsy's dinner in a room at the Westwood Marquis Hotel, a favorite haunt of Alfred's.

Marvin Pancoast is hardly an unimpeachable source, and Vicki apparently never told this story to her ghostwriter Gordon Basichis. When asked, Ed Meese denied ever having met Vicki Morgan. However, Connie Laney, who never acknowledged in so many words that her daughter had had sexual relations with anyone, including Bloomingdale, was irate enough at Meese's denial that he had never met Vicki to reiterate that her daughter had confided to her about meeting Meese—both before and after Reagan's election, and both in Bloomingdale's company and alone. Whether the details of this anecdote are based on truth or fantasy, it reveals the mentality of the schemes that were being hatched by Marvin and Vicki in their all-night heart-to-heart talks.

Seeing Gordon as a rival—a viewpoint Basichis would have disdained to reciprocate—Marvin confided to Vicki some paranoid suspicions of his own. Gordon, he suggested, was "not a writer at all." "Someone" must be paying him to keep Vicki preoccupied and to sabotage the book project. Marvin's reasoning on this score was simple. Gordon had been on the scene for eight months, and so far, not a word of the book was on paper. If Gordon was a writer, why didn't he write? If he wasn't, why was he still hanging around?

Vicki laughed off Marvin's theory, but it helped to feed her own private fear that choosing Gordon as a collaborator had been a mistake. She was terrified that Gordon would walk out on her and, simultaneously, terrified that he wouldn't. If things continued to drag on as they had all year, the chance that her memoirs would ever earn her the money and the vindication she was counting would soon vanish altogether.

Something had to be resolved soon, one way or another, because by June Vicki's financial situation had become desperate. She was behind in her lease payments on the condo, and the

Epsteins, the owners, had served notice that they wanted their property vacated by no later than July 7, 1983. Vicki, a believer in numerology, found it all too significant that the deadline happened to fall exactly one year after she had signed the papers that initiated her palimony suit. It was almost like a sign that Betsy's powers of persecution extended to the supernatural, she thought.

The first person she turned to for help was Gordon. "Where am I going to go?" she wondered. Connie would be happy enough to have Todd back in Montclair with her, but Vicki felt that she and her mother would never be able to coexist happily under the same roof, at least not the way things had been going recently. Besides—and perhaps, much more importantly—what would she do with herself, stuck way out there in the sticks, with no money and not even a car to get into L.A.?

The two of them actually discussed the possibility that Vicki might move in temporarily with Gordon and his wife Marcia, who had so far been amazingly tolerant of her husband's nocturnal work sessions. The Basichis's prided themselves on having an open marriage, and besides, on the one occasion when the two women met, they had taken a liking to each other. Vicki found Marcia, a woman who exuded intelligence and ambition, to be "a doll." Marcia had decided that Vicki was really "extremely intelligent," not at all the dumb blonde that had been portrayed in the press.

Even so, it was obvious to all concerned that the prospects for the three of them to get along under one roof were not very good. Marcia had a job and an infant child to care for, and by this time, even Gordon found it trying to be around Vicki for more than a few hours at a time.

Marvin found the plan ridiculous.

"But there's nowhere else for me to go," Vicki argued. "If he can't help me, I'm sunk."

"You are not sunk. I'll take care of you, Vicki. We'll work everything out together."

And, in reality, Marvin's plan was not such a bad one. Vicki had a houseful of furniture but no money. Marvin had no furniture but could probably borrow enough from his family to get a lease on a halfway decent place. After that ran out, he could even get a job for a while, to tide the two of them over until some money came in from the book project.

What's more, Marvin had medical insurance—something Vicki was very worried about being without. They often joked about how their friendship had started in "the loony bin" and how, the way things were going, they might both end up there again. "But at least you'll be in a nice, private loony bin," Vicki would say. "I'll end up in the state loony bin." Despite the attempt at humor, it was one of her worst fears. She'd heard enough about places like Camarillo State from Marvin to doubt that she's survive there very long. Marvin now had a solution even to this problem. "We could always get married," he pointed out. "At least then you'd be covered on my policy."

"Can you believe it," Vicki told Gordon the next day. "Marvin wants to *marry* me!"

Of course the idea was ludicrous . . . outrageous! Marvin was a fag and more than a little nutty. But even though she laughed, Vicki did halfway consider accepting.

After all, Marvin *did* have that insurance. And she couldn't completely dismiss Marvin for being gay, since she wasn't totally sure of where she stood on the same scale.

Marvin, of course, hadn't been joking.

He'd been close to Vicki for more than four years, a long time in the troubled history of his life. And, since Alfred's death, he'd seen the coterie that once flocked around the uncrowned queen of Beverly Hills dwindle away. The users were the first to go, the ones who were only hanging around to rip Vicki off for presents and cash. Then, one by one, her old friends had given up on her. Gordon was sure to drop out of the picture sooner or later, and Connie, whom Marvin liked, would have her hands full taking care of Todd. That left only him.

Marvin had never been at ease with his homosexuality. He wanted to go straight. And, in Vicki, he'd finally found a woman who needed him. Through sheer endurance, he was in line to become the successor to Alfred Bloomingdale.

Suddenly, everything was falling into place.

Late on Thursday night, June 30, or rather, early Friday morning, Gordon and Vicki had a terrific row. The August 8 deadline specified in their contract was fast approaching, and Gordon had managed to put together a draft of a first chapter for Vicki's approval. When he learned that evening that she hadn't managed to find time even to read it over, he lost his temper.

Vicki protested that she had no time for reading at the moment. She was worried about Todd. She had to pack up and get out of the damned condo within a week. She didn't even know where she was going to live, for chrissakes. And now that she'd hit bottom, Gordon was threatening to walk out on her. . . .

Vicki got more hysterical, and there are two versions of what happened next: According to Gordon, he took Vicki by the arms and tried to "sit her down" to give her a good talking to. Marvin, who was awakened by the noise and came downstairs just as the argument was ending, says there was more to it than that: Vicki had tried to struggle free of Gordon's grasp, and when Marvin first saw them, they were tussling near the balcony railing that separated the elevated dining area from the living room. Either way, Vicki came out of the quarrel with black-and-blue marks on her arms and an ugly bruise the size of a quarter under her right eye.

After the fight, Vicki fled upstairs and closed herself up in her bedroom. Gordon paced around in the living room for a few minutes, then went up to Vicki to say he was sorry. Wouldn't she at least accept his apology? Then they could sit down and talk out their problems like civilized people.

Vicki said, "No way. I want you out of this house." As far as she was concerned, their partnership was over—period.

That night Marvin got Vicki to go to an AA meeting, something he'd been after her to do for weeks. Address conscious even when it came to Alcoholics Anonymous, Vicki insisted that they pass up Marvin's regular group for the Rodeo Drive meeting in Beverly Hills.

On Monday, July 4, Marvin took Vicki to his mother's house for a holiday dinner. His grandmother liked Vicki and, no doubt pleased to see that Marvin was thinking of settling down with a young woman, she agreed to lend him $3,500—enough for moving expenses and the security deposit and first-month's rent on a new apartment.

Marvin's impossible dream seemed to be coming true, but like so many impossible dreams, this one started to look like a nightmare almost as soon as it came within reach.

After the Independence Day gathering, Marvin decided to spend the night at his family's home in Thousand Oaks. Vicki went back to Colfax Avenue, but she no sooner got home than she was on the phone, wanting Marvin to come over. She'd had an argument with Todd and needed Marvin to "handle it."

The demand was nothing out of the ordinary. It was the timing that irked Marvin. Here, he'd just managed to get a bankroll from his family that would keep Vicki from landing out on the street, and instead of being appreciated, he was getting ordered around. He'd been telling himself that, once Gordon was gone, Vicki would start treating him better, and now that he saw it wasn't going to work out that way, the frustration he'd been denying started bubbling up to the surface of his consciousness.

"They called me a hanger-on," Marvin would say later, "but it was Vicki who was hanging on to me. . . . Still, you couldn't just walk away."

Early Tuesday morning, Marvin went out to look at a one-bedroom condo in the Burbank Hills that had been advertised for lease. Since he couldn't convince Vicki to get up her energy to go househunting with him, the decision had been left in his hands. The condo was nothing special, but the price was right, and Vicki had to get her stuff out of Colfax Avenue the next day, one way or another. He told the agent they wanted the place and gave her the go-ahead to put the paperwork through.

While Marvin was gone, Connie showed up to do the packing that her daughter clearly wasn't up to managing herself. Connie had seen the results of the quarrel with Basichis—the bruise on Vicki's cheek and marks on her arm "just like someone would grab you"—and she'd been shocked by them. Despite her mother's misgivings, Vicki called Gordon at home and left a message on his answering machine, saying that she was willing to patch up their differences if he still wanted to.

Marvin, meanwhile, had gone on to his appointment with Dr. Cantalupo. When he returned to Colfax Avenue late in the afternoon, he strode into the living room where Connie was working and announced, "I've just fired my shrink." Cantalupo, he said, had ordered him to break off his relationship wtih Vicki, something he would never do.

Connie was somewhat taken aback. What relationship? As far as she'd heard, Marvin and Vicki were becoming roommates purely as a matter of convenience.

Even so, Connie had other things to do that day than sit around worrying about Marvin. The packing was an overwhelming job, plus she had just been through the unpleasant business of trying to get her daughter to straighten out the quarrel with Gordon. Then, around dinnertime, Todd came back from Hollywood wearing a ring in his nose, of all things. He'd had his nose pierced that day, a move that, however unconsciously, guaranteed that he would finally get some of his mother's attention. Vicki was hysterical.

In the midst of all the turmoil, Marvin took Vicki's Jeep Cherokee and drove to his AA meeting in the Fairfax district. When he came out, it was getting dark, but the headlights on the Jeep wouldn't work. Afraid to drive without them, he left the vehicle parked on Fairfax Avenue and took a taxi home. It was definitely not a good day, but the worst shock was still ahead of him.

Gordon, as usual, had slept during the hot hours of the day. He found Vicki's message on his machine when he woke up, and around 10:30 in the evening, he showed up at her place. Marvin was seated in the living room when he came in. "He was very red-faced. He seemed very surprised to see me," Gordon later said. "Physically, he was trembling. We didn't talk very much."

Almost immediately, Marvin left the room and went upstairs. As he later put it, "I was given a kiss on the lips and told to go to bed."

Gordon and Vicki stayed on the couch talking, except for a period of about forty-five minutes when Gordon went out to pay a quick visit to a friend who lived nearby. When he returned, it was about quarter to twelve. He and Vicki continued their discussion and could hear Marvin pacing back and forth in the spare bedroom.

Gordon, who had reached his own boiling point with Vicki only a week earlier, recognized the signs of simmering frustration. "You'd better cool it with Marvin for a while," he told Vicki. "Go easy on him."

Nevertheless, when Marvin came downstairs again, around seven-thirty A.M., to find Gordon and Vicki still in the living room, Vicki immediately ordered him, "Go out and get some breakfast things for us. And we need coffee, too. We're all out." Marvin went, spending more than $10 on bagels and the fixings and a pound of coffee, only to be lectured by Vicki for having brought back the wrong brand. "Gordon likes Chock Full o' Nuts," Vicki told him. "You should have got that."

After breakfasting, Gordon and Vicki retired to her bedroom. In theory, there was nothing to stop Marvin from just walking out, except that emotionally he didn't have the strength. He was afraid that being without Vicki might turn out to be even worse than being with her, and anyway, he could never resist Vicki when she called him up to summon him back. At least if he stuck this day out, they might end up living together.

Connie Laney also woke up around seven-thirty, in her own home on Harvard Avenue in Montclair. The first thought that flashed through her mind after she opened her eyes was, "I mustn't go back to the condo by myself." Although she had good reason to want another pair of hands for packing and some moral support, Connie, who considered herself to have psychic tendencies, would later be convinced that at that moment she'd had a premonition of disaster ahead.

After she'd had her morning tea, Connie called up her neighbor, Sharon Porto. "Sharon, how would you like to come in with me today to Los Angeles?" Connie asked.

"What for?" Sharon wondered.

"To help me pack up this stuff of Vicki's."

"Are you sure Vicki wouldn't mind?" Sharon asked.

"At this stage of the game," Connie said, "Vicki doesn't have a pot to pee in. If you want to come, come."

The two women arrived about noon, finding Marvin alone in the living room. "They're upstairs," he reported to Connie, waving his hand in the direction of the staircase.

"Who's upstairs?"

"Gordon and Vicki," Marvin said. "They really tied one on last night."

The two women set to work on the packing while Marvin sat at the kitchen table, chainsmoking and drinking coffee, clearly annoyed with Vicki for dallying with Gordon when she ought to be helping her mother pack her things. "She's taking advantage of you," Marvin told both women. "She's using you to do her dirty work."

"Look, Marvin," Connie said, "You go home. This is not your responsibility. We'll handle things here."

"No, I'm staying," Marvin replied. "I'm going to settle this today with Vicki once and for all."

Connie thought this was not entirely a bad idea. "Good," She told him. "I hope you do."

Marvin moved out of the kitchen and went and sat at the foot of the staircase, still smoking furiously. Later, he may have gone out for a while. Both women were doing their best not to ignore him.

Sharon, meanwhile, had discovered Vicki's collection of spices.

"I never saw so many spices in my whole life," she laughed. She started reading labels of the more exotic ones and speculating aloud on what they might be used for.

While this was going on, Gordon Basichis came down, grabbed a soda from the refrigerator, and left, not bothering to offer more than nod in Connie's direction. Vicki arrived downstairs a few moments later. "Hi," she said to Sharon with a smile, "I'm crazy Vicki."

It seemed that Vicki had asked Gordon, not Marvin, to drive her out to take her first look at the Burbank condo. Why she wanted Gordon to do this was not exactly clear, except that she may have already halfway made up her mind that her first look would also be her last.

After they'd left, Marvin insisted that Connie and Sharon come upstairs with him to look at some suicide notes he'd found on Vicki's night table. The notes, scribbled on pages torn from an unlined memo pad, weren't new. They were originally written by Vicki on March 31, the day she'd taken an overdose of Valium. The question was, why had Vicki hung on to the notes for three months, and why had she taken them out now and left them by her bed? Marvin claims that Connie was almost as upset by this discovery as he was. Connie remembers otherwise. Vicki kept everything, and it was no secret that she'd been morose and dwelling on the mistakes of the past.

Gordon dropped Vicki off at around two-forty-five and left without coming into the house. It was obvious that the Burbank condo had not met with their approval. Vicki surveyed the chaos in the kitchen, the stacks of half-filled cartons and half-empty cabinets, and languidly set about brewing herself a cup of tea. "Mom," she told Connie, "this thing with Marvin is not working out."

"Fine." said Connie. "You can always put your things in storage and come stay with me for a while."

After finishing her tea, Vicki announced that she was too wrecked to do anything useful. "I can't face all this," she said. "I'm going upstairs to take a nap." It was already three o'clock in the afternoon, and Vicki told them that she was going to set her alarm for six.

In the meantime, Sharon and Connie had been wrapping up the few possessions of value that were displayed in the dining room breakfront, mostly odds and ends of good crystal. They debated about whether to trust these items to the movers and decided it would be safer for Connie to take them to her house for the time being.

They were in the process of carrying some of the pieces down to the basement-level parking lot when Marvin joined them and apologized profusely. He and Vicki had just had a terrific argument, and he was sorry if all the yelling had disturbed them. His behavior was rather perplexing, since they hadn't heard a sound.

Around 4:30, Vicki appeared again and announced that she hadn't been able to get to sleep. She and Marvin retired to the dining alcove where they started thumbing through the real-estate listings in the paper. Vicki could be heard listing her reasons for being dissatisfied with the place Marvin had already found, reasons having to do mostly with the location. "It's the middle of nowhere," she complained. "It's the boondocks." Marvin, at this point, seemed more exasperated than angry. "What's the matter," he said, "Burbank's not fucking good enough for you?"

At some point during the discussion, however, Vicki did pick up the phone and place a call to Elephant Movers, a short-distance company serving North Hollywood.

The man at Elephant Movers would remember the call specifically because the woman on the line sounded "almost desperate," as if she were pleading with him to take the job at any price. He dealt with all kinds of nervous customers, the ones who were afraid to trust their precious belongings to him and the ones who were prepared to haggle endlessly over prices. But this was something new. The woman wanted to have her stuff moved out the very next day, yet she was either unable or unwilling to tell him where it was going to be moved to.

"Lady, I've got to have a destination to write down here," he complained.

"Can't I tell you tomorrow?"

"But without the destination, I can't give you a quote. See, the price is figured partly on mileage. It's thirty-six bucks an hour plus mileage."

"Oh, Thirty-four, did you say?" She sounded really spaced out, almost resentful over being asked to focus her attention on these boring details.

"Nah. Thirty-six. Plus mileage. If you'll tell me where you moving to, I can figure the charge right now."

"Oh, that's okay. It doesn't matter."

"Lady, it does matter. I told you, I got to have something to write on my trip order. Is it a long haul or what?"

Finally, just when he was about to hang up in exasperation, a man's voice came on the line and said they'd be moving to "somewhere up in the Burbank Hills."

Todd called a bit later in the afternoon to say that he and his girlfriend Lisa were in Hollywood and asked if his grandmother would drive down to pick them up.

"Where's Sunset and La Brea?" Connie asked Marvin.

He shook his head. "That's a bad area. You don't want to go down there alone. I'll drive you in the Oldsmobile."

Almost as soon as Todd and Lisa got into the back seat, Todd spotted his baseball bat lying on the shelf under the rear windshield. "That's my bat!" he exclaimed. "What are you doing with my bat?"

Marvin muttered something about how you never know who'll you meet or what might happen when you're driving in some areas.

They continued on, the air thick with tension. "I'm taking Lisa home first," Marvin announced, out of nowhere. "Lisa's not going to spend the night at your grandmother's."

Todd reacted angrily. "You're not my father!" he said. "What gives you the right to tell me what to do?"

Nevertheless, Lisa was dropped off first. They continued in silence until Marvin abruptly swung the car into a supermarket parking lot. He went into the market and came out carrying two cans of dog food. "Katy's got to eat," he announced reproachfully.

When they all arrived back at Colfax Avenue, Connie realized that she was not going to be able to keep her promise to Sharon to get her back to Montclair by dinnertime. Marvin then went out to the local McDonald's and brought back some hamburgers.

A few minutes after he returned, Vicki announced she'd just finished the little bit of white wine that was left in the fridge. Marvin waited until she'd left the room and then pulled Connie aside. "She wants wine," he said in a stage whisper.

Connie shrugged. Marvin went out for wine.

It was clear by now that then packing was never going to get finished, deadline or not. Sharon wanted to go home, for one thing. She had been feeling embarrassed and out of place all day. It wasn't easy being thrust into the middle of other people's quarrels.

Todd was also eager to escape. He'd been sleeping over at his grandmother's most nights recently, and though he'd originally planned to stay around that night to get his things ready for the movers, he was by now eager to get out of there. "Maybe I'll go home with you, Grandma," he suggested.

"Good," said Marvin. "That's a good idea. You go with your grandmother, Todd."

Todd went up to his room to throw together a few things. In the meantime, Marvin and Vicki sat down at the kitchen table and began to argue about their plans to drive over to Thousand Oaks to pick up the certified check for $3,500 from his grandmother. Marvin felt that Vicki owed it to the woman to at least make an appearance and thank her in person. "Go get yourself cleaned up, Vicki," he pleaded.

"Not tonight," said Vicki, "I'm tired. I can't deal with it. We'll get up early tomorrow."

"Tomorrow," Marvin pointed out, "the movers will be here. You know you'll never be up early enough to go over there and get back before they come."

It was shortly before nine when Connie, Sharon, and Todd departed, and Marvin announced that he was going to take the dog out for its evening walk. A chainlink fence separated the row of townhouse condos Vicki lived in from the all-but-bone-dry concrete viaduct that Angelenos call the Los Angeles River. In those days, though no longer, the gate in the fence was unlocked, and a number of residents had taken to using the viaduct corridor as a sort of oversize dogrun. Katy, the Doberman, loved the place, and Marvin Pancoast was conscientious about seeing that the dog got a chance to stretch her legs and romp. Todd had not been around much, and Vicki, though she walked the dog when it had to be done, didn't bother to give the animal the exercise it needed.

Although Marvin would have been just as happy to go alone, Vicki insisted on coming along. The time of day had arrived when she usually managed to shake off her lethargy and to gather enough energy to pursue her ongoing fight with insomnia.

During the walk, Vicki managed to tell him about her reasons for hating the place he'd chosen for them to share. According to Marvin, she confessed that she was "scared" by the prospect of ending in Burbank, in an apartment that was "beneath anything she'd ever had before."

"I don't want to be stuck way out in the boonies," she complained again.

"Vicki, we got no choice," Marvin said.

"I don't care."

"But tomorrow's D-Day," Marvin insisted, using the term they'd borrowed to refer to the date when the dispossess order came due. "The movers are coming first thing in the morning."

"There's still time to find another place. If I have to live in a dump, I at least want a dump in a better location. South of Ventura."

She then started talking about the possibility that she would have the movers put her things into temporary storage.

Others would later claim that Vicki had told Marvin at this point that she'd decided against moving in with him. This, after all, was the impression she'd given Connie earlier that day, and it fit with her relying on Gordon to take her out to inspect the condo that afternoon. Marvin insists she said no such thing. The live-together arrangement was still on, as far as he knew; it was just that the particular locale he'd selected was being vetoed. Vicki would be happy to live with him, happy to have him pay her way—but not in Burbank.

Marvin wasn't feeling rejected, just frustrated. A tendency to spend money he didn't have, to buy things he couldn't afford, had plagued him all his life, and his spending bouts usually preceded more serious symptoms of an impending breakdown. For once, though, he was being entirely sensible, and he was familiar enough with real-estate values in the area to know just how tough it would be to find an affordable place for three people and one large dog in the hills south of Ventura Boulevard.

He'd done everything he knew how to please Vicki. He'd made himself into her "little slave." All day long for the last three weeks, Vicki had sat around in her bedroom giving orders like "the queen of Sheba." All he'd heard was, "Marvin fix my hair, . . ." "Marvin, rub my feet, . . ." "Marvin bring me a cup of tea." And a little thing like making Vicki a cup of tea had become a major production number. Something was wrong with her tastebuds, probably from all the pills she'd been taking. He'd pour in seven teaspoonsful of sugar, so much that stuff just sank to the bottom of the glass and refused to dissolve, and still she'd complain to him about the bitter taste.

Still, there was no reason for him to assume that this particular whim concerning a better apartment amounted to an ultimatum. Vicki's bossy moods didn't last indefinitely, and knowing her,

she'd change her mind at least five more times before tomorrow
came. In the end, no doubt she'd follow the line of least resistance
and move into the place he'd already found.

When they got back to the condo, the two of them went upstairs
to Vicki's bedroom and settled down on her huge bed to watch
TV. *Dynasty* was on, and even in summer reruns, it was Vicki's
favorite TV show.

Curiously, Vicki also had a personal reason for taking an
interest in the show. Gordon's wife Marcia oversaw ongoing series
at ABC, and *Dynasty* was among her projects. Marcia claimed that
the decision to beef up the character of Alexis into a starring
vehicle for Joan Collins had been her idea. So it was just possible
that Alexis' growing resemblance to Betsy Bloomingdale—or, at
least, to Vicki Morgan's mental image of Betsy—was not entirely
coincidental.

Marvin watched the show, too, but with growing uneasiness. It
was on his mind that he ought to go to see his grandmother that
evening as promised, even if he couldn't get Vicki to bestir herself
to come along.

"I think I'll go over to Thousand Oaks," he announced when
the show ended. But Vicki wouldn't hear of it. "Don't leave me
here alone," she said. "If you do, the way I'm feeling I'll probably
start freaking out."

Marvin got up and took a shower and blow-dried his hair
anyway, but he couldn't quite find the energy to ignore Vicki's
pleas and get himself out the door. Vicki pointed out that there
was only one car now, not counting the wrecked Mustang that was
sitting in the garage. The Jeep was still over on Fairfax where
Marvin had left it the night before.

The Mustang was another sore spot with Marvin. He pointed
out that he had given her the Mustang to use, and she had
promptly gone out in it drunk and totaled it. The problem with
the Jeep wasn't his fault. As for the Oldsmobile Cutlass, he was
still making payments on it of $225 a month. If Vicki expected
him to keep it around to be at her disposal, maybe she should
consider helping him out with the payments. For that matter,
maybe she should pay him for the Mustang—he'd merely loaned
it to her for a while, never dreaming that she'd wreck it.

Twice before midnight, Vicki called up Gordon at home and
asked for his advice. She couldn't get any rest, she told Gordon,
and she was still debating what she should do about the condo
Marvin had found. Should they take it or not? She was also

wondering whether Marvin had a point about the Mustang.

Since Vicki had no money anyway, the latter problem was hardly of more than theoretical importance. Gordon suggested that it wasn't something that had to be settled that night. He sympathized about the moving-day crisis, but again there wasn't a whole lot he could do, considering the hour. According to Marvin, it was Gordon who eventually suggested that Marvin go out and pick up the early edition of the next day's paper so that they could check out the new listings.

Vicki thought it was a great idea. Surely they'd find something listed that was better than that dreary place she'd seen today. Maybe even a house! "Get dressed and go up to Dale's and get the Thursday morning papers," she told Marvin. "Gordon says lots of new listings come out on Thursday. And while you're out," she told Marvin, "pick me up a bag of chips. I'm hungry. I could use some munchies."

Marvin thought the whole idea was asinine. He'd spent the better part of the last three weeks househunting while Vicki couldn't be bothered focusing her attention on the problem. Now, at midnight on D-Day, she and Gordon thought that she could just pick up the next day's papers and find exactly what she wanted.

Marvin grumbled, but he went.

When he got to Dale's, he discovered that the morning papers hadn't come in yet and weren't expected until two A.M. He picked up a bag of Fritos and some candy bars. When he got back, Vicki tried to talk him into driving down Ventura Boulevard looking for a place that would have the papers on sale. He refused, and she seemed to lose interest. She nibbled at the contents of the bag of chips and agreed that she had been dumb to think that it would be possible to locate a new place at the last minute. She finished off what was left of the bottle of wine he'd bought earlier in the evening, took two more Valiums, and tried once more to get to sleep.

According to the story that Marvin later told the police and *Los Angeles Herald-Examiner* reporter Andy Furillo, instead of trying to rest, Vicki launched into a talking jag. She seemed to get more wide awake as the night went on. He, meanwhile, was exhausted after a lousy day on Tuesday and practically no rest the night before. Also, he felt guilty about not getting over to pick up the check from his grandmother—$3,500 was a substantial amount of money, and his grandmother had gone to the trouble of getting a cashier's check. And he hadn't even bothered to come pick it up. Tomorrow, he told himself, he'd have to get up at six A.M. to get the check and be back in time to greet the movers. The packing wasn't even done and, knowing Vicki, she'd still be in bed when the crew showed up.

As much to calm himself as her, Marvin found a bottle of baby oil among the jumble of cosmetics on the nightstand and began massaging Vicki's feet. It was a routine that sometimes succeeded in relaxing Vicki, but tonight it seemed to be having the opposite effect. She was really wired and getting more so as the hours passed.

While he was rubbing her feet, Vicki started reminiscing about Alfred. At first she talked about how much she hated him—hated him for breaking his promises to take care of her for life, hated him for dying on her and leaving her like this. Then, as usually happened, she shifted gears and put the blame on Betsy. "I could kill her for interfering with us," she complained. "It's all her fault."

By now, she changed her mind about Alfred. He was a wonderful man. If only he were still alive, she'd never be in this rotten situation.

Marvin had heard this refrain so often that he was able to tune out the details at will, but the gist of it was that Alfred had taught her to have high standards. With him, everything had been strictly first class. Houses in the canyons above Beverly Hills. A Mercedes for her to drive. The best hairdressers and aerobics instructors in town. The best masseurs, too. Really *top* people.

In self-defense, Marvin retreated into role of clown. "Well, honey," he said, affecting a very nelly drawl, "I . . . ain't . . . no . . . Bloomingdale, y'know."

Vicki giggled at this. Of course, he wasn't. The very notion was hilarious.

"Come on, Vicki," Marvin pleaded, putting away the bottle of baby oil. "I'm bushed. Let's call it a day."

But Vicki wanted to hear some music. If Marvin would just run downstairs and find the tape she wanted, she promised she'd listen quietly and try her best to doze off. What she wanted to hear was Michael Jackson—not the most soporific music in the world, but that was what she was in the mood for.

Once again, Marvin dragged himself out of bed and rummaged around in the packing boxes in the living room until he found the tape she'd asked for.

When he got back upstairs, she was sitting bolt upright in bed, wide awake and grinning at him. Deliberately, he reached over and turned off the light, then settled himself on the other side of the bed. "Lay your head down and count backwards one hundred, and you'll go to sleep," he told her.

For what seemed like hours but was probably more like ten or fifteen minutes, he lay in the dark, rigidly immobile, hoping that if Vicki thought he was out for the night she'd give up and go to sleep as well. But it was not good. He could feel her beside him, making small movements in time to the beat of the music.

He sat up. "Vicki, it's not good. I'm going to Thousand Oaks." At least there he could sleep and be reasonably refreshed for the ordeal of the next day.

"Don't go, Marv. I told you, I'll freak out if I have to be alone all night. Don't walk out on me."

Marvin turned to face the wall again, and this time he did manage to drift off. It was a troubled half-sleep at best, though, one of those false starts on the road to oblivion when he could almost watch himself sinking deeper and deeper into complete blackness, only to be jerked back to consciousness like a puppet on a string. Alert again, he noticed that the palms of his hands were drenched in sweat, and he'd begun to shiver uncontrollably. The tape had shut itself off by now, but beside him Vicki was still tossing and turning.

He ignored her.

She started to giggle again.

He ignored this, too.

Then she sat up in bed and fumbled around until she located her cigarettes and gum on the night table. He was aware of her lighting up, of the smell of cigarette smoke drifting in his direction, and finally, of the faint sizzle and sickly sweet smell caused by her stubbing out the half-smoked cigarette in a wad of barely chewed gum.

Over the years, the gum and cigarette routine had become a nervous habit, a personal tic that Marvin had seen so often that he called it Vicki's "trademark." Without ever having consciously analyzed why she did it, he was smart enough to sense that, on some level, it was a gesture of covert aggression, a way of expressing her contempt for the world. He seethed in silence as she repeated the whole ritual several times over. Then, unable to contain his irritation any longer, he fled the room.

Downstairs in the kitchen, he heated up yesterday's coffee and lit a cigarette of his own while he tried to figure out what to do now.

Marvin later told Andy Furillo that it was while sitting downstairs at the kitchen table, wondering how he could get Vicki to stop "needling" him, that he happened to think of the baseball bat he'd left in the back seat of the Oldsmobile.

But in a taped statement given to LAPD Detective Rush, a day and a half before he talked to Furillo, Marvin told a somewhat different story. Marvin told Rush that he'd found Todd's bat in the house. "They had cleaned out his room and there was some baseball things or tennis balls and the bat was there and I just grabbed it." He took the bat upstairs, where it occurred to him that it would be better to strangle Vicki, using the tie of the heavy velour men's bathrobe that he'd borrowed to wear earlier in the evening after his shower.

For some reason, he changed his mind. He dropped the tie in the hallway and then just sat there, thinking for an hour and forty-five minutes. Then he went into the spare bathroom and turned the taps on full force, to cover the sound of what he was going to do.

The light in the hall was on, but the bedroom light was out by now. Vicki was lying in the dark but still awake. "I was afraid she'd see me," Marvin told Rush. "I just walked in. I got the lighting just right, and walked in and just started hitting her."

The first blow of the baseball bat landed solidly, striking Vicki's skull with a sickening crack. But instead of succumbing silently, as he'd expected, she reared up in bed, whimpering and throwing her arms out in front of her to avoid further blows. Panicky, he hit her again. And again.

When he was sure that Vicki had stopped moving, that she wasn't going to bother him anymore, he went downstairs, put on his blue windbreaker, and stuck a pack of cigarettes in the pocket. He found his personal address book, one of his most precious possessions, and put it in the trunk of the Oldsmobile.

Marvin arrived at the North Hollywood police station shortly after three A.M. By ten minutes after five he was in the interrogation room, giving his taped statement to Detective Rush. At the beginning of the interview, his statements were somewhat rambling. He seemed more concerned with making sure Connie was notified before she could leave Montclair to go to the condo than with his own fate, and he was eager to make sure that Detective Rush knew exactly who Vicki was, or had been—about

Bloomingdale, and the palimony suit, and the book . . . and how her story was "very political."

Nevertheless, after a couple of minutes, the suspect settled down to give an account that was reasonably coherent and at times all too graphic. All the elements of a confession were there, except perhaps a completely straightforward statement about intent.

Marvin said that Vicki's behavior had been annoying him all day. "She didn't want to deal with anything. She didn't do anything at all today. And, anyway, she just went on about Vicki this, Vicki this, Vicki this. I couldn't take it anymore."

He said he'd hit Vicki because "she wouldn't shut up." And he added, "I hit her enough times on the head so she'd go to sleep."

"Okay," said Rush, "When you say *go to sleep,* you mean dead?"

"Go to sleep," replied Marvin. "She wouldn't complain anymore. She wanted to die." He then went on to talk about the March 31 suicide attempt.

A TALE OF TAPES

///

The *mobile camera crews arrived shortly before eight* A.M. *in time to film the corpse being removed to a waiting ambulance.*

At 8:30, a woman reporter from the Associated Press rang the doorbell on Condo C, the Graydons' townhouse, and said, "I came to talk to you about your neighbor."

Graydon, the ex-FBI man, had no idea what she was talking about. He and his wife had been awakened about three and a half hours earlier by a policeman who wanted to know if he'd heard any unusual noises coming from next door. Graydon hadn't made much of the police query. He and his wife had just returned from their second home in Palm Desert the evening before; they were exhausted from the trip and the unpacking, and Graydon had assumed that the police were just checking out a burglar alarm that had gone off. There'd been a rash of break-ins in the neighborhood recently so a lot of people had alarms, and the things were always getting set off by mistake. Graydon, whose condo shared a party wall with unit D, told the police that he hadn't heard a thing. "But then, I never do."

Now, just a few hours later, there was a reporter telling him that there'd been a murder next door and that the dead woman was Vicki Morgan, the one who had been suing for $10 million in palimony. Graydon couldn't think of much to tell her. "There was no gossip," he recalled later. "Nothing. Because no one knew who she was."

Connie Laney didn't get into North Hollywood until almost noon. Not up to driving, she'd called her son-in-law, Barbara's husband, Vern Gaston, to pick her up and go with her to see the police, and two of them went straight to the stationhouse, where they met Detective Bill Welch.

Connie never did go back to Colfax Avenue. "Bill Welch said to my son-in-law, 'Don't let her go in there,'" she recalls. "So I never went near the place."

Instead, Connie had Vern drive her over to the Daves' house, where there was some discussion about what to do next. Murder or not, the landlords were still going to want their property back, and there seemed no point in dragging out the process.

Sally Talbert had volunteered to be the one to go into the condo and see what needed to be done about getting the boxes and furniture moved out. Matt, her fifteen-year-old son, was worried about his mother having to do a job like that alone and so, while she was at the police station picking up the key, he went on ahead, expecting to meet her there and lend a hand.

At the condo, Matt found the door unlocked, so he just walked in. The place was a mess, packing boxes all around and drawers half open, partly as a result of the moving and partly from the police poking around. Matt went upstairs and stripped the blood-stained sheets off the bed where the body had been and turned the mattress, wanting to spare his mother the sight. Then he collected some things he thought might be valuable—a few pieces of jewelry, and a bunch of cassettes from the downstairs closet since he knew Vicki taped phone calls. He didn't think the video tapes upstairs were worth bothering about.

"We were worried," Connie said later, "because the door was open, and the door should have been shut." Reporters had been hanging around the area all morning, and Connie had assumed there would be a police guard or a seal on the door. Instead, the place wasn't even locked. "Somebody else had to have gone in here," she speculated.

The next day, Friday, Vicki's half-brother John, her sister, her sister's husband, and a few friends went down to the condo and supervised the moving of her belongings.

Aside from a lingering suspicion that someone might have been poking around inside the condo on Thursday, family members were shocked but not surprised by Marvin's confession. "He never seemed crazy to me," Connie said a few weeks after the killing, "but he was angry that day."

Cindy Stonehouse first heard about the murder when her ex-husband called her up to say, "Hey, you'll never guess who's in the news . . ." Her immediate reaction was that there had to be something cockeyed about the story. She just couldn't see Marvin as a murderer.

A dizzy, thirty-eight-year-old ash-blonde, Stonehouse was in some ways a less exotic version of Vicki Morgan, and like Vicki, she first got to know Marvin in a private psychiatric hospital. Suffering from depression and nervous exhaustion after a difficult divorce, according to Stonehouse, she had signed herself into Woodview-Calabasas hospital in early 1979; during her brief stay there, she and Marvin became buddies. Before that, she'd known him slightly for years as a customer of the 7-eleven store she'd managed on Wilcox Avenue in Thousand Oaks.

Marvin certainly had his emotional ups and downs, but during the several years that they'd been close friends, Stonehouse had never known him to be aggressive or threatening. On the contrary, his problem was that he was too meek and mild. Marvin was the kind of friend who was constantly offering to drive people places, running errands and doing favors that were sometimes a little embarrassing because no one could possibly return them all. He also apologized a lot.

Stonehouse was especially outraged that the papers were portraying Marvin as a nobody, a hanger-on in the so-called glamorous world of Vicki Morgan. In her view, it was exactly the opposite. "Everyone's treating him as if he were a non-sequential [sic] person, and he isn't, believe me. I've seen pictures of him with Rita Hayworth, Gene Kelly. This guy was really in the upper echelon of Hollywood. And now that Hollywood's turned their backs on him, that's their problem."

As soon as she saw the papers on Friday, July 8, Stonehouse decided to take it upon herself to call Marvin's mother, Christy Pancoast.

"Marvin's in jail and he's saying all these things that could really hurt him," Stonehouse told Christy.

Stonehouse had a suggestion. "I know this wonderful lawyer," she said. "He's just terrific—you know, super. You're in no frame of mind to deal with this stuff right now. Why don't you let me call him? Just put it in my hands."

As deliberate and phlegmatic as Cindy Stonehouse was excitable, Christy Pancoast saw no particular reason why this woman she hardly knew should be involved. As she recalled it, she didn't encourage Stonehouse to get in touch with the lawyer friend of hers, but perhaps she didn't forbid it in so many words either. She was so taken aback that she hadn't known quite what to say.

It wasn't until the next day, when Stonehouse called again, that Christy Pancoast realized she had better put her foot down. "Don't you worry about this, Cindy," she said. "I'll take care of this myself."

Christy called her longtime friend Arthur Barens to ask him to go down the jail that morning, Saturday, to see what could be done for Marvin, but in the meantime Stonehouse had already spoken to Robert K. Steinberg.

Stonehouse also made a few phone calles to reporters on Marvin's behalf, making sure they knew what Marvin was really like. "Marvin's, like, one of the best people I've ever known," she said. "But he's just had such a guilt trip laid on him from birth that if anyone says, 'You did something bad,' he believes it. I believe somebody else came in and killed her, and handed him a baseball bat and said, 'Look, you did it.' And he would believe it."

She added, for good measure, that her diaries were no doubt as interesting as anything Vicki Morgan could have written and that she was planning to sell them for $300,000.

Robert K. Steinberg was a familiar figure to his fellow L.A. county attorneys, a competent, even talented, courtroom performer but one whose personal eccentricities and insistent self-promotion had made him an object of scorn to many of his colleagues.

Beginning as an associate of the prominent celebrity attorney Samuel S. Brody, Steinberg had inherited much of the practice after Brody died along with actress Jayne Mansfield in a 1967 car wreck. Perhaps the high point of Steinberg's career came when he represented Virginia Graham, a cellmate of Manson family member Susan Atkins. Graham, who eventually claimed to have

knowledge of a Manson family hit list that included the names of
Frank Sinatra and Elizabeth Taylor, became a key prosecution
witness. It was as a result of this case that Steinberg became close
to Vincent Bugliosi, the chief prosecutor of Manson and author
of the best-selling book on the case. In the summer of 1983, the
two men were still sharing an office on Wilshire Boulevard.

While Steinberg, whose practice was a mix of criminal, divorce,
and personal injury cases, continued to have numerous satisfied
clients, his reputation for erratic behavior had grown during the
last several years. Steinberg had for instance recently told several
reporters that he had been hired to represent John Z. DeLorean
in his federal narcotics case—a claim prompting DeLorean's
actual attorney Howard Weitzmann to accuse him of attempting
to improperly "solicit the case."

On Saturday afternoon, July 9, in response to Cindy Stonehouse's call, Steinberg visited Marvin in jail. Whatever was said
during that brief meeting must have made a big impression.

Although Steinberg later claimed that he hadn't received the
tapes until Saturday evening, hadn't viewed the first segment of
the tapes with his two friends until eleven that night, and hadn't
finished identifying the participants until Sunday afternoon, immediately after his Saturday interview with Pancoast he began to
call reporters and spread the word he had been retained as
Marvin's defense attorney.

David Holley of the *Los Angeles Times,* one of the reporters who
promptly called Steinberg back to ask about his plans for the
defense, found him already very excited about the case. "You
know this case is really much bigger than anyone realizes," Steinberg said. "I mean, there are tapes. And there is, you know, so
much more . . ." Later, when asked how he could have predicted
the tapes' existence before his "mystery woman" even showed up,
Steinberg claimed that it was Holley who had said, "Yes, there are
tapes . . ."

Steinberg's calls to the press stepped up on Sunday, as he left
messages around town that there was more to the case than a
simple murder and that he was going to have major revelations to
make in a press conference called for his office on Monday
afternoon.

The story that Steinberg told at his Monday press conference
had all the elements of a Dashiell Hammett or Raymond Chandler parody: The hero alone in his office late on a logy Saturday
afternoon . . . The blond dame who appears out of nowhere,

leaves the evidence in a shopping bag, and then departs without so much as giving her name . . . scandal and rampant eroticism lurking in the background of what at first seemed to be an all-American crime of violence . . . and, finally, more loose ends than Chandler at his most cavalier would have left untied.

When he said goodbye to Pancoast at the county jail, Steinberg told reporters, he'd left him with a handful of quarters to use for making phone calls.

Later that afternoon, Steinberg continued, he was relaxing in his colonial-style Cheviot Hills home when he received a call forwarded from his answering service. The woman caller refused to give her name but insisted that she had some evidence relevant to the Morgan murder case. Intrigued, he agreed to cancel his afternoon racquetball game and meet the woman in his office on Wilshire Boulevard and Palm Drive.

It was an unusually hot Saturday, and Wilshire Boulevard was all but deserted, the office building itself empty except for a few cleaning people. He entered, leaving both the door to his private office and the outer door ajar, and waited to see what would happen.

He didn't have to wait long. Just minutes later, the mystery woman appeared. Steinberg described her as blond, about five-two, and average looking, neither young nor old.

The woman reached into a Gucci shopping bag and produced three Betamax-type video cassettes. "This is Vicki Morgan and some of her friends," she said.

"Fine, but who are you, and where did these things come from?" Steinberg asked.

But the blond still refused to give her name. She was just someone who thought that the tapes might "help Marvin."

Her attitude, Steinberg recalled, was, "Do you want them or don't you?"

Steinberg decided that he did want them.

He had invited two friends of his to drop in at his house that evening, one an attorney in private practice and one a lawyer with the Department of Justice strike force. One of the men happened to own a Betamax recorder, and Steinberg had him bring it along so that he could have a look at the tapes.

Steinberg popped one of the tapes into the Betamax, and much to their shock, he and his friends found themselves watching a black-and-white video of an orgy—consisting, said Steinberg, "of sadomasochistic sex acts that didn't appear to be violent" taking place in a "playroom or living room." One of the other two men, he said, recognized the participants on one of the tapes as Alfred Bloomingdale and Vicki Morgan.

Later, with the help of some magazines lying around the house, including an issue of *Fortune* magazine, Steinberg said, he was able to identify the other men shown in the tapes as a U.S. congressman, two Reagan appointees "of ambassadorial but not of cabinet level," and two prominent businessmen from the oil and gas industries who happened also to be Reagan supporters.

Even as they were busy scribbling down the details of this melodramatic story, some of the reporters present smelled a hoax. Among the skeptics was *Los Angeles Times* reporter David Johnston. Johnston hung around Steinberg's office for nearly three hours on Monday, listening to other reporters ply Steinberg with questions and watching as he taped interview segments for several news shows. It began to dawn on him that certain details of Steinberg's account were, well, evolving as the afternoon wore on.

After a while, he started challenging some of contradictions. "Wait a second," he'd interrupt, "you said there were three guys in this tape and three in the other, then later you said it was four and two. Which is it?"

And Steinberg would say, "Oh, it was four and two," or whatever.

What really bothered Johnston was that Steinberg had criticized his article on the murder that had appeared in Friday's *Los Angeles Times*. Johnston had included a few lines describing a sexual encounter between Morgan and Bloomingdale, saying that Morgan had often "watched in horror as other women stripped and crawled on the floor, partly bound with neckties, while Bloomingdale rode on their backs and beat them, his mouth drooling." Steinberg had complained that it was wrong of Johnston to have written such a thing and vulgar and irresponsible of the *Los Angeles Times* to have printed it. They shouldn't publish such things, Steinberg had said, because "this kind of thing feeds on itself."

And now, it seemed, Steinberg was doing his best to make his own prediction come true.

When Steinberg appeared on ABC's *Nightline* that evening, Ted Koppel immediately zeroed in on another bizarre twist in Steinberg's story—his claim that he was somehow doing the Reagan administration a favor.

By this time Steinberg had announced that he was not Marvin Pancoast's attorney after all—he had, he said, withdrawn from the case. And since Barens, the new attorney, was not interested in seeing the tapes, his plan was to offer them to the White House. If, after twenty-four hours, President Reagan hadn't taken him up on the offer, he planned to burn them.

"I would imagine," noted Koppel dryly, "that the President would want to stay three thousand miles away from those tapes if he possibly could."

Steinberg agreed that "this is the kind of thing the country doesn't need right now." But he went on to say that he hadn't really had any choice about releasing the story. "Ted, I'm not being good to you. . . . Unfortunately, the L.A. police department, when they came to the site [of the crime], picked up some books and some videos, it turns out now, that some reporters are checking out with some other names on them. UPI, when they called me, asked me about those videos, and it was my suspicion that Marvin, my ex-client, probably called on the telephone about it."

One of the early reports emanating from Steinberg's office press conference had came over the car radio as Michael Dave was heading for Vicki's memorial service at Forest Lawn. Dave had been mulling over the remarks he planned to make at the service, searching for the right words to express the qualities in Vicki that had inspired the affection and loyalty of her friends, in spite of her all-too-obvious failings. Steinberg's announcement was not only a shocker, but the timing couldn't have been worse. Dave had never heard of any tapes like the ones Steinberg was describing and was skeptical that any such things existed—still, with Vicki you had to allow for surprises.

Reluctant to upset Vicki's family and to destroy the mood of the service and the impromptu social gathering afterward, Dave nevertheless conducted a discreet "informal poll" of the guests, asking each in turn if they'd ever heard of such tapes. None of them had, Dave said later.

Dave was still at the postfuneral gathering at the Talberts' around ten P.M., when Detective Bill Welch got through to him. By that time, the mood of what had been planned as an informal, low-key evening was already deteriorating, with guests huddling in front of the oversize TV in the den, flipping from one channel to the next to catch Steinberg's successive appearances. Welch told Dave he was thinking about getting a warrant to search Connie's house and recover any tapes that might have been removed from the condo.

Dave protested. Connie, he said, was just getting over the ordeal of the funeral. It was already after ten at night, she was tired, and it would be wrong to put her through the experience of having her house and her daughter's belongings searched by the police.

"I can't help it," Welch said. "They're rattling my cage."

After further discussion with Deputy DA Mike Carroll, Welch agreed to drop the matter for the time being.

The next morning, as the saying goes, the plot thickened.

Concerned about Steinberg's promise—or threat—to destroy the tapes unless the White House asked him not to, Mike Carroll called Steinberg at home at 8:30 in the morning. Carroll warned that he and Detective Welch would like to see the tapes themselves to decide whether they had any evidentiary value in the Morgan homicide case. Either bring the tapes in voluntarily, Carroll said, or he might be forced to subpoena them.

When Steinberg arrived at his office about an hour later, it was already crawling with reporters, some waiting in the main reception area and others camped out in a side room that served as a combination conference room and law library. Steinberg made a brief statement that his wife, who sometimes served as his secretary, had been unable to get his call through to the White House as yet. He then retreated into his private office and shut the door, refusing all calls.

Around eleven, Steinberg phoned Mike Carroll. "The tapes are gone," he said, his voice vibrating with emotion, "they've been stolen."

Carroll, who'd been expecting some sort of stall tactics all along, could only manage a sarcastic, "Isn't that interesting?" before handing the phone to Detective Welch.

As Welch later recalled, Steinberg's first words to him were, "Bill, I fucked up." Steinberg said that since he'd been planning to play racquetball on Saturday when the mystery woman showed up at his office, he'd stashed the tapes she gave him in his gym bag. On Monday, he'd left the tapes, still in the gym bag, locked in the trunk of his El Dorado. Then when he saw how much fuss his press conference was generating, he'd become concerned that someone might break into the car and steal the tapes, so on Monday afternoon he'd brought the bag up to his office and left it in the law library. This morning a bunch of reporters had been using the law library to make phone calls, and now the tapes were gone.

Steinberg told Welch that the tapes had been taken by a member of the press and "I know who it is."

Welch in turn gruffly suggested that since Steinberg had apparently been the victim of a burglary, he ought to make a report to the Beverly Hills police.

A few minutes later, Steinberg emerged from his private office and angrily ordered the reporters to leave the premises, muttering that the tapes were gone, they'd been stolen.

At 11:50 he called the Beverly Hills police station and told the dispatcher, "Ah, I'm having a little difficulty with some reporters. . . . Ah, they, some, one of them has stolen some valuable tapes . . ."

The dispatcher sent out three uniformed officers, but by that time, quite a few of the reporters had left the building.

By Tuesday afternoon, Robert K. Steinberg was the most unpopular man in Los Angeles.

Deputy DA Carroll got a subpoena that very afternoon, ordering Steinberg to be prepared to testify and to produce the tapes— "just in case [he] decides he still has them," said Carroll—at an evidentiary hearing in Van Nuys on July 25.

The press, already suspecting that it had been manipulated into promoting a hoax, was collectively insulted by the attempt to pin the tapes' disappearance on them. Numerous articles appeared dwelling on the inconsistencies in Steinberg's own statements and on certain embarrassing episodes in his past—in particular, his ill-fated 1969 campaign for mayor, during which Steinberg had accused then City Councilman Tom Bradley of being an anti-Semite.

Filing a false police report was only a misdemeanor charge, but someone in the DA's office—no one cares to say who—decided that it might be interesting and worthwhile to put the matter before a grand jury. Deputy DA Marsha Revel was assigned to the matter, and she started investigating the case up one side and down the other. The sequence of events on Tuesday morning suggested that Steinberg had a motive to make a false claim and that his behavior was inconsistent with an actual theft—if someone in the office on Tuesday took the tapes, why kick everyone out after calling the police but before they could arrive to question the office occupants? Revel wasn't planning to rest with the obvious, however. She set out to show that the tapes couldn't have been taken because Steinberg never had them in the first place.

Then, just when it seemed that Steinberg's whole flap was deflating, Larry Flynt decided to pump a little more hot air into it.

If erratic was a word that had occasionally been used to describe Steinberg, Flynt was major-league erratic—off the charts.

The publisher of *Hustler* magazine, Flynt had long and loudly proclaimed his intent to exercise his First Amendment right to publish materials that were not only pornographic but, at times, obnoxious. Some of Flynt's antics over the years had the flavor of libertarian guerrilla theater. Flynt had used his considerable resources and bluster to challenge obscenity statutes in several states and then, in the late 1970s, announced that he had decided to forswear male chauvinist porn under the influence of Christian evangelist Ruth Carter Stapleton, the president's sister.

After 1978, when he was paralyzed by a would-be assassin who pumped four rifle shots into his back as he left a Georgia courthouse, Flynt's bluster began to take on more sinister overtones. In constant pain from his injuries, he became addicted to hard drugs and seldom emerged from the bedroom of his mansion in the Holmby Hills section of Bel-Air.

Flynt's mansion, next door to Joanna Carson's and, coincidentally, in the same section of Bel-Air as the Bloomingdale home, had always been something of a neighborhood conversation piece, best known for a certain bronze statue in the main entrance hall that depicted Flynt as a young boy having sexual intercourse with a chicken. By 1983, after changing his mind about selling out and moving to a condo in Beverly Hills, Flynt had converted the house into the headquarters of his "Larry Flynt for President" campaign and the fortress retreat where he intended to preside over the exposure of the myriad conspiracies he saw around him. He hired a private security force, very large men with eyes the size of coin slots who carried automatic pistols equipped with laser-guided sights.

Lapsed from his pro-Christian, antichauvinist phase, Flynt now believed that it was his mission to expose sexual hypocrisy among the nation's power elite. When he heard Steinberg's story about sex tapes, he became a man obsessed.

On Tuesday afternoon, just hours after Steinberg had reported the tapes stolen, a spokesman for Flynt announced that Flynt had the tapes and was planning to publish them—or, at least, selected stills from them—in *Hustler* magazine. An obvious inference to draw would be that someone had indeed stolen the tapes from Steinberg's office and hied on over to Flynt's mansion to offer them for sale. Whatever Flynt's other shortcomings might be, miserliness was not his problem; he was known to pay top dollar for material he wanted, so this would have been a logical course for a thief to take.

Within an hour of the first announcement, however, Flynt himself started telling the press that the whole thing had been a mistake. He didn't have the tapes and apparently hadn't known about the reported theft from Steinberg. What had happened was that he'd been *expecting* to have the tapes because he had made an agreement to buy them from Steinberg for $1 million. Then Steinberg had failed to show up for their 11:30 A.M. appointment.

On July 25, Steinberg appeared in Municipal Court in Van Nuys, where he refused to answer any questions about the tapes under oath. Ashen-faced and shaky, Steinberg lunged angrily at a photographer who snapped his picture at close range. The picture that emerged from this encounter, showing Steinberg wearing the panicky snarl of an animal at bay, was so painful that even some of the reporters who'd been most irate over being used found themselves feeling sorry for him.

"That photo said it all," one of them commented later. "The man was burned out."

And so, it seemed was the sex tapes rumor.

R EAL TINSEL

//

On August 18, 1983, twenty-two L.A. County grand jurors appeared before Judge Andrew J. Weisz in Beverly Hills Municipal Court to hand up an indictment of Robert K. Steinberg.

Not only was it unprecedented for a grand jury to devote its time to considering evidence of a possible misdemeanor, the evidence it heard had been marshaled with particular energy and meticulousness.

Deputy DA Revel had begun by producing Sam Gordon, the owner of the AM/PM Answering Service, his night manager who logged in the previous day's calls, and each of the employees who had been on duty on Saturday, July 9, when Robert K. Steinberg supposedly received an anonymous message from the woman with the tapes. No one remembered taking any such call—and it should have been memorable, since forwarding calls from an individual who refused to identify him- or herself was against office policy. Nor was there any record in the message slips routinely filled out for all callers.

The deputy DA also produced the parking-lot attendants who'd been on duty at the Wilshire Boulevard garage where Steinberg parked his tan El Dorado with its conspicuous TRIAL license plates—neither of whom had seen him return to his car on the Monday afternoon, July 11, and remove a gym bag from the trunk.

In addition, there were several reporters who'd spent time in Steinberg's law library on Monday afternoon and Tuesday morning, and who had failed to observe the gym bag that Steinberg claimed was stored there. Deputy DA Revel maintained that it was highly unlikely that a group of reporters hotly pursuing the tapes story would have allowed one of their number simply to walk away with the evidence, right under their noses. Whether Revel was correct on this point is debatable, since there were numerous cameramen and sound technicians milling around carrying similar looking bags, and no one had any reason to suspect the tapes would be sitting unguarded in the library anyway.

Nevertheless, she was surely accurate in suggesting that Steinberg's story about leaving the bag there in the first place was incredible. If he had been worried enough to fear that the locked trunk of his car was a insecure storage place, surely he would never have simply dumped the tapes in the law library, where any one of several dozen reporters and technicians had a perfect opportunity to take them. The story just didn't wash.

No doubt the most telling testimony the grand jury heard was that of Cindy Stonehouse, the woman who had set Steinberg on to the Pancoast case originally. Stonehouse, naturally had been everyone's prime candidate for the role of the mystery woman during the forty-eight hours or so after the story broke. She fit the general description Steinberg had given, though she did happen to be taller than five-two, the height he'd mentioned to the police, and her hints to the press about being invited by Pancoast to San Fernando Valley orgies had created suspicion that she might have been in possession of some films.

According to Stonehouse, she had been disconcerted enough by Steinberg's press conference to call him up and demand to know what was going on. Steinberg, she said, had assured her that the tapes existed, and he'd confided to her that the first name of the Justice Department strike-force attorney who'd watched the tapes with him was Joe. Also, he told her that his second witness, the prominent private-practice lawyer, was Vince—a reference,

Stonehouse assumed, to Vincent Bugliosi, who shared the same office.

It developed, however, that there was no Joe in the criminal division of the U.S. attorney's office in L.A. Nor had a confidential questionnaire distributed to all Justice Department attorneys in the L.A. office turned up anyone who would admit to being in a position to confirm Steinberg's story. As for Bugliosi, he flatly denied under oath that he had so much as been in Steinberg's home on the weekend in question.

The grand jury investigation established fairly conclusively that Steinberg's announcement about the sex tapes had been a hoax, a publicity grab that got out of control. Whether this meant that no such tapes existed was a matter of opinion. Deputy DA Revel's theory was that the tapes were a figment of Steinberg's imagination—and that his claim to have possession of them was a desperation strategy concocted to worm his way into the role of defense attorney in a notorious murder case.

Another possibility, supported by insider's rumors though no hard evidence, was that there were some tapes—though not necessarily featuring the same cast of high-level politicos described by Steinberg. If Steinberg had reason to believe that some orgy tapes actually had been filmed, then his motives for claiming to have possession of them no longer seem totally irrational. The individual who had the goods in hand would be in a very powerful position, and who knows what new information might be smoked out as the result of the bluff.

In the days after the tapes story broke, there had been no more energetic detractor of Robert Steinberg than Arthur Barens.

Barens, the same attorney who Vicki Morgan had once consulted about continuing her palimony case, had now been hired by Christy Pancoast to represent her son, Morgan's accused killer.

While he was not a criminal defense specialist, Barens had personal reasons for committing himself to Marvin's defense—reasons beyond the normal desire of an ambitious attorney to be associated with a case certain to achieve national prominence. Barens had known the Pancoast family for nearly twenty years, during which time Christy Pancoast's advice on investments in Valley real estate had helped to make him a moderately wealthy man. In addition, it had been Christy Pancoast who had steered him into attending Alcoholics Anonymous when his personal life became unmanageable in 1982. The AA program had proven to be a godsend for him.

So, when Christy called him on the Saturday morning after Marvin's arrest and asked him to take on her son's defense, Barens felt he owed her one.

The call from Christy had come around eight on Saturday morning, and by eleven Barens was at the L.A. county jail talking to his client. What he learned was not promising. Marvin had given a taped confession to the police within hours of turning himself in and had been talking freely to reporters ever since. Barens told Marvin that it would be a good idea if he'd be less loquacious from now on.

Naturally, he was not pleased when, only a few hours after he left the jail, he got a call from Marvin saying that the latter had just given yet another jailhouse interview. Marvin told Barens that his visitor had identified himself as Robert Steinberg, an attorney, and had offered to handle his case free on up through the preliminary hearing. Barens had never heard of Steinberg, and other than being vaguely upset that Marvin was still talking to anyone who showed up at the jail requesting a visit, he did not place any great importance on the incident. He made a mental note to get in touch with the other attorney and tell him that it was too late. Pancoast already had representation.

The next day, Sunday, Barens and his wife drove to Malibu to visit their daughter at her summer camp. They didn't get back home until after dinner, and it was about eleven P.M. when Barens got around to answering the messages Steinberg had left him. Barens figured the contact would be simply a matter of letting the man know that the family had decided to engage someone else.

Instead, he found himself being drawn into the most bizarre conversation. Steinberg, according to Barens, introduced himself as a "dear friend" of L.A. County DA Philibosian and insisted that if Barens would just turn the case over to him he could arrange to have Pancoast released without bail to the Thalians clinic.

"I've never heard of such an arrangement as long as I've been in practice," Barens told the caller.

But Steinberg, according to Barens, kept insisting that he indeed had a personal friendship with Philibosian that would make such an arrangement possible.

"Well, then," said Barens, "maybe you could get the same deal for me. Can't you call the DA, since he's such a friend of yours, and tell him that Art Barens is a nice guy. I'm a lawyer, too, so what difference would it make if they released him to me?"

Steinberg, says Barens, seemed tremendously agitated by Barens's refusal just to bow out of the case. "No, no," he said, "I can't do that. If it isn't me, it's no deal. And you can just say goodbye to Pancoast, because you just ruined it for him."

After he'd hung up, Barens went into the living room and said to his wife Maxine, "I just had a hell of a strange phone call with this guy. I think he's some kind of quack."

On Monday Pancoast was scheduled to appear for arraignment. Around 9:30 that morning, Steinberg called Barens at his office. This time, according to Barens, Steinberg brought up a subject he had not mentioned the previous night—video tapes. Steinberg now said that a woman interested in Pancoast's case had given him certain tapes "showing members of the administration in compromising sexual activity."

"I don't exactly see how that will help my client," Barens demurred.

"Well, you never know," he recalled Steinberg as saying.

"Can I see the tapes then?" Barens asked.

Steinberg said that would be fine with him, and Barens promised to call for a firm appointment after he returned from the arraignment later that morning.

From a legal standpoint, the proceedings that morning were a nonevent. Barens requested and got a week's delay. He needed more time to confer with his client before they'd be ready to enter a formal plea. In the meantime, considering Marvin's propensity for making self-incriminating statements, Barens thought his client would be better off behind bars.

Barens, meanwhile, had decided that he ought to at least look at what Steinberg had, in case it did turn out to be related to Marvin's situation. All afternoon, his secretary tried unsuccessfully to place a call to the number that Steinberg had left.

Around 3:30, Barens was going through some paperwork for another case when his secretary buzzed him. "You know that man Steinberg who called you this morning?" she said. "Well, he's on the radio right now and he's talking about sex tapes. I think you'd better check it out."

According to Marvin Pancoast, he was just about the last person in L.A. to hear about Steinberg's claim.

"I'd been under a suicide watch all weekend," Marvin said later.

"Someone, I don't know who, had told the jailer I might kill myself. When I got to the arraignment, the first one, there were these photographers there. I couldn't believe it. I was surprised to see so many. Then [after being returned to the jail] I was put on this [high security] floor where we didn't get to see the papers or hear the radio. So I had no idea what was going on. . . .

"The first thing I knew, a couple of days later, Larry Flynt sent these two goons down to see me in jail. They told me 'We'll give you a million dollars for the tapes. We'll make you rich.' It was the first I'd heard about the whole thing, and I was scared. So I called up Arthur and said, 'Who are these people? What do they want?' Arthur said, 'Well, I'll go up to Flynt's place and find out.' Later, on Friday I think It was, there was this guard up on my floor who showed me this newspaper. That was the first I heard about the whole thing."

Testifying before the grand jury in August, Barens was the first to attack Steinberg's credibility. "To this day," he testified, "I don't see how—unless someone could clarify it for me—how, even if they existed, which I doubt they exist, but even if they did, what relevance they would have to to a defense in a murder case is difficult for me to conceptualize."

These were words Barens would later have cause to regret.

Once he had settled into the routine at the jail, Marvin Pancoast seemed to be a different person. A psychiatrist employed by the county had studied Marvin's medical history and restored him to a regime of major tranquilizers, which seemed to have a calming effect. And Marvin now told Barens that he had no memory at all of beating Vicki to death. He had confessed only because Vicki was dead and he had assumed he must be responsible.

He now said that the last time he saw Vicki Morgan alive was shortly before midnight on Wednesday. She was sitting up in bed and smoking her cigarette and watching Johnny Carson on TV. In the middle of the monologue, Marvin dozed off. Sometime later, he awoke feeling dizzy and nauseated. He was aware of a sweet, sickish odor in the room, a smell that reminded him of medicine or, possibly, very pungent nail polish remover.

Still only half conscious, he saw Vicki's body on the bed beside him, her head a bloody mess. The hall light was on and there was water running in the bathroom. Disoriented, he staggered downstairs and out the front door, where he found Katy the Doberman not in the entrance courtyard but all the way out on the sidewalk. The front door had been closed but not locked.

In a daze, he let the dog back into the house and went down to his car. He had no plan, just this powerful urge to get out of there as quickly as possible.

"All of a sudden I realized that I was very hungry. You know, famished," Marvin continued. "So I decided to head for Bob's Big Boy on Moorpark. But when I got there it was closed. So I just kept going, with nothing particular in mind. Somehow I ended up at the North Hollywood station."

Marvin said he had no idea at all what he'd said to Detective Rush, much less why he'd said it. He'd just figured that if Vicki was dead he must have done it, and so he'd made up a confession that seemed to satisfy the police.

It was the damnedest story Barens had ever heard.

One thing was certain: It didn't take a whole lot of years trying criminal cases to know that this would not be a good account to give in front of a jury. Marvin seemed oblivious to the fact that a sudden yen for a hamburger was not the most sympathetic response to finding one's housemate bludgeoned to death. No rational human being would make up a thing like that.

Barens had known the Pancoast family since his client was a child. He knew Marvin had been in and out of mental hospitals and that his life was a perpetual guilt trip. He also knew that Marvin was gay, so it didn't make sense that he would be so screwed up over a woman that he would be driven to kill her. On the other hand, if someone else killed Vicki, Marvin would have been the perfect fall guy.

Marvin's mental state was so confused that he wasn't sure, really, whether he had killed Vicki or not. Either way, he was surely insane.

During the week after he took on the case, Barens brought in an associate who had extensive criminal experience. Charles "Ted" Mathews was a former L.A. county assistant DA, a heavyset man whose broad, planar face was nevertheless capable of projecting an expression of boyish earnestness. Mathews was repelled by Marvin's history—arrests for lewd conduct and hysterical suicide attempts over homosexual affairs that went wrong. But at the same time, he was fascinated by a case that posed a genuine element of mystery.

A man who described murder as "the stuff that Edgar Allan Poe and others write of . . . a word which carries a majesty and mystique that are legendary," Mathews knew only too well that he could try a thousand cases and not find one where there was any genuine doubt about the basic facts. This case, on the other hand, posed an almost classic conundrum—the sole witness to the slaying, the confessed killer, also happened to be a masochist, so he had a ready-made psychological motive for making himself appear guilty even if he wasn't. What's more, the victim was a glamorous woman, one who'd announced publicly that she was about to expose scandal and corruption in high places. Mathews would later describe her as the "silver" Vicki Morgan—glittering and enigmatic even in death.

On July 19, Marvin was arraigned in Van Nuys before Municipal Court Commissioner Robert L. Swasey, when he entered a double plea of not guilty and not guilty by reason of insanity.

The preliminary hearing a week later was a revelation. It developed that the LAPD indeed had no forensic evidence to disprove Marvin's claim that his confession had been sheer invention.

No fingerprint technician had been called to the scene of the crime—a departure from procedure that Mathews, a former assistant DA, could not recall in any case he'd ever been associated with. No one had as yet so much as attempted to raise fingerprints from the alleged murder weapon.

Nor had Hershel Arons, the investigator from the DA's office, begun to interview material witnesses. Notably, no one had troubled to attempt to interrogate the Gordon Basichis—this despite Marvin's statement to Detective Rush that there had been a fight only a week before the murder during which the writer allegedly "beat the shit" out of Vicki. Barens and Mathews began to wonder whether Basichis might be the ringer in the case.

In the meantime, Marvin was also telling his attorneys that even though Robert Steinberg happened to be a liar, the sex tapes really did exist.

Marvin said that he had first heard of the tapes one night when he and Vicki were sitting around in her bedroom watching TV, and he started talking about renting some porn films. "You don't have to rent them," Vicki laughed. "I've got some stuff here." And she went to black lacquer cabinet where she kept her video tapes and picked out three Betamax cassettes. One of the tapes showed Vicki with Bloomingdale; another, Bloomingdale with two other women; and a third, Marvin claimed, featured Vicki with a prominent member of the Reagan administration.

At first, Barens was more than skeptical. Marvin was talking about administration figures, but who was to say that he was even capable of recognizing an administration figure when he saw one?

Still, the tapes story wasn't necessarily any crazier than a lot of stuff Marvin said that later checked out as true: Vicki's affair with a prince or king from the Middle East, her lesbian relationship with a Saudi princess who was a major-league heroin addict, her almost-deal with William Morris, her paranoia and taping of phone calls . . .

Then, too, Barens was getting all this incredible feedback.

For one thing, Marvin Mitchelson, with whom Barens had worked for nearly three years, had come around to thinking that the tapes actually existed. On the Monday night that the Steinberg story broke, Mitchelson had gone to have dinner at the home of a friend who had good contacts in the White House. When he got there, his friend was really excited. He said that he'd talked to the President's counselor Mike Deaver on the phone and that Deaver was going wild. "There are these tapes!" Deaver had shouted. "And Meese and [William French] Smith are on them! There's a story breaking tomorrow in the [Washington] *Post!*"

Mitchelson put this story together with some other speculative gossip he had heard from an acquaintance who was ex-CIA, and concluded that the tapes had existed; that the White House knew about them; and that, most likely, someone representing the administration had gotten hold of them and destroyed them.

Mitchelson didn't tell this to any of the reporters who called in the wake of the murder, asking for on-the-record comments. He contented himself with enigmatic remarks about Vicki having been a woman "with a lot of secrets"—which was certainly true. Nevertheless, the story did eventually get to Arthur Barens via a reporter who'd heard it from Mitchelson.

Some months later, evaluating what he'd heard in retrospect, Mitchelson agreed that he wasn't all that sure that what he heard about the furor in the White House hadn't been misconstrued. It was possible that Deaver (if he really said that Meese and Smith were on the tapes), was reacting to the same rumors as everyone else.

But in the overheated atmosphere of the moment, it was easy to read more into the story than was actually there. The rumor mill had started to churn and Barens was hearing a lot of things from a lot of people, all of whom seemed to know someone who had heard something.

And then there was Flynt.

Flynt had developed a monomania about the Morgan murder; he was convinced that she'd been killed for tapes and had put out a standing offer to pay $1 million for tapes having to do with Morgan or John DeLorean. In early October, he actually managed to get his hands on the latter—a tape that showed DeLorean inspecting a suitcase full of cocaine, taken by FBI cameraman during their sting operation. There was no doubt that this tape, which Flynt said he'd gotten from "a friend of an FBI man" was genuine; Flynt had turned it over to CBS and the network's local affiliate, station KNXT, who eventually broadcast it on October 23, after a restraining order obtained by DeLorean's attorneys was overturned by a federal appeals judge.

Soon after he got the first tape, Flynt let it be known that he was negotiating with an anonymous source for a $25 million package that, he said, would contain FBI tapes showing that DeLorean had been a victim of entrapment—as well as the elusive Morgan sex tapes.

Also out there, on the outer fringes of the conspiracy front, was a certain man from western Pennsylvania, a source who had originally contacted writers at Flynt's soon-to-be defunct *Rebel* magazine, who claimed to be an ex-spook and talked about Vicki Morgan's connection with the renegade former CIA man Frank Terpil. Calling Barens collect at all hours of the day and night, the Pennsylvania man poured out an incredibly complex tale of intrigue, the gist of which was that Morgan participated in a sex and espionage ring with CIA connections.

On the night of her death, the Pennsylvania man said, another ex-spook working undercover on the DeLorean investigation had received a call ordering him to Vicki's condo to retrieve some compromising audio tapes.

Barens hardly knew what to make of this newest source, but the man had sent him a photocopy of a memorandum dating back to Watergate, apparently written by John Dean to John Ehrlichman, which discussed the source by name and said, in effect, "This guy is trouble." So he started thinking perhaps there was some foundation to it all. "It was," Barens said in a phone interview in early October, "the most fascinating fucking story. . . . I can hardly believe it myself."

Somehow or other, over the next two weeks, the core of suspicion and rumor and, undeniably, wishful thinking reached a critical mass. On October 13, Barens and Mathews issued a statement that was predominently featured in the tabloid press, making the front page of the *New York Post* the next afternoon.

"My client is an innocent man," declared Barens, and he went on to contend that Vicki Morgan was killed by a person or persons unknown who then ransacked her apartment for tapes while Marvin Pancoast slept. "At least one of those tapes survived the night Vicki was killed," added Mathews, attributing his information to a reliable source.

Not only that, said Barens, but they now had reliable witnesses who had seen the tapes, one of them "a lawyer . . . in hiding today for fear that he could become the next victim of the 'real' killer."

Toward the end of the month, Larry Flynt let the word out that he had actually acquired the second package of tapes, and on October 30, he invited the media to his mansion for a preview screening of one of the Morgan sex tapes. Supposedly, though no one believed it for a minute, the blurry footage showed the late Congressman Larry McDonald, recently killed in the Korean Airlines jet shot down by the Soviets, cavorting in bed with a very fat woman. Haranguing the assembled representatives of the media from his gold-plated wheelchair, Flynt said—and his remarks were reported in newspapers at the time—that Morgan's killing was somehow part of a plot directed by the ultraconservative foundation, Westerngoals, dedicated to promoting covert action and counterterrorism.

Flynt also played an audio cassette that, he claimed, recorded an attempt by DeLorean to back out of his drug deal with the feds.

At the end of his rambling and incoherent speech, Flynt admitted that even *he* wasn't saying that his bombshell tapes were authentic.

Then, while reporters stood around wondering what to make of the sideshow, Flynt began shouting. "The tapes are stolen! They're gone! One of you motherfuckers took them!"

And he kicked them all out of his house.

Larry Flynt had at last managed to one-up Steinberg, and it appeared that the entertainment value of Flynt's one-man guerrilla theater, and for that matter of the sex tapes rumor itself, was pretty well exhausted.

THE DEATH OF A VALLEY GIRL

///

Ironically, the trial of Vicki Morgan's murderer would confirm her lifelong belief in the overriding importance of a Beverly Hills address: Because she had the bad taste to die north of Ventura Boulevard, her alleged killer was being prosecuted in the northwest district of Los Angeles County, in downtown Van Nuys—an oxymoronic phrase.

As preliminary motions in the homicide case got under way in May 1984, the attention of the L.A. press corps and the nation was already focused on the federal court downtown where John Z. DeLorean was on trial for cocaine trafficking.

Not that the first-degree murder trial of Marvin Pancoast wasn't attracting its share of interest. TV crews were on the scene, camping in the hallway even during preliminary motions, and members of the press who'd been shuttling back and forth between Van Nuys and downtown reported that the Pancoast procedings attracted more courtroom spectators some days that DeLorean's. But DeLorean, with his chiseled Dick Tracy features and fashion-model wife, was the class act in town. Van Nuys was the territory of the tabloids, the beat of the six o'clock news crime reporters, and a mecca for the senior citizens who make an avocation of attending murder trials. They flocked to this one expecting exactly what they were going to get—the ultimate Valley Girl soap opera.

Arthur Barens and Ted Mathews, for the moment, the stars of the media sideshow, were doing their best to convince the skeptical press corps that they were sitting on evidence of a major political scandal. On the opening day of the preliminaries, they managed to capture a few seconds on the evening news with the announcement that they had subpoenaed none other than Edwin Meese III, at the time the attorney-general designate.

No one, least of all Barens and Mathews themselves, seriously expected Meese to make an appearance in the Department "R" courtroom where Pancoast was being tried. Nevertheless, Meese's name became a buzz word in the corridors—in part because he was an obvious target, in view of his well-publicized problems in getting his appointment as attorney general confirmed by the Senate, but also in part because members of Vicki's family recalled her having some strong negative opinions about the man. Connie Laney, had talked about a time when she happened to be watching a clip about Meese on the TV news, and Vicki had blurted out, "He's such a jerk," adding that Vicki said she had met Meese on several occasions both before and after the 1980 election.

Meese flatly denied that he had ever so much as met Vicki Morgan, and it was a good bet that if there was any reliable firsthand evidence to contradict him it would have surfaced long before Pancoast's case came to trial.

Before Marvin Pancoast had so much as shown his face in the

courtroom, the members of the press could already take their pick of conspiracy rumors, some of them positively byzantine in their complexity. Everyone, of course, had heard the account of what the elusive sex tapes supposedly showed—a stag party travesty of an S&M orgy that featured a unidentified dominatrix playfully pinning pink carnations to the pubic hairs of a certain administration officials.

As to what became of tapes after the murder, there was no shortage of theories. The simplest rumors had it that Vicki was killed by Pancoast after all, but that her condo was picked clean that same night by emissaries from the LAPD's notorious Red Squad. Other versions named, variously, the FBI, renegade spooks or Mafia-connected hit men. Or, for those who preferred the Chinese puzzle-style conspiracy, positing plots within plots within plots, there was the bizarre contention of a group of former reporters connected with *Rebel* magazine, who suggested that Arthur Barens himself was in league with *Time* magazine in an effort to make sure the most damaging evidence did not surface.

But Barens and Mathews, missing no opportunity to appear before the TV lights with their accusations of a police coverup, certainly did not behave like men who were engaged in trying to suppress a scandal.

Inevitably, the press nicknamed them the Odd Couple. Barens with his gold elephant-hair bracelet, his Southern California tan, and his impeccably tailored suits—not surprisingly he was once the foster child of a prominent Beverly Hills haberdasher—and Mathews, shambling and heavyset, sporting red suspenders under his shapeless blue suits, might have come to court straight from the casting agency. Yet it was by no means self-evident that their charges were without substance.

Just as jury selection was about to get under way, it developed that Barens's and Mathew's subpoenas had produced some results after all. A check of FBI records uncovered the information that Alfred Bloomingdale had named as far back as the late 1960s in connection with an investigation into organized crime and prostitution. According to the FBI, the investigation file had been returned to the LAPD, and according to the LAPD, the file had subsequently been lost.

While no one could say what, if anything, this decades-old investigation might have had to do with Vicki Morgan, the revelation was a nagging reminder of the LAPD's history of misplacing sensitive information about prominent citizens. For the last year and a half, citizens of Los Angeles had been following the scandal developing about intelligence files on prominent citizens maintained by the LAPD's Public Disorder Intelligence Division, (PDID); and only a week before Pancoast's trial opened, Detective Jay Paul, an LAPD officer who had been caught with a cache of the files in his garage, had been substantially cleared in a hearing before the police Board of Rights—a decision widely regarded as a rebuke to police brass for attempting to serve him up as a scapegoat.

Not surprisingly, there had already been a good deal of speculation about the PDID's possible interest in Vicki Morgan, and one of the "hot" rumors going around after her death was that Jay Paul himself had seen in the vicinity of Vicki Morgan's condominium on the night she died. Even Arthur Barens belittled the Jay Paul story, dismissing it as "just something a couple of people said, but the witnesses didn't come through." Nevertheless, the story of a "lost" Bloomingdale file suggested that perhaps a PDID connection was not such a farfetched notion after all.

The story surely did not make life any easier for Assistant DA Stanley Weisberg, who was faced with the task of defending the LAPD's shoddy policework both in court and to the press. Balding and slightly stoopshouldered, Weisberg looked like a grownup version of the one kid in a grade school class who'd come to school dressed in a sportscoat and tie. Reputedly an able and hardworking prosecutor, capable of occasional flashes of sardonic wit in one-to-one conversation, Weisberg was no match for the defense attorneys when it came to corridor banter.

Refusing to get involved in exchanging charges with Barens and Mathews, Weisberg dismissed their talk of a conspiracy and a coverup as "phony issues." However, his defense of certain lapses in the LAPD's investigative work—that the "police were busy with more important cases"—must have sounded lame even to his own ears. He was trying a homicide case, a case significant enough that the networks were spending the money to have a pool camera crew filming the entire proceedings, and his role consisted of having to push for a life sentence while simultaneously insisting that case had not been "important" enough to merit the LAPD's full attention; an unenviable position to be in.

While the opposing attorneys were exchanging opening shots in the war of the press conferences, forty-two-year-old Judge

David Horowitz was presiding over the tedious but crucial process of disposing of opening motions and selecting a jury.

Judge Horowitz ruled that five separate self-incriminatory statements made by the defendant, but now repudiated by him, would be admissible as evidence—a major though by no means unexpected blow to Pancoast's hopes of acquittal. He also denied a defense request that Pancoast's bifurcated plea of not guilty and not guilty by reason of insanity be heard by two separate juries. The judge was surely correct in concluding that the law that permitted two distinct pleas was never intended to give defendants two chances for acquittal, with the state bearing the burden and expense of having to empanel separate juries for each phase of the trial.

Empaneling just one jury took more than a month of the court's time. In view of the pretrial publicity surrounding the case, the judge had decided that each potential juror should be vetted in an individual interview, a time-consuming process considering that it was eventually necessary to vet ninety-seven jurors.

Jury selection is always an opportunity for defense attorneys to engage in a little pretrial education of the jurors, on issues that may or may not come up in the course of the actual proceedings. Barens and Mathews took advantage of the process to present potential jurors with a free-association word list that included not only *sex tapes* and *coverup* but a long list of proper names including Meese's.

Interestingly, while nearly all the panelists had heard of Vicki Morgan and Alfred Bloomingdale and the sex tapes, the name of Meese, which the defense attorneys were trying so hard to work into the proceedings one way or another, provoked mostly blank incomprehension. Quite a few of the panelists had never heard of him; others found the name vaguely familiar but couldn't place it beyond suggesting that he might have "something to do with the government."

Without doubt, the true beneficiary of the weeks devoted to jury selection was neither the prosecutor nor the defense attorneys but the judge. Good-looking enough to have his own coterie among the court watchers, Judge Horowitz was also unfailingly good-humored and solicitous of the jurors' welfare, whether their problems happened to be with employers reluctant to give leave for jury duty or with balky plumbing in the jury room. In the long run, the judge's capacity for inspiring loyalty no doubt worked against Marvin Pancoast by making a hung jury an extremely unlikely outcome.

Oddly, when it came to selecting the final panel of twelve jurors, it developed that both the prosecution and the defense had the same ideal juror in mind—a middle-aged female, preferably married, with a somewht better than average education.

The defense's reasoning was based on the conventional wisdom that male jurors are inevitably hostile to homosexual defendants, an effect that Mathews had encountered often enough in practice to make him adamant on the subject. "As soon as they start hearing about the guy's sex life, they're completely turned off," Mathews said. "You're standing up there talking about this stuff, and you can just see it in their faces."

Stanley Weisberg, meanwhile, had concluded that a mostly female group would be less likely to sympathize with a defendant who, gay or not, had been involved with a woman who might fairly described as a sexual tease.

Judging by the opinions that were being expressed outside the courtroom, Weisberg had the better strategy. A more or less typical view of the case was that of a courthouse cafeteria worker, who said with a confiding wink, "Oh come on. Is there anyone who thinks she didn't deserve it?"

Once attorneys start using their challenges to shape a jury according to a particular demographic profile, the results can sometimes be unpredictable. In this case, Barens and Mathews got their mostly female jury—a final panel of twelve women and two men—but only at the price of accepting some individuals who could hardly be thought to be ideal defense jurors:

One woman, who eventually became the jury foreman, was employed by the state's department of Labor Relations where her job was to organize administrative hearings.

Another had played tennis on occasion with the woman who, along with her husband, owned the condo Vicki had been leasing.

And still another was married to a retired family court prosecutor and—as she volunteered freely during her preliminary interview—had been a guest at the 1946 wedding of Alfred and Betsy Bloomingdale.

Finally, of the two men on the panel of twelve, one happened to be brewery worker born in Yugoslavia—a part of the world not noted for its tolerance of gays—a man, moreover, whose wife had never worked outside the home.

Whatever mental image the jurors may have had of Vicki Morgan's mother, Connie Laney, the prosecution's first witness, no doubt came as a revelation. A carefully groomed woman of sixty-two, Mrs. Laney carried her spine ramrod straight, her jaw in a determined set that signaled she was mustering all her composture in an effort to get through the ordeal at hand without breaking down. She looked like anyone's mother. And, as soon became evident from her testimony, her relationship with her grown daughter had been closer than most.

"Are you calm?" Weisberg asked after the oath was administered.

"I am trying to be," Mrs. Laney promised.

Laney began to explaining that in the summer of 1982, at the time Vicki filed her palimony suit against Alfred Bloomingdale, she had been in England visiting her family. When she returned to California in late August, she found Vicki in bad shape, emotionally and financially. Out of concern for her daughter and for her grandson Todd, she began spending several days a week at her daughter's house, helping out with various practical chores and keeping Vicki company.

She continued in this habit after Vicki moved to Colfax Avenue. By June 1983, Vicki's financial situation was "zero," recalled Laney. "I was helping her."

While she had never really understood why Marvin Pancoast spent so much of his time hanging around with Vicki, she had more or less come to accept him as a fixture of the household. On Wednesday, July 6, the day before the murder, however, she noticed almost from the minute she walked into the condo that Marvin was behaving strangely.

"Marvin met me as I was walking in the door," Laney remembered. "And he said, 'They're upstairs,' And I said, 'Who's upstairs?' And he said, 'Gordon and Vicki.' And I said, 'Why don't you go home. This is not your responsibility.' And he said, 'I'm not going home. I'm taking care of this tonight once and for all.' "

All that morning, while she worked on the packing with her friend Sharon Porto, Marvin kept a morose vigil on the bottom step of the staircase leading to the bedroom where Vicki and Gordon were asleep. "I'd never seen him so depressed," Laney recalled. "I'd never seen him this way before."

Then, as soon as Vicki went out with Gordon to take a look at the Burbank apartment, Marvin dragged both her and Sharon Porto upstairs, insisting that he had something very important to show them. When they got to Vicki's bedroom, Marvin pointed to some handwritten notes that were lying on the night table beside the bed. Laney, who recognized that the notes were several months old, couldn't figure out why Marvin was suddenly so upset over them. "What's the big deal?" she recalled asking in exasperation. "She doesn't want to live," Marvin replied.

All that afternoon, Marvin moped around, complaining that Vicki was behaving like the "Queen of Sheba" while leaving all the work of the packing to her mother and Sharon Porto. He had squabbled with Todd, who questioned what his baseball bat was doing in the back seat of Marvin's Oldsmobile, and then seemed especially eager to get the boy out of the house for the night. When Todd mentioned casually that he was thinking of going out to Montclair that night, Marvin had seemed to light up.

In hindsight, Laney could find all sorts of portents in her memory of Marvin's behavior during that day, perhaps none more disturbing than the fact that as the women prepared to leave the condo, he made a point of asking the two of them to give him a goodbye kiss. Sharon Porto, who had never met Marvin before that day, had found the request disconcerting. "Do you kiss him goodbye every night?" Laney recalled her asking as soon as they were out the door.

"I said no. He never asked me before."

The remainder of Laney's direct testimony, which occupied the entire afternoon session, consisted of her being asked to identify nearly fifty snapshots taken by a police photographer at the scene of the crime. During the preliminary hearing, Detective Welch mentioned that the apartment had looked "ransacked"—a choice of words that the defense was fully expected to exploit during the trial.

Laney's comments, as she carefully studied each of the photos in turn, suggested that she too might have her suspicions on that score. In general, she agreed that the state of extreme disarray shown in the snapshots reflected her daughter's poor housekeeping and the preparations for moving rather than evidence of an intruder. Nevertheless, she pointed out a number of details in the pictures that differed from her recollection of the way the upstairs rooms had looked when she left them at nine o'clock on Wednesday night—drawers pulled out of the dresser in Todd's bedroom, a pile of papers on the floor that she had not noticed before, and in the master bedroom, a number of tote bags that had been pulled from the closet and were lying around open on the floor.

Weisberg, meanwhile, had been handing Laney the crime-scene photos in a carefully organized progression, beginning with snapshots of the condo exterior and moving, painfully slowly but nevertheless inexorably, towards the bed where Vicki Morgan's body had been found. By the time, at long last, he produced a photo of the bed itself, with the corpse mercifully but perfunctorily hidden behind a stapled-on square of paper, Mrs. Laney burst into tears. It did not bode well for the defense that several of the jurors were crying along with her—among them the Yugoslavian brewery worker.

About the best that the defense could do on cross-examination was to remind Mrs. Laney that her memories of Marvin's behavior that day may have been considerably distorted by hindsight. Obviously, if she had anticipated that Marvin intended to harm her daughter, she would never have left the two of them alone for the night, much less parted from Marvin with a kiss.

Laney conceded that a phrase she used in her direct testimony—"I was as frustrated as anybody else"—accurately described her own feelings that Wednesday.

The testimony of Mrs. Laney's friend Sharon Porto gave a somewhat different perspective.

According to Porto, Marvin's complaint when she and Laney first arrived on Wednesay was not so much that Vicki and Gordon Basichis were in bed together as that they had stayed up all night, drinking and snorting coke. Marvin, Porto recalled with some puzzlement, had complained that "the noise from the hole in Gordon's nose kept him awake all night long."

Porto, who had been present when Marvin showed Connie the purported suicide notes left on Vicki's bedstand, couldn't recall hearing Marvin say "she doesn't want to live." Nor could she confirm Laney's assertion that Vicki had made a firm decision to go stay in Montclair with her mother instead of moving into the Burbank place Marvin had found—a decision that would inevitably have created the basis for an angry confrontation with Marvin when Vicki finally got around to delivering the news to him. "She didn't know what she was going to do," Porto recalls. In fact, by the time Porto left the condo with Connie and Todd, Marvin and Vicki were seated at the kitchen table arguing about whether they would go to see Marvin's grandmother that night or the next day—hardly an indication that Vicki was planning to give up on Marvin entirely.

Mrs. Porto also remembered a small but bewildering incident that occurred while she and Connie were discussing what to do about Vicki's "better pieces of glass." Marvin, who had been up in Vicki's bedroom, came down to the dining area where the two women were working and offered to help move the valuables to the trunk of Connie's car. "He asked us if we'd heard him yelling," Porto said, and he then went on to tell the two women that he'd just had a knock-down argument with Vicki about her behavior, shouting at her to "act like a lady" and to get herself together so that she would be presentable enough to drive over to see his grandmother.

Under cross-examination, Mrs. Porto agreed with Ted Mathews that Marvin's account had made no sense. The walls of the condo were thin—sound carried easily, and even normal activity in the upstairs bedrooms could be easily heard on the ground floor." "If he'd been yelling," Porto said, "I think I would have heard him."

In that case, prompted Mathews, "He'd be telling you something that isn't true."

"Possibly," conceded Porto.

On Tuesday afternoon, at the end of only the second day of the prosecution's case, Weisberg began to call on his police witnesses.

Officer Keith Wong, who was on desk duty at the North Hollywood station when Marvin Pancoast turned himself in, admitted that he conducted only a "cursory" patdown of the suspect before handcuffing him to the bench outside the detective's room. Nor had he noticed any bloodstains or other telltale signs of a violent struggle on the defendant or on his clothing. He hadn't thought to examine the prisoner for that kind of thing, and neither had anyone else.

Cynthia Slauson, a fingerprint analyst with the LAPD's Scientific Investigations Division, led off the next morning's session of court, attempting to explain her failure to lift fingerprints from the alleged murder weapons. Slauson, a veteran of three thousand major crime-scene investigations and two thousand cases analyzed in the lab, told of applying four separate fingerprint tests, including a sophisticated laser examination that was possible only because her lab happened to have the equipment on a one-month loan.

The failure of all four tests was not especially unusual, Slauson explained, since fingerprints are recoverable only 30 to 40 percent of the time. "There are many factors as to why fingerprints may not be left behind on a surface. Some people tend not to secrete perspiration as much as other people. In other words, when they touch an object they may not leave a print, where another person may touch the same object and leave a print."

Another factor in the failure may have been the porous, scarred surface of the bat, which Slauson characterized as generally "not conducive" to retaining prints.

On cross-examination, however, Slauson conceded yet a third possible explanation: The bat was not delivered to her lab until July 26, a full nineteen days after the homicide. Prints do deteriorate over time, Slauson allowed, and such a long delay between the crime and the delivery of the bat to SID was by no means normal procedure. In her experience, it occurred in "only a very small percentage" of cases.

An even more dismal picture of the forensic investigation emerged from the testimony of Eston Schwecke, the SID serologist. Schwecke did not even receive the bat for testing until August 9, after Slauson's lab was finished with it. Since the entire bat, not just the handle, had been exposed to various chemicals in the process of testing for fingerprints—all without taking the simple precaution of removing a sample of dried blood in advance—Schwecke was unable to obtain any meaningful results.

This in itself was not necessarily a major calamity. No one seriously questioned that the blood on the bat was Vicki Morgan's—although conceivably the killer may have left some traces of blood behind as well.

More importantly, Schwecke recalled that at the time the bat was delivered to him it was wrapped in a green plastic garbage bag—as, apparently, it had been since the night of the murder. Storage in plastic, Schwecke said, tended to create a sauna effect, degrading the integrity of biological samples, including fingerprints and as bloodstains.

"So, if somebody wanted to destroy evidence," asked Ted Mathews, "[if] somebody had it in their mind to make it impossible to tell whose blood was on the bat, one very good way to do it would be to put it in a plastic bag and leave it there for a long period of time before giving it to you, isn't that right?"

"Could be, yes," agreed Schwecke.

Following Schwecke, Weisberg called Harry Tarello, the civilian jailer at the North Hollywood police station. Tarello said that around 3:45 A.M. on the morning of July 7, he was starting to think about heating up some breakfasts for the prisoners in custody. He left the lockup area, glanced down the hall, and saw the defendant sitting there on the prisoner's bench. "I walked toward him. . . . I was going to look for the arresting officer to find out if he was going to be booked," Tarello testified. "As I approached . . . I said, 'What are you here for?

"And he looked up at me and replied, 'Murder.'

"I was a little startled, and I repeated the word, 'murder.' And he said, 'Yeah. At least I think she's dead. I beat her with a baseball bat.' "

Testimonies continued, with Officer Henkle, a member of the first field unit to arrive, describing the condo the night of the murder, and then the jury heard from Bill Welch, the veteran homicide detective who was in charge of the crime-scene investigation.

Welch recalled that there had already been one killing in the precinct that evening. He had just arrived back in the homicide room from that investigation when Detective Ramsdell stuck his head in the door and scowled. "We just had another one. The guy just walked in and confessed."

About fifteen minutes later, a call came from the field unit confirming that the victim was dead.

"I was just walking out the back door," Welch said, "[when] I looked over and observed [a prisoner] handcuffed to the bench. I asked him what his name was. He told me his name was Marvin Pancoast. . . . He then immediately stated, "I did it. I killed Vicki. I hit her with a baseball bat.'

"I immediately said, 'Now look, wait a minute. I'm not here to interview you. One of my detectives will be interviewing you in a short period of time.' "

Welch arrived at the condo at around 4:25 A.M. and took only a brief look around before heading back to the stationhouse. He had decided to call in additional detectives, and it was routine practice to meet new men coming on shift at the station before proceeding to the crime scene.

As it happened, the only off-duty man he could reach was Detective Phil Sowers. While waiting for Sowers to arrive, he did some paperwork on the earlier homicide of the evening. He and Sowers rendezvoused at the station and were back at Colfax Avenue by approximately 5:50 A.M.

Welch now took his first good look around the premises. There were stacks of packed cardboard boxes downstairs and, throughout the condo, the sort of disarray that might be expected in a household in the midst of preparing for a move. Welch recalled that he "opened a few drawers" in the master bedroom and in the spare bedroom. He also unzipped a white duffle bag, a brown carry-all, and possibly one or two other small pieces of luggage that were sitting closed on the bedroom floor.

Welch didn't say in his testimony exactly what he was looking for, though presumably he may have been making a quick check for the presence of guns or drugs. However, he did not appear to have taken any special notice of the lacquer bowl filled with pill bottles that was sitting on the nightstand beside the victim's bed.

In the course of this search of the premises, Welch agreed on cross-examination, he also looked into the downstairs closet and discovered some three dozen audio cassettes stored on a shelf. He also saw a number of video tapes stored in the lacquer cabinet on the north wall of the master bedroom.

At this admission, Arthur Barens pounced triumphantly, "And what did you do with them?"

Welch, a ruddy-complexioned man to begin with turned even redder. "I didn't go downstairs and watch movies, counselor," he retorted indignantly.

Police photographer Makasuki arrived about 6:15 and began to take pictures of the crime scene. There were objects strewn on the floor throughout the condo, particularly in the master bedroom, where the police had found an empty bottle of Soave, the Fritos bag from Vicki's last snack, newspapers, and myriad other small items, yet Welch singled out the velour bathroom tie that happened to be lying in the carpeted hallway near the second bathroom. He then took the tie into evidence—a good indication that he had already heard the substance of the confession made by Pancoast at the stationhouse.

Welch made the decision that it would not be necessary to have a fingerprint technician come out to the scene. Nor did he consider taking the blood-spattered bed sheets into evidence. Nor did he ask Officer Henkle to demonstrate how the bat, which Henkle had placed on end in the hall, had been positioned at the time the police arrived—a significant omission, since Pancoast in his confession said he thought he had thrown the bat, not placed it carefully over the body.

Over the next several hours, Welch went on, he left the condo at least once, and possibly twice, on unrelated business. He also made several phone calls—calls that were not noted in the police log and which later led to some confusion on the part of the family when they appeared on the final phone bill.

One of his last acts prior to leaving the premises for good, shortly before nine A.M., was to take the baseball bat, still standing on end in the hall, and stuff it into a plastic trash bag that had come from the kitchen. The coroner, meanwhile, had already arrived and supervised the removal of the body.

Welch took the plastic bag containing the murder weapon with him and placed it in the evidence locker at the North Hollywood station. Normally, unless he decided to deliver it downtown personally, the bag would have been routinely transferred to the crime lab.

It wasn't until several weeks later, as he was preparing for the preliminary hearing, Welch recalled, that he called for the results of the lab tests. Then Welch learned for the first time that, through some mixup, the weapon had never been transferred to SID. Even then, he did not leave any special instructions for the testing.

Under cross-examination, Welch amplified his account by noting that he was not aware of the option of testing only the handle of the bat for prints in order to preserve the integrity of the blood samples. Nor did he much care. He was not particularly interested "in knowing the victim's blood type."

This was not, in short, the most thorough homicide investigation ever conducted.

There was, of course, an obvious explanation for Welch's lack of rigor. The perpetrator was already in custody. He'd turned himself in.

Welch had every reason to assume that this was one case that would never go to trial at all. The overwhelming probability was that Pancoast would eventually plead guilty—and, despite the official position of DA Philibosian that plea bargaining did not exist under his tenure—no doubt to a lesser crime than first-degree murder. Welch was a veteran officer, just a year and a few months away from retirement, and he was on his second homicide call on a hot July night. It would have been only human of him to have concluded that there was no sense in making a lot of busy work for himself and others.

Notwithstanding Barens' and Mathews' broad hints that the LAPD team at the condo had been engaged in some sort of coverup, nothing emerged from Detective Welch's testimony or any other source to support this view. Pancoast, after all, came to the LAPD, not the other way around, so even a putative motive for a coverup would be difficult to reconstruct.

Nevertheless, a few of the police's actions at the condo seem to have gone beyond routine slovenliness.

For one thing, Welch made a discretionary decision not to seal the scene of the crime. Under cross-examination Welch defended this as having been done out of "courtesy to the family."

This explanation sounded perfectly reasonable except that, as no one thought to point out to the jury, the press was already swarming all over the neighborhood by the time Welch left, nine o'clock in the morning. A mobile TV crew had been camped in the parking lot where it filmed the removal of the corpse. Reporters were going door-to-door, waking neighbors and asking questions. And either then or soon after, an enterprising AP photographer managed to take photos of the interior of the condo through an uncovered window—not a simple task, considering that to do so he had to have been inside the walled courtyard adjacent to the front door.

In view of all the hubbub, the decision not to seal the house would have appeared to have been a mixed blessing for the family.

Although the premises were not sealed, Welch testified, he did lock the door—a dead bolt requiring a key to lock from the outside—when he left for the last time. However, the first representative of the family to enter the condo, Sally Talbert's teenage son Matt, found the door unlocked when he arrived early in the afternoon.

It's possible that someone came in through the garage-level entrance—which Henkle and the other uniformed officers never checked. Once the news of Vicki Morgan's death was broadcast, any number of individuals might have had an interest in snooping around her apartment. If one of them did, he or she would have had a clear field. The condo was wide open.

* * *

*T*he reporters who remembered Pancoast's taped statement to Detective Jay Rush from the preliminary hearing called it the "Vicki This" confession—a reference to Marvin's complaint that, "She just went on about Vicki this, Vicki this, Vicki this, Vicki this. I couldn't take it anymore."

By the time Rush took the stand at the trial, it was apparent that the confession was going to be the linchpin of the prosecution's case. Keith Wong, Harry Tarello, and Detective Welch had all reported hearing Pancoast make self-incriminatory statements, but none of them had been in contact with him long enough to be able to say that he was not making the whole thing up, as the defense claimed—and for that matter, the prisoner's behavior, which Tarello had called unique in his experience, might even be interpreted in support of the idea that Pancoast was a compulsive confessor.

Normally, when a defendant repudiates a confession, he charges coercion. Barens' and Mathews' claim, novel but more difficult to disprove positively, was that Marvin had been too eager to confess, and Rush had credulously led the process along. In particular, the defense attorneys pointed to a moment early in the confession when Pancoast, who so far had been talking of other matters, told Rush, "I'm confused. You ask me questions."

When Rush took the stand to play the actual tape for the jury it turned out to be scratchy and, at times, inaudible. Nevertheless, Rush's tone of voice on the recording hardly suggested a high-pressure interrogation. Nor, at least until the subject of motive came up, was he ever close to putting words in Pancoast's mouth.

There was, however, an eerie quality of emotional displacement in Marvin's account. Although only hours away from a traumatic experience, Pancoast expressed neither remorse over Vicki Morgan's death nor, even more strikingly, any particular concern about what was going to become of him now.

At first, in fact, he hardly seemed conscious of being a central figure in the drama at hand. Instead, he sounded like some sort of minor functionary, intent on making the police's job easier for them. Obsessed with the worry that Connie Laney would leave Montclair on her way to the condo before being informed of her daughter's death, he refused to discuss the crime itself until he was sure that Rush had the phone numbers of Vicki's mother and sister, as well as the name of her lawyer, Michael Dave. Then, less understandably, he explained the location of the Jeep, which had been abandoned on Fairfax Avenue two days earlier, and extracted an assurance from Rush that his phone book, obviously a prized possession, would be turned over to the care of his mother.

Next, he shifted into the role of Marvin the explainer, eager to make sure that Rush understood "the history" of his victim. Impatient when the detective couldn't recall the name of the man Vicki Morgan lodged the palimony suit against, Marvin hurried to remind him:

> "Alfred Bloomingdale, of course, is Bloomingdale's department store—"
> RUSH: "Right."
> PANCOAST: "—in New York. And Diner's Club, he founded that. And Vicki was his mistress for twelve years."

Marvin's insistence on laying all this out, in making absolutely sure the detective knew Vicki's identity and that her situation had been "very political" was so striking that Stanley Weisberg would later characterize it acerbically as "establishing the credentials of his victim."

Finally, the voice of a man deeply distressed did come through on the tape. Growing increasingly agitated, Pancoast explained to Rush that he'd been staying with Vicki for three weeks "catering to her and being her little slave boy. Camp, not camp, but lackey, or whatever you want to call it . . . getting her glasses of water, going out and walking the dog, and giving her this and giving her that and getting her that. . . ." And after all that, on Wednesday night, she had told him she didn't want to move to Burbank, but she still had no idea what she was going to do the next day. "She was so coked out, so Valiumed out, so alcoholicked out."

Marvin told Rush that Vicki had been unable to sleep despite taking "two more Valiums" and drinking "a whole thing" of wine—the bottle of Soave he bought for her late Wednesday afternoon and that was found empty by her bedside. Unable to take it any longer, he first considered using the sash from the bathrobe that was hanging on the door of the hall bathroom. Then he abandoned that idea, went downstairs and found Todd's baseball bat "downstairs. . . . They cleaned out his room and there was [sic] some baseball things or tennis balls and the bat was there and I just grabbed it."

Marvin's account of the location of the bat was, of course,

wrong. The bat was in the back seat of the Oldsmobile, a detail of the story he later changed when he talked to reporter Andy Furillo.

After that, Marvin went on, he waited in the hall for either forty-five minutes or an hour and forty-five minutes until the light was "just right"—whatever that means—so that he could creep into the bedroom without Vicki seeing him. He also turned on the taps in the spare bathroom to muffle any sounds that might alert the neighbors—though it isn't clear how he could do this without risking tipping off Vicki that he was upstairs.

It was perfectly true that there were some factual discrepancies between this account and what Pancoast later told Furillo. In talking to Furillo, he omitted the business about the robe tie, got the location of the bat right, and said that he had spent the unaccounted-for time between his last words with Vicki and the crime itself downstairs in the kitchen, drinking coffee and trying to figure out what he was going to do. Whether these changes might be interpreted to mean that Pancoast had rationalized his fantasy over the intervening two days, as the defense suggested, was another matter—one, however, that the jury did not have a chance to consider since they never heard the contents of Furillo's version.

Barens and Mathews also contended, this time not at all unreasonably, that Pancoast's continual statements that he just wanted Vicki to "go to sleep" showed a lack of rational motive. One exchange on the tape, however, pointed to the fact that Pancoast, however twisted his reasoning may have been, knew exactly what he was doing:

> RUSH: "And you were trying to make her go to sleep?"
> MARVIN: "She wouldn't shut up."
> RUSH: "Marvin—"
> MARVIN: (unintelligible)
> RUSH: "Marvin, was the reason you hit her so many times was to kill her so that this wouldn't go on: Is that why you hit her?"
> MARVIN: "She was suffering."
> RUSH: "She was suffering?"
> MARVIN: "She asked to die. When we took Katy for a walk, she said she wished she was dead."

Dr. Willard Bucklin of L.A. county coroner's office saw the body of Vicki Morgan shortly before eleven A.M. on July 7, some eight hours after her death. In his preliminary examination he noted that the deceased was a "well nourished, well developed" but "slender" adult Caucasian female who "appears to be about the stated age of thirty years." She had died wearing light blue bikini-type panties, a yellow T-shirt, now heavily blood-soaked, and "a small quantity of red polish on her toenails." Her hair, untended for months, he described "as mottled light and dark brown measuring up to sixteen inches in length."

There was no difficulty in determining the cause of death, which he listed as "multiple skull fractures and intercerebral hemmorhage due to blunt force trauma." In layman's terms, the right side of the woman's head had been beaten in—crushed so thoroughly that "separation of individual injuries is difficult." Bucklin estimated, however, that there appeared to have been at least six distinct blows to the skull. In addition, there were multiple lacerations on both hands and on the right forearm as well as fractures of the fingers of both hands—classic defense wounds. Vicki Morgan had not been killed in her sleep.

Describing the autopsy procedure on the witness stand, Dr. Bucklin explained that the attacker had confined his blows to the right side of the skull. Here there were "gaping blunt lacerations" of the scalp and "numerous bone fragments up to one inch in diameter." The face, by contrast, was unmarked, except for one bruise on the cheek—which, he noted, appeared to be "not . . . very fresh" and unrelated to the cause of death.

More than one of the blows, possibly as many as four of them, would have been sufficient to kill, Bucklin added, and that death must have occurred "rather quickly," judging from the absence of fluid in the cranial cavity. Indeed, a liver temperature taken approximately ten minutes after eight in the morning gave an estimated time of death of four hours earlier. Allowing for a two-hour margin of error, Morgan died at two A.M. at the absolute earliest, suggesting that very little time elapsed between the killing and the time Pancoast turned himself in.

When it came time to explaining the results of the lab tests, Dr. Bucklin conceded that these did not jibe with the testimony that had been presented so far. The blood tests reflected an alcohol level of .05—a significant amount though not consistent with inebriation, but no traces of either cocaine or Valium.

Pancoast, whose statements are admittedly subject to question, described Vicki in his statement to Detective Rush as "all coked out, all Valiumed out." Specifically, he'd claimed that Vicki had drunk the bottle of Soave he purchased for her earlier in the evening and that she had taken several of the Valiums from his prescription that evening to help herself get to sleep.

Both Mrs. Laney and Sharon Porto also recalled Vicki using drugs that day. Mrs. Laney had said that she had seen Vicki sit at the kitchen table and take two Valiums. Porto recalled her calling from upstairs later, around three in the afternoon, to say that she planned to take two Valiums and try to rest. Porto had also seen Vicki drink about four ounces of wine that was left in a bottle in the refrigerator before asking Marvin to go out for a replacement.

How could these statements by eyewitnesses be reconciled?

In part, at least, they couldn't.

"Cocaine," explained Dr. Bucklin, is an "evanescent" drug, with a half-life in the bloodstream of under two hours. Nor is it likely to be detectable in the urine after twelve hours. As for alcohol, the burnoff ceases at death. An .05 reading could indicate, at normal burnoff rates, that the victim's blood level had been as high as .13 four hours earlier.

The absence of any finding of Valium, however, made no sense.

A tall, spare man with a snow-white beard, Dr. Bucklin permitted himself a scientist's show of impatience at the methods of the police, which made it impossible to take earlier, more accurate forensic readings. "The policy of the police department," he said mournfully, "is not to call the coroner when the body is found. They call the coroner when they want the coroner to come. And that is very unfortunate."

A delay in the arrival of the medical examiner, however, should not have interfered with the detection of Valium in Morgan's blood. In contrast to cocaine, Valium has a half-life in the blood of twelve to twenty-four hours. Under cross-examination by Ted Mathews, Dr. Bucklin readily conceded that as small an amount as one tablet taken twelve hours before death ought to have shown up in the blood tests.

Why didn't it?

A possible explanation is that the blood test for Valium was not made until July 14, a week after the murder; the cocaine test was not run until the nineteenth. Due to a lack of facilities at the morgue, the blood samples used were refrigerated, not frozen, and therefore could have deteriorated, which would have affected the test results.

Still, Dr. Bucklin could not see deterioration as a particularly likely explanation. "I would probably feel that there is no Valium there. That the tests were correct," he insisted in summary.

If he was correct, it could only mean that Porto, Laney, and Pancoast were all wrong and that Vicki, despite her habit of taking at least five to six Valiums daily, had suddenly gone cold turkey on one of the most stressful days of her life. Either that or Bucklin was wrong, and the medical examiner's bloodtests were so inaccurate as to be meaningless.

Before court adjourned on Monday, the beginning of the second week of the prosecution's case, Gordon Basichis took the stand to give his version of the fight between himself and Vicki a week before she died.

Basichis said the fight started when he reproached Vicki for her inability to concentrate on the book and for her general malaise. "I shoved her," Basichis recalls. "It was just a shoving contest. . . . She was hysterical. At one point I grabbed her by both arms and sat her down forcibly." Vicki then went upstairs. "I did not feel too good about what had taken place," Basichis said, but Vicki spurned his apology and ordered him out of the house. So he assumed that the relationship was finished.

On Tuesday, to his surprise, Vicki called and asked him to come to her place early that evening to talk things over. Although Basichis didn't say so on the witness stand, according to Marvin, Vicki had decided that the collaboration would never work and that she wanted to replace Gordon with another writer. She was hoping, however, that he would agree to turn over the tapes they had made so far to his successor. Gordon presumably talked her out of it.

At any rate, when Marvin arrived home from his AA meeting three hours later, already upset because he'd had trouble with the Jeep's headlights and had to leave it parked on Fairfax Avenue, Vicki and Gordon were still seated in the living room having a very amiable discussion.

"He saw us there," Basichis recalls. "[And] he was very red-faced. He seemed very surprised. Physically, he was trembling. We didn't talk very much."

He and Vicki stayed up in the living room, "talking mainly about the book," until 9:30 in the morning. Until nearly 2:30, they could hear Marvin in the spare bedroom "pacing continually overhead." By 7:30 A.M., Marvin was awake again, at which time Vicki sent him out to pick up bagels and coffee.

Bizarrely enough, the only conversation Basichis could recall having with Marvin on the day of the murder concerned baseball. Marvin, he said, complained bitterly to him that because of Vicki and her problems he'd missed a lot of the Dodgers' games during the first half of the season and would now most likely miss that night's all-star game as well.

"I didn't know you were a fan," Basichis recalled saying.

Finally, Basichis disclosed that he spoke with Vicki by phone twice on Wednesday night after her mother and her son had left the condo. During the first call, which came at 10:15 and lasted ten minutes or so, he could hear Marvin in the background, telling Vicki that she ought to pay him for the car leased in his name that she had recently wrecked. Vicki wanted to know whether Gordon felt this was fair. During the second call, around 11:20, Vicki mentioned that Marvin was planning to get up at six A.M. to go to his grandmother's house. Again, Marvin's voice could be heard over the line, this time saying that he was planning to get up at four A.M., not six. Despite the disagreement over the car, Basichis had no sense that there was anything drastically wrong.

It had been no secret that Arthur Barens hoped to convince the jury that Gordon Basichis was the real killer. Nearly every day, he'd given carefully worded quotes to the reporters in the corridor, noting that Basichis "could not be ruled out as a suspect."

On the stand, Basichis missed no opportunity to signal his contempt for Barens and, seemingly, for the entire proceeding. He squirmed in his seat in an exaggerated parody of boredom, smirked broadly, and delivered his replies in a voice dripping with arrogance.

Asked by Barens how many times he slept with Vicki, he said, disdainfully, "I didn't keep count."

And, seemingly unaware of the unpleasant implications, since he'd just admitted to a fight that had left Vicki with an ugly bruise on her cheek, he volunteered an account of a discussion he'd had with Vicki a few weeks before her death. He and Vicki, he said, happened to get into a conversation about different modes of death. "They can do anything they want to me," Vicki had joked. "They can draw and quarter me. As long as they don't touch my face."

"She was proud of her face," Basichis explained helpfully.

But it was during a sequence of questions about cocaine that

Basichis blundered into real trouble. Despite the testimony of Sharon Porto and Connie Laney's earlier statements to the police and to reporters, Basichis denied ever bringing cocaine to the condo.

"Did Vicki ever use drugs in your presence?" asked Barens.

"I was not aware of it," Basichis replied.

". . . Did you ever use cocaine in your life?" Barens persisted.

And again, Basichis answered in the negative.

The reply sent a ripple of surprise through the packed courtroom. No doubt there exist aspiring Hollywood script-writers who have never so much as snorted a line at a party, but on the face of it, Gordon Basichis would not have seemed to be one of them—particularly in view of Sharon Porto's vivid account of her arrival at the condo that morning.

Perhaps it was unfair that the question should have been asked at all. Gordon Basichis was not on trial, and whether he used cocaine during his lifetime had no particular relevance to the issue at hand. Nevertheless, it was asked, and Basichis's denial had opened up the opportunity for the defense to call its own witnesses to impeach his testimony.

Basichis left the witness stand looking quite pleased with himself, apparently unaware of the can of worms he had opened.

The first witness to be called on Tuesday morning was Marcia Basichis, Gordon's wife of ten years. Tall and angular, with white blond hair, Mrs. Basichis had only recently left ABC, where she oversaw ongoing network series, to join Aaron Spelling, the independent producer of *Dynasty*. A tightly wound, intense woman with the look of one who has given a good account of herself in many a high-pressure meeting, she seemed determined to be equally combative on her husband's behalf.

Mrs. Basichis allowed that she "suspected" her husband's affair with Vicki Morgan but had decided not to press the issue. As for the night of the murder, she and her husband stayed home and watched the all-star game on TV with a friend. After the friend left, they stayed up talking until shortly after four o'clock in the morning. She remembered the time specifically because she'd been planning to get up for work the next day. Instead, she was awakened early the next morning with the news that Vicki had been murdered.

The defense had produced not a shred of evidence to suggest that Gordon Basichis was anywhere but at home on the night of the murder. Still, it was not out of the question that the jury might find his wife's claim to have stayed up until after four on a work night just a bit too neat.

And as it turned out, the Basichises were to be the prosecution's final witnesses. Stanley Weisberg had been planning to end his case on a more compelling note, with the confession that the defendant made to *Herald-Examiner* reporter Andy Furillo—an account more detailed and complete than the one he gave to Detective Rush. But Furillo, understandably concerned that testifying might be betraying an implicit trust, not to mention making his job more difficult in the future, decided to invoke the California shield law that protects reporters from having to answer questions beyond affirming what had already been published under their names. This meant that defense attorneys would have no opportunity to ask Furillo about Marvin's demeanor at the time they talked. Was he coherent? Rational? Or, possibly, behaving in a manner that might have given Furillo some reason to doubt the truth of what was said?

Under the circumstances, Judge Horowitz ruled that Furillo's article and his testimony about it could not be admitted into evidence at all. In effect, the ruling meant that the entire case against Marvin Pancoast rested on his statements to the LAPD—and the police work on the case had so far been shown to be singularly inept and unreliable.

Suddenly, a conviction no longer seemed inevitable.

SOME STATEMENTS ABOUT OTHER PEOPLE'S MOTIVES

///

For several days now, the press had been hearing hints from Arthur Barens and Ted Mathews that they intend to introduce dramatic new fingerprint evidence. As their expert witness, a young woman named Carol Hunter Rhodes, had other commitments later in the week, Judge Horowitz had agreed to allow her to take the stand immediately, before the opening statements for the defense.

Rhodes, proprietor of the California Laboratory of Forensic Science in Orange County, California, was a petite redhead who could easily have passed for sixteen. She wore a navy blue suit and a blouse with a Peter Pan collar, an outfit that had the no-doubt-unintended effect of making her look like an earnest student at a Catholic girls' high school, dressed for an important interview with the mother superior.

Rhodes started off by explaining that her attempt to test the dried blood on the bat was even less successful than the LAPD's. The best she could do was to establish that the blood was human. She could not even get an ABO blood typing result. However, Rhodes did contest the contention that the surface of the bat was too porous to retain fingerprints. In fact, she was prepared to perform a demonstration on the spot that would prove otherwise.

Stanley Weisberg immediately objected, pointing out that Rhodes's primary expertise was in serology.

"Right now you're trying to branch out into fingerprinting?" he asked sarcastically.

Obviously unused to being personally attacked, Rhodes let herself get flustered. Although her answers to Weisberg's substantive questions about her knowledge of the expert literature were in fact much the same as the LAPD's Slauson, she was soon all but apologizing "To my knowledge, which is not extensive," she said in prefacing one of her replies—a phrase that did not help her chances of being credentialed as an expert.

Weisberg won the skirmish but lost the battle. Although Judge Horowitz refused to let Carol Hunter Rhodes attempt her demonstration, Barens and Mathews were permitted to try the same test with the LAPD's own Cynthia Slauson the next morning.

At Arthur Barens's request, Slauson produced a fingerprinting kit of the type that routinely used by crime scene technicians. While Slauson described the black powder test, Barens, who had been mediatively grasping the alleged murder weapon in both hands, wondered aloud if Slauson would be prepared to demonstrate the dusting technique on the spot, right there in this courtroom.

This time, the judge ruled that the demonstration could proceed.

Barens surrendered the bat and watched anxiously as Slauson applied the sootlike powder to the handle.

And nothing happened!

Barens looked briefly distressed, then pulled himself together enough to ask the witness, rhetorically, if it wasn't true that some individuals were less likely to produce fingerprints than others. For example, a cool, calculating person might be able to handle an object without creating prints while a highly emotional one, prone to agitation and sweaty palms, would leave prints galore.

Slauson agreed that, yes, this was a good possibility, and Barens shot a well-timed glance in the direction of his associate Ted Mathews, telegraphing that it had just occurred to him that Mathews might indeed be the sweaty-palmed-type.

By now, the densest spectator had to realize that he was witnessing a prescripted performance. Nevertheless, it was hard not to feel caught up in the suspense as Mathews took the bat in his large hands and then passed it mournfully back to the witness, who began to apply another coat of dusting powder.

Mathews had good reason to be perspiring in earnest, since if Slauson failed, he would look foolish indeed. When a series of white ovals, clearly visible even from the back of the courtroom, materialized against the black background of the dusted bat, he seemed hugely relieved.

Theatrical, even hokey, the black powder demonstration did serve its purpose by underlining a point the jurors must have already grasped on their own: The LAPD's failure to take prints from the bat was more likely to be the fault of mishandling of evidence than of the bat itself.

In hindsight, it would seem that Weisberg's attack on Carol Hunter Rhodes had misfired. Now it was obvious to all that she had been telling the truth when she said that she would have no trouble getting prints from the bat. And if she was no great expert in fingerprinting, so much the worse for the prosecution's position. On the other hand, the defense may well have gone too far in tacking on the observation that a highly emotional, distressed individual would be more likely to leave discernible prints.

Whatever his state may have been in the early hours of July 7, 1983, the man seated at the defense table appeared to be anything but the sweaty-palmed type, as Barens would put it. Although it was an unusually hot June in Southern California, with temperatures in the high nineties, and the courtroom air conditioning by no means excessive, Marvin Pancoast had been appearing in court every day wearing a crew-neck sweater between his shirt and suit jacket.

In the corridor that noontime, a few reporters engaged Detective Welch in some goodnatured banter: "I bet you'll never put a murder weapon in a plastic bag again," joked Rich Varenchik of the L.A. *Daily News*.

Although the comment was by no stretch of the imagination accusatory, Welch seemed offended. "Of course, I will. I'll do the same thing next time," he retorted.

Thus die all illusions that real-life LAPD homicide investigations bear any resemblance to the plots so familiar from *Columbo* and *Quincy* reruns.

In the meantime, out of the hearing of the jury, Judge Horowitz had issued a stern warning to the counsel for the defense. "During the course of the trial there've been some statements with regard to other people's motives," the judge observed. "I am concerned that during the course of an opening statement you may make statements about things you intend to prove . . . [and] later there would be a decision that some of this would not be admitted." Horowitz reminded the defense that the mere fact that someone else had a motive to commit the crime in question was not admissible, unless they could produce some actual evidence pointing to guilt.

Stanley Weisberg would have liked to go farther. He even suggested that the defense's opening statement be vetted during an *in camera* hearing—an unusual move which the court immediately vetoed.

Perhaps in response to the judge's warnings, Arthur Barens' delayed opening statement turned out to be brief and fairly circumspect. However, Barens's outline of the defense version of the crime marked the first time that the jury had heard Marvin's story of the murder—that he was in the bed beside Vicki, unconscious and presumably chloroformed by the real killer or killers.

Surely, it would have been easier to leave the jury under the impression that Marvin was asleep in the spare bedroom, perhaps sedated by Valium, when the killing took place. If so, an unknown assassin could have entered and left without even realizing that Marvin was present. There was only one car in the garage, the blue Oldsmobile, and Marvin may well have left it unlocked when he returned from his unsuccessful errand to pick up the next day's papers. The baseball bat, clearly visible on the shelf inside the rear windshield, would have been a opportunistic choice for any outsider who did not want a weapon that could be traced back to himself.

Such a scenario would have been difficult to disprove positively—but it happened not to be what Marvin said had happened. To believe his account, the jury would have to assume that a killer saw him in bed with the victim, immobilized him with chloroform or by some other means, and then departed, leaving him alive to take the blame—which would no doubt have fallen on him whether or not he confessed. There had to have been, in short, a deliberate plot not just to kill Vicki Morgan but to cover up the real reason for the murder.

And this was exactly what Barens contended: that Vicki Morgan was killed because she had possession of video tapes that she may or may not have been attempting to use in a blackmail or extortion scheme. "The defense will show," Barens promised, "[that] Vicki Morgan had an insurance policy consisting of at least three video tapes consisting of her in sex activities with three members of the administration."

Barens said little about Gordon Basichis in his opening remarks, except to charge that Basichis had lied "on several important occasions." Once the opening statement was out of the way, however, it became clear that Basichis was still Barens' and Mathews' prime target.

The first defense witness of the afternoon was Jewell Seaver, a thin, olive-complexioned brunette who owned the Stone Canyon house where Gordon and Marcia Basichis were living in the summer of 1983. Mrs. Seaver recalled that at first she and her tenants had been quite friendly; she and Gordon Basichis had discussions about the benefits of hypnosis, and Gordon had even offered to hypnotize her himself. After some months, though, relations between the landlady and her tenants went sour.

In the early summer of 1983, said Mrs. Seaver, Gordon called her in the middle of the night to say that a pipe had broken in the house and that he wanted her to send for a plumber right away. Seaver tried to explain that it would be impossible to get anyone to fix the pipes after midnight. At that point, she recalled, Basichis became abusive and began "threatening me."

After that argument, continued Seaver, the Basichises stopped paying rent. In September she went to court, where she was awarded a default judgment of "$2,651.80" and eviction proceedings were set in motion.

Around the beginning of October, however, a gardener she employed to care for her rental properties informed her that the house was empty. Still nervous about Gordon Basichis' threats, which she took seriously, Mrs. Seaver had a policeman accompany her when she went to the house to verify that it was unoccupied.

The Basichises had left behind them a number of personal possessions, including old papers and phone bills, and, according to Seaver, in the upstairs bathroom some razor blades and a "cut-down" straw. Later, while inspecting the living room, Seaver testified, she noticed the corner of a white envelope protruding from a heating vent located above eye level. On inspection she found "some paraphernalia" secreted in the vent and, in the envelope, a small amount of white powder. She placed a few grains of the substance on her fingertip and tasted it, and when she found that it made her tongue slightly numb, concluded that it was cocaine.

During the recess following Seaver's testimony, Stanley Weisberg entertained members of the press out in the hall with some belittling comments about Mrs. Seaver's performance on the stand. Although she had admitted to having encountered cocaine "once, at a party," the witness was hardly an expert at drug analysis, Weisberg pointed out. How could she have been so sure that the substance she found was cocaine? Furthermore, he added, what's so unusual about finding razor blades in a bathroom? Presumably, the "cut-down" straw would have been used to drink tiny little glasses of lemonade while shaving.

At any rate, the thrust of Mrs. Seaver's testimony was confirmed by the second witness of the afternoon, Vicki's attorney Michael Dave.

Dave described an incident that occurred on the evening of Vicki's memorial service, at the postfuneral gathering at the Talberts' house. According to Dave, Gordon Basichis showed up while the "party" was still going on and demanded a private discussion. Since the TV news had just broadcast Robert Steinberg's announcement about the alleged sex tapes, it was a particularly bad moment for the family and no one was in any mood to discuss practicalities. Dave suggested that the two of them retreat to an upstairs bedroom.

While they were talking, Dave testified, Basichis "pulled out a vial . . . a small glass vial, clear glass, and then asked if I would forgive him his nasty habit." Basichis then proceeded to treat himself to a snort of coke. Describing the scene with the detached precision of an anthropologist reporting on some obscure tribal ritual, Dave noted that Basichis had administered the powder to himself with a "small, spoon-shaped implement . . . one nostril at a time."

The significance of Dave and Seaver's testimony was not so much that Gordon Basichis used cocaine, but that—assuming they told the truth—he lied. The defense was all too clearly hoping that the jury would conclude that a man who used drugs and then lied about it under oath, and who deceived his wife by starting an affair while she was nine-months pregnant, would also be capable of murder—a wild surmise at best. They were, however, remarkably successful at making the proceedings not the trial of Marvin Pancoast but an inquisition into the character of Gordon Basichis.

Strikingly enough, even those who were utterly convinced that Pancoast was the actual killer often seemed to be reserving their deepest antagonism for Basichis. Connie Laney, in her testimony, had not only pointedly dismissed the writer as "a person called Gordon Basichis" but had startled the courtroom on several occasions by substituting his name for Marvin's in the course of negative remarks. And later, Weisberg, obviously unhappy at the performance of his own witness, took to referring dryly to Gordon and Marcia as "the Basichi."

When they moved from casting suspicion on Basichis to attempting to prove a blackmail connection, the defense's case soon got mired in the quicksand of unsupportable rumor.

Cindy Stonehouse, the woman whose call to Robert Steinberg set the tapes brouhaha into motion in the first place, appeared as a character witness for the defendant, declaring effusively that Marvin was "just a wonderful person" and a loyal friend. Sure, he was a manic-depressive, but "no one is more fun than a manic when they're up" she added—a statement that may not have seemed quite so self-evident to the jury.

Marvin did have an irrational tendency to take the blame for anything that went wrong, Stonehouse qualified. When they were in Woodview-Calabasas together, she noticed that Marvin would go into a state of extreme depression and remorse over other patients' setbacks—"He'd go around saying, 'It's my fault. I should have been nicer to him.' "

Unfortunately for the defense, however, Stonehouse could not confirm the rumor that Marvin was a compulsive confessor who at one time attempted to turn himself in for the Manson family slayings.

"Did the defendant ever take the blame for any criminal acts?" asked Barens. There was a long pause, suggesting that perhaps Stonehouse may have had some indirect knowledge that she was weighing. "Not to me personally. No," she finally answered.

On the subject of the tapes, the defense found itself falling back on Robert K. Steinberg, a problematic witness, to say the least.

Pasty-faced and visibly shaky, Steinberg appeared in court looking a good twenty years older than he had in July 1983, when he went public with his story about sex tapes. During recess, while his attorney Peter Brown, a dapper Pierre Trudeau lookalike, gave interviews in the corridor along with Barens and Mathews, Steinberg could be found sitting almost unnoticed in the spectator session of the courtroom. "I've been keeping my mouth shut," he said when approached for a comment, "which is something I should have learned to do a long time ago."

Still under indictment for filing a false police report about the tapes' theft, Steinberg refused to answer any questions about the tapes on Fifth Amendment grounds, and the defense promptly requested that Judge Horowitz confer immunity on Steinberg for the misdemeanor charge so that he could testify freely.

The jury was exiled from the courtroom for the better part of the day while the attorneys wrangled, and in the course of the arguments, it developed that there was still another obstacle to Steinberg's testimony: His conversation with Marvin Pancoast at the LA county jail was protected by the attorney–client privilege—and Barens, though he'd called Steinberg as a defense witness, refused to waive the privilege on his client's behalf. So, even if Judge Horowitz did grant immunity, Steinberg still could not be cross-examined about anything Marvin may have said to him.

For example, when asked, "Were you told [by Marvin] that Vicki was killed for tapes?" Steinberg refused to say one way or another. "I'm not trying to pass the buck," he apologized to the court. "I'd like to answer if I could."

It did not take a great deal of imagination to see that if this dialogue continued in the presence of the jurors, some of them might come to the conclusion that information supporting the defendant's innocence was being suppressed.

By now, Weisberg was reminding Barens in front of the courtroom that he himself told the grand jury in August that he considered Steinberg a "crank" and the tapes irrelevant to Pancoast's defense.

"The quotation that Mr. Weisberg quotes," Barens could only reply lamely, "was before I'd had an opportunity to interview any witnesses in this case."

"If there are such witnesses," Weisberg shot back, "where are they?"

By this time, sentiment in the press section was almost unanimously with the prosecution. It appeared obvious that Barens was bluffing and, moreover, that the entire premise of the defense was completely cynical. Ironically, perhaps, the latter was not quite true. There was indeed one individual in the courtroom who might have been able to affirm the existence of sex tapes, if only Steinberg's legal problems were safely out of the way—an individual whose identity would not be disclosed until months after the trial.

The problem was that no one except Marvin Pancoast (and Steinberg, who may well have heard it from him) had ever asserted that the tapes, even assuming they did exist, involved political figures—and the entire logic behind the defense's contention that Marvin's confession was false arose from their claim that their client was a pathological liar, incapable of telling truth from fiction. Eventually, Judge Horowitz ruled that the entire subject of tapes was inadmissible for exactly that reason. The judge had already allowed a good deal more leeway for fishing expeditions than the defense would have been permitted in many another courtroom.

Even so, Barens and Mathews could not resist trying to slip in one more reference to the elusive tapes. In the closing minutes of the afternoon's proceedings, Barens called on a surprise witness—Carol Helen Gwenn. A heavy, round-faced woman, with intelligent brown eyes that signaled her extreme unease at finding herself on the witness stand, Gwenn admitted with no particular enthusiasm that she had been a friend and co-worker of Marvin Pancoast during the time he was employed by the William Morris Agency.

"Did you periodically at that time speak with Mr. Pancoast?" asked Ted Mathews.

"Yes," agreed Gwenn.

"Can you tell me if at any time before the date of July seventh of 1983 if Mr. Pancoast ever spoke to you about sex tapes involving Vicki Morgan and anyone else?"

"Yes," said Gwenn, in a barely audible voice.

Stanley Weisberg jumped to his feet. "Objection. Hearsay. Move to strike that answer."

The objection was sustained.

Outside in the hallway, Gwenn confirmed that Marvin was talking about tapes "one and a half to two years" before Vicki Morgan died.

Did she believe the tapes existed? Gwenn was asked.

She nodded her head and seemed prepared to elaborate when a swarm of TV technicians, fully armed with floodlights and sound equipment, suddenly swooped down on her. Someone thrust a microphone in front of Gwenn's lips. "I really don't think I should be talking about this," she blurted out and promptly fled in the direction of the elevators.

Gwenn made good her escape, taking off from the parking lot in an ancient blue VW Beetle, as those who'd birddogged her steps all the way stood around feeling semi-abashed. In a case populated with publicity seekers, it was just the press's luck that the one individual who promised to have something interesting and novel to say would turn out to be the one who could not be tempted by the promise of fifteen seconds' exposure on the evening news.

THE DOG THAT DIDN'T BARK IN THE NIGHT

So far, Marvin Pancoast had been the forgotten man of the trial. The witnesses who had referred to him—Connie Laney, Sharon Porto, and Gordon Basichis—had each in different ways left the impression that he was a shadowy figure, always hovering in the background but so easily dismissed that even his dramatic shift in mood just prior to the murder was scarcely taken seriously.

Tuesday morning's session opened with an expert who might be able to give a more substantive profile of Marvin's personality. Dr. William Vicary, one of the three psychiatrists appointed by the court to interview Pancoast after his arrest, was a youngish man who wore a neat mustache and had the mannerisms of a bright, eager-to-please graduate student. His credentials, which included both a degree from Harvard Law School and an M.D. from the University of Southern California—belied any suggestion that he might be a lightweight. Nor, it soon became apparent, was Dr. Vicary one of those psychiatric experts who come into the courtroom in the spirit of a missionary about to preach enlightenment to the heathens. A forensic specialist, Dr. Vicary was as much at home on the witness stand as in a hospital ward, which may have been precisely the reason why Barens and Mathews called on him. He could be counted on to give concise, understandable answers to their questions without blundering into areas that the defense might have preferred to leave unexplored.

Although the question of the defendant's sanity had been reserved for the second phase of the trial, what the defense wanted from Vicary was a portrait of Marvin the masochist—a man who sought out abuse and humiliation and who therefore had no rational motive to kill the woman who gave him exactly the treatment he craved.

To some extent, Dr. Vicary's testimony confirmed this picture. Despite numerous suicide attempts, Vicary agreed, Marvin had no history whatsoever of violent behavior towards others.

Marvin, he went on, was a "highly suggestible personality," easily led and tormented by guilt. "Throughout his life," Vicary explained, "[Marvin] has been useful or comfortable in a one-down position. That is, where he is the slave and the other person is the master." Recalling his own evaluation interview with the defendant, Dr. Vicary said that Marvin "was constantly apologizing. Saying that it was hard for me to come to the jail and interview him. And wasn't I getting tired?" He then apologized abjectly for lighting a cigarette, "as if it were a significant sin."

During the course of this interview, which took place in August 1983, Marvin also expressed dismay that the doctors he'd seen since his arrest now said he did not have AIDS after all, only a cluster of opportunistic infections including hepatitis and mononucleosis. He told me, said Vicary, "If I don't have AIDS, I want to have AIDS."

Unfortunately for the defense, while there was nothing in the Marvin's medical records to show that he ever engaged in violent behavior, there was plenty to suggest that he harbored aggressive, even homicidal fantasies. One reference in the defendant's file—a prediction by two of Pancoast's doctors that he might be "capable of mass murder"—so troubled Judge Horowitz that he interrupted Vicary's testimony to warn attorneys from both sides that he considered this speculative phrase so "explosive" that he has no intention of allowing it into evidence at this stage of the trial. However, the judge did allow Weisberg to question the witness about his own expert observations during the sanity-determination interview.

Did not Dr. Vicary note in his report of that interview, Weisberg asked, that Marvin Pancoast was living with "an accumulation of frustration, hostility, and anger"?

> VICARY: Yes.
> "Is it directed against any particular person or persons?"
> VICARY: ". . . Several persons."
> Including his mother, father, his brother's four children?"
> VICARY: "Yes, and the patient himself."

And in the Cedars-Sinai records, Weisberg went on, "Is there a reference to the relationship with Vicki Morgan mirroring his relationship with his mother?"

> VICARY: "Yes."
> And isn't there a reference to the patient that says, 'The patient can become actively suicidal or homicidal and therefore should not be allowed to live with Vicki Morgan'?"
> VICARY: "Yes."
> "In the records of Camarillo, is there a reference to the patient having suicidal and homicidal tendencies beyond his control?"
> VICARY: "Yes, there is."

Trying to undo some of the damage, Ted Mathews had Vicary read aloud from the file of Dr. Cantalupo, Marvin's therapist during the early summer of 1983:

> May 23, 1983—I can't help him, Mark (Pancoast's AA sponsor) can't help him, unless he stops lying and tells the truth. . . . I

have absolutely no way of knowing whether he is telling the truth. He is getting drunk and lying to me.

June 6–8—His diagnosis is now clear as a psychopathic personality. He is definitely not psychotic and not a danger to himself or to others. . . . There appears to be no danger whatsoever that he will ever make a homicidal gesture towards his mother.

June 10—I pointed out to him that there's no way I could continue to work with him when he was so dishonest and so manipulative.

June 20—I am considering discharging him since we are not getting anywhere.

June 23—[The patient] seems to have his impulses well under control except for his sexual promiscuity.

June 27—He admitted that he did not really know if he wanted to live with her [Vicki Morgan]. He is not suicidal and no longer talks about wanting to kill his mother.

June 30—[Moving in with Vicki may not be] in his best interests. He disapproves of what is going on between her and her lover.

And finally, after his last session with Pancoast on July 5, Dr. Cantalupo wrote, "Not suicidal. . . . He feels angry that the writer [Basichis] is not helping [Vicki], but takes advantage of her instead. He doesn't want to live with her. . . . No current evidence of danger to himself or to others."

Although some of the statements in these notes could cut both ways, what Mathews wanted the jury to extract from them was that Cantalupo could see no signs whatsoever that Marvin was about to break out of his lifelong pattern and commit a violent act. Furthermore, Mathews suggested, Dr. Cantalupo's records show that Marvin was a confirmed homosexual and thus could not possibly have had a sexual motive for being jealous of Gordon Basichis.

"Yes," Dr. Vicary said helpfully, "[but] he *was* having a sexual relationship with Vicki Morgan. According to what he told me . . . He told me that he'd had heterosexual intercourse with her on several occasions. Indeed, when he first met her at Cedars-Sinai."

Mathews looked stunned. "And you believed him?" he asks.

"Yes, I did," says Vicary.

"Did it occur to you that he might be lying?"

"Yes," insisted Vicary. Naturally, he was always skeptical in dealing with patients and was particularly so in this instance. Still, both the content of what Marvin said about his relations with Vicki and his manner while saying it suggested powerfully that he was telling the truth. Marvin had confided that he'd had sex with Vicki perhaps twenty times over the course of their four-year relationship—hardly the statement of a man laboring under delusions of grandeur.

To Mathews's dismay, Dr. Vicary went on to say that he couldn't agree that Marvin was a pathological liar. Although Pancoast may well have been easily influenced by authority figures and might lie on occasion to further what he perceived as his own interests, that didn't mean that he wasn't perfectly capable of distinguishing truth from falsehood. Dr. Vicary volunteered that he found Pancoast's confession to Detective Rush completely credible and that, judging by the tape-recorded transcript of the conversation, Pancoast's "demeanor was consistent with an individual that is basically not fabricating."

What's more, Dr. Vicary added, Marvin told him during the evaluation interview that he had originally planned to commit murder and suicide simultaneously, by driving his car over a cliff while Vicki was in the passenger seat.

After Dr. Vicary, the jury heard briefly from Dr. Cantalupo himself. Cantalupo confirmed that, while seeing Marvin several times weekly, he had no sense that he might be on the point of committing a violent act. Even though mandated by law to contact any individual potentially endangered by a patient, he "never felt it necessary to warn Vicki Morgan or Marvin Pancoast's mother."

On cross-examination, Stanley Weisberg contented himself with a single question: "Dr. Cantalupo," he asked, "did you ever make a mistake in your life?"

Cantalupo, braced for quite a grilling at the hands of the prosecution, looked first wary then relieved. "Yes, of course," he sighed.

Weisberg nodded. "Nothing else."

An ancient gambit, but seldom used in such an apropos situation, the sally drew laughter from the spectators and even a few smiles from the jurors.

Wednesday afternoon ended with a minidrama in the form of return appearances by Gordon and Marcia Basichis. Belatedly realizing that they, too, could get in a few shots in the media war, the Basichises had arrived at the courthouse equipped with color snapshots showing the damage done by the plumbing leak at the house they rented from Mrs. Seaver—evidence, they said, that they were within their rights in withholding the rent.

On the witness stand for the second time, Basichis gave a repeat of his earlier performance. He dismissed the statements of Jewell Seaver, the landlady, and Michael Dave as patently "absurd." He also denied that the collaboration agreement between himself and Vicki was on the point of breaking up. Neither of them, he said, had ever accused the other of being in breach of contract. Nevertheless, after more than eight months of work, only six hour-long minicassettes had been filled with taped interviews and only eighteen of nineteen pages of the first chapter were actually written—though these, Basichis added, had been "honed and rehoned." The work with Vicki was going slowly "because it took a while to loosen her up, and the process became more informal as time went on."

TV correspondents present in the courtroom on Wednesday were quick to focus on the most titillating moments of the day's testimony and draw the obvious inference. "Marvin had AIDS— May have given it to Vicki" was the lead story on one local news show that evening. This was not at all what Vicary had said. Still, the story was not as farfetched as those who relied solely on the trial record were led to believe. Barens and Mathews had engaged two physicians to examine their client. One had concurred with the county doctor's position that Pancoast was AIDS-free, but the second believed that he was in the early stages of the disease. The defense had concluded that no useful purpose would be served by introducing these ambivalent findings in court.

Surprisingly, in the wake of the dispiriting events of the last few days in court, Barens and Mathews were in an ebullient mood as they prepared to wrap up their presentation of evidence. They had new witnesses, they boasted to reporters that morning. There had been a major breakthrough in the case.

But the witnesses, when they appeared, turned out to be drawn from the already familiar cast—Detective Welch, Connie Laney, and Michael Dave, along with one new face, Vicki's longtime friend Sally Talbert. The subject was audio tapes, a minor variation on the old theme.

Belatedly, Barens and Mathews had seized on the fact that Vicki Morgan's family was not satisfied that the six research tapes acknowledged by Basichis were the only ones in existence. Talbert and Mrs. Laney were both prepared to testify that they had reason to believe Vicki had recorded more than six hours of reminiscences.

Once again, the judge made the expected ruling, cutting off the new line of inquiry as irrelevant and hearsay. However, this final group of witnesses did add a bizarre footnote to the case.

Detective Welch disclosed for the first time his reason for never bothering to examine the tapes that had been found at the condo to see if they might have some bearing on the murder. "I had several conversations with Mr. Dave," Welch explained, "and I've known Mr. Dave since high school, and he told me they were of no evidentiary value. . . . and I took him at his word."

Friendship or not, Welch contradicted Dave's earlier account that he had originally talked of obtaining a search warrant to seize the tapes and groused about being under pressure from higherups. None of this, said Welch, ever happened.

Michael Dave in turn testified that he had scanned the tapes only "very briefly," sampling segments at random and then fast-forwarding through the remainder once he had satisfied himself that the contents were unremarkable. Dave, normally so precise and meticulous in his speech, could not even say with any degree of certainty just how many video tapes there were. Dave said that Vicki's half-brother Patrick had turned over to him "eleven or thirteen" Betamax tapes that were found in the black lacquer cabinet in Vicki's bedroom. Three of these were commercial movies. Dave mentioned one title—Steve Martin's *The Jerk;* he had previously told the grand jury that two of the tapes contained X-rated films, *Emmanuelle, Joys of a Woman,* and *800 Fantasy Lane.* The remainder of the tapes—"eight or nine or ten" of them, estimated Dave—had been purchased blank and used to record various TV broadcasts, including news shows. Presumably, at least some of these reels would have been the ones Marvin Pancoast had used to make a record of news reports on the palimony suit.

Purely as a matter of speculation, it was interesting that the number of tapes obtained and vetted by Dave appeared to be nebulous by a factor of three. Of course, there could be innocent explanations for the uncertainty over numbers, beginning with a simple lapse of memory on the witness's part. Perhaps the most curious aspect of the revelations was that Arthur Barens, who had staked his entire case on the existence of sex tapes, appeared to be as incurious about the subject as Welch and Dave were. From the defense's point of view, the tapes were only of interest as a hypothetical motive for murder. If, by some remote chance, it should turn out that they had been around all along—overlooked and dismissed by everyone as of no importance—their existence would be as embarrassing to the defense as to anyone else.

As closing arguments in the trial got under way on the morning of July 3, Stanley Weisberg served notice that he was not going to be satisfied with anything less than a first-degree-murder conviction. Weisberg urged the jury not to be sidetracked by the notion that Marvin Pancoast may have killed Vicki Morgan in an explosive and uncontrollable burst of frustration. The attack was, he argued, not only committed with malice aforethought—that is, with intention to kill—but it was rationally and coldly premeditated over a considerable period of time, a classic instance of what the law calls murder "by lying in wait."

It was Marvin, Weisberg reminded the jurors, who had first referred to July 7, the day scheduled for Vicki's eviction, as "D-Day," a name that seemed a harmless bit of black humor at the time. And on Wednesday the sixth, according to Connie Laney, Marvin had behaved "like a different person. . . . He was acting as though he was sick and tired of Vicki."

By insisting on showing Connie the suicide notes left over from Vicki's attempt to take her own life the previous March, Weisberg theorized, Marvin had been attempting to justify to Connie the course of action he had already settled on.

To prove his point, Weisberg held up the notes in question, a fistful of dog-eared, notepad-size sheets and began to read. One of the notes, addressed to several of Vicki's closest women friends, said simply:

> My four friends: I love you all. Sorry I wasn't stronger. I tried really hard. Please forgive me.

A second was to "Mom, Barb, Pat and John:"

> I love you all so much. Please forgive me. I guess I had too much love and never knew what to do with it. It was always mistreated. That makes me sad. Oh, so sad. Love you all.

And on the same sheet:

> Todd, be strong. Todd, my darling, whatever is left it's all yours. Don't let anyone take it from you. The book will help. I've taught you to be strong.

Honey, don't forget—don't forget that. Watch your money, and most of all your emotions. Life is tough. Your father loves you, believe it or not. You can always talk to him.

Still another, dated March 21, more than three months before the quarrel with Gordon, was addressed to him and urged him:

Finish the book. What you don't know you know who will. Please, Todd needs the money and all the help and love he can get. He really doesn't know how much I loved him.
I molded my own life around him and yet never knew how to show him.
Good God, how ugly.

On the same sheet of paper as the note to Gordon was the name Alfred Bloomingdale connected by an arrow to the words:

He didn't mean it, but I really think I realized tonight that the man was so selfish he came first. What a surprise.

Marvin, theorized Weisberg, had transferred the intense feelings of love and resentment that he once felt for his mother on to Vicki. When she seemed to be on the point of rejecting him just as the transference became complete, he simply couldn't take it anymore. So he convinced himself that Vicki "didn't want to live," anyway.

The one witness who might have been able to counter this all-too-plausible and damning hypothesis was, of course, Marvin Pancoast himself, the defendant whose voice was never so much heard in the courtroom. The reason for Marvin's failure to testify on his own behalf was, quite simply, that even Barens and Mathews had no assurance that he would not change his mind and reaffirm his original confession on the stand. According to them, Pancoast's state of mind had been fluctuating wildly since the trail began. There were days when he utterly denied the killing and insisted on the chloroform story, and other days when he insisted that he had killed not only Vicki Morgan but Marvin Gaye, the pop singer whose murder had recently been in the news.

In the meantime, since the defense had obviously failed to prove the blackmail theory outlined by Arthur Barens in his opening statement, Ted Mathews felt compelled to offer the jury some scenario that would make sense of the confused presentation they had watched over the past two weeks. In essence, Mathews hypothesized that Gordon Basichis, his hopes for a successful collaboration fading, had somehow been tempted or blackmailed into joining forces with one or more hit men, hired by someone who wanted Vicki Morgan silenced.

But the key to the killing, Mathews suggested, was the book: "What does the book contain? It's not going to be the life and times of Grizzly Adams. It's going to be about Vicki Morgan, Alfred Bloomingdale, and the people that they travel with. It's going to be about Betsy's scorn for Vicki Morgan, and Vicki Morgan's scorn for Betsy. It's going to be about the president of the United States and Nancy Reagan. It's about many people with whom Alfred Bloomingdale and Vicki Morgan had relationships and affairs."

Once Vicki had begun to grow disillusioned, Mathews went on, Basichis might have been vulnerable to an offer to suppress the tapes: "Now if you were somebody in a powerful position," said Mathews, "so powerful, and had the ability to go to a guy like Basichis and say to him, 'You are going to do what we want. We are going to pay you a lot of money. We are going to keep you in good shape for your dope. You are going to do what we want. You are going to tell us what Vicki's writing. You are going to tell us what's there so we know about it before it hits print."

Basichis's testimony about his phone conversations with Vicki just hours before her death was "fascinating," said Mathews. It showed that Gordon Basichis knew there was no one at home at the condo that night but Vicki and "Marvin Milquetoast." The time was right for Basichis's anonymous ally to go to the condo and kill her, setting up Marvin to take the fall.

But why would such a person need Basichis's aid? Surely, it would seem, if Basichis was involved in such a plot, he would want to be as far from the condo as possible when the actual killing went down.

"The sleeper in the case," Mathews concluded, "is Katy. Remember Katy is the Doberman. . . .

"Do you think Katy would have stood idly by and let anybody hit Vicki? Uh-uh."

"Could not Gordon have grabbed the dog, held the dog while the killer went in—a cold, professional, deliberate killer who subsequently took Vicki's life?"

Later, added Mathews, wrapping up this oratorical flight of

fancy, Gordon Basichis, the amateur hypnotist, programmed "Marvin Milquetoast" into believing he had done the crime himself:

"I suggest to you, ladies and gentlement, that Gordon Basichis one way or another called the house and woke Marvin up and told him, 'Marvin, you just killed Vicki. Look at her. You used the baseball bat, and beat her to death with it. You are responsible.' "

There were snorts of laughter from the daily reporters in the courtroom as Mathews wound up his exposition of what one wag later called his "Manchurian Candidate" scenario. And, for that matter, *The Manchurian Candidate* was not the only work of fiction Mathews had drawn on. The clue of Katy, the "dog who didn't bark in the night" happened to be straight out of Sherlock Holmes' famous story "Adventure of the Naval Treaty." Unfortunately for the sake of the theory, the real Katy the Doberman, however, appeared to have been a different sort of beast entirely from the watchdog who solved Holmes' case for him. Katy, it will be recalled, did not even bark at the police when they showed up but docilely allowed herself to be locked away in the basement.

A point-by-point rebuttal of this conspiracy hypothesis hardly seems called for. Even Mathews didn't claim that he actually believed this was what happened. Still, it is worth pointing out that if Gordon Basichis had wanted to kill Vicki—and there was not so much as a shred of evidence to suggest he had—he would hardly have had to pick a time when Marvin Pancoast was physically present in the room. For that matter, a hypothetical individual who happened to be both "powerful" and ruthless enough to arrange for Vicki to die and for Marvin to be framed for the killing would hardly be likely to stop short at eliminating Gordon Basichis as well.

The jury certainly had no difficulty deciding between Mathews's version of the crime and Weisberg's. Returning to deliberate after the Fourth of July holiday, it took only six hours, including a break for lunch, to agree on a verdict of first-degree murder.

Ironically, though there never was a conspiracy to murder Vicki Morgan, it would not be too farfetched to conclude that there was a mystery man manipulating the course of the trial from behind the scenes. And that man was the defendant himself, the man whom even his own lawyer Ted Mathews dismissed as "Marvin Milquetoast."

Marvin killed Vicki out of jealousy and frustration, but since he also loved Vicki and identified with her, he managed to ensure that she would, posthumously, enjoy the revenge and continued celebrity she had craved.

Marvin had not worked in public relations off and on for a decade for nothing. Even when he spoke with Detective Rush hours after the murder, he was fixated on making sure that the police, and ultimately the reporters, would not overlook his victim's identity. And though he later denied it, it was surely he who planted the seed of the sex tapes rumor with Robert K. Steinberg.

Later, while in the L.A. county jail, Marvin was told that he did not have AIDS after all. Since he could no longer rely on the disease to punish him, he invented a scenario that, while it might lead ultimately to his conviction, would cause embarrassment to his and Vicki's enemies along the way. Never able to compete with Basichis for Vicki while she was alive, he devised a confession that pointed suspicion toward the writer, then sat back and watched while Arthur Barens, his surrogate, did his best to link Basichis to the crime.

Barens and Mathews were not as easy to convince on the subject of the tapes as Steinberg had been, but ultimately they could not resist the temptation to base their defense on the assumption that Marvin was either hopelessly crazy, or the victim of a convoluted frame-up, or—just conceivably—both things at once. The possibility that they were being manipulated to some degree by their own client, who suddenly became incoherent and incapable of testifying on his own behalf once the trial was under way, never seemed to have occurred to either of them.

Pancoast was surely a more clever and more complex individual than anyone, with the possible exception of Dr. Vicary, gave him credit for being.

But did this mean that he was also sane—or insane, but just pursuing his paranoiac rush to destruction in a particularly effective manner?

INSANITY

///

Over the last decade there has been a nationwide backlash against the insanity plea. In large part, this trend has been an unforeseen consequence of the movement to protect the civil rights of mental patients. As long as juries believed, rightly or wrongly, that potentially dangerous individuals were going to be locked up for a good long time anyway, commitment was often seen as a humane alternative to a prison. When it became clear that a defendant exonerated by reason of insanity might be back on the *street within ninety days, a lot of people were encouraged to scrutinize the logic behind psychiatric testimony a little more closely.*

As it is so often, the state of California was in the vanguard of the reaction. Also not untypically, sentiment in the state crystallized around a case that presented some unusual complications—the notorious assassination of San Francisco Mayor George Moscone and Supervisor Harvey Milk by their erstwhile political opponent Dan White.

The crime had all the earmarks of premeditated murder. White had entered San Francisco's City Hall through a basement window to avoid a metal detector he knew was located at the main door. He fired five shots into the mayor, then reloaded and walked calmly to the office of Milk, where he emptied his gun into his second victim.

When the case came to trial, however, psychiatric witnesses for the defense testified that White had been under extreme mental duress at the time of the killings, so much so that he was incapable of meaningful deliberation on the nature and consequences of his actions. As evidence that White was not quite rational in the period before the killings, one psychiatrist noted that the defendant had been subsisting on junk food—the infamous "Twinkie defense."

A sympathetic jury passed up charges of first-and second-degree murder and found White guilty only on the lesser count of voluntary manslaughter.

To the majority of Californians, however, the Twinkie defense sounded like so much baloney. Reaction to the White verdict led to the passage of Proposition Eight, otherwise known as the Victim's Bill of Rights. Among other provisions, Prop Eight specified that the burden of proof in an insanity plea lies with the defense, not with the prosecution. Moreover, the defense must show both that the defendant was incapable of distinguishing right from wrong at the time of the crime *and* that he was unable to appreciate the nature and quality of his actions.

Of course, Dan White had not been exonerated on an insanity plea. He had benefitted from the more common, and more often successful, claim of diminished capacity. Even before Prop Eight went to the voters, the California legislature took care of this loophole by eliminating diminished capacity as a defense. Largely as a reaction against one unpopular verdict, homicide juries in the state of California were no longer to be permitted to consider the defendant's mental state at the time of the crime as a mitigating factor.

Practically speaking, this meant that Marvin Pancoast and his defenders were caught between a rock and a very hard place indeed. Once he had decided to plead innocent and go to trial, Pancoast had little realistic hope that a jury would bring in a guilty verdict of less than first-degree murder, since the jurors were not permitted to consider diminished capacity. He *was* entitled to a separate hearing on the sanity question. It was just that he had virtually no hope or winning. Even theoretically, it is difficult to imagine how anyone capable of functioning even minimally outside of an institution could *prove* beyond a reasonable doubt that he did not appreciate the consequences of an act that caused the death of another.

Naturally, none of this had been explained to the jury ahead of time.

Since testimony about Pancoast's mental state had not been allowed during the first phase of the trial, the jurors returned to the courtroom after the Fourth of July holiday and found themselves listening to a lot of information that had previously been withheld about the defendant's background.

Notably, they learned for the first time that on the occasion of his only previous felony arrest Pancoast had been determined unfit to stand trial.

This 1969 arrest was on a charge of attempting to pass a stolen credit card. Pancoast had not stolen the card himself, or at least so he said. He claimed it had been given to him by a woman friend who said it would be "all right" to use. In police custody, the nineteen-year-old Pancoast seemed disoriented and potentially suicidal, so the court ordered a psychiatric evaluation. The interviewing psychiatrist, Dr. Edward Vogeler, made a preliminary diagnosis of chronic schizophrenia and concluded that Pancoast was incapable of understanding the charges against him and participating in his own defense.

In consequence, Pancoast was committed to the state hospital at Camarillo, where he received more individual attention than the average patient. Young, articulate, middle class, and apparently healthier than most of the inmates, Pancoast at first seemed outgoing and cooperative. However, staff members who went out of their way to befriend him soon became the subject of his bitter complaints to the next shift. Pancoast was a bundle of grievances. The orderlies had a grudge against him. Nurses treated him unfairly. Patients with whom he had been friendly for a time inevitably "betrayed" him.

As one nurse noted in his record, he was "obsessed with justice"—or, rather, with his inability to get it.

Also, during these first months of incarceration, Pancoast made two attempts at suicide—first by overdosing on a stash of medicine he had surreptitiously accumulated and later by stabbing himself with a contraband knife.

In November, this difficult but interesting patient was selected to be the subject of a case conference—a partly diagnostic and partly educational exercise in which a resident-in-training was assigned to do a complete patient workup that he would then defend at a meeting of senior staff. In the course of a long interview with the resident, Pancoast described in detail homocidal fantasies that centered on massacring his entire family—his mother, his brother, and his brother's four children.

The resident was so disturbed by these revelations that two senior consultants were asked to conduct followup interviews. According to hospital records, "Both of these consultants were quite concerned about the patient and felt that he was definitely capable of a mass murder."

Marvin also told the doctors that he was miserable about his homosexuality. "Can't you do something to make me change?" he pleaded.

At the conclusion of the conference process, Pancoast's original diagnosis was refined to "schizophrenic reaction, paranoid type." The panel recommended electroshock, and Pancoast eventually underwent two separate courses of shock therapy, twelve separate treatments in all. Pancoast's request for aversion therapy to change his sexual orientation was denied.

In January 1970, Camarillo informed the courts that Pancoast, while requiring continued inpatient treatment, could be certified as fit to stand trial. The hospital records leave no doubt that the doctors' attitudes toward Pancoast were protective. They believed that treatment at Camarillo State could do him some good, and they were hardly anxious to turn him over to the uncertain mercies of the courts.

"It is proposed . . . that existing criminal charges be positively acted upon," said the official report, "thus eliminating speculation from the patient's thoughts. This present uncertainty is considered an impediment to threapeutic progress. The patient is competent to face these charges and cooperate with his attorneys. Medication should not interfere with his judgment and may indeed enhance it. . . .

"Incarceration and prison will not be therapeutic in any sense."

Under the circumstances, with Pancoast having already been locked up for more time than he was likely to get on conviction, the DA's office decided to take a pass.

Between 1970 and 1975, Pancoast was in and out of Camarillo State. In July 1970, Drs. Lyons and Stephens repeated the diagnosis of schizophrenia. In March 1971, Drs. Plagens and Kramer reached essentially the same conclusion. So did Dr. Slote, who observed him during a nine day-commitment in December 1974. And Dr. Liberman, who saw Pancoast in 1975.

For nearly four years after this, from 1975 to 1979, Marvin Pancoast managed to stay out of California psychiatric facilities.

In the mid-seventies, Pancoast suffered a ruptured colon as the result of participating as the passive partner in a homosexual fistfucking orgy and had to be rushed to UCLA hospital for emergency surgery. He recovered and moved to New York, where he had an office job in the Manhattan offices of the Rogers & Cowan public relations agency, but his East Coast sojourn ended with another suicide attempt, precipitated by an unhappy love affair. In early '79, Pancoast was involved in a minor auto accident. The other driver, a woman in a red coat, became the focus of his paranoid fantasies. Ultimately, convinced that this woman was following him, Pancoast abandoned his car on the Ventura freeway and wandered across several lanes of traffic, apparently hoping to be run down and killed.

When Pancoast was recommitted that year, it was to the first of a series of private hospitals and nothing more was heard of the diagnosis of schizophrenia. The doctors who treated Pancoast at Woodview-Calabasas and at Cedars-Sinai did, however, continue to classify him as a psychotic, subject to delusions and out of touch with reality for significant periods of time.

The records of Pancoast's stay at Thalians during the period when he met Vicki Morgan were typical. The patient, they noted, "has a great deal of paranoid thinking, much of it revolving around the lady who was in the auto accident with him. It appears he believes that she was sent to harm him, that the accident was intentional, and that she continues to try to harass him.

"He feels that she may be from another life and may be punishing him for sins from another life of his. . . .

"On admission he was highly anxious, agitated, and depressed. He was hallucinating and delusional. He had paranoid fantasies and was obviously suicidal.

"He's overwhelmed with fear and suppressed rage. . . . He saw [the woman in the red coat] a number of times while [in] the unit. . . . He avoided occupational therapy for a while because of the self-destructive fantasies engendered by seeing the sharp tools there. . . . He tried jumping out of a window while in the hospital and tried to hang himself. He ruminated about destroying himself and various ways he could [accomplish this], and required involuntary commitment because he would threaten to sign out against medical advice while he was thinking these self-destructive thoughts."

However, the records went on to note, when he was on Stelazine—a powerful antipsychotic drug—"The hallucinations disappeared."

Pancoast also continued to be an unusually troublesome patient to treat. During the time he was at Thalians, his admitting threapist, Dr. Wallens, found it necessary to resign from the case and ask that Pancoast be transferred to another doctor on the grounds that he had become the focus of the patient's paranoid delusions.

When Pancoast was admitted to St. John's Hospital in Santa Monica in 1983, he encountered a set of doctors who, for the first time, suspected that his reported hallucinations were not genuine. Among other imagery he described, Pancoast talked of a recurring dream or hallucination during which he saw himself on a beach, surrounded and threatened by white-robed women who seemed to belong to some sort of black magic cult.

The doctors were skeptical. At most, they felt, the delusions were transitory, the result of the use of LSD and other psychedelic drugs rather than of any organic disease. At worst, the complaints of visions could be ascribed to the "squeaky wheel" phenomenon—in other words, Pancoast had learned over time that he could get attention by telling his doctors what they wanted to hear.

Dr. Paul Cantalupo, the analyst who saw Pancoast after his release from St. John's, was one of those who subscribed to the theory that Pancoast was a psychopathic personality—but not psychotic. Regardless of this conclusion, Cantalupo ultimately found Pancoast just as intractable in treatment as the doctors at Camarillo and Thalians had.

On July 5, 1983, after his final session with Pancoast, Dr. Cantalupo wrote:

> [A] letter will be sent telling Mr. Pancoast that I consider that he has decided to terminate treatment with me because I feel it is practically impossible for me to do any further work with him because of his lack of capacity for insight-oriented work, his lack of commitment to working on serious emotional issues. His refusal to make even a minimal [illegible word] and oral arrangement with me even for a reduced fee. I will discharge him.

Fourteen years after his initial commitment, Pancoast had exhausted the patience of his last therapist. And forty-eight hours later, Vicki Morgan was dead.

The jury, which heard this information in disjointed form over four days of testimony, could hardly be blamed for finding it completely confusing.

Needless to say, the contradictory diagnoses in Marvin Pancoast's medical history were complicated by equally contradictory conclusions from the expert witnesses called by both sides.

Dr. Edward Vogeler, the psychiatrist who originally concluded that Pancoast was schizophrenic back in 1969, appeared for the defense to reiterate that he believed that his diagnosis was correct then and that it was still correct as of 1984.

Dr. Irvin Matzner, one of three psychiatrists appointed by the court to examine Pancoast in August 1983, agreed with Vogeler, testifying that in his view the defendant was psychotic, schizophrenic, and legally insane. However, Dr. Matzner's assessment was undercut somewhat when he admitted on cross-examination that in his opinion perhaps 10 percent of the general population suffers from schizophrenia—a breathtaking estimate.

Nevertheless, a certain rough logic suggested that Matzner and Vogeler's view of Pancoast was the correct one. After all, the same psychiatrists who labeled Pancoast schizophrenic correctly pre-dicted back in 1969 that he was a potential killer—a possibility Dr. Cantalupo failed to foresee only hours before Pancoast murdered Vicki Morgan.

On the other hand, the jury had to weigh the testimony of two other court-appointed psychiatrists who argued forcefully that Pancoast must be found legally sane.

Dr. Ronald Markman, a veteran of both the Manson and Hillside Strangler cases, told the jurors that Pancoast should be correctly diagnosed as a "borderline personality"—seriously dis-turbed but nonpsychotic, as he had been labeled at St. John's—and well within the parameters of sanity as defined by the law.

But it was left to Dr. Vicary, the same expert witness who did so much to torpedo the defense contention that Pancoast was a harmless masochistic personality, to offer a novel explanation on how the St. John's doctors could have been right and previous doctors wrong.

"If you or I went out to Camarillo State Hospital today, this afternoon," Vicary told the jurors, "[if] we drove out there, and we were waiting in line and we got to talk to the admitting doctor out there, and you told him that you were hearing voices and they were saying nasty things to you and you had a vision of a woman in a red dress that was chasing you, I'll bet you a thousand dollars they would admit you to the hospital and diagnose you as being schizophrenic because they would accept at face value what you were telling them. . . .

"The tendency is to accept at face value—God forbid that you should make a mistake and somebody that was really sick should slip through your fingers . . . and it does have a momentum. Once you get started with this stuff, if you say this again over time or even if you don't. . . . Once that label is on you, you're proven to be schizophrenic until you show me you're not."

And once the label is in place, Vicary added, there is a tendency to continue to diagnose psychosis in one form or another. Furthermore, all kinds of psychiatrists "in Beverly Hills and wherever," will be prescribing "all kinds of powerful medication to you, which can be quite dangerous, merely on the basis that on some record from Camarillo or some other place it says *schizo-phrenic*. It is a very powerful word."

Although he chose his words judiciously, what Dr. Vicary was implying was that Marvin Pancoast, and indirectly Vicki Morgan, had been victims of medical error. At the age of nineteen, when he was first admitted to Camarillo State, Pancoast may have been merely an emotionally maladjusted teenager and, possibly, a drug abuser. By the age of thirty-three, after unnecessary shock therapy and more than a decade of exposure to the contraindicated medications, his condition had deteriorated sharply.

There is a good deal of recent though still controversial research to support this interpretation. According to a report on diagnostic practices in state hospitals written by Dr. William Carpenter, director of the Maryland Psychiatric Research Center, Thorazine, Stelazine, and other powerful psychotropic drugs commonly prescribed for schizophrenics can do irreversible harm when mistakenly given to nonschizophrenics. These powerful tranquilizers may also have the effect of masking the patient's symptoms, making a successful rediagnosis unlikely. "If you make the mistaken assumption of chronic schizophrenia, the patient may never recoup his losses," says Carpenter.

Interestingly, some experts investigating the same problem of misdiagnosis have suggested that the dangers are especially severe in the case of depressed patients—a substantial percentage of the mental patients who ultimately attempt suicide are thought to be depressives wrongly diagnosed and treated as schizophrenic.

Ironically, Dr. Vicary's interpretation meant that Dr. Cantalupo, however uninsightful he may have been when it came to evaluating his patient's potential for violence, was technically correct in his diagnosis. Deprived of the powerful medications he had taken in the past—and, incidentally, of the Valium Cantalupo had prescribed, since Pancoast was passing these pills on to Vicki—Pancoast gave way to his violent impulses for the first time in his life. Still, he was rational enough to turn himself in to the police promptly and to make a reasonably coherent confession. Later, in jail and restored to a regime of heavy tranquilizers by the prison doctors, he repudiated his confession and began fantasizing that he was the victim of a frameup.

Another inference that might have been drawn from Vicary's testimony, though no one seized on it at the time, was that Pancoast was sane at the time he committed murder but insane when he pleaded innocent and during the trial—incompetent by reason of being dosed with the wrong medications.

Fortunately for the jury, perhaps, nearly all the murky and wildly contradictory testimony was largely irrelevant to the sanity question, as defined by Prop Eight. A jury that could agree on a verdict of first-degree murder within a few hours ought to have had no trouble concluding that Pancoast could not prove that he did not understand the consequences of smashing Vicki Morgan's skull with a bat. After all, he certainly understood the consequences when he turned himself in to Keith Wong minutes later and when he told Detective Rush that Vicki "wanted to die."

It took this jury four and a half days.

The jury's lengthy deliberations reflected not so much confusion over the facts as frustration over their options under the law. Whether the jurors would have chosen a lesser verdict than first-degree homicide if they had known all the facts from the beginning is a moot point—but at least the choice would have been theirs.

As it was, their only option was to ignore the language of Prop Eight entirely and to bring in a verdict of not guilty by reason of insanity. Such a verdict would have absolved Marvin Pancoast of all responsibility for his actions, without necessarily ensuring that he would be committed for any length of time or even that he would receive appropriate treatment. Indeed, the chances were good of his ending up in the hands of doctors who would agree with the diagnosis made at St. John's, in which case he could be expected to be released in short order.

Faced with this unpalatable possibility, the jury eventually gritted its collective teeth and brought in a second verdict of guilty.

Judge Horowitz eventually sentenced Marvin Pancoast to a term of twenty-six years to life.

AFTERWORD

///

*Draw your chair up close to the edge
of the precipice and I'll tell
you a story.*

F. SCOTT FITZGERALD
THE JAZZ AGE

SURVIVORS

//

E*ven as the Van Nuys jury was debating the fate of Marvin Pancoast, Betsy Bloomingdale ended her two-year self-imposed retreat by appearing as the cover girl of W's special California issue. Photographed in the garden of her Holmby Hills mansion, she posed with a diminutive pair of gardening shears and a pink rose of truly Californian proportions, looking sleek and amazingly youthful. In the accompanying interview, headlined "Betsy in Bloom," Mrs. Bloomingdale talked of her passion for roses—a rose garden she was quoted as saying, "is like the stock market. It's very temperamental."*

Mrs. Bloomingdale also talked to the *W* interviewer, Maureen Sajbel, about her late husband. "I can only say that he was the most wonderful husband and had the most wonderful sense of humor. We had a fabulous thirty-five years and he was a fabulous father. That's all. . . . People who knew my husband knew he was a fabulous man. And those who didn't, well, that's their problem." Sajbel, writing in a publication not noted for questioning the sincerity of its interview subjects, did not forbear to note that these comments were "not resentment-filled protests, but more staunch and rehearsed defenses. Bloomingdale chooses to shape her world according to her own ideas of privacy and gentility."

Nevertheless, the interview went on to make it clear that a good deal had changed in Betsy Bloomingdale's life since her husband's death. "My husband wanted me to run his house and to dress well, to do everything as well as one could. He thought I was a dodo, and maybe I am—I'll find out," she observed with no apparent resentment. Since her husband's death, the article continued, Mrs. Bloomingdale had taken over his Westwood Boulevard office, his business interests, and the management of his Florida real-estate holdings, in addition to launching a "little designing venture" of her own.

Mrs. Bloomingdale, who does not sound the slightest bit like a dodo when the subject turns to business, told the *W* interviewer that her favorite reading material was now the *Wall Street Journal*—"Alfred never took [it], but I get it and love it." Her model and inspiration was her neighbor, industrialist Armand Hammer—"I read the other day that [he] was retaining all his coal interests and I said, 'Listen, if Armand Hammer is hanging on to his coal, we'll hang on to ours.' " Her chief complaint about her new role as a businesswoman was the dilatory pace—"I'm used to making a decision here, a decision there, and something happens. In business, they all move like snails. I remember Alfred saying to me that it takes forever. . . . But this is the way it goes. I have to do it alone. . . . I'm getting to like it now and it's getting on two years."

Among Mrs. Bloomingdale's more expeditious business moves, within weeks of her husband's death was the dissolution of the Bloomingdale/McComas investment company's holdings in Showbiz Pizza. According to Craig Sweeney, treasurer of the Brock Hotel Corporation, the parent company of Showbiz Pizza, Bloomingdale/McComas had held two area development agreements, one in the Washington, DC, area and one in Memphis,

Tennessee. Just before the first DC area outlet opened in Laurelton, Maryland, on October 27, 1982, the agreement was sold back to the parent company. Similarly, the Memphis agreement was sold to an outfit calling itself the McBiz Corporation.

Papers filed at the time showed that Vicki Morgan had indeed been listed as 10 percent owner of record in Bloomingdale/McComas, along with Bloomingdale himself, the daughter of Bill McComas, a man who had been maitre'd at the Marina Bay complex in Fort Lauderdale, and three other individuals—none of them politically prominent. But since the agreements were resold before any Showbiz Pizza outlets actually opened for business, and for amounts said to cover only the development monies already spent on establishing the franchises, there were no profits. Thus, Vicki Morgan died owning 10 percent of nothing.

Michael Dave nevertheless continued to pursue the remnants of Vicki Morgan's palimony suit against the Bloomingdale estate. With no profits showing from the Showbiz Pizza venture, the basis of the suit was reduced to the February 12, 1982, letter signed by Bloomingdale from his hospital bed, promising Vicki an allowance of $10,000 a month for two years. Bloomingdale lawyers argued that the letter represented Vicki Morgan's shameless attempt to "squeeze out the last drops of money" from a dying man and had been signed under emotional duress. A civil court jury, however, decided otherwise. Since Vicki had received four months' worth of support payments between the time the letter was signed and June 1982 when Betsy Bloomingdale ordered her cut off, the jury awarded her estate the balance of what had been promised, a total of $200,000.

In retrospect, both sides in the litigation were partially right. Vicki Morgan was greedy, just as Alfred Bloomingdale was a man who gave free rein to his baser impulses. Yet it was not so much corruption as the complicating factor of love that propelled their affair to its scandalous conclusion.

A man with a less troublesome conscience than Alfred Bloomingdale happened to possess would never have found it necessary to spend millions in an attempt to exorcise his guilt. A truly calculating woman would have milked the affair for whatever she could get and then gotten out, without letting the relationship destroy her life.

Beverly Hills may be no more or less sexist than any other community in the United States—it just happens to be richer.

And anywhere that big money is being made, men are likely to
make the most of it. Vicki Morgan was just one of the legion of
attractive young girls who flock to L.A. every year counting on
finding success on the screen, only to learn that their best hope,
often their only hope, of moving up from a shabby Hollywood
studio to a house in Beverly Hills lies in finding a good husband.
She wanted money, but she also wanted to cling to her romantic
fantasies. And like "other wives" from time immemorial, she
wanted to believe that the married man who loved her would
eventually leave his wife to marry her.

Vicki Morgan was hardly the first woman to wake up at age
thirty to the discovery that men in general, and her married lover
in particular, couldn't be relied on to take care of her forever. Nor
was she the first to focus her resentment on her lover's wife. The
self-delusion and spite were hers, though she did receive more
than the usual amount of reinforcement. Marvin Mitchelson
encouraged her to think there was nothing unreasonable in
expecting that Alfred's widow would pay her support for the rest
of her life, and no one saw anything unrealistic about her plan to
make a fortune from her memoirs. Indeed, she might well have
converted her notoriety into a modest but fairly lucrative career.
It wasn't the sleaziness of her story that made her success impossible, but her inability to play the role of the shady lady with the
requisite brassy good cheer. Self-pity is the one unforgivable sin
for a would-be celebrity.

And what of the alleged sex tapes?

The charges against attorney Robert K. Steinberg were not
settled until May 1985. The L.A. County DA's office agreed to
accept a plea of no-contest on a misdeameanor contempt charge
that had been filed against Steinberg for his refusal to answer
questions about the tapes under oath. The original misdemeanor
count, for filing a false police report, was dropped.

According to Assistant DA Lawrence Longo, the latter charge,
so carefully investigated at the time of the grand jury hearing,
had now become difficult to prosecute due to the death of one
witness, an employee of the AM/PM answering service, and the
unavailability of another. "We had to prove a negative, that the
the things never existed," said Longo, a difficult feat to manage in
the absence of a seamless web of evidence.

Steinberg, described by his attorneys as "totally mentally relieved" to have the issue resolved at last, received a six-month suspended sentence and a fine of $1,190.

It would seem that the disposal of Steinberg's legal problem would put to rest the sex tapes rumor once and for all. This certainly appeared to be the opinion of Longo, who called them a figment of Robert K. Steinberg's imagination. But in a bizarre turn of events, Steinberg's own attorney, Peter Brown, revealed after the plea that he had reasons of his own for thinking all along that there was such a thing as Morgan–Bloomingdale sex tapes.

In a recent interview, Brown said he first heard about the existence of some tapes back in 1974, when he was an associate of Paul Caruso. Vicki, he recalled, had come to see Caruso about pursuing a lawsuit against Alfred Bloomingdale and, said Brown, "In a case like that, one of the first things you ask is, 'Suppose the guy says he never heard of you?' " Vicki's reply at the time was that she could prove it, that there were films—"either under her control or somewhere where she could get her hands on them." Brown emphasized that Vicki never said anything about who else, if anyone at all, was shown on the tapes. Nor did he ever see them.

It seems likely that, at some point in her life, Vicki Morgan was in possession of some cassettes that could fairly be described as sex tapes. If the tapes had involved anyone with a political career to protect, however, then her vague plans to get money and revenge through blackmail would hardly have remained stalled at the talking stage.

As for Marvin Pancoast, he was by no means resigned to serving out his sentence of twenty-six years to life.

Shortly after his sentencing, while he was being transported to the state prison at Chino, Pancoast confided to the deputy who was escorting him that his cellmate at the county jail, Richard Ford, had made certain admissions to him. Pancoast was interviewed at Chino by Detective Bill Gailey of the LAPD's major crime division and summoned to appear at Ford's preliminary hearing. Although Pancoast never actually took the stand—the prosecutor having decided that his testimony would not be necessary to establish the charges—his appearance served to stir up conspiracy rumors that seemed to have died in the ashes of the trial. Here was Marvin, the pliable, "compulsive" confessor turned into a police stooge with his life sentence barely begun!

Marvin continued to hope for a new trial. He and Arthur Barens had parted company in state of mutual impatience and disillusionment. Asked why he was off the case, Barens first said it was because Christy had run out of money for attorney's fees, but then admitted that he and his client were no longer seeing eye-to-eye.

Marvin, meanwhile, was very unhappy about the way his attorneys had portrayed him at the trial. "It was humiliating just to sit there and listen to the things they said about me," he complained—all that "fag stuff" and clucking over the Dr. Vicary's testimony about a sexual relationship with Vicki, which was true. If only he had been able to speak for himself, he felt, the jury would have come out on his side. He even began to think that maybe Arthur had been working against him all along. Someone had told him that Barens and Norman Brokaw, the head of William Morris, belonged to the same country club. So it could be that they'd gotten together and agreed to keep him off the stand. That's how it worked—the people with power, with influence, were all connected . . .

Barens was disgusted. He felt bad for Christy Pancoast, but he'd broken his back to get her son off and had almost succeeded with the insanity thing, but Marvin wasn't the least bit appreciative. Gratitude—gratitude and remorse were two emotions that were missing from Marvin's makeup. "I still think the guy's insane," Barens said, "for what it's worth."

Ted Mathews continued to think that the judge's ruling against his motion for two juries had prevented Marvin from getting a fair trial. In March 1985 he filed an appeal on Marvin's behalf before the Second Appellate Court in L.A.

Drugs had also surfaced as an issue. Christy Pancoast had been appalled at the way her son looked during the trial. She'd written a letter to Judge Horowitz complaining that Marvin was so drugged up he "looked like a zombie."

Another player now entered the case—Jack Kimbrough, a self-described "assassination truth activist" who had spent more than a decade spinning theories about the deaths of JFK and RFK. Kimbrough contended that the L.A. county psychiatrist responsible for medicating Pancoast while he was in custody had intentionally prescribed a combination of major tranquilizers that would leave him dazed and disoriented. The medication regime—which combined Trilafon and Mellaril, potent tranquilizers, and Benadryl, a commonly prescribed antihistamine well known for its potential to produce drowsiness, even confusion, and hallucinations when used in combination with tranquilizers—

was strikingly different from what the doctors at St. Johns had found appropriate only a year earlier. Kimbrough suggested that its purpose was to make Pancoast incapable of participating in his own defense, much less of taking the stand on his own behalf. Kimbrough made these assertions the basis of a Friend of the Court brief, filed in support of Pancoast's appeal for a new trial.

Certainly it was true that the history of Marvin Pancoast cast no glory on the psychiatric profession. More than a decade of psychiatric treatment, much of it the best that money could buy, had failed either to help Marvin or to protect his eventual victim. Indeed, it could be justifiably argued, as Dr. Vicary had suggested on the witness stand, that the misdiagnosis of schizophrenia at Camarillo State and the years of treatment with the wrong drugs were responsible for turning a self-destructive, emotionally troubled youth into a dangerous, irreversibly depressed adult.

It might well be asked why the doctors all along, right up to the last set of physicians at St. Johns, seemed to underestimate the significance of Pancoast's abuse of street drugs on his condition. And why Dr. Cantalupo, who was seeing Pancoast three or more times a week just prior to Vicki Morgan's death, failed to see an approaching crisis—one that was predicted accurately by Gordon Basichis.

But ultimately, the blame for the confused handling of Pancoast's psychiatric case would seem to fall less on any one individual than on the mental-health establishment as a whole. At a time when there was optimism over the potential of tranquilizers for controlling schizophrenic behavior, Marvin was called schizophrenic. When lithium was discovered to be beneficial for many manic-depressives, Marvin was reclassified as manic-depressive. And so on, until the doctors had run out of chemical options. At which point, they labeled their patient an antisocial personality and washed their collective hands.

It didn't happen just to Marvin Pancoast. Thousands of patients who passed through institutions during the 1970s went the same route—mislabeled, mismedicated, and then released into society to cope as best they could because medical science had run out of answers, the doctors out of hope, and the law said that hospitals could no longer hold on to patients they could not meaningfully treat.

The trouble with Kimbrough's thesis that the medication was given purposely to keep Pancoast quiet during the trial was that it was the defense lawyers who were most insistent that their client receive his medication. It was they who complained to the judge when their client was permitted to come to court unmedicated one day during the pretrial period, they who demanded assurances that such a lapse would not occur in front of the jury.

Far from being afraid of what Marvin might say if he took the stand, Prosecutor Weisberg would have liked nothing better than to have a go at him—a defendant who has confessed five times is ripe for cross-examination. No assistant D.A. in the country would be other than salivating at the prospect. No, it was the defense who wanted Marvin tranquillized, not because they wanted to suppress his evidence but because they were increasingly nervous about some of the things he was saying to them.

And it wasn't until the psychiatric testimony in the final phase of the trial that the possibility finally hit home that the medication itself might be responsible for generating the fantasies. When Pancoast confided to Ted Mathews during the trial that he thought he might have shot Marvin Gaye, that was the drugs talking. The story about seeing Vicki's corpse and getting a sudden yen for a hamburger was the drugs talking, too. The question was, how exactly did you distinguish among what the drugs said, what Pancoast said, and the truth.

Marvin Pancoast, like Robert K. Steinberg, had been discredited. What once threatened to become a major scandal had turned out to be nothing more than a mad fantasy, and probing distinctions among the various levels of madness was beside the point. The conspiracy buffs started from the opposite set of assumptions, reasoning that what the establishment didn't seem to want heard was ipso facto well worth hearing. Smoke equals fire, and just as surely, a whiff of sweetish odor at a murder scene means chloroform.

Ted Mathews position as a defense attorney put him between the two camps. By the time he filed Pancoast's appeal in March 1985, he'd known his client for twenty months. Twenty months— and he still couldn't be entirely sure exactly what had happened between Marvin and Vicki Morgan. He'd drawn laughter and derision during his summation at the trial by trying to suggest to the jury some of the outside possibilities, to stretch their capacity for doubt. Yet reduced to its essentials, his position was doggedly logical, blatantly consistent: Since Marvin Pancoast was not a competent witness, his statements couldn't properly used to convict anyone.

Not even Marvin Pancoast himself.

Pancoast might not in fact be innocent. But it wasn't the business of attorneys and courts to determine innocence in any case. Their business was deciding between guilt and nonguilt.

Strictly speaking, no one was guilty in the matter of Victoria Lynn Morgan's death.

But everyone was to blame.

Blame Marvin's doctors.

Blame the courts.

Blame the lawyers for gambling on a plea they couldn't win with.

Blame Vicki for the rotten way she treated Marvin.

Blame Alfred Bloomingdale for corrupting a seventeen-year-old girl.

Blame Vicki again for her hunger to be corrupted.

Blame society for sending out so many seductive messages to both Vicki and Marvin, for whispering in their ears that there were no rewards worth living for except money and celebrity—really big money, really supercelebrity, instant and totally beyond moral judgments.

Somewhere in the list of who was to blame, there had to be a line reserved for Marvin Pancoast.

There could be no real doubt that Marvin Pancoast wielded the baseball bat that beat the life out of Vicki Morgan. But why exactly did he do it? Was he crazy or just cunning? And which of his various accounts of the crime did he himself really believe?

In April of 1985, when we interviewed Marvin in a windowless, unventilated conference room at San Quentin Penitentiary, Pancoast appeared to be not only articulate and in touch with reality but eager, he said, "to get a lot of things off my chest." He had continued to gain weight since his trial, and despite a slight puffiness in his face that made him seem older than his years, he appeared healthy.

Perhaps in deference to the presence of the prison's public-information officer, who was sitting in on the interview, Pancoast began by protesting his complete and total innocence. The police witnesses at his trial—Wong, Tarello, Welch—had all lied, he insisted. He never made the self-incriminatory statements that they recounted in their testimony. Nor did he ever say all those things he supposedly said to the "tall, handsome one."

Realizing that this was a reference to Detective Rush, who took his signed confession, we protested, "But it's on tape!"

"Well, then I have no idea why I said those things," was Marvin's reply. And he went on to recite the same story he'd told his lawyers, the one about waking up in the double bed to find the room filled with a smell "like nail polish remover," finding Vicki bludgeoned to death, and driving off in search of a late-night snack. "Suddenly, I was so hungry. Empty. I don't know why."

For a man who was supposedly either a pathological liar or at least a very clever one, Pancoast was notably unconvincing. He seemed bored with the subject of the murder and equally bored with that of the tapes, limply denying that he had ever told Steinberg, Barens, or anyone else that they existed.

What Pancoast truly did care about, it developed, was what others thought of him. "You were at the trial," he kept saying. "What was the press saying about me? What did they think? . . . What does Connie Laney think of me now? . . . What do you think? Did you think I was guilty?'

"Not as a premeditated thing," we ventured, "but it seemed that you might have done it—"

"—you mean, in a moment of rage?" As he finished the sentence on his own, Marvin brightened visibly. Suddenly, he was interested, involved. And suddenly he began discussing how Vicki Morgan might have been killed—always in hypothetical terms, without ever broaching the delicate question of actuality—but in terms suggesting that, hypothetically, mind you, his statements to Rush and Furillo might have not been far from the mark.

What Marvin would not agree to, even hypothetically, was any criticism of Vicki Morgan. "It occurred to me," we said at one point, "that Vicki got men to do a lot of things for her. To give her what she wanted. She wanted to die, and now she's dead. I wondered if maybe she hadn't goaded you into killing her."

"Not goaded," he protested. "Vicki was never mean. Let's just say that we talked a lot about dying. About how it might be done."

But he conceded that Vicki had never actually tried to take her own life, except that once when she took too many pills. She never speculated about killing herself other than with an overdose.

The interview ran into a second day, this time under somewhat more comfortable circumstances in a glass-enclosed visiting cubicle off the main visitor's area. The cubicle had an outside window, through which was visible, just barely beyond the prison court-yard, the blue waters of San Francisco Bay. Regular visiting hours were not on, and the main room was empty, except for an employee engaged in mopping down the much-scarred floors. The poker-faced Lieutenant Everly, the public-information officer who had observed our first interview, had been replaced by an attractive, cheerful young woman from his staff.

Marvin appeared in his dark blue prison denims, looking considerably more relaxed than he had been the day before, and talked easily and unself-consciously about his life and his relationship with Vicki.

"Vicki *was* special," he said, "I don't know how to put it into words. She had this quality. You just couldn't get enough of her."

What quality? he was asked.

"She could talk . . . in—intellectually about any subject," Marvin volunteered. After stumbling over the adverb, he then dismissed it with a chop of his hand. "That isn't the word. Not the word. But you know what I mean. And," he brightened, "she had a heart of gold."

A heart of gold—so that's what it had come down to. The sexy bad girl with a heart of gold.

But the mystique that had kept him in thrall, he conceded, wasn't based entirely on Vicki's goodheartedness or flair for amusing conversation.

"You have to understand about Vicki," he said. "She was an exhibitionist. She liked to have people watch her masturbate. She'd dress up in black garter belts. Put on lots of black eye makeup. Sometimes a wig. This went on right up until the night before she died."

"I couldn't say I was reluctant [to participate]." Pancoast said, making a face. But at a certain point, especially after Gordon came back into Vicki's life, his conflicted feelings had become almost unendurable.

There was no truth, Pancoast insisted, to the tapes-inspired rumors about orgies featuring prominent California Republicans. Nor, as had been whispered, did Vicki know any damaging secrets about goings-on at the exclusive, all-male Bohemian Club.

However, it was so, he insisted, that Vicki had once delivered $10,000 in a plain envelope to a high-ranking Republican upon his arrival at Los Angeles International Airport, and true also that she had a romantic assignation on one occasion with another Reaganaut.

Towards the end of our talk, Marvin volunteered, "Last night in my cell, I was thinking about what you said yesterday. And I realized, you're so smart, you'd figured it all out anyway. . . . Let's just say that there were plenty of times when Vicki and I discussed how it might end. But she always said, if it happened, it would have to be in a way that would do credit to Alfred."

"Do credit to him? How?" we asked.

"By getting a lot of publicity," Pancoast explained, as if it were the most obvious thing in the world.

Vicki, he went on, had repeatedly complained that she had nothing left to live for, now that Alfred was gone, and speculated in detail that, if she killed herself, at least the resulting publicity would hurt Betsy even more than the palimony suit had. "She wanted to make Betsy squirm."

The cells of San Quentin are filled with prisoners who will tell you that, for one reason or another, they don't deserve to be there. But Marvin Pancoast was no doubt unique in believing that the public, the courts, and even Vicki's family would not hold what happened against him if only they understood that his sole motive had been to get his victim's name into the headlines in the most sordid manner possible.

Tearfully, he kept insisting that he had been Vicki Morgan's only true friend. All the others, with the possible exception of her mother and her sister, had been out to exploit her in one way or another. He was the only one who had never tried to use her, the one who had been there by her side to the bitter end.

Two months after this interview, Pancoast sent a letter filled with news of his still-unresolved appeal and an updated list of those who had betrayed him. He was more convinced than ever, he wrote, that he wouldn't have been convicted if it weren't for his lawyers—"I was screwed by Arthur and Ted."

But he had also concluded by now that he was a victim of the media and its "irresponsible, bloodthirsty pursuit of a 'story' at the expense of the human being whose story it is."

Fortunately, he added, he was going to have an opportunity to indict the media before a larger audience, since he was "doing a documentary film for Home Box Office"—his way of saying that there was a possibility he might be interviewed for a series that aimed, he wrote, to show how excessive publicity can "severely damage [people's] private lives and careers even though they may have been exonerated of the charges against them."

Vicki, the perpetual, self-willed victim, was dead, and Marvin Pancoast had survived, and her story had become his story.

It was a very cheerful letter.

But fate still had one more reversal in store for Marvin Pancoast. Shortly after this letter was written, his health began to deteriorate. He was transferred from San Quentin to the state facility at Vacaville for treatment and further diagnostic tests. In November of 1985, the Vacaville physicians confirmed that the prisoner was terminally ill. The man who once told Dr. Vicary, "If I don't have AIDS, I want to have it," had been granted his self-destructive wish.